AF725648

Catholic Social Thought

This series focuses on Catholic social thought and its application to current social, political, economic, and cultural issues. The titles in this series are written and edited by members of the Society of Catholic Social Scientists. They survey and analyze Catholic approaches to politics, sociology, law, economics, history, and other disciplines. Within these broad themes, authors explore the Church's role and influence in contemporary society.

The Society of Catholic Social Scientists was formed in 1992 to rejuvenate a distinctively Catholic scholarship in the social sciences.

1. *The Public Order and the Sacred Order*, by Stephen M. Krason, 2009.
2. *Bioethics, Law, and Human Life Issues*, by D. Brian Scarnecchia, 2010.
3. *Pope Pius XII on the Economic Order*, by Rupert J. Ederer, 2011.
4. *Economics As If God Matters*, by Rupert J. Ederer, 2011.

Pope Pius XII on the Economic Order

Rupert J. Ederer

Catholic Social Thought, No. 3

THE SCARECROW PRESS, INC.
Lanham • Toronto • Plymouth, UK
2011

Published by Scarecrow Press, Inc.
A wholly owned subsidiary of The Rowman & Littlefield Publishing Group, Inc.
4501 Forbes Boulevard, Suite 200, Lanham, Maryland 20706
http://www.scarecrowpress.com

Estover Road, Plymouth PL6 7PY, United Kingdom

Copyright © 2011 by Rupert J. Ederer

All rights reserved. No part of this book may be reproduced in any form or by any electronic or mechanical means, including information storage and retrieval systems, without written permission from the publisher, except by a reviewer who may quote passages in a review.

British Library Cataloguing in Publication Information Available

Library of Congress Cataloging-in-Publication Data
Ederer, Rupert J.
Pope Pius XII on the economic order / Rupert J. Ederer.
p. cm. — (Catholic social thought ; no. 3)
Includes bibliographical references and index.
ISBN 978-0-8108-7797-9 (hardcover : alk. paper)
1. Pius XII, Pope, 1876-1958. 2. Economics—Religious aspects—Catholic Church—History of doctrines—20th century. 3. Catholic Church—Doctrines—History—20th century. I. Title. II. Title: Pope Pius the Twelfth on the economic order.
BX1795.E27E34 2011
261.8'5—dc22 2010052700

™ The paper used in this publication meets the minimum requirements of American National Standard for Information Sciences—Permanence of Paper for Printed Library Materials, ANSI/NISO Z39.48-1992.

Printed in the United States of America

THIS BOOK IS DEDICATED TO MY BROTHER BAVARIAN

POPE BENEDICT XVI

The time has come to repudiate empty phrases, and to attempt to organize the forces of the people on a new basis; to raise them above the distinction between employers and would-be-workers, and to realize that higher unity which is a bond between all those who cooperate in production, formed by their *solidarity* in the duty of working together for the common good and filling together the needs of the community. If this *solidarity* is extended to all branches of production, if it becomes the foundation for *a better economic system*, it will lead the working classes to obtain honestly their share of responsibility in the direction of the national economy[Italics added].

The Future of Trade Unions—An Address by Pius XII to Delegates to the Convention of the Italian Catholic Workers' Association on 11 March 1945

Contents

Foreword

Few historians have the expertise that may be attributed to Rupert J. Ederer. Undoubtedly his new book, *Pope Pius XII on the Economic Order*, will be hailed as a great contribution to the science of economics and the study of Pope Pius XII.

Following his birth in Rome, Italy to Filippo and Virginia Pacelli on 2 March 1876, Eugenio Pacelli was immediately christened. Also on March 2, 1938, his 64th birthday, he became Pope Pius XII. Although his family name suggests "peace," his lifetime, including his years as the temporal head of the Roman Catholic Church, involved some of the most devastating events in the history of the world. These included World War I and II, the deadliest wars of all times, and violent revolutions which assured that even the intervals between wars would not be genuinely peaceful. In fact, after his death in 1958 there were those who created turbulence by their false and unhistorical accusations about his character and actions. Unjustly such accusations continue to be propagated.

Many writers published works about Pope Pius XII during the years after his death, especially after the play, *The Deputy*, presented by the German playwright Rolf Hochhuth in 1963. These directed their energies largely to undoing the harm done to the image of a truly great and saintly pope. In a certain sense, the need to do that was unfortunate. Pius XII was a holy man. The Catholic Church has acknowledged his sanctity publicly by advancing his cause toward eventual canonization with the title Venerable. In a scholastic sense, he was also brilliant and intensely productive.

The forty illustrious encyclicals by Pius XII take up one entire volume of the five published by Sister Claudia Carlen IHM in 1981—a work that covers all papal encyclicals from 1740 until 1981. The Christmas Messages presented by him each year from 1939 through 1957 rank as legendary masterpieces. (They were published in English in one of a two-volume work by Father Vincent Yzermans in 1961). During his 19-year pontificate there were also countless radio messages and addresses before various groups of faithful. An indication of the great volume and extent of his many presentations is found in the expansive three-volume work (4038 pp.) by two Swiss Dominican scholars, Arthur-

Fridolin Utz and Joseph Fulko Groner. Presented as *Soziale Summe Pius XII*, this collection is confined to his social thinking. Beyond that, Pius XII has often been presented as the most frequently cited reference, after Sacred Scripture, throughout the documents of the Second Vatican Council.

Regrettably, amid all of the tumult caused by the falsification of the actions of Pius XII during the critical time in world history that he was pope, not enough attention has been directed to that highly productive aspect of his papacy. It is time now therefore that scholars like Dr. Rupert J. Ederer, convinced of the outstanding character and brilliance of Pius XII, may proceed with their analysis of what Pius XII had to say in their various areas of expertise. Clearly the great pope had a keen interest in certain aspects of the social order that had been addressed in earlier social encyclicals. Nor is it unlikely that his successors also built on some of his wisdom. Blessed John XXIII referred to him in *Mater et Magistra,* as did Pope Paul VI in *Populorum Progressio*, and also Pope John Paul II in his own great trilogy of social encyclicals. The social teachings of the Catholic Church are a work-in-progress, and Pius XII was a very important link in that magisterial enterprise. Since the time of Blessed John XXIII they are addressed to "All People of Good Will," but they need to be applied to the problems in various countries by persons who have expertise in their specific fields, like the author of this work.

Margherita Marchione, MPF

Acknowledgments

I am indebted to many persons who were helpful and instrumental in various ways for the inspiration and preparation of this work for publication. These include especially Dr. Stephen Krason, President and Founder of the Society of Catholic Social Scientists. It was he who presented this work to the Scarecrow Press as meriting publication.

My very special thanks are in order to persons here spanning the generations from my parents, the late John and Frances Ederer, to my son, Dr. Martin Ederer. It was my parents who aroused my early interest in and admiration for Eugenio Pacelli who, as Papal Nuncio to Bavaria and then to all of Germany, resided in my native city Munich when I was born there in 1923. After I came of age, they told me stories about his perilous encounters with the Communists who were contending with the Nazis for control of Bavaria and eventually all of Germany in that city during those desperate and climactic years.

My son, Dr. Martin Ederer, is already of the cybernetic generation. His computer skills far exceed those of his father who was never that good even with the old-fashioned typewriter or, for that matter, with pen and ink. His help during my very senior years has been indispensable for getting my messy manuscripts publication-ready.

I am deeply grateful also to Sister Margherita Marchione, of the Religious Teachers Filippini, who is of my generation, and who has been kind enough to provide a *Foreword*. She has valiantly and tirelessly defended the reputation of Pope Pius XII against groundless unhistorical accusations over a period of many years. This misrepresentation of history may well have discouraged potential scholarship directed toward demonstrating how valuable the teachings of Pius XII were in so many areas including the social one addressed by this book.

Great respect and gratitude are owed to the two Dominican friars Fridolin Utz and Joseph Groner at the University of Fribourg in Switzerland. Between 1954 and 1961 they accomplished the mammoth and valuable task of gathering and arranging in three volumes all of the Pius XII social teachings. The great usefulness of that work is of course limited somewhat by the fact that it is in

German. I take full responsibility for the accuracy of all translations from their original text.

My personal interest in the social teachings by Pope Pius was first nurtured by the presentation of select addresses in the documentary section of the monthly publication *The Catholic Mind* published by the America Press of the Jesuit fathers in the United States. Later, there appeared the very useful quarterly publication, *The Pope Speaks*, which was devoted exclusively to presenting papal addresses, both the shorter addresses and longer documents like the encyclicals. Although it is included in the Bibliography, I would like to mention here as especially useful in my work the very excellent two-volume *Major Addresses of Pope Pius XII*, edited by the Rev. Vincent A. Yzermans.

Chapter 1
An Age of Great Popes

The present difficult era in the history of the Roman Catholic Church has been marked by a singularly strong and exceptional papacy. Unlike the period during the Renaissance which witnessed the installation of some dubious characters as popes by rival families and political factions, no pretender, anti-pope or political opportunist has occupied the Chair of Peter within the memory of any living person and well beyond.[1] One may begin at least with Pius IX, whose papacy extended from 1846 to 1878, and who has since been beatified by the Church. He was followed by Leo XIII (1878-1903) whose prophetic teachings included social encyclicals which he pioneered and for which he established the pattern.[2] His successor, Pius X (1903-1914), was the first pope to be canonized a saint since the 16th century Counter-Reformation pontiff St. Pius V was declared a saint in 1712. The all but forgotten and under-appreciated Benedict XV (1914-1922) spent himself trying to end the insane carnage of World War I. Pius XI (1922-1939) was forced to contend with the depredations of two of the most brutal tyrants in history, Joseph Stalin and Adolf Hitler, along with the dictator Benito Mussolini in his native Italy; he addressed three definitive encyclicals, *Noi Abbiamo Bisogno* (1931), *Mit Brennender Sorge* (1937) and *Divini Redemptoris* (1937) respectively to the Fascist, Nazi, and Communist cults which they represented. The embattled pope also issued the landmark sequel to *Rerum Novarum,* known as *Quadragesimo Anno* (1931), for the context of the world-wide economic depression.

Following the great pope whose teachings are the subject of this book, there was the brief and dramatic pontificate of Blessed John XXIII (1958 -1963) who left an indelible mark on church history. Aside from his two significant social encyclicals, *Mater et Magistra* in 1961, and *Pacem in Terris* in 1963, this Pope peremptorily convoked an ecumenical council to the amazement of all. It fell to his successor, Paul VI (1963-1978), to guide the Second Vatican Council through to its completion and to begin implementing its revolutionary directions intended to guide the Catholic Church's progression into the next millennium. In the process he suffered the dry martyrdom of witnessing an encroaching disciplinary disarray in his Church, with many thousands of religious renouncing their vows and abandoning their vocations, at the same time that there occurred a calamitous decline in new religious vocations. Perhaps as a consequence, the remarkable pontiff embarked on a revolutionary new strategy. In an effort to "show the flag," so to speak, and to shore up morale and discipline in the Church worldwide, Paul VI undertook a number of precedent-setting world travels, emulating his chosen namesake, St. Paul.

After the pontificate of John Paul I (1978) was dramatically cut short by his death after just 33 days as pope, Karol Wojtyla of Poland was elected. The first non-Italian pope in over four centuries chose the name John Paul II. If the martyrdom of Paul VI was "dry"—witnessing the diabolical disarray in his Church— that of John Paul II would have been bloody except for what he himself perceived as the intervention of the Mother of God. Shot and critically wounded by a would-be assassin in St. Peter's Square, on May 13, 1981, the Pope recovered miraculously in the opinion of many, including himself. Following and vastly accelerating his predecessor's visits to his worldwide flock, his own world travels became legendary. So too have his voluminous writings, which include a masterful trilogy of social encyclicals: *Laborem Exercens* (1981), *Sollicitudo Rei Socialis* (1987), and *Centesimus Annus* (1991). Soon after his death on 2 April 2005, the many thousands gathered in St. Peter's Square began calling for his canonization with the chant "*Santo subito!*" Meanwhile many refer to him already as "John Paul, the Great." I personally expect that he will one day be declared a *Doctor of the Church*—a title which presupposes prior canonization—along with Pius XII, the man whose social teachings are the subject of this work.

Eugenio Pacelli was born on 2 March 1876. Elected pope on 2 March 1939, his 63rd birthday, he chose the name, Pius XII. His family name is a diminutive form of the Italian word for peace, *pace.* Pacelli suggests "little peace." In truth, that characterized the man's nineteen-year pontificate marked, as it was, by the deadliest war in history, and followed by the frightful period which came to be known as the Cold War. Pius XII was thrust into a role of world leadership at the same time that the two dictators, Stalin and Hitler, terrorized their own countries and eventually the entire world. World War II began just six months into his papacy. The diminutive Vatican City over which he presided lies wholly within an Italy then ruled by Benito Mussolini, whose alliance with Adolf Hitler already made life difficult for the newly elected Pope. Mussolini departed from the scene shortly, and Hitler's own *Götterdämmerung* would follow soon afterwards. Joseph Stalin survived until 1953 after extending the Soviet Empire throughout Eastern Europe and with it, the Cold War. That episode saw buildings throughout America marked as public fallout shelters, while the world shuddered at the prospect of nuclear war throughout the remaining years of the Pius XII pontificate.

The teachings of this great pope over his nineteen-year pontificate were prodigious, providing astute commentary on an astounding range of topics. They were contained in 41 encyclicals and 19 singularly exalted and prophetic *Christmas Messages*, in addition to 1371 addresses categorized variously as allocutions, homilies, and discourses to groups meeting with him at the Vatican, and the *Radiomessaggi* which went out to other nations from the Vatican radio. His audiences ranged from beekeepers and farmers, to distinguished scientists, medical professionals, and diplomats. Commentators often expressed surprise and admiration at the depth of the Pope's insights into so wide a variety of topics, as well as at the number of languages in which his messages were delivered.[3]

Foremost among the admirers of the breadth and depth of Eugenio Pacelli's teachings was his immediate successor. With characteristic ebullience Blessed John XXIII, in his first *Christmas Message* on December 23, 1958, unofficially declared Pius XII to be a Doctor of the Church. He said: "Apart from any official declaration which would be premature, the triple title, '*Doctor optimus, Ecclesiae sanctae lumen, divinae legis amator,*' [Most excellent doctor, light of the holy Church, upholder of the divine law] would be most suitable to his memory." Since being proclaimed a Doctor of the Church presupposes canonization, that too was foretold by the enthusiastic pontiff: "Already we like to think of him as one of God's saints in heaven where he dispenses renewed strength to those Christians who survive him, and who will continue to venerate for generations his beloved and sacred memory."[4] The canonization process is underway. One might add parenthetically that no single personal source is more frequently referred to in the Vatican II documents than Pius XII.[5]

There have been many publications over the years including in their various dimensions the texts of the papal messages by Pius XII, as well as commentaries about them. Why now, so many years after his death, should anyone present a commentary on the teachings of Pius XII? First of all, this work is written by an economist; therefore it will confine itself to what that pope had to say directly as well as inferentially about the economic order. Also, it is intended to complement a previous work by this author.[6] That dealt exclusively with papal encyclicals about the economic order, and Pius XII did not deliver any of such. Popes of the Roman Catholic Church have been addressing that order specifically, starting with the 1891 pioneer encyclical *Rerum Novarum* by Leo XIII.

Pius XII is generally not credited with encyclicals which fit into the category of *social encyclical.* However, that designation is not an official one. It has come to be assigned to certain teachings because of their explicit implications for the social order, which would include the family and the political as well as the economic orders. Accordingly, in this writer's opinion, the very first encyclical by Pius XII, *Summi Pontificatus* (1939), could be classified as a social encyclical since its content ranges widely in its application over the entire social order.

In any case, it is safe to say that no Roman pontiff has addressed the problems confronting the social order as frequently and as widely outside the formal structure of encyclicals as Pius XII. This applies in a special way to his masterful and prophetic *Christmas Messages*. Overall, the Pope's approach may reflect his convictions expressed in a radio message to the Roman people on February 10, 1952:

> This is not the time for the discussion or seeking out of new principles, nor the time for assigning new aims and objectives. In substance, both the principles and the objectives are well known and firmly established, because they have been taught by Jesus Christ Himself, they have been clarified and worked out by the Church in the course of the centuries, and adapted to the immediate circumstances by recent popes; they need only one thing, and that is to be put into actual practice.[7]

Putting the principles into practice is by no means an accomplished mission. In some significant respects, our world is no better off today than it was when Leo XIII issued *Rerum Novarum.* Today, as in 1891, we have worldwide exploitation of female and child labor. Concomitantly, there is at large a widespread inability or unwillingness to pay a just wage that will enable the rank-and-file worker to support his wife and family at a respectable level of living. That applies also in wealthy nations like the United States. To an increasing degree mothers must once again enter the work force in order to supplement underpaid or underemployed fathers—a process which involves the neglect of young children and is gravely detrimental to family life and society. Nor are these phenomena unrelated. In the so-called free market economy the wage is regarded as simply another market price paid for a commodity, which in this case happens to be human labor. Thus, where exploitable female and child labor makes itself readily available, the level of wages deteriorates to the point where the presence of the mother in the work force becomes less an option than a necessity.

At the same time, by and large, the ground has been cut from under labor unionism, so the right of workers to organize into effective organizations has been reduced toward the level of impotence prevailing when Leo XIII championed that right as *natural.* The deterioration of the workingman's condition is a part of a wider effort to restore liberal capitalism which had receded somewhat following the Great Depression of the 1930's. This restoration has been heralded by a renewed dedication in various quarters to so-called *free markets* during the decades following World War II. Pope Paul VI expressed concern about what he called a "renewal of the liberal ideology."[8] Pope John Paul II has referred to the ideology subsequently as "neoliberalism."[9]

The astute reader will recognize the continuing relevance of Pope Pius XII's teachings to the present condition.

Finally, there is one other important matter regarding Pius XII that needs to be addressed. It is perhaps symptomatic of our post-Christian condition that anyone presenting and extolling any aspect of this saintly pope's teachings must include an *apologia* because of a persistent, nefarious campaign underway since 1963 in particular. I refer to the accusation that Pius XII maintained a cowardly silence while Nazi Germany was embarking on its systematic massacre of Jews during World War II. There is implicit in this bit of unhistorical nonsense the naïve notion that if Pius XII had spoken up righteously and loudly, Adolf Hitler would have discontinued his activities and run for cover. The campaign also involves the insinuations that the Pope secretly supported Hitler's "crusade" against Communist Russia. The vilification campaign of unhistorical defamation stemmed originally from a play entitled *Der Stellvertreter* (The Deputy) by Rolf Hochhuth, which first appeared in 1963.

I will not attempt a systematic refutation of the Hochhuth-inspired thesis here. The matter has since been addressed definitively and in scholarly fashion by, among others, the nun-historian, Sister Margherita Marchione Ph.D., and the law professor, Ronald J. Rychlak.[10] The cowardly silence thesis rests on the flawed assumption that, if Pius XII had used the authority of his office to issue a blunt proclamation to the world about what was happening to Jews in the Nazi empire, Hitler and his cohorts would have ceased their genocidal campaign. That is based at best on a naive contextual misunderstanding of the mentality of the Nazi leaders during their desperate war against the world. It also ignores the fact that the Pope had by stealth and at grave personal risk to the parties involved, including ultimately himself, provided shelter for many thousands of Jews in religious houses around Rome and even in the Vatican. It is estimated that at Castel Gandolfo, the papal summer residence, some 15,000 Jews were quartered virtually under the noses of the occupying Germans. Besides, the Vatican understood what the Dutch hierarchy, like Hochhuth, apparently did not, that an inflammatory statement against the Nazis would simply lead to an extreme reaction. Such reaction did in fact occur tragically in the Netherlands, costing the lives of thousands of Dutch Jews. Five days after the archbishop of Utrecht had a pastoral letter read in all churches protesting the treatment of the hapless victims, they were rounded up. By August of 1942 some 40,000 Jews including the now canonized convert nun, Teresia Benedicta (formerly Edith Stein), were transported to Auschwitz. Dr. Joseph Lichten, then head of the B'nai B'rith Anti-Defamation League, said in 1963,[11] "The Pope did not speak out more strongly against the Jewish persecution by the Nazis, because anything he would have said was liable to make matters even worse for the Jews."

In any case, it seems that, notwithstanding Hochhuth's second-guesses, twenty years after the fact, surviving Jews who were much closer historically to the scene of the horror had a better appreciation of Pius XII's efforts on their behalf. For example, in October 1945 the World Jewish Congress donated 2 million *lire* to Vatican charity in recognition of the Pope's efforts to rescue Jews. The chief Rabbi of Rome, Israel Zolli, was so impressed by Pius XII's actions that he converted to Catholicism and took as his Christian name the Pope's baptismal name, Eugenio.

Over the years there were many other Jewish accolades before Hochhuth muddied the waters of history. On May 26, 1955, the Israeli Philharmonic Orchestra gave a concert at the Vatican to express Jewish gratitude for the acknowledged efforts by the Pope on the behalf of Jews during their dark hour. Jewish expressions of gratitude to Pius XII came from persons like Chief Rabbi Herzog, World Jewish Congress Secretary-General Leon Kubowitzky, Italian Jewish Welfare Committee President Raffaele Contoni, Moshe Sharret of the World Jewish Congress (later to become Prime Minister of Israel), and Maurice Edelmann, President of the Anglo-Jewish Association. These occurred in the period immediately following the War. When Pius XII died in 1958, Golda Meir, then Foreign Minister of Israel, called the Vatican, expressing sympathy for the loss of the "voice speaking out on the great moral truths above the tumult of daily conflict...." Others who sent condolences include President Ben-Zvi of Israel, Dr. Eli Toaff, the Chief Rabbi of Rome, and Nahum Goldmann, President of the World Jewish Congress. Leonard Bernstein preceded a New York Philharmonic concert with a moment of silence, "for the passing of this very great man."

Many of these facts were brought to the foreground by Pinchas E. Lapide, a journalist and former member of the Israeli diplomatic corps, in his book, *Three Popes and the Jews.*[12] The book's cover indicates that Lapide began this work as a "protest against Hochhuth's *The Deputy.*" After his detailed study of the matter, Lapide concluded:

> To which we may add, in the light of the preceding chapters that the Catholic Church under the pontificate of Pius XII was instrumental in saving at least 700,000, but probably as many as 860,000, Jews from certain death at Nazi hands.... These figures, small as they are in comparison with our six million martyrs whose fate is beyond consolation, exceed by far those saved by all other churches, religious institutions and rescue organizations combined.[13]

No belated egregious distortion of history should stand in the way of analyzing the important contributions to the body of his Church's social teachings by Pius XII. This book attempts to enumerate and provide commentary on his teachings dealing specifically with the economic order. Being an economist, I shall confine my efforts to the Pope's addresses regarding the economic order. His first concern was not to analyze how the economic system looks or operates, but how pertinent moral principles should apply in the economic order for its proper functioning. That represents an entirely appropriate part of magisterial role for the head of the oldest and largest Christian church.

I am indebted to many who made my own work in this area possible. These include Father Vincent Yzermans, whose presentation of selected major addresses by Pius XII first inspired my respect for the range, profundity and continuing relevance of that Pope's teachings.[14] His two-volume work also includes a useful listing of the Pope's allocutions, letters and discourses during his pontificate. Many of these appeared in English translation in two periodicals, *The Catholic Mind*, and *The Pope Speaks.* The forty-one encyclicals by Pius XII are contained in the major work, *The Papal Encyclicals,* by Sister Claudia Carlen IHM.[15] For certain hard-to-find discourses, the author relied on his translations of the pertinent German texts by two Swiss Dominican scholars, Arthur-Fridolin Utz and Joseph-Fulko Groner, who undertook the enormous task of gathering into their three-volume *Soziale Summe Pius XII* all of the specifically social teachings of Pius XII.[16]

Notes

1. During the early years, all popes until the 6th century were canonized saints; many, starting with St. Peter, by virtue of martyrdom.

2. Cf. Etienne Gilson, *The Church Speaks to the Modern World* (Garden City: Doubleday & Co., 1954). Following guidelines set down by Leo XIII himself, Gilson presented with commentary eleven of the Pope's encyclicals as an integral *Leonine Corpus*. These include encyclicals which establish the basic philosophy behind the Church's social teachings, and encyclicals addressing marriage and the family, the political order, and what is perhaps the best known of Leo's encyclicals, *Rerum Novarum*, dealing with the economic order.

3. These eventually comprised 21 volumes known as *Discorsi e Radiomessaggi di Sua Santità Pio XII*.

4. Michael Chinigo, ed., *The Teachings of Pope John XXIII* (New York: Grosset & Dunlap, 1967) 106; also, John XXIII, "The Legacy of Pius XII," in *The Pope Speaks* - Vol. 5, No. 2 (Spring 1959), 127-133.

5. Vincent Miceli (author of *The Gods of Atheism*), who as a Jesuit had been both a student and a professor at the Gregorianum in Rome, confided to me that Pius XII was often referred to there as *Pio Massimo*, i.e., Pius the Great.

6. Rupert J. Ederer, *Economics as if God Matters* (South Bend: Fidelity Press, 1995).

7. Vincent A. Yzermans, ed., *The Major Addresses of Pope Pius XII* (St. Paul: The North Central Publishing Co. 1961). 1:193.

8. Paul VI, *Octogesima Adveniens* (London: Catholic Truth Society, 1971), par. 35.

9. John Paul II, "Ecclesia in America," *The Pope Speaks*, vol. 44, no. 4, 237.

10. Cf. Sister Margherita Marchione, *Pius XII: Architect for Peace* (New York: Paulist Press 2000); also, Ronald J. Rychlak, *Hitler, the War and the Pope* (Huntington IN: Our Sunday Visitor, 2000).

11. Joseph L. Lichten, *ADL Bulletin*, October 1959.

12. Pinchas E. Lapide, *Three Popes and the Jews* (New York: Hawthorn Books, 1967) 247.

13. Ibid. 214-215.

14. Vincent A. Yzermans, ed., *The Major Addresses of Pope Pius XII* (St. Paul: North Central Publ. Co., 1961).

15. Claudia Carlen, IHM, ed., *The Papal Encyclicals, 1740-1981* (N.p.: McGrath, 1981).

16. Arthur-Fridolin Utz, O.P., and Joseph-Fulko Groner, O.P., *Soziale Summe Pius XII* (Freiburg, Switzerland: Paulusverlag, 1954-1961), 3 vols.

Chapter 2
Encyclicals

Summi Pontificatus (1939)

Summi Pontificatus was the first of forty-one encyclicals by Pius XII. It was delivered on October 20, 1939, seven months into his pontificate. The encyclical was intended to reach the faithful in time for the Feast of Christ the King, and its leitmotif is the spread of the kingdom of Christ. "We shall make of it the Alpha and Omega of Our aims, of Our hopes, of Our teachings, of Our activity, of Our patience and of Our sufferings by consecrating them all to the spread of the Kingdom of Christ"(*Summi Pontificatus*, par. 2).[1]

That emphasis may explain why the document is not generally classified as a social encyclical. Yet, in one English translation it is entitled *The Function of the State in the Modern World.* The various titles used for vernacular renditions of encyclicals were typically derived from the translators' perceptions of the content. These clearly suggest a dominant social perspective in *Summi Pontificatus,* and they place it in the tradition of certain Leo XIII encyclicals dealing with Civil Government (*Diuturnum,* 1881), the Christian Constitution of States (*Immortali Dei*, 1885), Christian Citizenship (*Sapientiae Christianae,* 1890), and Christian Democracy (*Graves de Communi,* 1901).

Given its dedication to the spread of the Kingdom of Christ, *Summi Pontificatus* follows even more directly the theme of two early encyclicals by Pius XI, his immediate predecessor. *Ubi Arcano* (1922) is commonly entitled in English, *On the Peace of Christ in the Reign of Christ.* And for *Quas Primas* (1925) we find the English title: *On the Kingship of Christ.* These are in fact included in a significant compilation of Pius XI encyclicals where they are characterized as *The Social Encyclicals of Pius XI.*[2] Even a quick reading indicates their overriding concern with the social order which was by then slipping into a clearly post-Christian condition. If that is indeed a valid designation, then the Pius XII encyclical, which built on them explicitly, also deserves the designation of social encyclical. The successor of Pius XI referred to *Quas Primas* when he wrote:

> We see ever more clearly the sacred significance of that consecration of mankind to Christ the King. We see its inspiring symbolism; we see its power to refine and to elevate, to strengthen and to fortify souls. We see, besides, in that consecration a penetrating wisdom which sets itself to restore and to ennoble all human society and to promote its true welfare (*Summi Pontificatus*, par. 3).

The quotation involves a twofold message indicating that a true dedication to Christ the King was once widespread, and that it has since been lost. It was to the end—restoration—that Pius XII affirmed his intention: "We place this first Encyclical of Our Pontificate under the Seal of Christ the King...." (*Summi Pontificatus*, par. 10).

Summi Pontificatus appeared shortly after World War II had begun on its course of devastating the remnants of old Europe; and the Pope addressed these prophetic and plaintiff words to the continent about to undergo the worst bloodbath in its history:

> The denial of the fundamentals of morality had its origin in Europe, in the abandonment of that Christian teaching of which the Chair of Peter is the depository and exponent. That teaching had once given spiritual cohesion to a Europe which, educated, ennobled and civilized by the Cross, had reached such a degree of civil progress as to become the teacher of other peoples, of other continents. But cut off from the infallible teaching authority of the Church, not a few separated brethren have gone so far as to overthrow the central dogma of Christianity, the Divinity of the Savior, and have hastened thereby the progress of spiritual decay (*Summi Pontificatus*, par. 24).

These words clearly suggest the overall destruction of Christian culture in Europe. Throughout the encyclical there are copious references to the application of the Christian moral principles, most specifically justice and charity, in the various segments of the social order. And the political order at the international and national levels is singled out with expressions of concern about the harm which the absolute state does to "private enterprises" (*Summi Pontificatus*, par. 55), the family (*Summi Pontificatus*, pars. 56, 57, 58), and in the area of education (*Summi Pontificatus*, pars. 61, 62, 63), as well as at the level of relations among nations (*Summi Pontificatus*, pars. 64-70).

Whereas there is scant specific mention of the economic order, except near the end, *Summi Pontificatus* inaugurates what was to become in subsequent papal social teachings a key principle for re-establishing social order. That principle, stated here as the *law of human solidarity*, came to be applied subsequently also to the economic order in significant ways.

Actually, the principle or "law" of solidarity as it came to be employed in the Church's social teachings originated in a monumental but largely overlooked work by the German Jesuit economist, Heinrich Pesch (1854-1926). Pesch is the author of what is until now the most comprehensive economics text ever written.

His five-volume *Lehrbuch der Nationalökonomie* appeared through several editions from 1905 to 1926.[3] The learned Jesuit's intention was to provide the guidelines for an economic system that steered between liberal capitalism, which had caused untold devastation especially among the working classes, and socialism, which, when he began his work, was looming ominously as a snare for the workers. He called his system the *social* or *solidaristic system of human work*, based on the social philosophy, *solidarism*, which stood opposed to individualism and collectivism. Ensouling the system and the philosophy was the *principle of solidarity* as it came to bear on the social order generally, but specifically on the national economy.[4]

Due to the widespread irreligiosity of the time frame in which Pesch operated, his work was largely ignored and eventually set aside by economists. Pesch's Church, however, incorporated salient principles from his large work into its social teachings. That process began with Pius XI, who issued the important encyclical *Quadragesimo Anno* within five years of the great scholar's death. Involved specifically in the process of drafting that encyclical were two Jesuit confreres, Oswald Nell-Breuning and Gustav Gundlach. They were understudies of Pesch in full concordance with his work and ideas. Subsequently, Pius XII came to rely heavily on Gundlach in particular for information about the economic order and the relevance of Christian moral principles to it.[5] The influence of the solidarist idea is clear throughout that Pope's pronouncements addressed to economic matters.

Whereas Pesch was a trained economist who wrote an economic text, he had previously received the excellent training in philosophy and theology which the Jesuit order was providing for its men during the latter half of the 19th century. He wrote extensively also on social philosophy, and he understood how to apply Christian principles to the social order overall. Thus, when he presented his pivotal *principle of solidarity*, he indicated its application specifically to four levels of society: the basic solidarity which binds all members of the human race; the solidarity uniting all citizens of the same nation; and in economic life specifically: the solidarity among members in the same work place and, more broadly, in the same occupation or industry; finally, and most basically, the solidarity binding members of the same family.[6]

In *Summi Pontificatus*, faced with the tragic wartime situation, Pius XII began using the term *solidarity* in papal pronouncements, emphasizing there the first level of application indicated by Pesch—the worldwide level based on the "supernatural brotherhood of peoples around their common Father...." (*Summi Pontificatus*, par. 12). That echoed the Jesuit's own explication of the application of solidarity at that level:

> The universal solidarity of the entire human race...enables us to see in our fellow man a natural companion and, in fact, a brother, because of the common relationship which we all share toward God and to Christ, so that it assures him just and charitable treatment.... [M]ankind is not merely a species which has certain features in common. It is in fact a community—the unique great family

> of God. Anyone who denies that is not in a position to pray the Our Father, without lying to himself.[7]

It is evident that Pius XII used the concept of solidarity as representing something more than simply a pious sentiment. Lamenting the dissension which was then tearing Europe apart, and indicating that it stemmed from a "surge of rebellious passion, but also from a deep spiritual crisis," the Pope said: "The first of these pernicious errors, widespread today, is the forgetfulness of that law of human solidarity and charity which is dictated and imposed by our common origin and by the equality of rational nature in all men, to whatever people they belong, and by the redeeming Sacrifice offered by Jesus Christ on the Altar of the Cross to His Heavenly Father on behalf of sinful mankind" (*Summi Pontificatus*, par. 30). Thus, we have solidarity affirmed as a "law," at the same time that it is linked with the foremost Christian virtue, charity. Spanish translators of the encyclical apparently considered solidarity to be central enough to *Summi Pontificatus* that they gave the Spanish edition the title of *Solidaridad humana y estado totalitario.*[8]

At the time, it was customary to assign vernacular titles to encyclicals that reflected their essential content. Since the various ecclesiastical jurisdictions might sometimes have different perceptions of the content, the traditional method of using the first words of an encyclical as its title circumvents the problem of preserving uniformity.[9]

Pius XII used the expression, solidarity, with increasing frequency throughout his pontificate as did his successors John XXIII and Paul VI. The matter appears to have come full circle subsequently in the teachings of Pope John Paul II, who made solidarity a leading principle in the Church's social teachings. In his 1987 encyclical *Sollicitudo Rei Socialis*, the Polish Pope stated that, "Solidarity is undoubtedly a Christian virtue...." (*Sollicitudo Rei Socialis*, par. 40). He devoted an important part of that encyclical to defining the concept as "...the correlative response as a moral and social attitude, as a 'virtue,' stemming from a recognition of the interdependence in the contemporary world, in its economic, cultural, political and religious elements and accepted as a moral category...." (*Sollicitudo Rei Socialis*, par. 38) Later, in the third of his impressive trilogy of social encyclicals, *Centesimus Annus* (1991), Pope John Paul II closed the ring on the explication of the virtue of solidarity (cf. *Centesimus Annus*, par. 10):

> In this way, what we nowadays call the principle of solidarity, the validity of which both in the internal order of each nation and in the international order I have discussed in the Encyclical *Sollicitudo Rei Socialis*, is clearly seen to be one of the fundamental principles of the Christian view of social and political organization. This principle is frequently stated by Pope Leo XIII, who uses the term "friendship," a concept already found in Greek philosophy. Pope Pius XI refers to it with the equally meaningful term "social charity." Pope Paul VI, expanding the concept to cover the many modern aspects of the social question, speaks of a "civilization of love."[10]

That illustrates a continuing development of doctrine in the most positive and acceptable sense of that word, never suggesting for one moment an essential alteration or departure from the original meaning. The important thread of continuity running through papal social teachings is sometimes overlooked, with an excess of energy expended on stressing differences among the successive popes, as though their obvious differing personality traits presuppose also doctrinal juxtaposition.

Summi Pontificatus, Pius XII's first encyclical, is addressed predominantly to the political order, in particular at the international level. The economy and its problems are not featured prominently. However, since the *principle of solidarity* relates to the social order overall it applies also, importantly, to the economic life of a nation. As we shall see, later during his pontificate Pius XII made frequent reference to it in addressing the economic order. Meanwhile, the only specific mention of the economic order in *Summi Pontificatus* comes late in the encyclical where we find:

> For true though it is that the evils from which mankind suffers today come in part from economic instability and from the struggle of interests regarding a more equal distribution of the goods which God has given man as a means of sustenance and progress, it is not less true that their root is deeper and more intrinsic, belonging to the sphere of religious belief and moral convictions which have been perverted by the progressive alienation of the peoples from that unity of doctrine, faith, customs and morals which once was promoted by the tireless and beneficent work of the Church. If it is to have any effect, the re-education of mankind must be, above all things, spiritual and religious. Hence, it must proceed from Christ as from its indispensable foundation; it must be actuated by justice and crowned by charity (*Summi Pontificatus*, par. 76).

Here Pius XII leads us back to the cardinal principles presented in precise terms by his predecessor Pius XI: justice and charity, as applied to the social order, therefore: social justice and social charity.[11]

Quadragesimo Anno was, of course, addressed specifically to the economic order. That highlights the link between the teachings of Pius XII with his predecessor. As for his immediate successor, John XXIII, the emphasis on worldwide solidarity introduced in *Summi Pontificatus* anticipates the way in which Pope John XXIII was to bring the social virtues, including solidarity, to bear on the entire family of nations at the worldwide level. That, indeed, was the distinctive hallmark of that remarkable Pope's social teachings in his two social encyclicals: *Mater et Magistra* (1961), and *Pacem in Terris* (1963). It also marks the road traveled by Pope Paul VI in his only social encyclical, *Populorum Progressio* (1967).

There can be little doubt that *Summi Pontificatus* was a *social* encyclical, in the relevant sense of the word. It provided important insights into what is required for the ongoing problems afflicting the social order in its various dimensions. Pius XII's other encyclicals, even while they could not properly be designated as social encyclicals, make reference to the social teachings and their application to certain problems. One example is his unique, little noted encyclical addressed to the United States.

Sertum Laetitiae (1939)
"To the Church of the United States"

While he was still Eugenio Cardinal Pacelli, Pius XII traveled widely in the United States. In a sense that made him the first Catholic pope to have seen America first hand, with both its promise and its problems. In *Sertum Laetitiae* he demonstrated his awareness of what aspects of the social problem afflicted this country in particular.[12]

The encyclical was issued on November 1, 1939, just ten days after *Summi Pontificatus*; the occasion was the 150th anniversary of the establishment of the Catholic hierarchy in the United States. In addition to being congratulatory, however, this encyclical also contains a significant note of prophetic warning. There is remarkable prescience in these words about what happens to "the public weal and the glory of civilized life...when right is subverted and virtue despised and derided" (*Sertum Laetitiae*, par. 18).

> Thence arise immoderate and blind egoists, the thirst for pleasure, the vice of drunkenness, immodest and costly styles in dress, the prevalence of crime for ill-gotten wealth, the flight from the land, levity in entering marriage, divorce, the break-up of the family, the cooling of mutual affection between parents and children, birth control, the enfeeblement of the race, the weakening of respect for authority, or obsequiousness, or rebellion, neglect of duty towards one's country and towards mankind (*Sertum Laetitiae*, par. 19).

The Pope also revealed his understanding and sympathy with regard to the festering underlying problem which could be characterized as stemming from America's "original sin" as a nation: slavery.

> We confess that we feel a special paternal affection, which is certainly inspired by Heaven, for the Negro people dwelling among you; for in the field of religion and education we know they need special care and comfort and are very deserving of it. We therefore invoke an abundance of heavenly blessing, and we pray fruitful success for those whose generous zeal is devoted to their welfare. (*Sertum Laetitiae*, par. 9)

While the words in the foregoing passages are not addressed to the economic order in particular, their relevance to it is apparent. Moreover, the entire latter portion of this brief encyclical is directed to economic problems afflicting the social order in the United States.

In *Sertum Laetitiae* there is specific reference to what came to be known as "the social question," and also to the social encyclicals, *Rerum Novarum* and

Quadragesimo Anno. Pius XII indicated that "The fundamental point of the social question is this, that the goods created by God for all men should in the same way reach all, justice guiding and charity helping" (*Sertum Laetitiae*, par. 34). We also find here an early expression of that "preferential option for the poor" suggested first in *Rerum Novarum*, and mentioned frequently in social encyclicals by Pope John Paul II: "Worthy of honor are the poor who fear God because theirs is the Kingdom of Heaven and because they readily abound in spiritual graces." Lest the wealthy take umbrage at that "option," Pius XII added directly: "But the rich, if they are upright and honest, are God's dispensers and providers of this world's goods; as ministers of Divine Providence they assist the indigent through whom they often receive gifts for the soul and whose hand —so they may hope—will lead them into the eternal tabernacles" (*Sertum Laetitiae*, par. 34).

That was followed by what could be interpreted colloquially as a "plug" for the middle class.

> God, who provides for all with counsels of supreme bounty, has ordained that for the exercise of virtues and for the testing of one's worth there be in the world rich and poor; but he does not wish that some have exaggerated riches while others are in such straits that they lack the bare necessities of life. But a kindly mother of virtue is honest poverty which gains its living by daily labor in accordance with the scriptural saying: 'Give me neither beggary, nor riches, give me only the necessaries of life' (Proverbs 30:8) (*Sertum Laetitiae*, par. 35).

Clearly the way to such "honest poverty" for the vast majority of mankind is the just wage; and the paragraphs following its mention are addressed precisely to the just wage doctrine as formulated by Pius XI in *Quadragesimo Anno.*

> Now if the rich and the prosperous are obliged out of ordinary motives of pity to act generously towards the poor, their obligation is all the greater to do them justice. The salaries of the workers as is just, are to be such that they are sufficient to maintain them and their families (*Sertum Laetitiae*, par. 36).

What that means is explained further by a direct quotation of the important just wage doctrine as stated in *Quadragesimo Anno*: "Every effort must therefore be made that fathers of families receive a wage sufficient to meet adequately normal domestic needs." The problem of interpreting that lofty doctrine in precise dollars and cents terms is not inconsiderable. It has nevertheless already been managed successfully even while such attempts may always be amenable to improvement.[13]

Indeed, the question of what family size must be accommodated by the just wage was already anticipated and addressed by Pius XI when he suggested along with his statement of the doctrine itself: "In this connection We praise those who have most prudently and usefully attempted various methods by which an increased wage is paid in view of increased family burdens and special provision made for special needs" (*Quadragesimo Anno,* par. 71).

That all-important just wage doctrine, first presented in its modern aspect by Leo XIII in *Rerum Novarum*, has been restated and reaffirmed in social encyclicals by all popes since. What Pius XI was praising in his statement of it was the family allowance program which has been approached by some employers on their own, and which has since been incorporated as an important part of social welfare programs by many nations of the world. Supplementing the wage paid by the employer with payments according to family size is an important if not indispensable step to resolving the thorny problem of how many dollars constitute a just wage. Most recently, Pope John Paul II in *Laborem Exercens* suggested "...social measures such as family allowances or grants to mothers devoting themselves exclusively to their families," as one of two alternate approaches to establishing the just wage. The other approach was "a single salary given to the head of the family for his work, sufficient for the needs of the family without the other spouse having to take up gainful employment outside the home" (*Laborem Exercens,* par. 90).

There is further significant concordance between what the two popes had to say about the just wage. Pius XI insisted that "If under present circumstances this (payment of the just wage) is not always feasible, social justice demands that reforms be introduced without delay which will guarantee such a wage to every adult working man" (*Sertum Laetitiae,* par. 36, quoting *Quadragesimo Anno,* par. 71). Pope John Paul II raised to the ultimate level the urgency of promoting a situation where the just wage is paid "to every adult working man." He declared the just wage to be "the concrete means of verifying the justice of the whole socioeconomic system" (*Laborem Exercens,* par. 89). The full significance of that statement, which was repeated twice in *Laborem Exercens*, has not been fully appreciated. It is not profit, the level of production, the well-being of entrepreneurs, or for that matter, of consumers, but the prevalence of the just wage by which we can determine whether an economy is functioning as it should be, i.e., justly!

Pius XII turned from his affirmation of the just wage doctrine to another serious problem which was at the time still having a devastating effect on the American economy: unemployment. Although the worst was past by 1939, the problems underlying the Great Depression had not by any means been completely resolved. Full employment would not be restored except by the high levels of spending and the reallocation of manpower caused by World War II. Accordingly, the Pope took the occasion to express his continuing concern about the problem:

> May it also be brought about that each and every able-bodied man may receive an equal opportunity for work in order to earn the daily bread for himself and his own. We deeply lament the lot of those— and their number in the United States is large indeed—who though robust, capable and willing, cannot have

the work for which they are anxiously searching (*Sertum Laetitiae*, par. 37).

As a matter of fact, the official unemployment statistics for the year in which the encyclical appeared still stood at 17.2% and 25.2% for the total civilian labor force and for non-farm employees respectively. Those figures are in sharp contrast with the equivalent figures—3.9% and 5.4%—for the postwar year 1947 which was generally regarded as a year of "full employment." The contrast is even more stark when we look at the last year of World War II when the two figures respectively were 1.9 and 2.7!

In the meantime, the struggle for just wages was in the forefront of issues championed by the embattled labor union movement which by 1939 was achieving some significant success. Organized labor was enjoying unprecedented support stemming from progressive labor legislation at both the federal and state levels in the United States. Pius XII took the occasion of this encyclical to reaffirm the workers' right to form unions, first upheld as natural by Leo XIII in *Rerum Novarum.* "Because sociability is one of man's natural requirements, and since it is legitimate to promote by common effort a decent livelihood, it is not possible without injustice to deny or to limit either to the producers or to the laboring and farming classes the free faculty of uniting in associations by means of which they may defend their proper rights and secure the betterment of the goods of soul and of body, as well as the honest comforts of life (*Sertum Laetitiae*, par. 39).

To justify the particular form which the union movement was taking at the time, as opposed to the "unions...which in past centuries have procured immortal glory for Christianity and for the professions an untarnishable splendor," the Pope indicated that "one can not everywhere impose an identical discipline and structure which therefore can be varied to meet the different temperament of the people and the diverse circumstances of time" (*Sertum Laetitiae*, par. 39). In *Quadragesimo Anno,* Pius XI proposed a return to the guild-like vocational orders of the Middle Ages which included both parties in the labor market: workers as well as employers. Indeed, he suggested that such groups are "at least natural to civil society" (*Quadragesimo Anno,* par. 83). That remarkable and under-appreciated statement suggests that perhaps not much of the economic order which prevailed in 1931, or in the years afterwards, was "natural." Instead we were faced with the unnatural situation where "the so-called labor market separates men into two divisions, as into battle lines, and the contest between these divisions turns the labor market itself almost into a battlefield where, face to face the opposing lines struggle bitterly" (*Quadragesimo Anno,* par. 83).

That is not an indictment of the labor movement as such, where workers organize to secure their rights vis-à-vis their employers. Such unions certainly come under the heading of the "sociability (which) is one of man's natural requirements and, since it is legitimate to promote by common effort decent livelihood, it is not possible without injustice to deny or to limit." What Pius XI had indicted was the bitterness which turns the partners in production into warring parties. That is why Pius XII, in this encyclical addressed to the people of the

United States, urged them to "...let unions in question draw their vital force from principles of wholesome liberty," and to "let them take their form from the lofty rules of justice and of honesty and, conforming themselves to those norms, let them act in such a manner that in their care for the interests of their class they violate no one's rights, but instead "continue to strive for harmony and respect the common weal of civil society" (*Sertum Laetitiae*, par. 40).

One may hope for better days when the cooperation of labor and management overall becomes the order of the day. There have indeed been movements in that direction in the years since *Quadragesimo Anno* and *Sertum Laetitiae* appeared. Nevertheless, the right of workers to organize as workers, for their own separate legitimate interests, like the right of employers to organize as employers for theirs, is a right which cannot be denied either by employers or by the state.

Sertum Laetitiae closed on a hopeful note, offering what is at the same time a compliment and a challenge to "the American people, by nature inclined to grandiose undertakings and to liberality" (*Sertum Laetitiae*, par. 42).

> It is a source of joy to Us to know that the above cited Encyclical, Quadragesimo Anno, as well as that of the Sovereign Pontiff Leo XIII, Rerum Novarum, in which is indicated the solution of the social question in accordance with the postulates of the Gospel and of the eternal philosophy, are the object in the United States of careful and prolonged consideration on the part of some men of keener intellect whose generous wish pushes them on towards social restoration and the restrengthening of the bonds of love amongst men, and that some employers themselves have desired to settle the ever-recurring controversies with the working man in accordance with the norms of these Encyclicals, respecting always the common good and the dignity of the human person (*Sertum Laetitiae*, par. 41).

Optatissima Pax (1947)

This very brief but urgent encyclical was issued by Pope Pius XII on December 18, 1947. It was entitled in English, "On Prescribing Public Prayers for Social and World Peace."[14]

Optatissima Pax represents a lament about the continuing lack of peace internally, even among the nations so recently devastated by World War II. The Pope was confronted by the renewed messianic frenzy with which Communist agitators tried to promote their agenda, aglow now with the great victory in which the Soviet Union shared. While Joseph Stalin was absorbing the Eastern European states into the Soviet Empire, his agents, including indigenous Communist Parties outside that empire in countries like Italy, felt that their hour had now struck. Their frenzied activity was widespread during the immediate postwar years. Pius XII, clearly disheartened by the state of affairs, warned, using the Psalmist's words: "Unless the Lord build the house, they labor in vain that build it."

Also, World War II had scarcely ended when what came to be known as the "Cold War" began. With it came years that involved the waste of vast resources sorely needed to rehabilitate the devastated economies of Europe, and to bring the awakened "Third World" into the 20th century.

Once again, while nowhere listed as a "social encyclical," the overriding tone of *Optatissima Pax* is social in its tone, and it addresses the economic order explicitly.

> The crisis is most serious indeed. Remedies must be found and found without further delay. On the one hand the economic system of many nations, as a result of fabulous military expenditures and enormous destruction wrought by the war, has been dislocated and weakened to such an extent as to be powerless to meet the problems with which it is faced, and to provide the materials for appropriate constructive enterprise where work might be available for the unemployed who now must live their lives in forced and fruitless idleness. On the other hand, there is no lack of those who, sad to say, embitter and exploit the working man in his distress following a secret and astute plan, and thus obstruct the heroic efforts which the forces of justice and order are making to rebuild scattered fortunes (*Optatissima Pax*, par. 3).

Overall, the tone of the earlier social encyclicals is also clearly present in that paragraph, and in passages like this: "At the same time it is the duty of all to realize that the world crisis is so serious today and so menacing for the future that it is imperative for all, especially the rich, to place the common welfare above their private advantage and profits" (*Optatissima Pax*, par. 6).

Important material in future social teachings was foreshadowed in *Optatissima Pax*. Reference to the scandalous waste of vast resources consumed by wars and preparation for war, as in World War II, became an urgent theme in encyclicals by successors of Pius XII. Pope John XXIII would express his dismay at the way billions were expended for military hardware which, paradoxically, everyone hoped would never actually be used. For example, in *Mater et Magistra* written fourteen years later by Blessed John XXIII we find: "And in other countries a notable percentage of income is absorbed in building up an ill-conceived national prestige, and vast sums are spent on armament." (*Mater et Magistra*, par. 69) In another context after speaking about the mutual distrust between world powers, the same Pope wrote: "The result is a vast expenditure of human energy and natural resources on projects which are disruptive of human society rather than beneficial to it; while a growing uneasiness gnaws at men's hearts and makes them less responsive to the call of nobler enterprises" (*Mater et Magistra*, par. 204).

The same topic surfaced later in *Pacem in Terris* where John XXIII made reference to the preposterous nuclear balance of terror that had emerged between the superpowers.

> On the other hand, We are deeply distressed to see the enormous stocks of armaments that have been, and continue to be manufactured in the economically

> more developed countries. This policy is involving a vast outlay of intellectual and material resources with the result that the people of these countries are saddled with a great burden, while other countries lack the help they need for their economic and social development (*Pacem in Terris*, par. 109).

Later, in 1967, Pope Paul VI too made that anomaly the subject of a most passionate plea in his only social encyclical:

> Countless millions are starving, countless families are destitute, countless men are steeped in ignorance, countless people need schools, hospitals, and homes worthy of the name. In such circumstances, we cannot tolerate public and private expenditures of a wasteful nature; we cannot but condemn lavish displays of wealth by nations or individuals; we cannot approve a debilitating arms race. It is Our solemn duty to speak out against them. If only world leaders would listen to Us, before it is too late (*Populorum Progressio,* par. 53)!

Finally, Pope John Paul II made a powerful statement involving the same theme in *Redemptor Hominis* which, while not a social encyclical, is heavily laced with the implications of Catholic teachings for the social order. Referring to the last judgment, he wrote:

> This eschatological scene must always be applied to man's history; it must always be made the "measure" for human acts as an essential outline for an examination of conscience by each and every one: "I was hungry and you gave me no food...naked and you did not clothe me...in prison and you did not visit me." These words became charged with even stronger warning, when we think that, instead of bread and cultural aid, the new States and nations awakening to independent life are being offered sometimes in abundance, modern weapons and means of destruction placed at the service of armed conflicts and wars that are not so much a requirement for defending their just rights and their sovereignty but rather a form of chauvinism, imperialism, and neocolonialism of one kind or another. We all know well that the areas of misery and hunger on our globe could have been made fertile in a short time, if the gigantic investments for armaments at the service of war and destruction had been changed into investments for food at the service of life (*Redemptor Hominis*, par. 57).

These early warnings, starting with Pius XII, were, once again, prophetic. Both the Soviet Union and the United States brought themselves to the brink of economic bankruptcy by the profligate arms race which began even as that Pontiff was lamenting the outrageous cost in lives and economic resources occasioned by World War II.

Pius XII was therefore a bridge figure—a *pontifex*—between the world which suffered through the deadliest of all wars, and the foreboding future of the space-nuclear age. As is perhaps not yet recognized widely enough, in his teachings he was also in many other ways the precursor of the Second Vatican Council, standing as a critically important link between the pre-conciliar and the post-conciliar Church.

Although he issued no landmark social encyclicals, Pius XII provided a plethora of insightful social teachings. These were included in certain encyclicals wherever he regarded them as contextually proper. They also abound throughout his discourses and messages that are legendary in their scope and number. Nevertheless, perhaps most important as a corpus of social teachings by Pius XII are his masterful and eloquent *Christmas Messages*. We turn to them now, concentrating once again on those addressed specifically to the economic order.

Notes

1. Pius XII, *Summi Pontificatus* (Paulist edition), 1939.

2. *The Church and the Reconstruction of the Modern World*, edited and with commentary by Terence P. McLaughlin, C.S.B. (1957). This Doubleday Image Book was designed as a follow-up work to the earlier one, *The Church Speaks to the Modern World* (1954), edited by Etienne Gilson.

3. Heinrich Pesch, *Lehrbuch der Nationalökonomie*, rev. ed., (Freiburg im Breisgau: Herder, 1923-1926); English translation: *Lehrbuch der Nationalökonomie/Teaching Guide to Economics*, trans. Rupert J. Ederer, (Lewiston: Edwin Mellen Press, 2002-2003). Significant excerpts are also to be found in Rupert J. Ederer, *Heinrich Pesch on Solidarist Economics* (Lanham, Md.: University Press of America, 1998).

4. Pesch/Ederer, vol. I, bk.1, 36-39.

5. The late Msgr. Eugene Kevane (d. 1996), noted professor at Catholic University of America, spent many years as both a student and teacher in Rome. He informed me of this connection between Pius XII and Pesch, via the Jesuit scholar Gustav Gundlach.

6. Pesch/Ederer, vol. I, bk. 2, 221.

7. Pesch/Ederer, vol. 1, bk. 2, 221-222.

8. Jose Garcia, ed. *Doctrina Pontificia* II (Madrid: *Biblioteca de Autores Cristianos*, 1958), 749.

9. For example, for the official English translation, the National Catholic Welfare Conference assigned the title: *On the Function of the State in the Modern World*, which is used also for the Daughters of St. Paul edition. The Jesuit translation published by the America Press bore the title: *The Unity of Human Society*, which is also used in Claudia Carlen's 1958-1981 volume of *The Papal Encyclicals*. The British edition published by the Catholic Truth Society of London bears the title *Darkness Over the Earth*. The Paulist edition, on the other hand, carries the English title *Exhorting Unity in Opposing World Evils*.

10. See Aristotle on Friendship: cf. Richard McKeon, ed., *The Basic Works of Aristotle* (New York: Random House, 1941), 1058-1076.

11. Cf. Pius XI *Quadragesimo Anno* (1931). Whereas Leo XIII clearly inferred the relevance of those principles throughout *Rerum Novarum*, when dealing with the social problem confronting the workers, he did not mention them specifically by name. Pius XI, speaking of the inability of free competition, on the one hand, and "economic dictatorship" on the other, to guide economic life, stated that "other and nobler principles—social justice and social charity—are required." (*Rerum Novarum*, par. 88)

12. Pius XII, *Sertum Laetitiae* (1939) in Claudia Carlen IHM, ed. *The Papal Encyclicals, Vol. IV (1939-1958)* (N.p.: McGrath, 1981), 23-30.

13. Rupert J. Ederer, *Economics as if God Matters* (South Bend: Fidelity Press, 1995), 28n.

14. Pius XII, *Optatissima Pax* (1947) in Claudia Carlen IHM, ed. *The Papal Encyclicals, Vol. IV, 1939-1958* (N.p.: McGrath, 1981), 155-156.

Chapter 3
The Christmas Messages

The nineteen annual *Christmas Messages* by Pius XII had an elegance and a special magisterial quality which placed them in a class by themselves. They were normally delivered a day or two before Christmas. The earlier messages dealt principally with problems arising from the calamitous episode of World War II as it spread from Europe throughout the entire world. The *Messages* included recurring, persistent appeals for a just peace, for humane treatment of the victims of war, and for a much desired shortening of the war itself. Economic aspects surfaced more and more frequently, since it is impossible to isolate them fully from problems engulfing the political order overall.

Christmas Message of 1939

The first *Christmas Message* in 1939 includes passing reference to problems in the economic order associated with the war and the pervasive damage stemming from it. What Pius XII had to say about such matters echoed the concerns he mentioned in *Sertum Laetitiae.* The demands of wartime on the economic capacity of nations is such as "to inspire great anxiety in those concerned with the future economic, social and spiritual conditions of Europe, and not of Europe alone."[1]

> The more the war monster strives for, swallows, and allots itself material means which are placed inexorably at the service of war needs—mounting from hour to hour—the more acute becomes the danger for nations directly or indirectly struck by the conflict, of what We might call pernicious anemia, and they are faced with the pressing question: "How can an exhausted or weakened economy, at the end of the war, find means for economic and social reconstruction among difficulties which will be enormously increased, and which the forces and artifices of disorder, lying in wait, will seek to make use of in the hope of giving the final blow to Christian Europe?"

To its credit, the United States, which suffered less direct harm on the home-front than most other major participants in World War II, undertook to assist the other countries, friend and foe alike, in their economic reconstruction efforts after the War, to get through that "pernicious anemia." Had such benevolent action been of a purely altruistic nature, it would even then have marked a historic departure from the treatment which victors normally accorded to the vanquished after wars ended. Actually, without taking away from the benevolence of such measures, as was also present in postwar assistance, the foreign aid program of the United States, in its various aspects, soon became also a part of its Cold War policy. The alternatives which appeared to present themselves were either to help the nations left in desperate and dire need, or see them fall into the hands of the aggressive, expanding Soviet Empire. The Pope too may have been thinking in those terms when he spoke of "the forces and artifices of disorder, lying in wait" and seeking to deliver "the final blow to Christian Europe." In retrospect the helping hand turned out to be providential. And it also perhaps served to affirm the trait of "liberality" in the American people which Pius XII had mentioned in *Sertum Laetitiae*.

Christmas Message of 1940

The 1940 *Christmas Message* already offered guidelines for the postwar period. These came as precautionary in the context of talk among the warring parties about "a new order." Otherwise that "new order" could involve a "liberty-destroying mechanism enforced by violence, without sincerity, consent, joy, dignity or honor, oppressing souls."[2]

Here we find among the "premises for such a new order" specific mention of the economic life of nations. The Pope included among five premises: "Victory over those potential conflicts arising out of the disequilibrium of world economy. Therefore a new economic order has to be gradually evolved which gives all nations the means to secure for their citizens an appropriate standard of life."

Directly following that premise is one involving an appeal for "genuine Christian solidarity of a legal and economic character," and to "a brotherly co-operation of the nations, the sovereignty of which has been duly secured."[3] This would be required, according to Pius XII, to provide, "victory over the kind of egoism which, relying on its own power, aims at impairing the honor and liberty of individuals."

That represents the first time in his *Christmas Messages* that Pius XII mentioned *solidarity*, first referred to by him in *Summi Pontificatus* as the "law of solidarity." It is a theme which occurred subsequently with increasing frequency in the Pope's teachings throughout his pontificate especially, but not exclusively, when he dealt with the economic order. It is noteworthy that he used the modifying adjective, "Christian," here. It would be nearly a half century later when Pope John Paul II would confirm, in his encyclical *Sollicitudo Rei Socialis,* that "*Solidarity* is undoubtedly a *Christian virtue*."[4]

Christmas Message of 1942

The next important reference to the economic order occurs in the *Christmas Message of 1942*. It is a message that addressed specifically the internal order of society that the Pope saw as "intimately related" to international relations among peoples.[5] Accordingly: "A social teaching or a social reconstruction program which denies or prescinds from this internal essential relation to God of everything regarding men, is on a false course; and while it builds up with one hand, it prepares with the other the materials which sooner or later will undermine and destroy the whole fabric."[6]

We find here an important reference to the then rival economic systems, both of which were on the "false course," since neither accepted "this internal essential relation to God of everything that regards men."

First there is liberal capitalism which marked Western civilization from the 18th century onward into the 20th century when it was seriously challenged by communism. The Pope referred to the juxtaposition of economic systems:

> After the fateful economy of the past decades, during which the lives of all citizens were subordinated to the stimulus of gain, there now succeeds another and no less fateful policy which, while it considers everybody with reference to the State, excludes all thought of ethics or religion. This is a fatal travesty, a fatal error. It is calculated to bring about far-reaching consequences for social life, which is never nearer to losing its noblest prerogatives than when it thinks it can deny or forget with impunity the external source of its own dignity: God.

Pius XII mentioned the "travesty" by name, and he addressed it with these words:

> Always moved by religious motives, the Church has condemned the various forms of Marxist Socialism; and she condemns them today because it is her permanent right and duty to safeguard men from currents of thought and influences that jeopardize their eternal salvation. But the Church cannot ignore or overlook the fact that the worker in his efforts to better his lot, is opposed by a machinery which is not only not in accordance with nature, but is at variance with God's plan and with the purpose He had in creating the goods of earth.[7]

What follows is highly relevant for the discussion of the juxtaposed economic systems: capitalism and socialism.

> In spite of the fact that the ways they followed were and are false and to be condemned, what man, and especially what priest or Christian, could remain deaf to the cries that rise from the depths and calls for justice and a spirit of brotherly collaboration in a world ruled by a just God? Such silence would be culpable and unjustifiable before God, and contrary to the inspired teaching of the Apostle, who, while he inculcates the needs of resolution in the fight against error, also knows that we must be full of sympathy for those who err, and open-minded in our understanding of their aspirations, hopes and motives.
>
> When He blessed our first parents, God said: "Increase and multiply and fill the earth and subdue it." And to the first father of a family, He said later:

> "In the sweat of thy face shalt thou eat bread." The dignity of the human person, then, requires normally as a natural foundation of life the right to the use of the goods of the earth. To this right corresponds the fundamental obligation to grant private ownership of property, if possible, to all. Positive legislation regulating private ownership may change and more or less restrict its use. But if legislation is to play its part in the pacification of the community, it must prevent the worker, who is or will be a father of a family from being condemned to an economic dependence and slavery which is irreconcilable with his rights as a person. Whether this slavery arises from the exploitation of private capital or from the power of the state, the result is the same. Indeed, under the pressure of a State which dominates all and controls the whole field of public and private life, even going into the realm of ideas and beliefs and of conscience, this lack of liberty can have the more serious consequences, as experience shows and proves.[8]

The shortcomings of both rival systems of economy are bared here in stark terms. The operative term is "slavery"! According to Pius XII it can arise from the irresponsible exercise of control over capital, or from total power wielded by the totalitarian state. The latter can be worse in that its dominion extends over "the realm of ideas and beliefs and of conscience." Nevertheless, capitalism is not extolled outright as the preferable option. Its acceptability is conditioned by general prevalence of the just wage doctrine which makes possible, among other things, "widespread private ownership." The Pope's message reached the heights of its moral imperative character while reaffirming one of the pivotal doctrines in the two prior encyclicals dealing with the economic order.

In referring to the task of "social reconstruction" that lay ahead, Pius XII made a striking allusion to the Crusades: "It is for the most distinguished members of the Christian family, filled with the enthusiasm of Crusaders, to unite in the spirit of truth, justice and love to the call: God wills it, ready to serve, to sacrifice themselves like the Crusaders of old."[9]

With no misgivings about the length and ardor of the journey, the Pope continued as if prophetically: "It is true that the road from night to full day will be long; but of decisive importance are the first steps on the path." He marked off this path with five "mile-stones." And the third of these, regarding the "Dignity of Labor," addresses the economic order directly by, among other things, repeating the just wage theme.

> He who would have the Star of Peace shine out and stand over society should give to work the place assigned to it by God from the beginning. As an indispensable means towards gaining over the world that mastery which God wishes, for His glory, all work has an inherent dignity and at the same time a close connection with the perfection of the person; this is the noble dignity and privilege of work which is not in any way cheapened by the fatigue and the burden, which have to be borne as the effect of original sin, in obedience and submission to the will of God.
>
> Those who are familiar with the great Encyclicals of Our predecessors and Our Own previous messages know well that the Church does not hesitate to draw the practical conclusions which are derived from the moral nobility of work, and to give them all the support of her authority. These exigencies in-

> clude, besides a just wage which covers the needs of the worker and his family, the conservation and perfection of a social order which will make possible an assured, even if modest, private property for all classes of society, which will promote higher education for the children of the working class who are especially endowed with intelligence and good will, which will promote the care and practice of the social spirit in one's immediate neighborhood, in the district, the province, the people and the nation, a spirit which, by smoothing over friction arising from privileges or class interests removes from workers the sense of isolation through the assuring experience of a genuinely human, and fraternally Christian solidarity.[10]

That passage, with its powerful endorsement of prior Catholic social teaching about labor and its problems and needs, reaffirms the aspect of the just wage doctrine insisting on the possibility of "modest private property for all classes of society." In addition, there was another dimension which was far from standard at the time when Pius XII delivered this urgent message. In the United States, as elsewhere, higher education was still out of the reach of the majority of people. The "majority of people" had to rely, then as now, almost exclusively on wages for their sustenance. They were of the "working class" which the Pope was talking about here. In the United States, graduation from secondary school was the prevalent educational endowment for the journey through life. After World War II, special programs for war veterans made a significant start to placing higher education within the reach of the working class. What Pius XII was proposing here was still beyond the range to which ordinary people could aspire, thus placing an added burden on the just wage doctrine to eventually make it possible, as became the case again in more recent times.

Considered in its broader aspects, that urgent "guideline" dealing with the dignity of labor presents us with a remarkable preview of where future social teachings of the Church would extend. Once again we have a Pontiff building a bridge between the foundation provided by Leo XIII in 1891, and what Pope John Paul II had to say about human work ninety years later. *Laborem Exercens* (1981), which presents a brilliant theology of work, was foreshadowed in this remarkable "milestone" message for reconstructing social order out of the chaos of World War II.

The almost rhapsodic elevation of simple human work, like the "Christian solidarity" appealed to in the previous sentence, is in full accord with what the Jesuit economist Heinrich Pesch had to say in designing his solidaristic system with human work fixed at its center. "Man who is ordained and empowered to be the lord over the environment accomplishes this dominion and makes use of it by his work."[11]

The centrality of human work as the predominant source of the national wealth was an aspect of economic reality, which both Adam Smith and Karl Marx as architects of contending economic systems also sensed. Unfortunately, they were unable to follow through to correct conclusions because they started on false premises. One ended up exalting self-interest, which inevitably worked to the advantage of the capitalist class at the expense of labor; the other installed the tyrannical state under the false pretext of a "dictatorship of the proletariat."

Finally, Pius XII offered in this important *Christmas Message* yet one more indication of forceful social teachings that would be brought to the forefront by his successors. Pope John XXIII went far to expand the social gospel, especially by extending the application of the virtues of justice and charity in the economic order beyond national boundaries to a worldwide basis. Pope Paul VI dedicated his one social encyclical precisely to the urgent need to extend the genuine benefits of modern industrial society, until then reaped by a few favored wealthier countries, to the underdeveloped nations of the world. We find in this 1942 *Christmas Message* by Pius XII a significant indication of what lay ahead for a world then still deeply immersed in World War II:

> The progress and extent of urgent social reforms depend on the economic possibilities of single nations. It is only through an intelligent and generous sharing of forces between the strong and the weak that it will be possible to effect a universal pacification in such a wise as not to leave behind centers of conflagration and infection from which new disasters may come.

That such "generous sharing" is not to be confined within national borders is suggested by the closing question: "Is it not true that deep thinkers see ever more clearly in the renunciation of egoism and national isolation, the way to general salvation, ready as they are to demand of their peoples, a heavy participation in the sacrifices necessary for the social well-being in other people?"[12]

That is an important prelude to an agenda which John XXIII initiated, and to which Paul VI would devote his impassioned plea in *Populorum Progressio* 25 years later.

Pius XII ended this important *Christmas Message* with a no less passionate plea. Calling for a "solemn vow not to rest until in all peoples and all nations of the earth a vast legion shall be formed...bent on bringing back society to its center of gravity, which is the law of God," the Pope said:

> Mankind owes that vow to the countless dead who lie buried on the field of battle: the sacrifice of their lives in the fulfillment of their duty is a holocaust offered for a new and better social order. Mankind owes that vow to the innumerable sorrowing host of mothers, widows, and orphans who have seen the light, the solace and the support of their lives wrenched from them. Mankind owes that vow to those numberless exiles whom the hurricane of war has torn from their native land and scattered in the land of the stranger; who can make their own the lament of the Prophet, "Our inheritance is turned to aliens; our house to strangers." Mankind owes that vow to the hundreds of thousands of persons who, without any fault on their part, sometimes only because of their nationality or race, have been consigned to death or to a slow decline....[13]

It is well worth bearing in mind that those words were delivered in December of 1942, several years before the deadliest of all wars had tallied near 50 million dead! That war would finally come to an end five years before Pius XII presented the next important message of solidarity to a world still struggling with the wretched baggage of its recent past.

Christmas Message of 1950

The *Christmas Message of 1950* was mainly an appeal for peace. The Korean War was raging and brought the super-powers face to face in what had become an era of awesome nuclear weaponry. Nevertheless, the Roman Catholic Pontiff, ever aware of the close interrelationship between the political and economic orders, used the opportunity to point out also that the underlying difficulty lay in "a more serious evil of a spiritual and moral character." He saw that as "...evidenced by the number of men with narrow minds and mean spirits, of egoists and 'go-getters,' of those who follow fortune's favors." And he perceived how, as a result "the foundations of the industrial and capitalistic systems have undergone essential changes that after a long period of preparation have been accelerated by the war.... The thirst for social security that is ever growing in intensity and extent is but a symptom of the present state of society in the various countries, where many things that once seemed traditionally solid have become unreliable and uncertain."[14]

The presence of those symptoms throughout the political and economic orders prompted the Pontiff to make a fervent renewed appeal for *solidarity*:

> Why, then, does not this common uncertainty and doubt, arising from present circumstances, create a certain solidarity among the peoples in different countries. Is not the interest of the employer and the employed in this respect identical? Is it not true in every country that industrial and agricultural production are now more than ever linked together on account of the reciprocal influence they exert one upon the other? And you, you who remain insensible to the hardships suffered by the wandering and homeless refugees, should you not have a fellow-feeling for him whose unhappy lot today may well be yours tomorrow?
>
> Why should not this solidarity among all those peoples who are restless and in danger become for all the secure way of leading to safety? Why should not this spirit of solidarity be the basis of the natural social order in its three essentials—the family, property and the state—and make these elements collaborate in one organic whole that is adapted to present conditions? These present conditions are, after all, despite all their inherent difficulties, a gift of God; why should they not conduce to the strengthening of the Christian spirit?[15]

Reference to the application of "this spirit of solidarity" in three essential parts of the "natural social order" is clearly Peschian. The Jesuit economist had indicated how the principle of solidarity, in addition to the bond among all people worldwide, was to apply specifically at the level of the family, at the basic economic level of common occupations, and among citizens of the same national state.[16] These four levels of application are all represented in this *Christmas Message*, as conducive to "the strengthening of the Christian spirit." It is noteworthy also that Pesch devoted the third chapter of the first volume of his *Lehrbuch*, in three parts, to: the family, private property, and the state—precisely what Pius XII refers to here as "the natural social order in its three essentials—the family, property and the state." Peschian solidarity assumes a prominent place in subsequent Christmas addresses, which are addressed predominantly to the economic order.

Christmas Message of 1952

The *Christmas Message of 1952,* like the one following it in 1953, dwells on the theme of over-organization to the detriment of the human person. The 1952 *Message* involves an eloquent defense against a certain depersonalization by what Pius XII called here "the demon of organization."[17] It is in a real sense a Jeremiad—a lamentation about the Frankenstein monster that modern mankind had created and over which it was now in grave danger of losing control:

> One would say that humanity today, which has been able to build the marvelous, complex machine of the modern world, subjugating to its service the tremendous forces of nature, now appears incapable of controlling these forces—as though the rudder has slipped from its hands—and so it is in peril of being overthrown and crushed by them.
>
> Such inability to control should of itself suggest to men who are its victims not to expect salvation solely from the technicians' production and organization. The work of these can help, and notably, to solve the grave and extensive problems which afflict the world only if it is bound up with, and directed toward, bettering and strengthening true human values, but in no case—oh, how We wish that all, both on this Continent and beyond the sea, would realize it—will it avail to fashion a world without misery.[18]

Reference to the contending economic systems recurs here: "Men either attribute salvation to some order rigorously uniform and inflexible, embracing the whole world, to a system that ought to act with the certainty of a proven medicine, to a new social formula reduced to cold theoretic terms—or, on the other hand, rejecting such general prescriptions, they hope for salvation from the spontaneous forces of the natural instinct and, in the best hypothesis, from sentimental impulses of individuals and peoples, without troubling whether the overthrow of existing order follows as a consequence, even though it is quite clear that salvation cannot be born of chaos."[19]

Both collectivistic socialism and individualistic capitalism were rejected:

> Both these ways are false, and so are far from reflecting the wisdom of God, Who is the first and exemplary cause of the alleviation of misery. It is superstition to expect salvation from rigid formulas mathematically applied to the social order, for this attributes to them an almost prodigious power which they cannot have, while to place one's hope exclusively in the creative forces of vital action of each individual is contrary to the designs of God, Who is the Lord of Order.

The totalitarian approach to organizing economic life is then singled out:

> We wish to draw the attention of those who come forward as benefactors of mankind to both these aberrations, but particularly to the first: to the superstition which holds for certain that salvation must spring from the organization of men and things in a strict unity designed for the highest productive capacity. They think that if they succeed in coordinating the energies of man and the resources of nature in a single organic structure for the highest possible produc-

> tion, by means of minutely designed and executed organization, then every kind of desirable benefit will spring forth: prosperity, security for the individual, peace.

Although Pius XII was clearly indicting total centralized planning of economic life in the communist states, his reference to "rigid formulas mathematically applied to the social order" could to some extent be applied also to some economies in the non-Communist world. Planning national economic life on the basis of such formulas had also insinuated itself there. Especially since the Keynesian influence on so-called *national income analysis*, and with the contrivance of elaborate input-output tables, economists in the West too had begun to play games with mathematical models that supposedly represented actual or even normative depictions of economic reality. They felt they could thereby promote a desired outcome, e.g., full employment, with greater certitude than by leaving the course of events simply to free market impulses. The movement to depict economic life in all of its critical sectors in terms of mathematical equations had, of course, gained significant impetus long before John Maynard Keynes triggered the movement into so-called macro-economics.

Previously, there were attempts to represent the interrelationships of prices, including the prices of the factors of production labor and capital, i.e., wage and interest rates, in terms of sets of equations. The implication was that the economy could perform at some supposed optimum equilibrium level. Factors like the realities of practical politics and the active ongoing intervention in economic life by various economic pressure groups made the dreams of mathematically oriented economists into little more than fascination with stimulating theoretical games.

Even in the totalitarian socialist states where the official planners supposedly sat at the actual levers of control over economic life, other stark realities, like the vagaries of indomitable human nature, inserted themselves as if to affirm the words of the Poet Robert Burns: "The best laid plans of mice and men gang aft agley." The horrendous inefficiency of the entire top-heavy planning process finally contributed greatly to bringing the system down in the bloodless revolutions which amazed the world after 1989. That eventuality too made the words of Pius XII appear, once again, prophetic.

Pius XII wisely proceeded in this *Message* to forestall a flawed reaction. Throughout the period in history that followed the Industrial Revolution, there have emerged time and again romanticist reactions opposed to modern industrial organization. These involved not only legitimate indictments of exaggerated bigness in enterprise and the depersonalization of workers that often stemmed from it, but also less valid initiatives against the mechanization of industry as such. Referring to "the gigantic enterprises of modern industry," the Pope said:

> We do not intend here to express an opinion on the necessity, utility and disadvantages of these forms of production. Indubitably, they are a marvelous manifestation of the inventive and constructive genius of the human spirit. It is right for the world to admire enterprises which in the area of production and management succeed in coordinating and mobilizing the physical forces of men and

> matter. And the present age may take legitimate pride in the stable way in which these enterprises are organized and in the often novel and characteristic beauty of their external set-up. But what must be denied is that modern social life should be regulated by them or made to conform to them.[20]

However, giant enterprise is not the whole story. "History teaches that other forms of economic organization have always had a constructive influence upon all society, an influence which benefited both the basic institutions of family, state, and private property, and those freely formed by men." In other words, we should not be overly impressed with the genius that is certainly involved in designing and operating the gigantic enterprises of our time, to the extent that we make them the universal norm for economic life in our time. That is where Pius XII perceived a threat in modern society. "Modern industry has unquestionably had beneficial results, but the problem which arises today is this: will a world in which the only economic form to find acceptance is a vast productive system be equally fitted to exert a happy influence upon society in general and upon the three fundamental institutions of society in particular?" He offers the answer in the threat which he perceives in the resultant depersonalization of man brought on by the "demon of organization":[21]

> We must answer that the impersonal character of such a world is contrary to the fundamentally personal nature of those institutions which the Creator has given to human society. In fact, marriage and the family, the state and private property tend of their very nature to form man as a person, to protect and render him capable of contributing through his own voluntary cooperation and personal responsibility to the similarly personal life and development of human relations. The creative wisdom of God is therefore alien to that system of impersonal unity which strikes at the human person, who is origin, and end of society, and in the depths of his being an image of his God.

Enter here the "demon of organization" which the Pope indicates is already "a sad reality," and which "invades and tyrannizes man's spirit," reflecting "the signs of a false and abnormal orientation of society." In "some countries," the movement is glaring and obvious, because "the modern state is becoming a gigantic administrative machine" which "extends its influence over almost every phase of life...bringing under its administration the entire gamut of political, economic, social and intellectual life from birth to death." The vast socialist empire of the Soviet Union as well as the Asian giant, Communist China, can be recognized in the way "society itself has been transformed into an impersonal system and into a cold organization of force." However, one must not overlook the papal reference to "some countries," because the depersonalization process occurs in its own way also in the "other world" of capitalism.

The Pope turned to the problem of unemployment, which in the postwar years again became in the capitalist world the recurring, nagging problem that refused to go away. As examples of the "depersonalization" process, he referred to "different classes of the indigent" in "the teeming world of misery." As an example, Pius XII cited "the father of a needy family, a constant visitor to the bureau of public charity, whose children cannot wait for the distant and vague realization of the golden age which is always in the future."[22] The inquiry followed: "What is the answer which modern society often gives to the unemployed person who presents himself at an employment office, disposed, perhaps through habit, to accept one more disappointment, but not resigned to the unmerited fate of being considered useless?" As if to confirm that the "unemployed person" is not an isolated case, we find: "And what is the response to be given to a people who, despite all efforts, have not succeeded in freeing themselves from the atrophying clutches of mass unemployment?"

The eventual solution is not to be found in pipe dreams about "guaranteeing full employment with a constantly rising standard of living." The problem is that in all such fantasies "the standard of living and employment of labor" are treated as "purely quantitative factors," instead of as "human values in the full sense of the word." The next passage is highly significant in that it points away from mechanistic solutions and toward the "human approach" to solving the problem at hand:

"Every plan or program must be inspired by the principle that man as subject, guardian and promoter of human values is more important than mere things, is more important than practical applications of scientific progress, and that above all it is imperative to preserve from an unwholesome 'depersonalization' the essential forms of the social order which We have just mentioned, and to use them to create and develop human relationships."[23]

What follows comes as close to an appeal for the establishment of a solidaristic system of economy as any pope before or since has dared propose. After pointing out that "the forces of society have the task of encouraging full and reciprocal solidarity among individuals and among peoples," Pius XII made this remarkable statement:

> It is upon the basis of this solidarity, and not upon worthless and unstable systems, that We call upon men to build the social fabric. Solidarity demands that outrageous and provoking inequalities in living standards among different groups in a nation be eliminated.

Here we have no less than appeal that "the social fabric" be woven on the basis of the *principle of solidarity*! And such a "social fabric" is being juxtaposed to "worthless and unstable systems"! Thirty-five years later John Paul II, the Pope who more than any other articulated the precise meaning of *solidarity*, while declaring it to be a "Christian virtue," stated: "For the Church does not propose economic and political systems or programs, nor does she show preference for one or the other, *provided that human dignity is properly respected and promoted, and provided she herself is allowed the room she needs to exercise her ministry in the world* [italics added]." (*Sollicitudo Rei Socialis*, par. 41)

Could it be that Pius XII was so totally disenchanted with the alternative existing systems, each in its own way guilty of the "depersonalization of man," that he had already despaired of seeking salvation for man in those contending economic orders? Thus, he may have been resorting precisely to the proviso included many years later by Pope John Paul II as italicized above. There is no question but that the Communist system, then in operation, failed the test of allowing to the Church "the room she needs to exercise her ministry in the world." And so far as the capitalistic system is concerned, what Pius XII was saying about depersonalization and the loss of dignity among the masses of unemployed workers also indicted the reliance on the dubious leadership of the "men of narrow minds and mean spirits, of the egotists and 'go-getters'" that he mentioned in his 1950 *Christmas Message.*

In the best of circumstances, the popes and the Church need not have gotten involved in pedestrian economic matters, let alone questions of economic methodology. However, circumstances have been far from optimum since individualistic capitalism, along with the collectivistic socialism which was triggered in response to it, turned economic life upside down. Now man, the human person, is no longer the dominant factor—the "subject"—of the economic order. In the solidaristic system of human work envisioned by Heinrich Pesch, it is precisely man who is at the core of economic life. For Pesch, the working human person is not merely a factor of production, and he is certainly not a mere commodity in the market. He is the subject of economic activity, as well as the reason for which it takes place. The influence of Pesch's ideas are perhaps more apparent in this *Message* than anywhere else in the social teachings of Pius XII. As indicated earlier, that may well reflect the influence of Pesch's disciple, Gustav Gundlach, S. J., who was that Pope's principal advisor on matters relating to the economic order.

The "voice of conscience" to which the Pope appealed in establishing solidarity as the basis for "the social fabric" also echoes Pesch. The Jesuit economist placed the conscience of the individual first among the factors which were to serve as regulating forces to assure that his solidaristic system would function in a satisfactory manner: hence his stress on the virtues of justice and charity in their social application. The intermediate structures, like occupational (or vocational) orders and, in the final analysis, the state, would support conscientious individuals in a *subsidiary* fashion. Pius XII went on to explain the role of conscience, and in the process he also suggested the essence of solidarity.

> Conscience will know how to set limits to expenditures for luxuries, and likewise persuade those of more modest means to provide before all else for what is necessary and useful, and then save whatever is left over. This solidarity of men with each other demands, not only in the name of brotherly love, but even of mutual advantage, that everything possible be done to maintain and increase employment. Therefore let those who are able to invest capital consider in the light of the common good—and with due regard to their economic condition, to risks involved and opportunity offered—whether they can reconcile with their conscience their neglect and failure to make investments because of unreasonable caution.

Once again, the appeal to "mutual advantage" is precisely what *solidarity* is all about. In other words, people need to help each other not solely out of charitable impulses, i.e., "brotherly love," but because in the context of society, including the economy, such help is "of mutual advantage." As Pope John Paul II would explain thirty-five years later in *Sollicitudo Rei Socialis*, "When interdependence becomes recognized in this way, the correlative response as a moral and social attitude, as a 'virtue,' is *solidarity*." (*Sollicitudo Rei Socialis*, par. 38) It is the recognition and appreciation of *de facto* interdependence at all levels of society which, when acted upon in a habitual manner ("as a moral and social attitude"), is a *virtue*. In this case it is what John Paul II termed the "Christian virtue" of solidarity, and what Pius XI in his encyclical *On Reconstructing the Social Order* (1931) had identified as "social charity." According to that Pontiff, "social charity was to be the soul of this order" (*On Reconstructing the Social Order*, par. 88). The Jesuit Heinrich Pesch whose ideas inspired essential elements of that encyclical, established the "principle of solidarity" early in his *Lehrbuch*: "When we speak of solidarity with regard to social life, we have in mind in a most general sense, first of all social interdependence, the actual mutual dependence of people on one another."[24]

Pius XII then went on to extend the application of the *principle of solidarity* beyond the confines of the workplace and the national economy at large, across the borders of individual nations. The paragraph that follows clearly foreshadows the teachings of John XXIII and Paul VI in the way that they extended such application of the virtues of social justice and social charity—the latter now equated by Pope John Paul II with solidarity—to bridge the vast gaps in wealth between the developed and underdeveloped nations of the world:

> But also to nations as such, We extend our invitation to render operative this sense and obligation of solidarity: that every nation develop its own potentialities in regard to living standards and employment, and contribute to the corresponding progress of nations less favored. Although even the most perfect realization of international solidarity would hardly bring about perfect equality among nations, still there is an urgent need that this solidarity be put into practice at least enough to change perceptibly the present situation, which is far indeed from attaining a just harmony. In other words, solidarity among nations demands the abolition of glaring inequalities in living standards, and so in financial investments and in the degree of productivity of human labor.

Contained therein is the stuff of which an entire social encyclical, *Populorum Progressio* (1967), was later made! Pope Paul VI subsequently emphasized the need for the poor nations to, first of all, do all in their own power to improve the economic lot of their own people. "Nations are the architects of their own development, and they must bear the burden of this work; but they cannot accomplish it if they live in isolation from others...." (*Populorum Progressio*, par. 77).

Two more specific topics relating to economics are addressed in the *Christmas Message of 1952*. Pius XII aired the population problem and the impact that it has on immigration policies. He also spoke of labor unions and their position in the "depersonalization" process. Both matters were dealt with in terms of conscience to which in this *Message* he was assigning such a large role for resolving the problems confronting the economic order.

The problem of so-called overpopulation was made into a pressing issue by certain interests during the years following World War II. That was somewhat ironic, inasmuch as the world had just lost some 40 million people in that war. To the extent that propagandists were successful in assigning the blame for poverty and hunger in the world, and later for environmental depredation, on overpopulation, some persons who were misled by them alleged problems in conscience with regard to how they would conduct their marital unions. Also, nations faced with population influx from poorer neighbor states began to factor into their immigration laws the prospective impact of such population gains. As Pius XII pointed out,

> When married couples wish to remain faithful to the sacrosanct laws of life established by the Creator, or when to safeguard this fidelity they seek to break loose from straitened circumstances which shackle them in their own country and find the only possible solution in emigration—in former times counseled by the desire for gain, today often imposed by misery—then see how they run up against the provisions of organized society as against an inexorable law, against pure mathematics which has already determined how many persons in such and such circumstances a given country can or ought to support, not only now, but in the future.

The Pope scored here the use of "pure mathematics" leading to "an inexorable law," to frustrate people's consciences in the important matter of family size and the exercise of "the natural right of the individual to be unhampered in immigration or emigration."[25] He added: "Such interior conflicts between the economic system and conscience are disguised under the terms: the question of the birth rate and the problem of emigration." For that, he blamed "modern society, which wishes to plan and organize all things" so that it "comes into conflict, since it is conceived as a machine, with that which is living, and which therefore cannot be subjected to quantitative calculations." Hence, we are face to face once again with that "demon of organization" which approaches society as "inflexible" and "static," operating with mathematical precision, "as though it were a machine." Ultimately then, "by means of such prophetic mathematics an attempt is made to mechanize even consciences." The Pontiff made reference here to "public prescriptions for birth control."

Conceding that "this or that region is at present burdened by a relatively excess population," he is unwilling to accept as a solution "a formula that the number of inhabitants should be regulated according to the public economy" because that would "subvert the order of nature and the entire psychological and moral world which is bound up with it." That "would be to blame natural law for the present miseries of the world, when it is clear these derive from the lack of mutual solidarity of men and peoples."

The important straight-forward position adopted here by Pius XII once again foreshadows messages in future social encyclicals by his successors John XXIII and Paul VI. Both of these pontiffs admitted along with him that "*this or that region* is *at present* burdened by a *relatively excess* population." The italics added here indicate what is of the essence in considering the correct approach to resolving the problem. The areas under immediate population pressure represent a small number of cases. A look at a world map showing population densities reveals that by far the greater portion of the world is sparsely populated. In addition, several of the most densely populated countries of the world (e.g., Netherlands, Belgium, Great Britain) are also among the economically most prosperous. Also, the term, "*at present,*" suggests that the problem is temporary, not one which is destined to confront the world for all time as by some natural law expressed in terms of arithmetical and geometric progressions, until the planet approaches its doom. Ultimately, the "excess" is *relative*, in that it relates to given circumstances of time and place, in this case to the particular state of economic development. One may say therefore that the problem is not absolute but *cultural,* i.e., relative to certain cultural factors present in each nation. The apparent overpopulation surfaces in certain economically underdeveloped nations, many of which are in fact very sparsely populated. It often stems from the still primitive circumstances of their economies, rather than from the mere numbers of their inhabitants. In other countries, what looks like excess population results from disastrous political management, whether due to inherently inefficient socialistic experiments, or the kind of political corruption that seems almost endemic in some nations which gained their independence following the dissolution of empires after World War II. It is important to note that in such situations, reducing the populations would simply result in fewer people whose economic plight remains as bad as it was before!

In any case, the genius of this Pope is manifested by the way he led the way for his successors. Both John XXIII and Paul VI picked up on the theme in that one very pregnant passage about a "relatively excess population," and about the frequently projected solution and its associated problem for the conscience.

For example, Blessed John XXIII devoted a significant portion of the encyclical *Mater et Magistra* (1961) to precisely that problem.[26] In terms of what Pius XII had referred to as "prophetic mathematics," he wrote:

> According to sufficiently reliable statistics the next few decades will see a very great increase in human population, whereas economic development will proceed at a slower rate. Hence we are told, if nothing is done to check this rise in population, the world will be faced in the not too distant future with an increasing shortage in the necessities of life" (*Mater et Magistra*, par. 186).
>
> As it affects the less developed countries, the problem is stated thus: The resources of modern hygiene and medicine will very shortly bring about a notable decrease in the mortality rate, especially among infants, while the birth rate—which in such countries is unusually high—will tend to remain more or less constant, at least for a considerable period. The excess of births over deaths will therefore show a steep rise, whereas there will be no corresponding increase in the productive efficiency of the economy. Accordingly, the standard of living in these poorer countries cannot possibly improve. It must surely worsen, even to the point of extreme hardship. Hence there are those who hold the opinion that, in order to prevent a serious crisis from developing, the conception and birth of children should be secretly avoided, or, in any event, curbed in some way (*Mater et Magistra*, par. 187).

The amiable John XXIII, regarded by many as naturally optimistic, was of another opinion:

> Truth to tell, we do not seem to be faced with any immediate or imminent world problem arising from the disproportion between the increase of population and the supply of food. Arguments to this effect are based on such unreliable and controversial data that they can only be of very uncertain validity (*Mater et Magistra*, par. 188).

He had another solution. Echoing precisely what Pius XII had stated in his 1952 *Christmas Message*, he wrote:

> As for the problems which face the poorer nations in various parts of the world, We realize, of course, that these are very real. They are caused, more often than not, by a deficient economic and social organization, which does not offer living conditions proportionate to the increase in population. They are caused, also, by the lack of effective solidarity among such peoples (*Mater et Magistra*, par. 190).

Rejecting the proffered solution of artificial birth control, he proposed instead:

> The only possible solution to this question is one which envisages the social and economic progress both of individuals and of the whole of human society, and which respects and promotes true human values. First, consideration must obviously be given to those values which concern man's dignity generally, and the immense worth of each individual human life. Attention must then be turned to the need for worldwide co-operation among men, with a view to a fruitful and well-regulated interchange of useful knowledge, capital and manpower (*Mater et Magistra*, par. 192).

John XXIII lamented that instead of productive cooperation among nations, there is instead "a vast expenditure of human energy and natural resources on projects which are disruptive of human society rather than beneficial to it; while a growing uneasiness gnaws at men's hearts and makes them less responsible to the call of nobler enterprise." (*Mater et Magistra*, par. 204)

After the brief, hectic pontificate of John XXIII, his successor, Pope Paul VI devoted two encyclicals to both aspects of the problem indicated above. The encyclical *Populorum Progressio* (1967) addressed the need to bridge the gap between the poor and rich nations of the earth. Like his two predecessors, he also acknowledged, first of all, that there *is* a problem: "There is no denying that the accelerated rate of population growth brings many added difficulties to the problems of development where the size of the population grows more rapidly than the quantity of available resources to such a degree that things seem to have reached an impasse." (*Populorum Progressio*, par. 37)[27]

Again, like his two predecessors Paul VI indicated what the implications of the problem are for the entire family of nations: "The duty of promoting human solidarity also falls upon the shoulders of nations: 'It is a very important duty of the advanced nations to help the developing nations.'" (Here he was quoting the Vatican II decree, *The Church in the Modern World.*) Beyond that there was the same admonition about using to far better advantage vast amounts of wealth spent for armaments:

> A further step must be taken. When We were at Bombay for the Eucharistic Congress, We asked world leaders to set aside part of their military expenditures for a world fund to relieve the needs of impoverished people. What is true for the immediate war against poverty is also true for the work of national development. Only a concerted effort on the part of all nations embodied in and carried out by this world fund will stop these senseless rivalries and promote fruitful, friendly dialogue between nations (*Populorum Progressio*, par. 51).

The urgent need to assist the underdeveloped countries to once and for all eliminate the horrendous imbalance between the rich and poor nations of the world was the theme of an entire social encyclical by Pope Paul VI. Having dealt with the positive approach to the supposed overpopulation problem, in the following year he issued an encyclical on human life which rejected the widely proffered negative solution. Generally hailed, and also censured in many circles, as "the encyclical against birth control," *Humanae Vitae* (1968) was a positive defense of human life in a post-Christian world which had come to view it as cheap and dispensable. The encyclical ruled out artificial contraception as a solution to, among other things, the problem of supposed overpopulation. It thus brought to full definition the issue which Pius XII addressed in his 1952 *Christmas Message*, whether "*this or that region* is *at present* burdened by a *relatively excess* population."

The digression into encyclicals by two successors is undertaken here because it demonstrates once again how the social teachings of later pontiffs build on, and thereby develop further, those of their predecessors, in this case Pius XII. Seekers after novelty and drastic departures from the steady direction of the Church's teaching are thus, time and again, destined for disappointment.

The final point with regard to the economic order that Pius XII addressed in his 1952 *Christmas Message* involved the matter of labor unions. He suggested that these too, unfortunately, have sometimes allowed themselves to be seduced by the "demon of organization," so that they come to deal with workers in the same cold, impersonal way as does society at large. He singled out the practice of making employment "depend on registration in certain parties, or in organizations which deal with the distribution of employment."[28] That is scored as "an inexact concept of the proper function of labor unions and their proper purpose, which is the protection of the interests of the salaried worker within modern society, which is becoming more and more anonymous and collectivistic."

Turning to what he regarded as "the essential purpose of unions" the Pope questioned whether that is not "the practical affirmation that man is the subject, and not the object of social relations?" Furthermore, "Is it not to protect the individual against collective irresponsibility of anonymous proprietors?" And, "Is it not to represent the person of the worker against those who are inclined to consider him merely a productive agent with a certain price value?"

Modern labor organizations, some of which had grown large, perhaps needed to contemplate those words and those which followed:

> How, therefore can it be considered normal that the protection of the personal rights of the worker be placed more and more in the hands of an anonymous group, working through the agency of immense organizations which are of their very nature monopolies? The worker, thus wronged in the exercise of his personal rights, will surely find especially painful the oppression of his liberty and of his conscience, caught as he is in the wheels of a gigantic social machine.

Those words delivered in 1952 may have been applicable also to some portions of American organized labor. After many years of militancy developed in the face of harsh treatment at the hands of powerful employers, as well as by the courts, they grew in size and influence. Predictably there were complaints also among their own members about the way their newly found power was exercised. Before long legislation was passed which began to roll back some of the gains made in the years since the *Wagner Act* was passed in 1935. In 1947 the *Taft-Hartley Act* began the process of curbing union power. For example, it outlawed the closed shop, which gave the unions virtually the kind of power over hiring which Pius XII was addressing in this *Christmas Message*. Union hiring-hall practices became abusive in some instances. Eventually the *Landrum-Griffin Act* of 1958 placed further restrictions on union actions. Since unions are by nature "monopolies," as the Pope pointed out, it was especially urgent that they exercised their power judiciously and with restraint. Had the labor movement itself been more sensitive in that respect, perhaps it could have averted such repressive legislation.

The Church's "preferential option for the poor" found eloquent expression in the closing portion of the 1952 *Christmas Message*. It included a stirring reference to the plight of the world's poor and to its author's own personal frustration with the failure to marshal more of the world's resources in order to come to grips with the immense problem. Pius XII addressed these words to "those families over whom hangs, like a menacing specter, the danger of being cut off from the source of all livelihood by sudden unemployment. For others, to this precariousness of wages is added their insufficiency, which is such that it does not permit them to obtain decent clothing, nor even food necessary to ward off sickness." He also indicated his awareness of the desperate housing problem which confronted Europe in particular as it painstakingly sought to recover from the devastation left by World War II. Unfortunately, much of what the Pope had to say about poverty and the human desolation to which it contributes is not confined to the period following the War. "Whole masses of population are brought up as enemies of law and order, so many poor girls gone astray, pushed down into the bottom of the abyss, because they believed that was the only way out of their shameful poverty." Also, "not rare is the case where it is wretched misery that leads to crime."

Christmas Message of 1953

While the 1952 *Message* attacked the "demon of organization," the *Christ-*

mas Message of 1953 dealt with a related theme—the technological spirit and what it could do to humanity. Thus, it too was implicitly addressed to the economic order.

Now Pius XII was himself a great admirer of technology and the spectacular achievements in the physical sciences. That is clear from many of his allocutions addressed to various groups of scientists and their areas of expertise. Nevertheless, he offered here a highly significant warning to a world that had replaced a truly human spirit with a "technological spirit." The Pope was concerned with the unhinged pursuit of technological progress—unhinged, because it extolled technology to the exclusion of higher spiritual values and even of God Himself. He referred to "excessive and sometimes exclusive esteem for what is called 'progress in technology,'" even while asserting, "the aforementioned erroneous consequence does not follow necessarily, nor are our present criticisms to be understood as a condemnation of technological progress in itself."[29] Indeed:

> The Church loves and favors human progress. It is undeniable that technological progress comes from God, and so it can be and ought to lead to God. In point of fact, while the believer admires the conquests of science and makes use of them to penetrate more deeply into the knowledge of creation and of the forces of nature, that by means of machines he may better master them for the service of mankind and the enrichment of human life, it most often happens that he feels himself drawn to adore the Giver of those good things which he admires and uses, knowing full well that the eternal Son of God is the "first born of every creature. For in Him were created all things in the heavens and on the earth, things visible and things invisible."(Col. 1: 15-16)

In keeping with the spirit of Christmas, we are told in eloquent terms how to sublimate this gift of technological genius— a hallmark of the modern world. Man should "find it natural to place beside the gold frankincense and myrrh, offered by the Magi to the Infant God, also the modern conquests of technology: machines and numbers, laboratories and inventions, power and resources." Then came this highly significant statement:

> Furthermore, such an offering is like presenting Him with the work which He Himself once commanded and which is now being effected, though it has not reached its term. "Inhabit the earth and subject it" (Gen. I: 29), said God to man as He handed creation over to him in temporary heritage. What a long and hard road from then to the present day, when men can at last say that they have in some measure fulfilled the divine command![30]

Therein is contained a remarkable theology of technology which "has, in fact, brought man's domination of the material world to a level of perfection never known before." There are no subtle or disguised Luddite overtones in the Pope's treatment of modern technology. Instead there is profuse praise: "The modern machine allows a mode of production that substitutes for, and multiplies a hundredfold, human energy for work, that is entirely independent of the contribution of organic forces and which ensures a maximum of extensive and intensive potential and at the same time of precision." The sublimation process reaches its summit with the statement: "Now it is clear that all search for and discovery of the forces of nature, which technology effectuates, is at once a search for and discovery of the greatness, of the wisdom, and of the harmony of God. Looked at in this way, there is nothing to disapprove of or condemn in technology."

One can perhaps sense that a *monitum* is destined to follow the paeans for technology. Human nature in its fallen state has from its outset shown itself capable of turning paradise into tribulation. The Pope indicated "that this technology which in our century has reached the height of its splendor and fruitfulness is through certain circumstances changed into a grave spiritual danger." The "golden calf" is an ever-present temptation to mankind in its pilgrimage through life's desert. Thus: "...it seems to give modern man, prostrate at its altar, a sense of self-sufficiency and satisfaction of his boundless thirst for knowledge and power." Indeed, "In its many varied uses, in the absolute confidence which it awakens, in the extraordinary possibilities that it promises, modern technology displays before man so vast a vision as to be confounded by many with the Infinite Itself." The Golden Calf revisited—the "technological spirit" triumphant! That prophetic warning was issued even before anyone but specialists were aware of the dawning of the computer age, and before scientists began attempting to concoct human life in science laboratories, and to mimic its awesome profundity in cloning!

Subtly germane to the "demon of organization" dealt with in the previous *Christmas Message of 1952*, we are now face-to-face with another demon: "the technological spirit." Man, ever Faustian in his aspirations, makes his deal with yet another toy of creation, allowed by the Creator of all.

> There is a fundamental falsehood in this distorted vision of the world offered by the technological spirit. The seemingly boundless panorama unfolded before the eyes of modern man, however extensive it may be, remains but a partial projection of life, in reality only expressing its relations with matter. Accordingly, it is a deceitful panorama that finishes by shutting up as in a prison those who are too credulous with regard to the omnipotence and immensity of technology, a prison that is vast indeed, but nevertheless circumscribed, and hence in the long run insupportable to their true spirit. Their glance, far from reaching out over infinite reality as they thought, (for reality does not consist only of matter) will feel chafed by the barriers which matter of necessity opposes. From this results the deep anguish of contemporary man, made blind for having willfully surrounded himself with darkness.[31]

Another Babylonian tower?

The Pope then moved into the area of the pitfalls confronting those who yield to the "technological spirit." At the personal level, they find "with difficulty the calm, the serenity, the inwardness essential for discovering the way that leads to the Son of God made man. In fact they, "will even go so far as to belittle the Creator and His work, pronouncing human nature a defective product, when the necessary limitations of the human brain and other organs stand in the way of fulfillment of technological plans and projects...." As indicated, all of this was prior to the full flowering of the computer age, where man perhaps approaches the pinnacle in aping the human intelligence mechanically! There could be a hint of what was to come in the sentence which followed: "Their thought is along different lines and follows other patterns, under the one-sided influence of that 'technological spirit' which only recognizes and reckons as real what can be expressed in mathematical formulas and utilitarian calculations."[32]

The recurring papal challenge to positivism and the dominant methodology which came with it in the social sciences followed directly:

> They think that they are thus breaking up reality into its elements, but their knowledge remains on the surface and deals with but one aspect. It is evident that whoever adopts the method of technology as the sole way of seeking truth must give up any idea of penetrating the profound realities of organic life, and even more so those of the spiritual life, the living realities of the individual person and of human society, because these cannot be analyzed into quantitative relationships.

One of the most memorable and masterful statements by Pius XII in all of his *Christmas Messages* involved the consequences of this triumph of the "technological spirit." Unless "the narrowness of his (the technologist's) knowledge will be broken through...this era of technological progress will achieve its monstrous masterpiece, making man into a giant of the physical world, at the expense of his soul, reduced to a pygmy in the realm of the supernatural and eternal."

As man had previously managed to subvert by the capitalistic spirit the finer providential benefits of the Industrial Revolution, he appeared to be continuing on the same course now as technology advanced far beyond that earlier stage, by bowing obsequiously before the "technological spirit." With positivism enshrined in modern thinking, the infant social sciences, and therefore their practical ramifications into the social order, bred the perversity before which we now cower. Those range from ecological depredation to the even more serious devastation of the family, which the Pope sought to salvage here as, "the strongest principle of order in society."

Long before the term "ecology" became current jargon, Pius XII issued this warning:

> We refrain from showing more at length how this system, inspired exclusively by technological considerations, contrary to what was expected of it, causes a waste of material resources, no less than of the principal sources of energy—among which certainly man himself must be included—and how in consequence it must in the long run prove a costly burden on the world economy.

That prescinded from the gravest threat of modern technology—the ultimate Frankenstein monster—the atomic bomb and the various hazards of even the peace-time uses of nuclear power: products of the great scientific geniuses of our time. With the prayerful hope that what men feared most of all from modern science will not come to pass, we have still the more pedestrian ravages of our technological age: the massive pollution of air and water which afflicts especially our cities, the real threat of global warming, along with the profligate waste of resources brought about by the too facile use of technological advances. What people have eventually become painfully aware of, sometimes even to an obsessive degree, Pius XII was drawing attention to in 1953.

But there is another threat stemming from the rampant "technological spirit," which is in certain respects even more serious:

> And with particular anxiety We consider the danger threatening the family.... For the family is capable of inspiring in its members innumerable daily acts of service, binds them to the home and hearth with bonds of affection, and awakes in each of them a love of the family traditions in the production and conservation of useful goods. Wherever on the contrary the technological concept of life penetrates, the family loses its personal bond of unity, is deprived of its warmth and stability. It remains united only to the extent that is demanded by the exigencies of mass production, which is being pursued with more and more insistence. No longer is the family a work of love and a haven for souls; it is rather a desolate depot, according to the circumstances, either of manpower for mass production, or of consumers of the material goods produced.[33]

The *Message* ends on a sober note of warning about man's relying time and again on "a material approach to the problem of peace." That—notwithstanding the Pope's unquestioned enthusiasm about advances in modern technology, and economic improvement among the nations of the world. Significantly, he referred to what has now again become in certain circles a kind of formula for peaceful progress for mankind: "They think that the secret of the solution lies in bringing material prosperity to all nations through constant increase in productivity and in the standard of living. A hundred years ago, another similar formula aroused the absolute confidence of statesmen: "With free trade, lasting peace." He warned:

> But no materialism was ever an apt means to establish peace. For peace is above all an attitude of the mind, and only secondarily a harmonious equilibrium of external forces. So it is an error of principle to entrust peace to a modern materialism that corrupts the essence of man and stifles his personal and spiritual life. Experience induces the same distrust, for it proves that the costly distribution of technical and economical forces more or less equally between two parties causes reciprocal intimidation, from which would result a peace based on fear, not that peace which is security for the future.

What is needed instead is "above all a question of spiritual unity and of moral dispositions."

Toward the end of this remarkable *Message*, we find a plea for Christian social doctrine. The Pope admonishes the Christian statesman that he "must have tenacity in putting into practice Christian social doctrine, tenacity and faith in his own principles more than the adversaries show in their false tenets." That admonition culminates in this statement:

> If during the past hundred years and more, Christian social doctrine has developed and borne fruit in the practical policies of many nations—unfortunately not all—those who have come on the scene very late have no reason today to complain that Christianity leaves something to be desired in the social field, which according to them must be supplied by a so-called revolution in Christian consciences. The failure is not in Christianity, but in the minds of her accusers.[34]

Christmas Message of 1954

The *Christmas Message of 1954* was addressed to the perilous coexistence between the Communist world and the so-called free world: the "Cold War" and what Pius XII called also the "cold peace." That co-existence, in the Pope's words, "rests on fear."[35] While it involved a comparison and juxtaposition of the two armed camps, there was also some significant allusion to the opposing economic systems. He remarked about what he called "an intense rhythm of life pulsing therein." But that operated "almost exclusively in the economic field." There followed a remarkable papal admission: "It is undeniable that economics, taking advantage of the pressing progress of modern techniques, has by feverish activity attained surprising results, of such a nature as to foreshadow a profound transformation in the lives of all peoples, even those heretofore considered rather backward." That remark obviously applies to the Soviet Empire, and specifically to the Soviet Union, which was generally regarded as lagging behind Western Europe in industrialization and technology prior to the forced march imposed by the Communist regime. Giving the economics "devil" his due, Pius XII said: "Admiration unquestionably cannot be withheld for what it has done and what it promises to do." The predictable *monitum* followed directly: "Nevertheless economics, with its apparently unlimited ability to produce goods without number, and with the multiplicity of its relationships, exercises over many of our contemporaries a fascination superior to its potentiality, and extends to fields extraneous to economics."

The so-called free world was not exempted from this warning:

> The error of placing such trust in modern economics is again shared in common by the two camps into which the world is today divided. In one of these it is taught that, since man has given proof of such great power as to create the marvelous technico-economical composite of which he boasts today, he will also be able to organize the liberation of human life from all the privations and evils from which it suffers, and in this way effect a kind of self-redemption. On the other hand, the conception gains ground in the opposing camp that the solution of the problem of peace must be sought in economics, and particularly in a specific form thereof, that of free exchange.

The translation "free exchange" is the same as *the free market.* Both of the two contending systems were by now exploiting fully the providential Industrial Revolution and its updated manifestations during the 20th century. Advocates of each mistakenly attributed the real economic improvements in the lot of even the common man to the particular systems themselves. Communism was devoted doctrinally to full economic determinism, while the free market systems attributed to freedom in enterprise all of the remarkable progress in living standards due in large measure to the blessings of the technological revolution that happened to originate in England whence it spread to its former colony, the United States, and also to much of Europe. When the Soviet Union promoted industrialization under forced draft, it also realized some predictable dramatic economic growth, even while the benefits to the rank and file workers filtered through sparingly, as occurred also in the capitalist world. In both cases, the ruling classes benefited disproportionately from the economic progress that was made: in the Communist world that meant limited circles of officialdom along with the ruling bureaucracy; and in the world of the free markets, it was the capitalists and those who administered their capital.

The indictment of the free market system that followed included one of the very rare instances where in his social teachings a pope mentioned by name, with the source included in parentheses, a leading exponent of that system. This seems the more surprising since it was not Adam Smith or any other of the leading economic champions of free market economics, but Richard Cobden (1804-1865). Cobden was a Manchester industrialist and a leading exponent of free trade. As a member of parliament he was instrumental in getting the restrictive Corn Laws repealed, and in negotiating a reciprocal trade treaty with France. The naive reliance on free trade, and also on free markets internally, came to be known as "Manchester liberalism." Naive, because it awaited optimum results from allowing markets to follow imagined natural laws at work in economic life. The work cited by Pius XII in this *Message* was: Richard Cobden, "*Speeches on Questions of Public Policy*," London, Macmillan, 1870; Vol. I, pp. 362-366. In his words:

> We have already had occasion at other times to expose the baselessness of such teachings. About a hundred years ago, followers of the free commerce system expected wonderful things from it, attributing to it an almost magical power. One of its most ardent converts did not hesitate to compare the principle of free exchange, insofar as its effects in the moral world are concerned, with the principle of gravity which rules the physical world, and he attributed to it, as its proper effect, the drawing of men closer together, the elimination of antagonism based on race, faith, or language, and the unity of all human beings in unalterable peace.[36]

Such "innocence" about economics and economic life has resurfaced in our own time, in particular, after the principal antagonist, the Soviet Empire, dissolved after 1989. Indeed, the demise of that empire is attributed triumphantly by not a few to the superiority of free market economics. Papal social teachings have, of course, been of another mind as expressed here by Pius XII:

> The course of events has shown how deceitful is the illusion of entrusting peace to free exchange alone. Nor would the result be otherwise in the future if there were to persist that blind faith which confers on economics an imaginary mystic force. At present, moreover, there are lacking those foundations of fact

> which could in any way warrant the over-rosy hopes nourished today, as in the past, by followers of this teaching. As a matter of fact, while in one of the camps coexisting in cold peace this highly vaunted economic freedom does not in reality exist, it is in the other completely rejected as an absurd principle.

The Pope was indicating that in the Western world, whatever talk there was about economic freedom both in domestic economies and in relations among national economies, that was an exaggeration which contradicted the way in which actual economic policies were conducted. In the Communist world, of course, based on economic determinism in theory, and operating in practice as a centrally planned economy, there was no room at all for even a legitimate amount of economic freedom. Thus: "There is between the two, a diametrical opposition in their ways of conceiving the very fundamentals of life—an opposition which cannot be reconciled by purely economic forces."

A sound approach to reconciling the two opposing camps, both ideologically and in practice, was then proposed by Pius XII.

> Nay more, if there are—as there actually are—relations of cause and effect between the moral world and the economic world, they must be so ordered that primacy be assigned to the former, that is, the moral world, which must authoritatively permeate with its spirit the social economy. Once this scale of values has been established and its actual exercise permitted, economics will, insofar as it is able, consolidate the moral world and confirm the spiritual postulates and forces of peace.

That important passage highlights the link between morality and economic policy, with the primacy of morality clearly established.

The final portion of this *Message* dealing with the economic side of the peaceful coexistence equation once again anticipated what was to become a major theme in encyclicals by John XXIII and Paul VI. It indicated a danger in dependence on the economic factor if "employing erroneous systems" were to lead to a weakening of one of the groups of people. Without using the term, *solidarity*, it was clearly implied here.

> This could occur if, among other eventualities individual people of one group were to engage, without consideration or regard for others, in a ceaseless increase of production, and a constant raising of their own living standard. What might happen then? In such a case, an upsurge of resentment and rivalry on the part of neighboring peoples would be inevitable, and consequently also the weakening of the entire group.[37]

That refers to the economic imbalance among nations which Pope John XXIII addressed in *Mater et Magistra,* foreshadowing an entire encyclical dedicated to the problem: *Populorum Progressio* by Pope Paul VI.

The parting comment on the economic issue does away once and for all with the notion that harmony in economic life can be left to the automatic workings of laws in the economy or, for that matter, wherever human relations are involved.

> Let it be held for certain that in relations between men, even merely economic relations, nothing is produced spontaneously—as does occur in nature, which is subject to necessary laws—but everything depends substantially on the spirit. Only the spirit, the image of God and the executor of His designs can establish order and harmony on earth, and it will succeed in doing so to the same extent that it becomes the faithful interpreter and docile instrument of the only Savior Jesus Christ, Who is Himself Peace.

That reference applies to the aboriginal fallacy in contemporary free market economics which commenced with the physiocratic system and its total reliance on "natural laws," ending up as a surrealistic mathematical jumble. However, it applies also to the rival Communist system which aped the economics of liberal capitalism by its scientistic reliance on *necessary* laws for bringing it to fulfillment.

The Pope's concluding remark once again resonates what the originator of solidarist economics, Heinrich Pesch, wrote in 1924:

> For too long has the name of God been either totally excluded from scientific discussion, or it has at best been mentioned with a certain reticence or with tongue-in-cheek. Actually, this most holy Name should be professed before the whole world, so that at least where God's dominion is acknowledged and where divine moral law is regarded with reverence, the true common good of nations can find a secure safeguard and a powerful affirmation. The practical application of a divine moral law whose norms are unchangeable does not deprive morality, as science today understands it, of a firm basis. On the contrary, it reaffirms respect for what tradition has provided thus far, and for what has already been accomplished in our science. In addition, it alone secures for the highest social norms the stability, the constancy, and the universal validity which a merely historical and human tradition would never be able to provide.[38]

Christmas Message of 1955

The *Christmas Message of 1955* contains a warning about the possibility of man's over-reliance on "the power of his instruments, his organizations, his weapons, the precision of his calculations, the vastness of his production, of the distance he can reach with his words, his gaze, and influence."[39] We detect here again the papal preoccupation with the ongoing idolatry of technology and reliance on man's own organizational powers. Pius XII used a plain-spoken analogy about the threat facing men: "Like the construction of the Tower of Babel, they are dreaming false dreams, 'The Divinization of Man,' suitable and sufficient for every exigency of the physical and spiritual life."

Once again we have man, the self-reliant engineer, building a tower that will enable him to reach paradise! The Pope had another idea. "Modern achievements, certainly remarkable in scientific and technical development, will assuredly be able to give man an extensive mastery over the forces of nature, over sickness and even over the beginning and end of human life; but it is also certain that such mastery will not be able to transform the earth into a paradise of assured enjoyment." That is, among other things, because his approach is based on "the one-sided character of an idea which would wish to control life exclusively on the foundation of quantitative analysis and synthesis...." And that "above mentioned purely quantitative method...takes no account of the order of nature as is the wish of those who entrust men's destiny to the tremendous industrial power of the present age."

In the following paragraph it becomes clear that the Pontiff was targeting the Marxian myth of *full communism* that was supposed to follow an intense and difficult period of the "dictatorship of the proletariat:"

> They think they are establishing complete security in the ever-increasing productivity and in the uninterrupted flow of an every greater and more fruitful production in the nation's economy. This, they say—on a basis of a full and ever more perfect automatic system of production and supported by better methods of organization and accountancy—will guarantee to all workers a continuous and expanding return for their labor. In a subsequent phase this will become so great that, by means of community measures, it will be able to satisfy the security of those who are not yet, or no longer able to work—the young children, the old, the sick. To establish security, they conclude, there will therefore no longer be any necessity to have recourse to property either private or collective, either in goods or in money.[40]

That approach flatly disregards the real underlying "natural order" mentioned earlier. "There is in fact a natural order, even if its outward appearance changes with historical and social developments, but the essential lines are, and ever remain, the same: family and property as the basis of provision for individuals, then, as complementary factors of security, local and professional groups and finally, the state."[41] That "natural order" persists so that, "a quantitative method, however perfected, neither can, nor ought to control the social and historical reality of human life." Also: "The ever quickening pulse of life, the constantly multiplying technical productivity are not criteria which of themselves provide authority of declaring that there is a genuine improvement in the economic life of a nation."

Thus, we are reminded again here of the three "demons" previously identified by Pius XII in his *Christmas Messages*: the demons of over-reliance on organization, on technology, and on the quantitative method for assuring human welfare, peace and security. Much has happened since then, including a growing awareness of what the Pope warned against long before ecological concerns became modish: "rash consumption of reserves and of the treasures of nature."

Also, there was the collapse of the Soviet Empire which had continued to offer lip service to the emerging "paradise," where components of what the Pope had called "the natural order" like the family and private property, and even the state itself would become relics of a past, benighted era. That demise, however, brought with it another temptation, all too real now, which Pius XII already cautioned against in a multi-faceted prophetic warning in 1955:

> In this industrial age, the man who accuses, and rightly accuses communism of having deprived of freedom the people over whom it holds sway, should not omit to note that in the other part of the world also liberty will be a very dubious possession if man's security is not derived to a greater extent from a condition of things which corresponds to his true nature.

Also:

> The erroneous belief which makes security rest on the ever-mounting process of social production is a superstition, perhaps the unique one, of our rationalistic age of industry. But it is also the most dangerous, because it seems to deem impossible economic crises which always bring in their train risk of a return to dictatorship.

There followed this admonition, highly relevant for the post-Soviet era: "But at the same time We again warn Christians of the industrial age, in the spirit of Our immediate predecessors in the supreme pastoral and teaching office, against being satisfied with an anti-communism founded on the slogan and defense of liberty which is devoid of content."

Such satisfaction with "anti-communism" has, since the end of the communist system in Russia, become in certain influential circles erected into a kind of triumphalism, as if the *good* system has now triumphed over the *evil* one. The best antidote for such aberrance is to link the teachings of the "immediate predecessors," mentioned by Pius XII, to his immediate successors. The message of Leo XIII and Pius XI has since been reinforced and updated and developed further by the social encyclicals of John XXIII, Paul VI, and John Paul II.

In this *continuum* of magisterial teachings, one should include also the important but largely overlooked *Apostolic Letter* by Paul VI, *Octogesima Adveniens* (1971) where that Pope cautioned about the "renewal of the liberal ideology." He was referring to that individualistic cult which had propelled the free market economies of the Western world during much of the 19th century and into the 20th. In the context of his warning he also used the term "technocratic capitalism" (*Octogesima Adveniens*, par. 36), suggesting quite clearly that he was continuing in the tradition of social teaching by Pius XII.

The exaggerated reliance on technology and technical genius came up for review briefly again in the *Christmas Message of 1956* where Pius XII used the term "second technical revolution." The term was in quotation marks, since the Pope was perhaps not prepared to accept what may in the broad sweep of history be viewed as simply a historical continuation of the original Industrial Revolution. In any case, he scored the attitude which "treats everything in a technical manner and fosters complete confidence in technological ability":

> It is the prerogative of the men of the present technical age, they declare, to be able to construct society ever anew, in step with that progress in technological ability and without the need to learn from the past. The past, on the contrary, being linked with all manner of prejudices, but particularly with those inspired by religion, would weaken confidence and temper its constructive impulse.

> Modern man, conscious of and proud to live in this world as in a house which he, and he alone, is building, allots to himself the function of creation. What once was, does not interest him nor detain him. The whole world becomes for him a laboratory where he is ever gathering together again, with strict mathematical connections, the forces of nature, distributing them again according to fixed proportions and shaping and ordering events in advance...
>
> Hence there is no reason to wonder that modern man, in approaching social life, does so with the gesture of a technician who, after having dismantled a machine into its constituent parts, sets himself to reconstruct it according to a pattern of his own design....[42]

The theme of over-reliance on technology and on quantitative analysis of all of reality recurs in the thinking of this Pope with a final warning: "Those who through atheism, in theory or even in practice, make gods of technology and the mechanical progress of events inevitably end by becoming enemies of true human liberty, since they deal with mankind as with inanimate objects in a laboratory." What will happen now that scientists have at last succeeded in replicating life by cloning? Perhaps that is the ultimate step towards the emergence of "a class of men among whom the *homo faber* takes precedence over the *homo sapiens.*"[43]

Notes

1. Pius XII, *Christmas Message of 1939* ("International Peace") in Vincent A. Yzermans, ed., *The Major Addresses of Pope Pius XII, Vol. 2: Christmas Messages* (St. Paul: North Central Publishing Company, 1961), 27-32; especially 29.

2. Pius XII, *Christmas Message of 1940* ("Conditions for a New World Order") in Yzermans, 33-37; especially 36.

3. Ibid., 37.

4. John Paul II, *Sollicitudo Rei Socialis* (Boston: St. Paul Books & Media, 1987), par. 40.

5. Pius XII, *Christmas Message of 1942* ("The Internal Order of States and People") in Yzermans, 53-64; especially 53.

6. Ibid,. 54.

7. Ibid., 58.

8. Ibid., 58-59.

9. Ibid., 60.

10. Ibid., 61-62.

11. Heinrich Pesch, S.J., *Lehrbuch der Nationalökonomie/Teaching Guide to Economics*, trans. Rupert J. Ederer (Lewiston: The Edwin Mellen Press, 2002), vol. I, bk. 1, 10.

12. Yzermans, 62.

13. Ibid., 64.

14. Pius XII, *Christmas Message of 1950* ("Hope for the Future") in Yzermans, 145-146; especially 145.

15. Ibid., 145-146.

16. Pesch, I,1: 193-289. Pesch devoted the third chapter to what he referred to as the "three pillars of the social order": the family, private property, and the state.

17. Pius XII, *Christmas Message of 1952* ("The Rights of Man") in Yzermans, 159-

172; see especially 163. The theme of over-organization was widely discussed during this time, especially following the publication of the book by William H. Whyte, *The Organization Man* (New York: Simon and Schuster, 1956).

18. Ibid., 152.
19. Ibid., 160-61.
20. Ibid., 162.
21. Yzermans, 163.
22. Ibid., 164.
23. Ibid., 165.
24. Pesch, I, 1: 36-37.
25. Ibid., 167.
26. Claudia Carlen IHM, *The Papal Encyclicals,* 1958-1981: see *Mater et Magistra,* 185-204.
27. Ibid.; see Pope Paul VI, *Populorum Progressio* in Carlen, 183-201.
28. Yzermans, 168.
29. Pius XII, *Christmas Message of 1953* ("Modern Technology and Peace") in Yzermans, 173-183; see especially 174.
30. Ibid., 175.
31. Ibid., 176.
32. Ibid., 177.
33. Ibid., 179.
34. Ibid., 181.
35. Pius XII, *Christmas Message of 1954* ("Coexistence: Its Meaning and Future") in Yzermans, 184-197; see especially 186.
36. Ibid., 190.
37. Ibid., 190-191.
38. Pesch, I, 2: 321.
39. Pius XII, *Christmas Message of 1955* ("True Basis for Peace and Security") in Yzermans, 198-212.
40. Ibid., 203.
41. Ibid., 202.
42. Ibid., 220.
43. Ibid., 246: (Final *Christmas Message* by Pius XII in 1957).

Chapter 4
On Economics and the Economic Order

In the many discourses throughout his nineteen-year pontificate, Pope Pius XII often addressed various aspects relating to the economic order. He applied the Church's teachings to the economic system overall, and to specific areas of it according to the varying interests of the wide range of pilgrims who came to hear him, e.g., workers, managers, farmers, bankers. We shall examine first the more comprehensive statements on the economic order overall before turning in subsequent chapters to specialized sectors.

The Fiftieth Anniversary of *Rerum Novarum*
Address to Italian Workers
June 1, 1941[1]

Early in his pontificate on June 1, 1941, Pius XII delivered an important address to many thousands of workers gathered in St. Peter's Square to commemorate the 50th anniversary of the encyclical *Rerum Novarum* by Leo XIII. His discourse was also transmitted as a radio message to the workers of the world.

The Pope endorsed that encyclical as the "'*Magna Carta'* of Christian social endeavor," a designation which had already been assigned to it by Pius XI in *Quadragesimo Anno* ten years previously. He warned that, like the forty years which elapsed between it and *Quadragesimo Anno,* the ten years that followed the latter had been "...no less fraught with surprises in social and economic life than the years before it, and have finally poured their dark and turbulent waters into the sea of war whose unforeseen currents may affect our economy and society" (30). To deal with these "surprises," the Pope took the opportunity to offer some further directive moral principles "on three fundamental values which are closely connected one with the other, mutually complementary and dependent: the use of material goods, labor, and the family."

With regard to the use of material goods, Pius XII repeated the established position of Catholic social teaching: the goods of this earth are first of all intended to take care of the temporal needs of all men. Even the private property right and the jurisdiction of the State remain "subordinate to the natural scope of material goods, and cannot emancipate itself from the first and fundamental right which concedes their use to all men." Historically, as the Pope indicated, public authority had in the 19th century, "through excessive exaltation of liberty considered as its exclusive scope the safe-guarding of liberty." Actually, the State is charged with its own proper responsibility for the common good:

> To safeguard the inviolable sphere of the rights of the human person and to facilitate the fulfillment of his duties should be essential to the office of every public authority. Does not this flow from that genuine concept of the common good which the State is called upon to promote? (31)

This statement addresses precisely the error of nineteenth century liberalism; but the Pope then turned his attention to those who would attempt to correct past wrongs by moving history's pendulum to the opposite extreme—one which was likewise rooted in an intellectual eruption of that same century. The twin evils were mentioned specifically early in the message, where Pius XII pointed out that "the errors and dangers of the materialist Socialist conception" were "the fatal consequences of Liberalism, so often unaware, or forgetful, or contemptuous of social duties." Counteracting the "night-watchman state" by introducing the *total* state had by 1941 resulted in the subordination of countless millions of people to what was just then coming to be referred to widely as *totalitarianism.*

> Hence it follows that the care of such a common good does not imply a power so extensive over the members of the community, that in virtue of it the public authority can interfere with the evolution of that individual activity which We have just described, decide directly on the beginning or—excepting the case of legitimate capital punishment—the ending of human life, determine at will the manner of his physical, spiritual, religious, and moral movements in opposition to the personal duties of rights of man, and to this end abolish or deprive of efficacy his natural rights to material goods. To deduce such extension of power from the care of the common good would be equivalent to overthrowing the very meaning of the word common good, and falling into the error that the proper scope of man on earth is society, that society is an end in itself, that man has no other life which awaits him beyond that which ends here below.

The Pope indicated that so far as material goods are concerned, "the economic riches of a people do not properly consist of the abundance of goods, measured according to a purely and solely material calculation of their worth, but in the fact that such an abundance represents and offers really and effectively the material basis sufficient for the proper personal development of its members." This led him to the conclusion that the mere abundance of material goods is not of paramount importance, but that their just distribution is equally important. Even where there are goods in great abundance:

> ...the people in not being called upon to share them, would not be economi-

> cally rich, but poor. Suppose on the other hand that such distribution is effective genuinely and permanently, and you will see a people, even if it disposes of less goods, making itself economically sound.

Pius XII took the occasion in this important address to refer to his recent encyclical addressed to the bishops of the United States. "In our Encyclical *Sertum Laetitiae*.... We called the attention of all to the basic idea of these principles which consists, as We said, in the assertion of the unquestionable need, 'that the goods which were created by God for all men, should flow equally to all, according to the principles of justice and charity' "(30). Justice and charity in their specific social application, i.e., social justice and social charity, were the two cardinal principles proposed by Pius XI in *Quadragesimo Anno* as the appropriate "loftier and nobler principles," for regulating economic life. (cf. *Quadragesimo Anno*, par. 88).

With reference to labor, Pius XII restated earlier teachings regarding its dual nature: "it is personal and it is necessary.... It is *personal,* because it is achieved through the exercise of man's particular forces." That—as opposed to the widespread practice of treating it as simply another commodity in the market place! It is *necessary,* because "without it one cannot secure what is indispensable to life; and man has a natural grave individual obligation to maintain life." Since the duty and right to work are imposed on and conceded to the individual in the first instance by nature, and not by society, "it follows that the duty and right to organize the labor of the people belongs above all to the people immediately interested: the employers and the workers" (30).

That provided the appropriate occasion to reaffirm the *principle of subsidiarity*: "If they [the employers and the workers] do not fulfill their functions, then it falls back on the State to intervene in the field of labor and in the division and distribution of work according to the form and measure that the common good properly understood demands." Worth noting here is that the state is summoned to intervene also because the parties themselves "*do not* fulfill their functions. [italics added]" Such neglect involves, as is often the case, violation of the principle of subsidiarity by omission. In such situations the state is not to be faulted for intervening; instead, it would be derelict if it did not do so.

Turning to the family, we find here a distinctive emphasis on the ownership of "a homestead of one's own" (34). The Pope related the emphasis of disposal over private property to the father's ability to "fulfill the duties assigned him by the Creator regarding the physical, spiritual and religious welfare of the family." That familial function of private property is "a function in the natural order under certain aspects superior to all others" because, "in the family, the nation finds the natural and fecund roots of its greatness and power."

All of that was by then standard social encyclical material:

> Of all the goods that can be the object of private property, none is more conformable to nature according to the teaching of *Rerum Novarum* than the land, the holding in which the family lives and from the products of which it draws all or part of its subsistence. And it is in accord with the spirit of *Rerum Novarum* to state that, as a rule, only that stability which is rooted in one's own holding makes of the family the vital and most perfect and fecund cell of society, joining up in a brilliant manner in its progressive cohesion the present and future generations. If today, the concept and the creation of vital spaces is at the center of social and political aims, should not one, before all else, think of the vital space of the family and free it of the fetters of conditions which do not permit it even to formulate the idea of a homestead of one's own?

At this point, Pius XII established new ground in the Church's social teaching, ground which anticipated what his successor, John XXIII, would later include in his own social encyclicals, *Mater et Magistra* (par. 45) and *Pacem in Terris* (pars. 25, 105-6). We find here the pretext for the emigration/immigration right as one response to what was soon to emerge as a virtual "overpopulation" hysteria, in particular—and with some irony—among economically more favored nations of the world. Having insisted that the private property right implied "the idea of a homestead of one's own," how could this be reconciled with an alleged widespread overpopulation?

> Our planet, with all its extent of oceans and seas and lakes, with mountains and plains covered with eternal snows and ice, with great deserts and trackless lands is not, all the same, without habitable regions and vital spaces now abandoned to wild natural vegetation, and well-suited to be cultivated by man to satisfy his needs and civil activities; and more than once it is inevitable that some families migrating from one spot to another, should go elsewhere in search of new homeland. Then, according to the teaching of *Rerum Novarum* the right of the family to a vital space is recognized. When this happens, emigration attains its natural scope, as experience often shows; We mean the more favorable distribution of man on the earth's surface, suitable to colonies of agricultural workers; that surface which God created and prepared for the use of all (34).

This message ended on a prophetic note, especially in view of the fact that the European phase of World War II was well into its second year. First, we find the admonition not to let die "the insistent call of the two Pontiffs of the social encyclicals, that voice which indicates to the faithful in the supernatural regeneration of mankind the moral obligation to cooperate in the arrangement of society, and especially of economic life.... Do not let the external difficulties put you off; dear children, do not be upset by the obstacle of the growing paganism of public life."

Finally, the Pope intimated, perhaps optimistically, that better times are coming:

> If between the ideal and its realization there appears even now an evident lack of proportion; if there have been failures, common indeed to all human activity, if divergences of view arose on the way followed or to be followed, all this should not make you depressed or slow up your step or give rise to lamenta-

tions or recriminations, nor can it make you forget the consoling fact that the inspired message of the Pope of *Rerum Novarum* sent forth a living and clear stream of strong social sense, sincere and disinterested; a stream which if it be now partly perhaps covered by a landslide of divergent and overpowering events, tomorrow, when the ruin of this world hurricane is cleared, at the outset of that reconstruction of the social order, which is a desire worthy of God and of man, will infuse new courage and a new wave of profusion and growth in the garden of human culture (35-36).

Thoughts on Building a New Social Order
A Radio Address to the World
September 1, 1944[2]

As World War II had reached its full intensity of death and destruction, Pius XII delivered a *Radio Message* to the world on September 1, 1944, noting that this date marked the fifth year since the outbreak of the War. The tone was somber: "The dial of history today is registering a grave, decisive hour for the whole of humanity." And, "An ancient world lies shattered in ruins." The Pope, in fact, speculated about the possibility of a bad reaction, given the so-called pendulum-swing tendency in history. "Will the painful, deadly errors of the past perhaps be followed by others no less deplorable, and will the world swing indefinitely from one extreme to the other?" Yet, at the same time he issued an invitation for reconstructing "from the ruins a world more sane, juridically better organized and more in harmony with the exigencies of nature."

By benefit of hindsight, we are able to see how history would change from a Europe dominated by Nazi totalitarianism to a world overshadowed by the Communist menace, and under the threat of annihilation by atomic weapons which were not yet a known quantity when the Pontiff delivered this address. Many wars ensued before the deadly century would end, even though they were more limited in scope and did not assume the dreaded horrendous nuclear dimensions. Nevertheless the so-called body count was staggering.

Pius XII did not hesitate to lay the blame for the deadliest of all wars on the "systematic undermining of the very foundations of Christian civilization," even though "Europe and the other continents still subsist, in different measure, from the vital forces and principles which the inheritance of Christian thought had transmitted to them as in a spiritual blood transfusion."

From a discussion of those broad historical aspects of the calamity, the Pope turned to more specific economic ones. What he had to say about the economic order addresses what represented indeed a kind of pendulum swing from the socialistic attempt to erase private ownership toward a system which would go far to restore crass abuses of such ownership. Not long after the War ended, there were determined reactive endeavors to restore the so-called free-market capitalism which had led up to the great worldwide economic collapse during the 1930s. Various countries, including the United States, proceeded to a disturbing degree in that direction.[3]

In opposing both extremes of that pendulum-swing, Pius XII began by reaffirming the Church's traditional defense of private property, stating that "the Christian conscience cannot admit as just a social order which either denies on principle, or renders practically impossible or vain the natural right of possession, both over consumer goods and over the means of production." Echoing Leo XIII, he referred to "the right of private property...as an unshakable foundation." Having dealt thus with the socialist system, he then turned to capitalism which violated that right from another direction: "But it (the Christian conscience) cannot likewise accept those systems which recognize the right of private property according to a wholly false concept, and are therefore in contrast with the genuine and sane social order.... Hence where, for example, 'capitalism' is based on such erroneous conceptions and unduly claims for itself an unlimited right of property, without any subordination to the common good, the Church has reproved it as contrary to natural law." The Pontiff became quite explicit in what he meant by that kind of capitalism.

> We see, in fact, the ever increasing ranks of workers often faced with those excessive concentrations of economic goods which, frequently hidden under anonymous forms, succeed in evading their social obligations and place the worker in the near impossibility of creating property of his own.
>
> We see medium and small property diminish and lose vigor in social life, compressed and restricted as it is to a defensive struggle ever more harsh and without hope of positive success.
>
> We see, on the one hand, tremendous riches dominate the private and public economy and often even civic affairs, and, on the other hand, the vast multitude of those who, deprived of any security, direct or indirect, in their life, lose all interest in the true and high values of the spirit, bar themselves against aspirations toward genuine liberty, cast themselves in the arms of any political party, slaves to whoever promises them, in one way or another, bread and tranquility. And experience has shown of what tyranny humanity is capable in such conditions, even at the present time.

Since there were always those who charged the Church with being a defender of the *status quo,* Pius XII made it clear that the Church "does not intend purely and simply to sustain the present state of affairs, as if she saw therein the expression of divine will, nor to protect as a matter of principle, the rich and the plutocrat against the poor and destitute." Instead, it "follows a lofty ethical-social aim." This means that she has from her origins "been a guardian of the poor and oppressed against the tyranny of the powerful, and she has always championed the just protests of all classes of workers against every iniquity." However, her aim is to act so that "private property may become what it should be according to the designs of divine Wisdom and the dispositions of nature: an element of social order, a necessary prerequisite to private initiative, a stimulus to labor to the advantage of temporal and transcendental goals of life, and hence of the liberty and dignity of man, created in the image of God, Who from the very beginning assigned to him to use as he saw fit the mastery over material things."

The Pope then went on to state what has been viewed by some as one of the more radical aspects of the Catholic social teachings. While always defending in principle the right to private ownership of property, including the means of production, the Church has also acknowledged that "the State may, in the common interest intervene to regulate its use, or even, if it is impossible to arrive at another solution, decree expropriation, giving a fair and equitable indemnity."

Finally, there was in this message an important early indication of the kind of limitation on technology as such and on "technical progress" that would come up for serious consideration at various times in certain of this Pope's *Christmas Messages*. It appeared in the context of his appeal that "small and medium-sized properties in agriculture, in the arts and trades, in commerce and industry, must be guaranteed and promoted." That included "cooperatives which "assure the advantages of a large concern." And where the "large business concern...manifests itself to be more productive," the Pope reaffirmed a significant proposal made by his predecessor. Pius XI had urged that "where the large business concern today manifests itself to be more productive, the possibility should be offered to temper the labor agreement with some kind of contract of partnership" (*Quadragesimo Anno* 65).

Pius XII was saying in no uncertain terms that technology is, in any case, not the ultimate consideration:

> Technical progress does not determine, as a fatal and necessary fact, economic life. Too often it has bowed docilely before the demands of egotistical calculations avid to increase capital indefinitely; why then should it not also bend to the need of maintaining and assuring the private property of all, the cornerstone of the social order? Even technical progress, as a social fact, must not prevail over the general good, but must instead be regulated by and subordinated to it.

In the intervening years, since Pius XII delivered that significant message, much has happened in a fast-moving world. The Communist system as it found expression in the Soviet Empire has collapsed. Some nations in Europe established market economies while retaining important safeguards on behalf of the social welfare. In post-war Germany, for example, a system arose, nurtured by the exemplary Christian statesman Konrad Adenauer, which came to be known as a *social market economy*. That involved retention of the basic market mechanism, subject to appropriate social controls on behalf of the common good, including safeguards for workers and their families, like universal health insurance, security in old age, and family allowances.

In the United States, on the other hand, there eventually came about a renewed emphasis on the *free market*, with significant deregulation of important sectors of the economy, like banking and transportation. One outcome has been the kind of "excessive concentrations of economic goods" mentioned here by Pius XII with the result that, "the vast multitude of those who, deprived of any security, direct or indirect in their life, lose all interest in the true and high values of the spirit."

As in his teachings on other matters, Pius XII showed himself as a remarkable bridge-figure between his predecessors and his successors. For example, there is in this message a remarkable similarity to what Pope John Paul II said about "capitalism" nearly a half century later in *Centesimus Annus.* To the challenge as to whether, now that the Communist system has failed, "capitalism is the victorious social system so that it should be the goal of the former Communist countries that were endeavoring to rebuild their economy and society," the Pope responded in *Centesimus Annus* (1991) with these words:

> But if by "capitalism" is meant a system in which freedom in the economic sector is not circumscribed within a strong juridical framework which places it at the service of human freedom in its totality, and which sees it as a particular aspect of that freedom, the core of which is ethical and religious, the reply is certainly negative (*Centesimus Annus*, par. 42).

Over the many years of serious contention, including the Cold War period, between the Communist and the non-Communist worlds, the term "capitalism" came to take on many meanings. Some understood it simplistically as any economic system that was not communistic. For others, lacking fundamental historical perspective, capitalism meant the kind of system where private ownership of property, including the means of production, was in place. By still others, in view of certain developments following the Industrial Revolution, capitalism was identified with economies where the factor of production, *capital,* as opposed to labor and land ownership, came to play the dominant role in economic life. Elsewhere, the term "capitalism" was used interchangeably with the concept of *market economy*. Pope John Paul II indicated his awareness of the ambiguity when he politely suggested that, "it would perhaps be more appropriate to speak of 'a business economy,' 'market economy,' or simply 'free economy'" (*Centesimus Annus,* 42). Some economists have indeed attempted to rescue the designation, which had, in a certain sense, fallen victim to the ideological combat between the real-life socialistic command economies, and what their antagonists liked to refer to as the "free world."

Scientifically, the expression *market economy* is more descriptive, in that such economies entrust much of the operation of the production, exchange and income distribution processes to the "laws" or forces of the market. To the extent that the market processes are regulated where the common good requires it, the term *social market economy* originally applied to the post-World War II German economy would therefore seem more appropriate.

In fact, most economies throughout the history of the world, including the medieval cities, featured private ownership of property, including the means of production, without being therefore capitalistic. Also, so far as the primacy of capital in the economy is concerned, that factor was nowhere more emphasized than in the Soviet system as it actually developed in real life. In fact, the cogency of new and additional capital formation was of such high priority in the socialist central planning process, that consumers and their needs were time and again callously disregarded—a practice which contributed to the eventual demise of the Soviet system.

The use of the expressions "capitalism" and "capitalistic" in the Church's social teachings, as here in this Radio Message of Pius XII, came to seem pejorative, precisely because the primacy of capital in the economic order brought with it a coldly materialistic aspect. That involved harsh treatment of what will always be the most important factor in economic life: the working human person! The term itself suggests a basic ontological disorder to the extent that it intimates a priority of the purely *material* factor of production, capital, over the *human* factor, labor. In a correct ordering of things, the latter, or more precisely, the worker, necessarily enjoys primacy in the economic order over the material factors that are here to serve him and his needs (Cf. *Laborem Exercens*, para. 13, 15).

This important message therefore expressed in clear and eloquent terms the reaffirmation by Pius XII of various aspects of what was by then standard Catholic social doctrine, while at the same time providing the foundation for future teaching by his successors. He ended the portion addressed to the economic order with an earnest appeal to "our loyal sons and daughters in the Catholic world to act as heralds of the Christian social ideals, even if it costs them dearly, so that the kind of social justice will be realized for which all true disciples of Christ must hunger and thirst."

Freedom as the Foundation for Life in Society and The Dangers of Indiscriminate Nationalization
An Address to the Social Week of France
10 July 1946[4]

This short but significant letter to the prestigious French Social Week (*Semaine Sociale*) meeting in Strasbourg touched on a subject especially close to the hearts of Frenchmen—the much-abused and misunderstood concept of *liberty*. Pius XII began with challenging words:

> You are studying the various problems of the national community which you do not wish to present, as certain philosophers of a positivistic and anti-intellectual orientation wish to do so—in the sense of a collectivity where the instinctive drives and the herd instinct overshadow the rational, legal, and moral aspects; but you simply want to present in a better light what a country—especially when we are dealing with a country like France and with a nation like the '*nobilissima Gallorum gens*'—embraces: legitimate differences within its necessary unity, originality and free consensus, and reciprocal contribution within the bosom of this extended and transcendent family which is the fatherland.

He asked whether "this concept of community does not also have an explicit Christian character which was already sanctified by the original Church."

There followed a powerful message presenting the Church as the model for social life: "In the divine institution which our Lord Jesus Christ established we have an inimitable paradigm, so that societies at the human level could do nothing better than to adopt its spirit." This should not surprise anyone, "inasmuch as it was the Church which salvaged the real value of the human person from the level to which pagan philosophies and morals had degraded it. And it was the Church which has acknowledged and defended the human person—created in the image of God, as the root and goal of all social life." That significant statement in fact establishes the foundation for Catholic social teaching. It is worthwhile considering what Pius XII said here in terms of the doctrine of the Mystical Body of Christ, which the selfsame Pontiff had explained in the important encyclical *Mystici Corporis* three years previously.

From there the Pope went on the offensive against the totalitarian states which had been asserting themselves in various forms during the troubled times that marked his pontificate. He urged his French audience to emphasize "these great truths which must establish the foundation of the social body." Because now again "systems raise their heads which extend totalitarian demands in all areas and which have no other ideal than collective egoism, and recognize no other forms than that of the all powerful state, making human beings mere figures in a political chess game and figures in their economic calculations."

From there the address shifted to a theme especially close to the hearts of Frenchmen. He reminded them that while "a healthy communal spirit must indeed be operative in the members of the national community, it must also be present in the members of the mother cell, the family.... Only then will the great principles of liberty, equality, and fraternity blossom to which the modern democracies lay claim." The Pope reminded his audience that unless these are understood in terms of "the natural law, the law of the Gospel, and Christian tradition which are at the same time their authors, indeed their only authors, and their authentic interpreters," they will be "terribly distorted."

Getting down to specific economic terms, Pius XII turned his attention to the indiscriminate nationalization of business enterprises the *Semaine Sociale* was then addressing. Recalling that he and his predecessors had "more than once addressed the moral aspect of these measures," the Pope warned that "even where such measures are admissible they do not ameliorate the mechanical character of life and work in common, but rather increase this mechanical character." Thus "the advancement of true community, as you understand it, which they are supposed to bring about are to be regarded with great caution." Instead, the Pope proposed the "establishment of corporate associations or units in all branches of the national economy" as "much more advantageous for the goal which you are pursuing, and also for increasing the yields of business operations." Here was one more urgent appeal for the establishment of occupational organizations or the vocational orders which his predecessor, Pius XI, included as a significant part of his program for reconstructing the social order in *Quadragesimo Anno*. Pius XII cited that proposal as far more appropriate especially where the "combination of enterprises and the disappearances of the small independent producers ended up advancing only the interest of capital and not of the social economy." The Pope was forthright in proclaiming that there was "no doubt but that in present circumstances, the corporative structuring of social and especially of economic life served the practical advancement of Christian teaching about the human personality, about the community, about work and about private property."

That represented a powerful reaffirmation by Pius XII of Christian social teaching as it had been presented by his predecessors. And it offered at the same time a basis for what the successors of Pius XII would have to say in the future, in particular in terms of what the doctrine of the Mystical Body of Christ would mean in support of the Christian virtue of solidarity!

Basic Questions Concerning the Economic Order
Letter Addressed to the Leaders of the French Semaine Sociale
July 18, 1947[5]

Pius XII used this occasion to correct a false impression at large in certain circles regarding his position on state intervention to assure the material welfare of a nation. There have always been those, some with the best of intentions, who seized upon papal statements to justify a particular political agenda. "Socialization" measures have been justified in papal teachings if and to the extent that the common good would require it. The Pope had previously suggested that the state might take action in order to foster and nurture the growth of cooperatives. He indicated that he did so in order to promote small and mid-sized business operations then threatened by the onrush of mammoth enterprises.

Similar misunderstandings had gotten abroad regarding the occupational or "corporative" organizations first proposed explicitly in *Quadragesimo Anno.* Having become the subject of public polemical disputations where it was used in varying political contexts, this notion came to be distorted in varying ways. Pius XII here affirmed the validity of the *principle* of occupational organization to counteract the increasing tendency to fragment employers and workers into rival factions. He pointed out that, as opposed to such a dichotomy, *work* itself stands as a unifying force, since it involves a lifelong personal vocation to provide society with the goods and services needed for its survival and well-being. That structure could go far to counteract the present form of society that has lost all inner coherence and is now composed of a mass of workers. Control over society by such a "mass" can be as dangerous as "if the state comes under the dominion of capital."

Pius XII then turned his attention to the theme of the meeting in Paris: *Social Catholicism Confronting the Great Currents of the Time.* In this context, he made the interesting observation that much energy had been directed in the past to the important question of distribution. What was urgent now was the "problem of production." Given the condition of Europe in particular in the immediate postwar period, that was an understandable concern.

Even here, the Pontiff warned that the *principle of subsidiarity* is to be observed. He indicated that this was especially so in the period when the tendency to "*laissez faire, laissez passer*" receded into the background, so that an opposite extreme might move into the foreground. The intervention of society was always to be "subsidiary" to the activity of the individual, the family, and the occupational groups themselves.

In any case, there was praise here for the French endeavor to promote social Catholicism. As the Pope understood it, that meant bringing the Church's social teachings to bear in everyday life, "public as well as private."

The Church in Its Encounter with the Social and Political Questions of the Present Time
Address to the College of Cardinals
2 June 1948[6]

This rather extended address to the Cardinals included also a significant section dealing with the economic order. Dwelling on the disorder and destruction left in the wake of World War II, Pius XII warned that "it would be dangerous, because it would easily lead to bitter disappointments, if one were to put too much hope in many of the proposed reforms for full, quick and satisfactory results." What is at stake now is more than simply "a just distribution of the output of the economy." Displaying remarkable acumen about economic realities, the Pope said that, "Important as that may be, under present conditions, in particular given the enormous destruction and dislocations which the War brought, every social reform is closely tied with the question of a judicious ordering of production." Probably, this remark was directed at the ubiquitous Marxist agitation which was hard at work attempting to capitalize on disorganized postwar conditions.

Pius XII cited other considerations that also had to be taken into account. These included "the relationship between agriculture and industry in the particular national economies; and also among these economies, the nature and degree of participation by each nation in the world market." These were all problems, which, in the Pope's view, "have taken on new and different forms than previously." It is on "their reasonable solution that the productivity of the individual nations depends, and along with that the welfare of the individual persons, because it is clear that where there is not enough production, no adequate distribution is possible." That reflected the views of many economists during the postwar era, when there was a new emphasis on economic development.

The insightful analysis of the ongoing economic problem continued. "Certainly there are nations which pride themselves today on the kind of productivity whose increase they point to pridefully." A warning followed. "However, if such productivity is purchased by an unrestricted competition and an unscrupulous use of property, or by a despotic repressing and exploitation of labor and the needs of individuals by the state, then it cannot be healthy and genuine, for the social economy is an orderly complex of working persons, each of which is constituted with human dignity and freedom." In that indictment, there is clearly enough blame to include both the so-called free market economies and the statist socialist ones.

Then, in a reference which anticipated the ecological concern which was not yet a standard part of the human dialogue in those years, we find: "Such unbounded exploitation of the true value of the human person usually keeps pace with the exploitation of natural resources, especially of the soil; and sooner or later it leads to decline."

Pius XII gives no quarter in his conclusion to those observations: " It is only on the basis of the principles and the spirit of Christianity that those social reforms can be realized which are called for so desperately by the need and craving of our time." What that translates to, according to the Pope, is "restraint and sacrifice on the part of some, along with a sense of responsibility and patience on the part of others, and hard and dedicated work by all."

There is a potent bit of social teaching in those words. The Pontiff closed this portion of the address with a plea that "Catholics the world over should not be satisfied with good intentions and neat programs," but that "they should work diligently for their practical realization." Also, they should not be shy about presenting "the social teachings of the Catholic Church" even to those who are "not in their ranks." For what the Church offers is not "the way of violent overthrow, but the way of tested experience and effective resolutions."

The Social Problem
Radio Address to the German Catholic Congress in Bochum
4 September 1949[7]

This address offers an interesting insight into the character of Pius XII. Before presenting the heart of his message he related to the Congress gathered in the industrial center at Bochum an episode from his early experience as Papal Nuncio to Germany in 1927. In what were still the early, if not pioneering, days of aviation he had flown over the Rhineland from Trier, en route to a previous Catholic Congress held in Dortmund.

Now, he offered words of guidance for restoration and hope to a nation demolished physically as well as politically by the deadly War, which had ended a few years previously. Characteristically, he summed these words up under five points, the first of which hailed the memory of the nineteenth-century bishop of Mainz, Wilhelm Emmanuel von Ketteler, a leading pioneer of modern Catholic social teaching. In essence, much of the basis for what was later found in papal social teachings echoes the thought of that great bishop. Thus, the Pope made the point that "no right thinking man will dare to accuse the Church of not having in mind and at heart the problem of the workers and also, in general, the whole of the social question." He termed it of the essence that "the social doctrine of the Church should become the patrimony of all Christian consciences and that this doctrine be put into practice."

His second point was that "the social program of the Catholic Church is based on three powerful moral pillars: truth, justice and Christian charity." This threefold basis for order was echoed later in the social teachings of his successor, John XXIII (*Mater et Magistra*, par. 215; *Pacem in Terris*, par. 163). Here he indicated that, "the Church has always been on the side of those who seek justice and who are in need of help, but, in principle, she has never been opposed to any social group or class and always aims at serving the common good of all the members of the people or the state."

The third point includes an especially significant reference to the vocational orders or occupational groups which his predecessor, Pius XI, proposed specifically in *Quadragesimo Anno.* Pius XII proclaimed the Church's ongoing rejection of "the apparent conflict between capital and labor, between the employer and the worker." He proposed instead that this, "be transformed into a higher unity, which means to say, into that organic cooperation of both parties which is indicated by their very nature and which consists in the collaboration of both according to their activity in the economic sector and the professions."

What followed offers us an important indication of where the Church stands in its social teachings with regard to the origins and role of present-day labor unions: "May it please God that the day be not far off when those organizations of self-defense which the defects of the economic system, and especially the lack of Christian outlook have made necessary may cease to function." The key words here are "self-defense," and "necessary." Labor unions became *necessary* organs of *self-defense* amid the de-spiritualized and consequently also dehumanized capitalistic ambience developing since the eighteenth century. And the Church, to the displeasure of many, was an early supporter of worker organizations. It included that right of workers to organize as stemming from the natural right of association.

Yet, even while Leo XIII championed the embattled workers of his time, he already proposed an eventual restoration of "artificers' guilds" which should, however, "be suited to the requirements of this our age." (*Rerum Novarum* 49). Pius XI articulated this concept fully in *Quadragesimo Anno*, where he indicated that the organization of all members of an occupation or profession should be organized into one self-governing body, and not as at present, "into two divisions as into battle lines, and the contest between these two divisions turns the labor market itself into almost a battlefield." The predecessor of Pius XII indicated that organization according to occupational lines was, "if not essential, at least natural to civil society" (*Quadragesimo Anno*, par. 83).

Pius XII then made this interesting observation: "The tremendous catastrophe which fell upon you has brought with it the advantage that in important groups, freed from the prejudices and egoism of class, the class contrasts have been in great part leveled out and men have come closer one to the other." An interesting example of how good may stem from a disordered situation!

> The common misfortune and misery was and is a severe but salutary teacher of discipline. It forced all to learn the art of mutual support, comprehension and assistance one to the other to bear the years of misfortune. The precious fruit of

> those years must not be lost to you. It must never happen again that the contrast between the rich and the poor, which incidentally has been greatly reduced, the contrast between the owner and the man who lives from the work of his hands, be allowed to widen or deepen. Who, dear sons and daughters, who more than you are called to smooth the way for this decisive step in social reconstruction in order to effect the law and the spirit of Christ?

Western Germany, which was reconstructed almost literally from the ashes of World War II under the wise guidance of the Christian statesman, Konrad Adenauer, did indeed manifest important traces of "the law and spirit of Christ." Anyone who has visited and been able to observe first hand the German social market economy that emerged in the years following World War II will note the great leveling of social classes which Pius XII envisioned here. Like certain other members of the postwar European Community, Germany today is much closer to being a "middle class society" than it had been previously. Indeed, one may dare say, given its generous social welfare system and its well-paid and well-treated workers, that it came closer to that ideal than even the United States, where the vision is much vaunted, but nevertheless fading especially amid the resurgence of the so-called free market economy. Unfortunately, the bitter memory of those harrowing years directly after World War II has receded, and the prosperous nations of Europe seem once again to have drifted into Mammonism in its new form: consumerism.

The fourth point made by Pius XII in this message had to do with the need to combine "Christian cultural and social policy." They cannot be separated "because the same Christian man is both the source and the aim of each." He had in mind such factors as defending the Catholic schools, whose continued separate existence was then being challenged in Germany.

Here, once again, we find a remarkable concordance with the German Jesuit economist, Heinrich Pesch who, in fact, spoke of a "law" or "principle of cultural unity." As regards this interrelationship of the various areas of culture, we do not hesitate to talk about a law or principle of cultural unity, which is of the utmost importance for the study of economics in general.[8] Pesch went on to explain what he meant by that concept.

> However, we understand cultural unity here as meaning a principle of reason emanating from uniformity in the national life-style, and stemming from the internal relationship and bond that exists among the various spheres of human and social existence and activity. The proper understanding of cultural unity in this sense safeguards us against the radical rejection of humane and social considerations in the course of our economic analysis; and it protects us against the all-too prevalent exaggeration of the absolute maximization of material production and riches, so that there is room left for a proper consideration of the relative optimum—an optimum which takes into account the whole human person, the whole of society, the whole nation, and the whole state.

The fifth and final point appears to have become even more relevant now than when it was first presented: "It must not happen that the world of labor falls into atheistic materialism." While the danger of slipping into "atheistic communism" was still very real when this message was delivered, more recent developments suggest that the atheistic trap has assumed a broader secular humanistic form, which entails also the aforementioned consumerist cult. Indeed, when the East Germans were finally free to move through the infamous "Iron Curtain" and across the Berlin Wall, it soon became obvious that most of them were coming westward not to relish a lost spiritual freedom, but to stock up on various consumer goods so long withheld from them. Thus the message of Pius XII to Germans is still worth contemplating, also well beyond the borders of that particular materially rich, and somewhat spiritually impoverished nation.

Christian Justice and Charity as the Main Supports of the State
Address to Senators from the United States
17 November 1949[9]

This very brief message is worth recounting here because in it Pius XII reaffirmed what his predecessor had established as key principles in Catholic social teaching 18 years previously. In *Quadragesimo Anno,* Pius XI, who in turn referred back to Leo XIII (*Quadragesimo Anno*, par. 126), made the tandem virtues, social justice and social charity, the "lofty and noble principles" for regulating economic life (88). Indeed, even beyond economic life "all of the institutions of public and social life" are to be "imbued" with these social virtues. Now Pius XII told several United States senators, representing what was by then clearly the most powerful nation on earth, that peace can ultimately only be assured by qualities in the soul of a people. And that must find expression in "the defense of the family, of children, of workers and their employers where all, guided by the Christian principles of justice and charity, may enjoy the blessed fruits of brotherly love and contribute to the general welfare according to their abilities."

The Pope placed the message in the specific context of the time of the senators' visitation. Europe was still staggering economically from the devastation left by what he called here "a long and merciless war." So he repeated to them the central message: "The Christian principles of justice and charity—how indispensable they are for a world that is seeking peace!" Nor did he hesitate to lecture them that those principles "are and must be founded on religion." He concluded with a bit of practical advice about how the indispensable principles are best instilled in citizens' hearts. "Anyone who is convinced of the importance of the task will recognize that these principles must be instilled in the hearts of children already in the home, and then developed further throughout their school years."

It turned out to be an interesting sermon for a group of men who represented what was then the most powerful nation on earth. They had perhaps expected something more platitudinous or even congratulatory.

`Production for Human Needs
Address for the Catholic International Congress of Social Study in Rome
3 June, 1950[10]

We have here an especially important message with regard to shaping an economic system that is in harmony with Christian principles. Pius XII summed up in one expansive statement what he cited as: "... the great social problem with its challenge at the crossroads in this present hour!" Indicating that "the vast problem of unemployment" cannot be reduced simply to providing a "better distribution of the total individual and physical labor forces in the world," the Pope said: "The time has come to face squarely in its full dimension, the duty of providing for countless families, in their natural moral, juridical and economic unity, a just living-space which meets, however modestly but at the very least in sufficient measure, the demands of human dignity." He was talking of doing this on a worldwide scale:

> Away with the selfish preoccupations of nationality and class which may in the least degree hinder an undertaking loyally embraced and vigorously carried out by the joint action of all the forces actually at work or available over the whole face of the earth; an undertaking launched with the aid of every initiative and effort of private individuals and specialized groups, and with the world-wide collaboration of peoples and states, each contributing its respective share of wealth in raw materials, in capital, in manpower. All the participants in this common project should appreciate, finally, the assistance offered to it by the Church.

The Pontiff was indicating a prescient awareness of the worldwide dimensions of the social problem that used to involve mainly internal economic considerations of the individual industrialized nations. After World War II, with the release from colonial dependency the nations which were to make up the so-called Third World, he was already preparing the way for the important social teachings of his successors. John XXIII and Paul VI would begin to focus attention on the importance of worldwide economic solidarity. The technology emerging from World War II made the world a much smaller place than it had been previously, and that shrinkage had both positive and negative dimensions. Positive, were the remarkable advances in transportation and communication. Negative, was the irreversible leap into the nuclear era whose threat was immediately recognizable, and whose possible advantages were as yet unclear.

That, in the Pope's words, placed "the great social problem, with its challenge at the crossroads in this present hour!" He stated the promise that: "If that problem is put on the way to a successful solution, even at the expense of material interests, even at the price of sacrifices by every member of the great human family, the international situation will be rid of one of its most troubling factors, the one which more than any other keeps alive today the ruinous 'cold war,' and threatens to set ablaze the incomparably more disastrous hot war, the war that burns."

He indicated that the social problem had moved beyond the point where all that was needed was to assure the worker greater power in the work place, e.g., by "progressive evolution in labor legislation." In fact, there was evidence now that "a limit is reached where the danger arises that the working class may follow in its turn the mistaken course of capital." Where capital had more and more withdrawn responsibility from private owners and handed "it over to the responsibility of anonymous corporate groups," in some circles it is now being "claimed that the wage earners in a given industry have the right to economic joint-management."

Certain proponents of joint labor-management initiatives had reached the point where in their enthusiasm they elevated them to the status of *rights*. Indeed, some even appealed to the Church's social teachings to support that position. Pius XII clarified how this problem may have stemmed from a misunderstanding of what Pius XI had stated in *Quadragesimo Anno* about advantages which could derive from some ventures in the direction of labor-management partnership. There we find praise for workers and employers entering into arrangements where workers "become sharers in ownership or management or participate in some fashion in the profits received" (*Quadragesimo Anno*, par. 65). In fact, Pius XI even considered such amelioration of the work contract "advisable...in the present condition of human society." However, that advice followed directly his statement that, "those who declare that a contract of hiring and being hired is unjust of its own nature, and hence a partnership contract must take its place, are certainly in error and gravely misrepresent Our predecessor whose Encyclical not only accepts working for wages or salaries but deals at some length with its regulation in accordance with the rules of justice"(*Quadragesimo Anno*, par. 64).

As Pius XI had to defend Leo XIII against what were perhaps overenthusiastic interpretations of portions of *Rerum Novarum,* Pius XII was now forced to warn about an incorrect reading of his own predecessor's suggestion. He, in fact, spoke of a "danger" that is "present when it is claimed that the wage-earners in a given industry have the right to economic joint-management."

> As a matter of fact, neither the nature of the labor contract nor the nature of the business enterprise in themselves admit necessarily of a right of this sort. It is unquestionable that the wage earner and the employer are equally the subjects, not the objects, of a nation's economy. There is no question of denying this parity. It is already an established principle of social policy; it would be asserted still more effectively were that policy to be organized on the occupational level. But there is nothing in the private-law relationship as governed by the simple wage-contract, to contradict this fundamental parity....

Indeed, Pius XII saw a certain disadvantage in such problems in that "they make one lose sight of the problem of major importance and major urgency which broods like a nightmare especially over the old industrial countries, that is the imminent and permanent menace of unemployment, the problem of the reintegration and maintenance of normal productive enterprise, of that productivity which is intimately linked by its origin as well as in its purpose to the dignity and well-being of the family viewed as a moral juridical and economic unit." In other words, perhaps zealous people were getting ahead of themselves in some respects, while the serious long-standing problems continued to nag at the core of the old industrialized economies. At the same time, the Pope seized the opportunity to indicate that he had not given up on the notion of occupational organization as proposed his predecessor.

As for the newly industrialized countries, the Pontiff's suggestions here clearly foreshadow admonitions in the social encyclicals of his successors. For example, he warns of "a repetition of the grievous omissions of economic liberalism during the last century." A similar warning by Paul VI in *Populorum Progressio* (1967) would earn him the scorn of "conservative" commentators who were by then enthused about restoring, in updated form, the "economic liberalism" and the "laissez faire" approach to resolving economic problems, that was explicitly rejected here by Pius XII.

Clearly opposed to those nineteenth century formulae, we have this statement: "Equally blind is the well-nigh superstitious reliance on the mechanism of the world market to restore a balanced economy, and the trust in an omniprovident State to secure for each of its subjects and in every emergency of their lives the right to make demands which must eventually prove to be unattainable." By that brief statement, juxtaposed rival economic systems, along with volumes of wrong-headed economic analysis, are swept into the dust bin! The once discredited, now resuscitated liberal capitalism, along with the moribund socialistic system are both rejected.

Then, without mentioning the name of the economist Heinrich Pesch S. J., who devised the *solidaristic system*, Pope Pius XII introduced an element of that system which lies at its heart: "In the domain of social economy the duty pressing for attention is the judicious adjustment of production to consumption on the basis of human needs and human dignity." "In other words, economic life is not about profits or riches or power, but about adjusting human production to human needs." That would seem to accord perfectly with simple common sense. The problem is that very little makes good sense in a system of economy that has been burdened by centuries of philosophical malpractice. The Pope is explicit about that kind of thinking in his very next sentence:

> The solution of this question must not be sought from the theory of 'laws of the market'—a purely positivistic by-product of neo-Kantian criticism—nor in the mere formula, every bit as artificial, of 'full employment.' There before you is the problem on which We should like to see the theorists and practical men of the Catholic social movement concentrate their attention and bring their studies to bear.

That modern economic thought, and subsequently also practice, is based on positivism, its practitioners would scarcely deny. Basically, they are men of the Enlightenment, which, with its deistic naturalism and the positivism stemming from it, has long shaped the prevailing philosophy among the mainstream of social scientists.

There appears to have been little real progress in the economic science since that papal message in 1950. Even today, the theorists and practitioners are still pretty much divided between devotees of one or the other of the two sets of theories and formulae which the Pope mentioned here. Indeed, there has been renewed vigor devoted to rehabilitating a form of economy based on "the theory of 'laws of the market.'" In the opposing camp are residual Keynesians with updated versions of "the mere formula, every bit as artificial, of 'full employment.'" The latter group insist on what is assuredly a valid goal, full employment, for which they nevertheless rely to an invalid degree on the heavy hand of the state.

It seems remarkable that even those economists who professed devotion to their Church's social teachings did not pay closer attention to the advice offered here by Pope Pius XII in 1950. The Keynesian "revolution" was just then in the process of dividing serious economic thinking into the pre-Keynesian and post-Keynesian modes, into those who favored the so-called microeconomic approach as opposed to those who insisted on a macroeconomic approach to economic analysis and management.[11] The latter made of John Maynard Keynes a kind of messianic figure who had finally arrived to establish order and a definitive parting-of-the-ways for their disoriented science. On the other hand, here was the head of the Roman Catholic Church, by a simple, brief sentence laying the ax at the root of their twisted tree. Not surprisingly, the challenge was not picked up, and the science is as discombobulated now, a half century later, as it was then; and economic policies which are eventually based on some variation of these errant economic philosophies, demonstrates this state of economic thinking. Theoretical nit-pickers have long since unearthed what errors there are in the Keynesian approach; but this has served, among other things, to divert serious thought back toward rehabilitating Adam Smith and the massively flawed liberal free market approach which flowed from his Enlightenment-based economics.

One final point deserves to be mentioned with regard to this important address. Long before ecological concerns became prominent in scientific and popular discourse, we find Pius XII warning: "There has been too much experimentation with mass production, with the exploitation, to the point of exhaustion, of every resource of the soil and subsoil." We have here a prescient papal message, which while brief, is nevertheless powerful and still highly relevant for economic thought and for the economic systems based thereon in the new millennium.

The Meaning and Limits of State Intervention
Address to Scholars of the Science of Public Administration
5 August 1950[12]

What we have here is an explication of the *principle of subsidiarity* presented before a group dedicated to the study of the science of public administration. This address is included here among Pius XII's teachings on the economic order because of the important position that principle occupies in the teachings of the Catholic Church with regard to the economic order. It therefore has an important tangential relevance. It also provides an important message for those who seem to recognize only positive aggression against that hallowed principle of social order.

Pius XII began his address with the reminder that next to the family, the state is the most essential social institution, rooted as it is as "one of the constitutive elements of the natural law." There has been much loose commentary since the revival of liberalism in social thought suggesting that the state is to be minimized as though it represented an evil, and that instead of offering a solution to our problems, it is itself actually "the problem." Meanwhile, the negative violation of subsidiarity tends to be neglected completely, i.e., the failure of individuals and of the lower social organs of society to live up to their social responsibilities, thereby often forcing the state to get involved in matters which *could* be handled more effectively at a lower level.

Unfortunately 1950, when this discourse was delivered, still gave witness to much excessive incursion by an all-powerful state. As the Pope remarked, "and with what consequences!" Yet, he cautioned, "no one will contest the need for the state to extend its activity especially in the field of social activity, and even to increase its power there." He indicated that all of that could happen "without danger if there had been equivalent progress in the understanding and appreciation of the purpose and function of the state." In that case, "the state would have found a regulator and a control which could have prevented it from extending its power for reasons, other than economic and social needs, into areas of a cultural nature which would best be left to the free enterprising spirit of the citizens." Instead, all too often this grasp of what the state's purpose is "grew in inverse relationship to the increase in power, not only among those who see in the state only their source of profit, or among those who suffer under it, but even among those who have the responsibility to give the state its form and constitution."

The true concept of the state lies in being a "moral organism" which is based on the moral world order. "It does not have plenipotentiary power that suppresses all legitimate autonomy." "Its function, its noble task is to promote the active cooperation of its members so as to forge, support and bolster a higher unity among them who will serve the welfare of the whole community so long as they respect their subordination to the state's purpose." This means that "neither the individual nor the family is to be absorbed by the state.... Each is to retain its freedom of action to the extent that this does not pose the risk of harming the common good." The Pope offered specific examples of areas where this freedom of action is to apply: "the right to one's good name, the right and the freedom to honor the true God, the natural right of parents to raise and educate their children." He regarded it as a good omen, and he likened to the sunrise the fact that some new constitutions have embodied these ideas.

Pius XII concluded with a warning about luxuriant blossoming of "plans" and "standardizations," all of which are acceptable within proper bounds. What he opposed is "the exaggerated intervention by the state," especially since its actions are all too often left to "pure technicians in the area of organization."

The Church's Concern for Economic Life
A Radio Message to the Workers of Spain
11 March 1951[13]

This message, like others, did not come with a title. Titles are assigned by people who do the editorial work in various publications. In the German language version (Utz & Groner) it was presented as: *The Labor Problem and the New Order of Society*. It was addressed to workers in the broad sense as intended by the Church in its social teachings. That is to say, the category includes not only laborers in the widely used sense of wage-earners, but also working entrepreneurs and the salaried types of employees sometimes referred to as "white collar workers."

Pius XII began with a papal defense of the Church's role in speaking on behalf of workers and their problems in the social order. He alluded here specifically to its activity dating back to the *Epistle of St. Paul to Philemon* and continuing in the social teachings of the popes of the nineteenth and twentieth centuries. There was, as may be expected, special honorable mention of Leo XIII as having provided the workers with "the *Magna Carta* of their rights." That was followed by a statement which some may regard as rather startling, if not contra-ecumenical: "the social question of our time cannot be resolved without the Church!" Indeed, the Pope did not shrink from asserting that the social legislation of various countries in recent times reflected social principles set forth by the Church in recent times. He recalled that the Church in its nearly 2000-year history has had to deal with a great variety of social systems. These began with the ancient ones that included slavery as an integral institution, extending then to the modern systems, which are described by the words, "capitalism," and "proletarian."

Against the background of that history lesson, Pius XII launched into the traditional position of the Church on private property as an inviolable right. Nevertheless, there was always the moderating qualification that the right was not absolute, so that it involved a more just distribution of property and rejected as contrary to nature the condition where "a small group of privileged people and excessively rich stand opposed to an enormous impoverished mass of people." Thus, those who are in the position of power in society must see to it that conditions are such that people do not have to live from hand to mouth, but that savings are also possible for them.

That aspect—the ability to acquire savings—is implicit in the just wage doctrine presented by Leo XIII and Pius XI in their encyclicals addressed to the economic order. The Pope made that clear in his next statement indicating: "The just wage will always be the most important factor among those which will lead to a wider distribution of property." In fact, he stated:

> You know full well, dear Sons, that the just wage and a better distribution of the goods of nature constitute the two most urgent requirements in the social program of the Church. In the process, the Church also encourages whatever brings about improvements in the relationship between employers and employees, to make these more humane and more Christian so as to instill mutual trust. Needless to say, class struggle can never be a social objective.

The spiritual dimension for resolving the social problem is reaffirmed toward the end of this brief message. The Pope encouraged the workers to be "men of prayer," since what they hope to accomplish "can only be achieved with the help and providence of God." He pointed out that the Church need not apologize for insisting on that spiritual aspect, because, at the same time, its program for alleviating the ills of society here below in the world has not been surpassed by any other.

The Problem of Fair Distribution
A Letter addressed to Semaine Sociale of Dijon, France,
7 July 1952[14]

Pius XII returned in this message to the problem of how wealth and income are distributed—a problem which, he indicated, cannot be solved by simply increasing production. He referred to "the riches which have been created in such abundance in our period of industrialism." The increase in labor's productivity, and consequently in production, made the problem of inequitable distribution of the fruits of such increased production all the more glaring—a problem which, in the Pontiff's view, had "become ever more acute," since the end of World War II. The reason was the fact that with the dismantling of colonial empires and the newly won independence of many new nations, along with the legitimate aspirations of the emancipated millions of people, the problem "now forces itself upon us on a worldwide scale, where the contrasts are still striking." Once again, we have here the prescient suggestion of what would be a fully developed theme of social encyclicals by two successor popes, John XXIII and Paul VI: the international application of the original social teachings as established by Leo XIII and Pius XI.

Also, although it was scarcely seven years since World War II, Pius XII here sounded an early warning about the "consumerism" which would in the years ahead become a social affliction in the industrially advanced nations. The

Pope referred to "the intolerable increase in luxury spending and in superfluous and unreasonable expenditures, which contrast sharply with the misery of so many people, be they in the ranks of the urban or rural proletariat, or among those little people who are usually called the 'economically weak.'"

Pius XII introduced an important and widely overlooked passage about the just wage and the severe implications of withholding it from the worker, from the Epistle of St. James. "Behold, the wages of the laborers who reaped your fields, which have been kept back by you unjustly, cry out; and their cry has entered into the ears of the Lord of Hosts" (James 5:4).

The role of the twin social virtues, justice and charity, in the social order is then placed in proper perspective by the words: "...in order to be genuinely true, charity must always take into account the justice which must be established and must never satisfy itself with palliating the disorders and deficiencies of an unjust situation."

The theme of just distribution *vis à vis* simply increasing production recurs: "If it is true that the best and most natural means of satisfying this obligation is to increase available goods through a healthy development of production, it is still necessary, in pursuing this effort, to have care to distribute justly the fruit of the labor of all."

A significant figure of speech introduced by this Pontiff occurs here in discussing the cooperative role of managers and workers: it is the fact that

> ...all are eating at the same table.... Managers of industry and workers are here cooperators in a common task; both of them are called upon to derive their livelihood from the actual and total income of the economy.... Thus, even though there are differences in functions and responsibilities—the share given to each should conform to a common dignity which they have as men; and that, in particular, these shares should permit a greater number of persons to attain the independence and security which come from possession of private property, and to participate with their families in the spiritual and cultural goods to which earthly goods are ordered.

That brings up the question: "...if both employers and workers have a common interest in the healthy prosperity of the national economy, why should it not be legitimate to give to the workers a just share of responsibility in the organization and development of that economy?"[15]

Liberalism came up for discussion and rejection several times in this important message. The Pope pointed out that "to meet the demands of social life, this distribution cannot be left to the free play of blind economic forces." The present-day "conservative" or "neoliberal" school of thought would not be comfortable with that warning. Nor would it be likely to accept what Pius XII had to say about the role of the state in maintaining order in the economy: "Now, although the public authorities should not substitute their oppressive omnipotence for the legitimate independence of private initiatives, these authorities have, in this matter, an undeniable function of coordination, which is made even more necessary by the confusion of present conditions, especially social conditions." Nor would the neoliberal trend of thinking be easily reconciled with the papal suggestion that "without the cooperation of the public authorities it is not possible to formulate an integral economic policy which would promote active cooperation on the part of all and an increase of industrial production." While that merely reaffirms the principle of subsidiarity, in other words the *subsidiary*, not preemptive, position of the state and public authorities, it nevertheless suggests an active and not a merely a passive role for them.

From there, Pius XII went on to also affirm what has come to be known in the Church's social teachings as the "preferential option for the poor":

> It also devolves on the state to see to it that the very poor are not unjustly exploited. On this point, the teaching of Our predecessors is very explicit: in the protection of private rights the authorities should give special attention to the claims of the weak and the needy.

To support that teaching he cited a Pius XI quotation from Leo XIII: " For the rich are guarded by their own defenses and are in less need of governmental protection, whereas the suffering multitude without the means to protect itself, relies especially on the protection of the state" (*Quadragesimo Anno*, par. 25).

Things get worse for the so-called "conservative" viewpoint. First there is an endorsement of "some institutions" which "have endeavored for several years to correct the most flagrant evils caused by an over-mechanical distribution of the national income." The Pope made clear that "these institutions, remaining themselves adequately independent of the political power, can become for the low income group and the poor of every class an indispensable remedy for evils caused by economic or monetary disorder." Assuming that labor unions are among the "institutions" referred to here, there are nevertheless also admonitions for them: "However, the various forms and methods of such institutions should be studied with great care, and one could not possibly commit oneself unreservedly to a plan wherein policies of excessive taxation might endanger the rights of private property, and where abuses of collective security could weaken the rights of the person and the family."

What all of that amounts to, ultimately, is a reaffirmation of the position of the Church, as the Pope put it here, "midway between the errors of liberalism and statism." Ultimately, "the great misery of the social order is that it is neither deeply Christian nor really human, but solely technical and economic." That papal lament speaks volumes about the course of history over the past centuries since the secularization of society was accomplished. Once again, it also echoes precisely the economic philosophy of solidarism as developed by the Jesuit economist, Heinrich Pesch.[16]

To Austrian Catholics
A Radio Address to Austrian Catholics in Vienna
14 September 1952[17]

This address to the Austrian *Katholikentag* was the first since 1933, a fact which Pius XII noted while also reminiscing about cataclysmic events that transpired since that time. Actually Austria was the one country that the Soviet occupying forces departed from voluntarily for reasons which until this day remain unexplained. The Pope referred to the "fateful events which began with the first World War and shook our existence as a nation and as a state to its deepest foundations, in unimaginable upheavals and catastrophes...."

Little remembered is the dignity and scope of the great Habsburg Empire under which Austria-Hungary remained the largest territory in Europe only next to Russia. After its involvement in World War II as a part of Hitler's Third Reich, the now diminutive Austria was subjected to many years of Soviet occupation, from which it had at last been freed.

There was a poignant proposal that all of the "buildings, statues, paintings, which symbolize the full richness of Catholic religious and cultural traditions, which have been gathered by the faith of many centuries" should not "some day become a death mask, but always remain the face and figure of a living organism full of inner warmth and overflowing strength." The Pope was well aware that the Catholic religious beliefs of the vast majority of Austrians had been placed under severe strain during the period of Nazi domination and even before. His "death mask" allusion was a reminder that this historically very Catholic nation should now return to the solid Faith of its fathers. He followed that with similar admonitions about the sanctity of marriage and the need for solid "Christian upbringing of your children," along with warnings against "Sunday secularization," and "an almost pagan glorification of physical culture and pleasure." Those were to some degree legacies of the Nazi era between 1938 and 1945. Pius XII indicated his awareness of the implications for family life in the kind of "far-reaching housing projects" that were already underway. He warned that care should be taken "to assure that their planning and execution are in accord with the will of God concerning marriage and the family." Much new housing in Austria, as throughout Europe, was geared to the demographically fatal two-child family.

Turning to the broader social question, the Pius XII recalled that Vienna "has always been one of the focal points of Catholic social action." He cited "the problem of the workingman" as standing "...at the center of the modern social controversy." The Pope identified it as: "the distress of the proletariat and the task of lifting this class of society, exposed defenselessly to the caprices of economic ups-and-downs, to a status of dignity equal to that enjoyed by the other classes, and of endowing it with clearly defined rights." He proposed that "this task has been solved—at any rate in its essentials—and the Catholic world has honestly and effectively contributed to its solution." That was attributable at least in part to "the social principles and directives stated by the successors of St. Peter during the past sixty years." Accordingly he saw what still needed to be accomplished as "the second phase of the social dispute," and he regarded this as "of a different nature."

Pius XII addressed this "second phase" by drawing attention to two specific aspects.

The first was "overcoming the class struggle through an organic coordination of employer and employee, for class struggle can never be a goal of Catholic social ethics." In all but name, this refers to one important dimension of the principle of occupational organization which was part and parcel of the Pius XI encyclical addressed to reconstructing the social order: *Quadragesimo Anno.* That principle involved the incorporation of both sides of the so-called labor market within one body, which could deal in solidarity with problems confronting the respective industries or occupations as a whole.

The second aspect of the ongoing "social dispute" was the then continuing threat of socialism. Thus Pius XII saw the need for "the protection of the individual and of the family against the vortex which threatens to draw them into an all-embracing socialization at the end of which looms the very real nightmare of 'Leviathan.'"

That led the Pope into discussing a tangential problem that had arisen among well-intentioned champions of the Church's social doctrine. He pointed out once again that the Church's steadfast defense of private property required also that it "declined to deduce, directly or indirectly from the labor contract the right of the employee to participate in the ownership of the operating capital and its corollary, the right of the worker to participate in decisions concerning operations of the plant (*Mitbestimmung*). At the time (1950) the Co-Determination Law (*Mitbestimmungsgesetz*) had been passed in Germany, which entitled workers and their labor unions to have seats on directorates enabling them to co-determine conditions affecting the workers in the respective industries. During the discussions leading up to passage of the law, there were overly zealous interpreters of what Pius XI had stated in *Quadragesimo Anno* about "the work contract" being "somewhat modified by a partnership contract..." (*Quadragesimo Anno*, par. 65). They mistakenly exalted certain prudential suggestions by that Pope into natural rights which therefore could not be denied to the workers. As indicated earlier, Pius XI had proposed variations of what are today called profit-sharing, ownership-sharing (like employee stock ownership plans), and management-sharing arrangements "as is already being done in various ways and with no small advantage to workers and owners." However, these were by no means to be regarded as natural rights of workers, as the same Pontiff made clear in a preceding paragraph. "First of all, those who declare that a contact of hiring and being hired is unjust of its own nature, and hence a partnership-contract must take its place, are certain in error and gravely misrepresent Our Predecessor." (*Quadragesimo Anno*, par. 64).

The paragraph (*Quadragesimo Anno*, par. 65) proposing modification of the "work contract" opened with the suggestion: "We consider it more advisable, however, in the present condition of society that, so far as is possible, the work contract be somewhat modified by a partnership contract...." The stringent qualifications need to be noted and not lost sight of. Key words are "advisable," "somewhat modified," "in the present conditions of society," (which Pius XI clearly considered to be socially disordered), "so far as possible," and "somewhat." What that Pontiff, like his predecessor Leo XIII proposed as the natural right of all workers was, like his right to private property, the right to a just wage. One has only to read the unqualified—because unqualifiable—insistence on such a wage in order to perceive the difference between prudential suggestions and inalienable rights: "...social justice demands that changes be introduced as soon as possible whereby such a wage will be assured to every adult workingman" (*Quadragesimo Anno*, par. 71).

Pius XII indicated that the newly discovered "right" had to be "denied because behind this question there stands that greater problem: the right of the individual and of the family to own property which stems immediately from the human person." Needless to say it is "a right...accompanied by social obligation." It is "a right, however, and not merely a social function." That right includes also the right of businessmen—stockholders in the case of corporations—to exclusive ownership of their enterprises and their capital.

Given the context in which the Pontiff presented this correction, it seems possible that he saw the attack on the private property right by those who claimed loyalty to the Church's social teachings about the right of private property as an extension of the ongoing socialist contestation of that right. In any case, he seized the opportunity to clarify the matter, which he clearly regarded with concern: "We feel compelled to exhort you and all other Catholics anew, to hue to the clearly defined line of Catholic social teaching from the very beginning of the new dispute, without deviating to the right or to the left."

It is significant that Pius XII was issuing an early warning that Catholics avoid "deviating to the right or to the left." In the years that followed, it appears that the warning was ill-heeded. Some time later, "liberation theology" was to put in an appearance among Catholics as a significant deviance to the left, especially among Latin American countries. At the same time there arose also a serious deviance to the right of Catholic social teachings, which Paul VI saw fit to warn against in *Octogesima Adveniens* (par. 35) in 1971, and which Pope John Paul II decried as "neoliberalism" in an *Apostolic Exhortation* to the Bishops of the Americas in 1999.

Perhaps Pius XII was once again being prophetic in this little noted address to the Austrian Catholics in 1952. His admonition rates being presented verbatim:

> We feel compelled to exhort you and all other Catholics anew, to hue to the clearly defined line of Catholic social teaching from the very beginning of the new dispute, without deviating to the right or to the left. A deviation from that line, even if only by a few degrees, may at first seem inconsequential. In the long run, however, it would lead dangerously astray from the right path and bring fateful consequences. Calm thinking, self-control, steadfastness in the face of temptations from either extreme must, then, be a watchword of our time.

The Anniversary of *Rerum Novarum*
Address to Italian Catholic Workers
14 May 1953[18]

In this address, Pius XII referred back to the primeval root of social disorder: "the same enemy who until the end of time will try to break through the front lines of goodness, in order to sow destruction and death."

In 1953 when it was delivered, the Communist Empire was still threatening in a militant and aggressive manner. One may assume that the Pope was addressing the Marxist demon when he issued this warning:

> In fact, whenever it suits him, the spirit of darkness is able also to clothe himself as an angel of light. Then adapting himself to situations and circumstances, and to the state of the soul that listens to him, he alters his tone and language; but the substance of his utterances never varies: "You men, do not look up to heaven; think only of things of earth."

One of the standard accusations made by Marxists against the Catholic Church was that it distracted the workers from dealing with the injustices inflicted on them in this world, by diverting their attention to the hereafter. The occasion of the anniversary of *Rerum Novarum* afforded Pius XII the opportunity to counter that charge with what Leo XIII had accomplished to direct attention also to justice here on this earth. "Did not that most wise Pontiff precisely combine the true Christian life with the right order of this world when, making his own the words of St. Thomas Aquinas, he confirmed in *Rerum Novarum* that the use of earthly goods 'is necessary for the exercise of virtue,' and therefore the leading on earth of a Christian life worthy of man."

Lest anyone might lose sight of the higher dimension, however, he warned:

> Yes, so it is. While Leo XIII sent forth his cry of truth and justice on the labor question, he wished that men, and particularly the workers, should remain with both feet on the ground. Here below, they were bound, as Christians, to take an interest in right order. However, man whom God created and saved cannot keep his two feet on the ground without keeping his eyes raised towards God, towards the real end of human life, namely, union with God in heaven, where alone all order and all justice will definitely be achieved.

Indeed, the Pope was quite specific about pitfalls that may confront even Catholic champions of social order, who sometimes display a special penchant for allowing their feet to leave the ground.

> Certain Catholics, promoters of a new social order, are in error when they maintain that social reform must come first of all and that afterwards care will be taken of the religious and moral life of the individual and of society. The first cannot, in fact, be separated from the second, because this world cannot be disjoined from the other, nor can man who is a living whole be broken up into

two parts.

That was followed by a sobering statement to readjust the vision of those who, in their preoccupation with social order in the world, overlook the importance of the more pedestrian roots of that order in "everyday, concrete, human relations between employers and employed, between management and the workers in the factories." That, said the Pope citing Leo XIII, is where social order begins, in "the reform of the mutual relations between persons engaged in economic activity."

Clearly, therefore, the admonition about exclusive preoccupation with the material welfare here below was not intended solely for the Marxists whose "pie in the sky" program has since been undermined by its own intrinsic, unnatural flawed view of man. The so-called free world suffered then, as now, from its distorted vision of reality, including economic reality. Pius XII referred here to "a colorless humanism devoid of all Christian faith." That humanism obviously was in force as much in the non-Communist world as it was in the Soviet Empire. Therefore, the Pope contrasted the regnant secular humanism in the modern world to the "wondrous riches of Christian humanism," lamenting that, "...when people exchange the latter for the former, they exchange riches for poverty, the real thing for what is only a substitute."

Although the obsession with consumption had not yet been exalted to the level of an "ism," i.e., "consumerism," its hallmarks were already apparent, at least to the prescient Pontiff, when he delivered this message in 1954. And it gave rise to a papal warning. Referring to the great expectations which some have for "the possibilities of technical science and of organization that make bright promises of producing even more at less cost," the Pope cautioned, "the more exclusively and incessantly one increases the tendency to consumption, all the more does the economy cease to have as its object the normal man in his reality, the man who orders and adjusts the demands of this earthly life to his last end and to the law of God."

There followed a prophetic note whose validity is perhaps more evident a half century later than it was in 1954: the consumerist urge that is especially virulent now in the opulent nations, even while it is being desperately aspired to in the emerging nations.

> Thus, the genuine relationship existing with a real and normal need would be reversed through demands artificially created. The income therefrom would necessarily increase, but very soon it would become no longer enough. The lack of security would remain, because the social economy would take its rise from and would suppose a mankind deviated from the right and just measure of its being.

At the end of his message, Pope Pius XII reaffirmed the insistence of Leo XIII "on the observance of Sundays and holy days." The great author of *Rerum Novarum* was facing one of the pitfalls of early industrialism, when the obsession with ever more production and profits often led to workers, young and old, male and female, being forced to forego the rest provided by Sundays and holy days. Progressive legislation and aggressive labor union activity led to a gradual amelioration of excessive hours of work and the blurring of distinctions between weekdays and Sundays. Therefore, in the United States perhaps some thirty years ago, this may have been regarded as a no longer widely relevant issue. Now at the start of the new millennium, the problem is back in all of its inhumane dimensions. In our allegedly affluent society Sunday-rest is now widely disregarded for workers, especially in mercantile establishments. What is more, manufacturers, in the competitive scramble for greater profits, increasingly export their work to developing nations, thus evading our own wage and hour legislation. There men, women, and children routinely work for inhumanely long hours for paltry wages—a scenario painfully reminiscent of the early years of the Industrial Revolution. So this issue too has urgent relevance once again, as it had when Leo XIII first drew the world's attention to it near the end of the nineteenth century.

The Benefits of Sound Technology
An Address before the First International Congress of Engineers
October 9, 1953[19]

After pointing out that engineers occupy a position of special importance in the modern world marked above all by an extraordinary development of technology, Pius XI addressed the question posed by them at this international congress: Why do engineers not enjoy higher status among occupations? He suggested that the engineer is confronted by direct practical applications, which are constantly being superseded by improved and less costly ones. Therefore he often succumbs to the temptation to abandon the strict scientific side of his profession and to favor instead the empirical process, over the correct and determinate theoretical solutions. He must often bow to the commands of business managers and to economic considerations, and so to sacrifice his own intellectual perspectives which would lead him to what is less practical in the short run, but of far greater significance for the long run.

Ultimately the engineer must have the courage to look beyond his own field. Even though his accomplishments in technology can enhance prosperity and increase the level of wealth in wide circles of the population, that is just a part of the story. History shows that the age of discoveries and inventions has also triggered widespread crises for the existing order and its morals. It takes a while until society can adjust itself to, and learn to master, the new techniques that are placed in its hands, since technology is only one aspect of overall human culture. Thus the engineer is in a sense a precursor. But what he accomplishes is not enough. He must appreciate the need for overall cultural development and progress. Technological concerns, for all of their importance and impact, do not satisfy all of the needs of mankind. In fact, by themselves in isolation they can be harmful and disruptive of social order.

One cannot expect the engineer to be expert in all fields relating to that order, but he must maintain a proper balance, a broadened view of the overall goals of human society in all of its various dimensions. Among other things, he must foster an appreciation for the natural law, which governs man and his activities both as an individual and as a member of the various communities of which he is a part. This requires a broader vision—one which also has an eye for the good and the beautiful as it unfolds both now and in past history.

The Pope proposed the Church as providing that kind of balanced perspective. Although it has labored for 2000 years at the religious and moral cultivation of mankind, it also demonstrated ongoing concern about man's other needs, including the material ones, his status with regard to the laws of nations, his education, and the familial and political order. Here its social teachings are of special importance, and they indicate attention to the needs of the whole person, both in body and in soul, as an individual and as a member of society, as a child of man and a child of God. "For that reason Christian principles provide the surest guarantee for a normal and happy development of mankind."

That plug for the Church's social teachings led Pius XII to conclude with a paternal admonition. Just as engineers express concern about their status in the overall productive structure, fearing that they are not adequately appreciated amid all of the immediate economic and business considerations, they should demonstrate a proper concern about those who work under them. That includes the "humblest of their subordinates." Indeed, after treating the rank-and-file worker for too long as simply a means of production which performs its duty in a servile manner, we appear to be concerned now mainly with the material aspects of his existence; and we recognize that this is not enough.

> If labor is a necessity for all human beings, work at one's occupation may not be permitted to frustrate its most natural and requisite impulses, but its dignity must be recognized fully and completely. This means that it is not enough to see in workers only producers of goods, but we should treat them as something more than mere material beings. Their work must afford dignity and they are entitled to expect understanding for their needs, and genuine fraternal sympathy from their employer even more so than from their own kind.

The Christian Way and Life Among Workingmen
Address to Catholic Association of Italian Workers
1 May 1955[20]

It was during the course of this address that Pius XII surprised the Italian workers gathered before him by instituting, at that moment, the Feast of St. Joseph the Worker and installing it on May 1st of the Church's liturgical calendar. As the Pope expressed it, he offered them this action in return for the "numerous and precious gifts bought to Us from all parts of Italy." Although May Day had been adopted in much of the Western world since the 1890s to mark an international labor day, the Communist world appropriated it as its special day to commemorate the workers' defiance of capitalistic oppression. This particular occasion also marked the 10th anniversary of the founding of the Catholic Association of Italian Workers (ACLI).

Along with a word of praise for the work of the Association and of the priests and laity "who serve as its teachers," the Pope warned of "false ideas about man and the world, about history, about social and economic structures" that had been spread about, and to which workers were especially vulnerable. He left little doubt about who might be spreading such falsehoods despite the Church's continuous concern for the workers as indicated in her social encyclicals: "Yet the monstrous lie is still spread about that 'the Church is allied with capitalism against labor.'" There followed a foreshadowing of the designation which his successor, John XXIII, would affix to the Church with special impact, just a few years later. "She, mother and teacher of all men, is always concerned especially for her children who are in more difficult circumstances, and in fact has made a strong contribution to the equitable progress already obtained by certain categories of workers."

It may be startling or even disconcerting to some that a pontiff of the Roman Catholic Church calls it a "monstrous lie" that "the Church is allied with capitalism against labor." Yet, from *Rerum Novarum* onward, it is clear that its social teachings did not propose a solution of liberal capitalism, but what Pius XII referred to here as "a world ruled by a just God, (which) appeals to justice and the spirit of brotherhood." Instead, the Pope made it clear once again that, "To enter into the world of social problems with its systems which do not derive from Him, whether they are called 'lay humanism' or 'Socialism stripped of materialism,' Jesus Christ does not wait for the door to be opened to him." After suggesting that "neither new laws nor new institutions are adequate to give to each the security to exist, protected against every misused restriction, and to be able to develop with freedom in society," the Pope indicated what was really required:

> All will be in vain if the ordinary man lives in fear of coming under arbitrary rule, and does not succeed in freeing himself from the feeling that he is subject to the good and bad will of those who apply the laws, or of those who, as public officials, direct institutions and organizations; if he perceives that, in daily life, all depends on connections which he—unlike others—perhaps does not have; if he suspects that behind the external show of what is called the state, there is hidden the manipulation of powerful organized groups.

Business and the Common Good
Address to the Italian Federation of Commerce
17 February 1956[21]

Like the previous address, this one too marked an anniversary: the tenth Anniversary of the founding of the *General Italian Federation of Commerce*. Pius XII defended the businessman against inferences that have confronted him since antiquity: that he is nothing more than a middleman who "uselessly prolongs and complicates the passage of goods from the producer to the consumer." He indicated here that, even as a middleman, the businessman "possesses a valuable experience which he has gained not without painful risks." However, the Pope made it clear that he has legitimate positive functions which go beyond that of a mere middleman. The businessman is "in the first place, a stimulating force in the economy," who not only assures "an opportune distribution of goods and services," but "likewise gives effective encouragement to the manufacturer to provide merchandise of higher quality and lower cost." What is more, "he has it in his power to afford to the consumer, in the fullest measure, a free access to the market."

That, along with what followed, offers a remarkable facsimile of what we find also in the writings of economists like Alfred Marshall who presented entrepreneurship as even a separate (fourth) primary factor of production in economic life.[22] It also reflects somewhat that key role of the "dynamic entrepreneur" as emphasized by Joseph Schumpeter.[23] For that role, the Pope suggested that the businessman "needs a thorough and well-balanced professional training; he must have a mind always quick to understand and follow up economic trends as they develop, in order to handle his business with success and to foresee the reactions of the masses of the people as well as their mental attitudes."

A pope would not be a pope if he did not add to requisite technical proficiency also the need for "sound moral qualities." Specifically, these include "courage in a period of crisis," and "tenacity in overcoming public apathy and misunderstanding." The businessman "must possess a spirit of optimism in revising his formulas and methods of action, and in estimating and making the best use of the probabilities of successful outcome."

From that array of qualifications, the Pope turned to the external framework required for a businessman to apply his capabilities most effectively, in other words, the economic system where "his way is not barred by too many obstacles set up by a regimentation that is too complicated or too strict." Also:

> He expects to face fair competition, operating under the same conditions in which he himself is placed; a competition that does not enjoy exclusive and unjustifiable privileges. At the same time he dares to hope that an excessive part of his well-earned profits will not be taken from him by taxes that are too numerous and too heavy.

What follows makes it clear that when Pius XII was taking about "fair competition," he did not have in mind the "free competition" of liberal capitalism. He allowed for "the growing desire to assure to all classes of society guarantees that will preserve them from the mishaps and chances inherent in the fluctuations of the economy; guarantees that will protect employment and its rewards; guarantees that will provide for sickness and incapacitating accidents that may reduce a man to idleness and deprive him of the means of livelihood." He even suggested that, "in many cases the present system of social security has not yet succeeded in putting an end to difficult situations or in healing wounds that are always open."

However, it is clear that Pius XII was not favoring a socialist so-called welfare state. Hence we find: "It is important, however, that the anxious desire for security should not prevail over the businessman's readiness to risk his resources to such an extent as to dry up every creative impulse; nor impose on the enterprise operating conditions that are too burdensome; nor discourage those who devote their time and energy to commercial transactions."

> Unhappily, it is an all-too-human tendency to seek out the way of minimum effort, to avoid obligations, and to exempt oneself from the duty of self-reliance in order to fall back upon the support of society and to live at the expense of one's fellows. These are, of course the easy solutions in which the responsibility of the individual is reduced to a minimum under the shadow of the nameless multitude.
>
> If the businessman has his own interests to defend and promote, if he bears the responsibility for his own activities, he will deal with and solve his own economic problems with greater enthusiasm, ability, and wisdom. No one will deny the need for assurances and vigilance exercised by public authority in the interest of the businessmen themselves as well as in that of the public.

That provided an opening for a predictable reaffirmation of the principle of subsidiarity:

> We may hope, then, that the State will be able to remain within the limits of its function of meeting the needs of private enterprise, by keeping a watchful eye upon its progress, and by lending a helping hand, should the need arise. But the State ought not to try to take the place of private enterprise, so long as the latter functions usefully and successfully. An equilibrium must be maintained between these two component parts of the economic movement, namely the forces of progress, and the element of organization; otherwise economic life will fall into either anarchy or stagnation.

The address typifies the approach followed by the Church in its social teachings. It seeks the middle ground between the old liberal capitalism and its opposite, the socialistic welfare state where private ownership of the means of production and private entrepreneurship are stifled. Addressing the businessman, the Pope told him: "Since it is your business to represent in the national economy the moving impulse that facilitates and stimulates exchange, you may claim with every right the liberty necessary to fulfill your function genuinely and effectively." But the qualifier follows directly: "It is your intention to make use of this freedom of action not only to serve your own private interests or those of a definite class of society, but to promote the advantage of the whole country." In that the Church's position departs from liberal capitalism where precisely the pursuit of private interests is presumed to lead, as if by magic, to promoting "the advantage of the whole country," but where in fact it simply serves "private interests or those of a definite class of society."

Those words of an outstanding pope at mid-century are remarkably appropriate to what was happening toward at the end of the century where liberal capitalism had been resuscitated. Thus: "Temptations, of course, are not wanting, if we consider the weakness of human nature; temptations to employ procedures that are not quite honest, to realize unlawful profits, to sacrifice moral dignity to the allurements of material goods."

> Every man must be convinced that his destiny is not limited to procuring the most comfortable situation in his temporal life. One who is contented with this idea will be unable to find in himself sufficient energy to resist the ignoble impulses arising from his lower nature, from the example and inducements of those in whose midst he spends his life, and also, unfortunately, from the need of defending himself from similar conduct on the part of others.
>
> Freedom of economic activity cannot be justified and maintained except on condition that it serves a higher freedom, and has the ability when need arises to renounce a part of itself, in order not to fall short of the moral imperative.

Following that indictment of what is precisely the basic flaw in liberal capitalism, Pius XII encouraged the businessman to "take pride in the exercise of his profession, and not merely from the hope of gain, but with a deep consciousness of fulfilling a necessary task, one that is extremely beneficial to the common welfare." That entails not losing sight of the "the really essential point, which is to say, the enduring values of the spiritual order, that are superior to all individualistic aims, and which remain the only means capable of assuring the survival of modern civilization."

The Christian Aspect of Business
Address before the Members of the Italian Waterworks Society
13 April 1956[24]

The translation of the name of the group being addressed here can be misleading. Pius XII is not addressing a government-run or -sponsored public utility, but a private enterprise which operated throughout Italy in the area of drainage, irrigation and canalization, and more recently also in installing waterlines as well as oil and gas lines.

The address by Pius XII therefore turned out to be a defense of private enterprise against unwarranted state intervention. Private initiative, said the Pope, "contributes to the wealth of the community, alleviates, as well, the burden of human toil, raises the efficiency of labor, diminishes the costs of production and develops the habit of saving." A defense of the principle of subsidiarity followed directly: "For this reason the Church has never ceased and will not cease to react unfavorably to the attempts which have been made in certain countries to attribute to the state powers and duties which it does not possess."

Simply inviting the state to intervene in economic life does not resolve the "social question." Indeed, where "this interference is extended to 'total planning' certain aims are realized, but only at the cost of inestimable losses brought about by an insane and destructive urge." In the process:

> The just liberties of the individual are destroyed. The serenity of labor is disturbed. The sacred character of the family is violated. The love of country is corrupted. The precious patrimony of religion is obliterated.

And while the Pope acknowledged once again that "...men who, while they work of course for their own legitimate interests, still are making an essential contribution to the welfare of all their fellow-citizens as well as to the prosperity of their native land," he was not thereby accepting Adam Smith's "invisible hand" economic philosophy. For, after supporting the proper sphere of private enterprise, and warning about the excesses of state intervention, he then hastened once again "with the same pastoral frankness" to the middle ground which the Church has occupied consistently in its social teachings. "One sometimes hears understandable but scarcely justifiable complaints about certain interventions of the state, which are directed, not towards hindering the productive impulse, but rather towards regulating in a more equitable manner distribution of the goods produced by human industry." Therein is a rejection of the individualistic philosophy that permeates liberal capitalism:

> Such interventions cannot be called unlawful without some qualifications. Our rejection of totalitarian planning which destroys all individual enterprise does not imply that a regime of absolute freedom in the economic field is acceptable. This would in fact set a premium on indifference to the welfare of others, and would engender contempt for certain indispensable principles dictated by considerations of human and Christian brotherhood. These principles are more urgent today than ever before. Such indifference and contempt must not be found among you, beloved sons.

Those words are as relevant now, if not more so, than in 1956 when they were delivered. Whereas the penchant for "total planning" is perhaps less rampant now, given the debacle of the planned economies in Communist countries, it is the resurgent economic liberalism which poses a grave threat to the resolution of the "social question." And before he closed his address, Pius XII returned to the Church's own proffered solution to that question which is, basically, treating workers as one would himself want to be treated.

> In this field you stand in need of clear and striking examples if you would cooperate in the building of a world founded on the teachings of Jesus Christ. You must meditate, therefore, on the truths enunciated by Our Predecessors and Ourselves concerning the elevated position of the laboring man, his dignity as a member of the human family, and his mysterious, yet real participation in the life of the Mystical Body of Christ. Think on these things, and, so far as lies in your power, try to make them actualities.

Specifically that would involve living the Gospel, "in relations that arise between those who provide work and those who perform it." For, "all of you are the sons of God and all are equally necessary to the enterprise, although in different degrees according to the different functions you perform." That followed the admonition to "practice Christian principles" not only in private life: but "be Christians in your corporate life as well." And that effort would be made "easier, as is just, by the expectation of a suitable remuneration that will provide a livelihood for you and your children."

In other words, even while the Pope was indeed looking forward to "the building of a new social structure on the ruins of the old edifice," he warned that "one must not look for hastily improvised reforms in the structure of society." That is where he pointed out the aforementioned measures at the microeconomic level in everyday work-place-level relations between workers and employers. Pius XII never left any doubt but that all of this would involve an earnest and widespread injection of Christian principles into the life of society at all levels. At this point, the Pontiff repeated a favorite theme of his about principles and their application: "The principles are well known nowadays; nonetheless it is a rare thing to see them intelligently and courageously applied, even when they are modified by a realistic Christian balancing of opposites."

He ended his message on a very moving, pastoral note:

> My dear children, Jesus desires to return to the world. Mankind 'weary and heavy-laden,' is seeking Him without knowing it. He desires to come back to palace and cottage alike, to the streets of the city and to the mines, to parliaments and to factories. Let Him come and dwell among you. Offer yourselves to Him; welcome Him as the undisputed Master of your hearts and of your families; above all make Him king and Lord of your industrial firm to such a degree that it may be wholly inspired by faith, sustained by hope, and enlivened by love.

Economics and Man
An Address to the First Congress of the International Association of Economists
9 September 1956[25]

This very important address never received the attention it deserved. The message it contains is no less urgent now for economists who are concerned about the shortcomings of the science of economics, especially with regard to methodology. As Pius XII pointed out, the International Association of Economists was founded in Paris in 1949 at the suggestion of UNESCO, and at the time it embraced twenty-four national organizations from four continents. This Rome gathering was its first international congress. No one with a serious interest in economic methodology should overlook what this Pope had to say about the economic science, demonstrating once again his remarkable insight into an astounding variety of specialized fields.

The 1956 Congress of Economists chose as its theme, "Stability and Progress in the World Economy." Using that as his point of departure, Pius XII indicated how in "the vast social organism whose different functions reciprocally influence and condition one another, it is impossible to touch on one without affecting all the others, and so having to take compensatory measures." He established his insight into the intricacies of the economic order by referring to the danger in increasing "industrial production without assuring the sale of the goods produced," and in modifying "the volume of monetary circulation without taking into account the corresponding volume of commercial transactions," and finally, in striving "for full employment while neglecting to prevent the risk of inflation."

Implicitly, that first danger implies papal rejection of the so-called "law of markets" which has resurfaced more recently as "supply-side economics." If supply generates its own demand as J. Baptiste Say proposed in the early nineteenth century, then the danger which the Pope suggested would not be real, or at least long-lasting. It would correct itself! The second suggests variations of what economists call "the equation of exchange," whether the "transactions" type proposed by the American economist Irving Fisher, or the so-called "cash-balance" type preferred by British economists.[26] The third danger alluded to here by the Pontiff echoes the ongoing preoccupation of those managing our Federal Reserve System in the United States, who seek to maintain economic prosperity along with stability in the price level.

The Pope also demonstrated his awareness of the particular weakness that has bedeviled modern economies throughout the capitalist era: "periods of crisis." European economists typically use the term "crises" for what American economists used to designate as "business cycles," when referring to recurring alternations of prosperity and depression.

Moving to the international level, the Pontiff remarked about the then growing sensitivity to the "grave discord between poor countries which are more and more aware of their great needs, and the nations which are generously supplied with necessities and superfluities." That is a problem which certain economists were beginning to point out with regard to its grave implications from a purely economic point of view.[27] At the same time, with Pius XII once again leading the way, the Church would make it a major chapter in its social teachings.[28]

Given all of the momentous problems facing the postwar world, economists scarcely need a reminder that their task "grows more extensive, more arduous and more charged with responsibility than ever before." Nevertheless, the Pope told them that "the decisions of each statesman and every technician who assists him have repercussions in the lives of millions and millions of people and bring about a great many fortunate improvements and a great many dramatic disturbances."

What followed was a frank exposition of what was wrong with economics as it had developed until our time. If Pius XII was a gentle person, schooled and experienced in diplomacy, the message he delivered was scarcely veiled in diplomatic language. "Truly there is no more time for adventurous theories, or for artificial structures which perhaps satisfy the reasoning mind in the abstract but are profoundly out of tune with reality through an error in basic principles."

Most collegiate economics students begin to sense early on, even if vaguely or instinctively, the problem which Pius XII was talking about here. It was nothing less than a devastating indictment of what had happened to this very important science virtually from its beginnings. Its theorists had abstracted from reality to a degree where much labor was lost over the years in chasing shadows down errant paths. How else should one interpret the papal words: "through an error in basic principles?" The Pope called economists to rectify their judgments and conclusions "verifying in them their scientific characteristics, that is, making them conform fully to the laws of thought and human nature and to the objective conditions of economic reality."

At that point, Pius XII lectured the economists about precisely what happened to their science at its outset to divert it from its proper course, even while backing away from what he called "a discussion of technical points."

> The science of economics started to build up, like other sciences in modern times, by observation of facts. But if the physiocrats and the representatives of classic economics believed they had built a solid framework by treating economic facts as if they were physical or chemical phenomena amenable to the determination of natural laws, the falsity of such a conception was revealed in the crying contradiction between the theoretic harmony of their conclusions and the terrible social misery which they allowed to exist in reality.

That terse paragraph speaks volumes about the birth defect which afflicted the economic science and from which it continues to suffer, given its origin in the halcyon days of the Enlightenment with its warped philosophies of man and nature. Pius XII used the word, "rigor," which modern economists often employ pridefully when describing the exalted mathematical terms they employ for describing what they propose to be economic reality. However, he added that this "rigor of their deductions could not remedy the weaknesses in their point of departure; in economic matters they considered only the quantitative, material elements, and they ignored the essential human element, the relations which unite the individual to society and impose upon him not only natural but also moral criteria for using material goods." When such quantitative, material elements are "diverted from their communal purposes, these elements become means of exploitation of the weak by the strong, under the law of sheer merciless competition." That is an astute commentary on the Darwinian direction that modern economics followed inevitably, once it was divorced by unrealistic theory from what is the true nature of man.

History was, of course, not long in providing a reaction, albeit a bad one. As the Pope said: "To remedy that defect, Marxism strives to restore to value the social aspect of economics and to prevent individuals from monopolizing the means of production for their own exclusive profit." What follows directly is highly significant: "But by a no less fatal error, it pretends to see men only as an economic medium, and makes the whole structure of human society depend on production yield." The world knows well how "fatal" that error has been. Now that the curse has been lifted, at least from European lands, if not yet from the most populous nation on earth in Asia, there is still a need to reflect on the exact words "a *no less fatal* error" [emphasis added] used by Pius XII here. It appears that we must conclude about liberal capitalism—the expression in real life of physiocratic and the subsequent classical and neo-classical economics—was also a *fatal* error! Or is that not what the Pope was referring to when he referred in the next paragraph to the hapless man who has been storm-tossed between the Scylla of liberal capitalism and the Charybdis of Marxist socialism?

"Though he is no longer delivered up to the arbitrary play of the power of money, man thus finds himself crushed and overwhelmed within the social framework of a society threatened by the elimination of spiritual values, and as merciless in its reactions and its demands as the caprice of individual whims."

Once again then, the Church emerges here on the high middle ground that typifies its social teachings. What is wrong is that, "Both sides have forgotten to consider economic factors in all their amplitude—human and material, quantitative and moral, individual and social—all at the same time." Instead, Pius XII proposed a balanced view of man: "Beyond the physical needs of man and the interests which they govern, beyond his inclusion in social production reports, it is necessary to envisage the activity—a really free, personal and communal activity—of man, the subject of the economy." The key expression there is: "subject of the economy."

One economist who has placed man definitively at the center of the economic order as its "subject" is the pioneer solidarist economist, Heinrich Pesch (d. 1926). In the very first chapter of his five-volume *Lehrbuch* we find the caption, "Man as Lord of the World According to God's Ordinance."[29] Consequently, his system of economics, solidarism, established itself between the two wrong-headed approaches Pius XII indicted in this important address. The concordance between that Pope's thinking on economic matters and Peschian thought is once again affirmed later in the message. The Pontiff stated:

> It is also one of the happy traits of the present epoch that it accentuates the feeling of interdependence among the members of the social body, and leads them on to recognize that the human person reaches his true dimensions only on condition that he recognizes his social and personal responsibilities and that human problems—or simply economic ones—will find their solution only through the medium of understanding and sincere mutual love.

This is an endorsement precisely of what Pope John Paul II many years later defined as the "virtue of solidarity."[30] That is the "feeling of interdependence among the members of the social body which leads them." And the expression "mutual love," as the same Pope indicated, is an alternate expression of the virtue of *social charity* which was introduced in *Quadragesimo Anno* (*Quadragesimo Anno*, par. 88) by Pius XI in 1931 as a cardinal principle for social order, along with its twin virtue, social justice.

Pesch likewise stepped out of the mainstream of traditional economics when he indicated the implication of ethics and religion in economic life.[31] The connection is there precisely because man, who is the subject of the economic order, also, "when he produces, buys, sells, or consumes goods, is moved by a determined purpose which could be simply to satisfy a natural appetite but also could be the expression of a totally subjective attitude, controlled by feelings or passion." That, as the Pope maintained here, could result in a situation where "motives of self-love, prestige or vindictiveness can completely reverse the direction of an economic decision." Therefore, to build a true science: "You must advance even further and appreciate the importance of the true, free and personal decision, that is, one fully reasoned and well-founded, one capable consequently of entering as a positive element into the building of a science of economics." That refutes definitively the too "abstract" approach to economics which the Pope scored earlier in his address.

The remainder of the papal message is devoted precisely to demolishing certain myths of traditional economics which had gotten out of touch with reality, for example, the always deliberately calculating, cost-conscious "economic man." The Pope alluded, as in his previous message, to the dynamic entrepreneur—whom he refers to here as "the enterprising man and his constructive action in determining economic progress." The corrective interpretation followed:

> One would be wrong to believe that such activities always coincide with their private interests or that they correspond only to selfish motives. One would rather compare such activity to a scientific invention or to an artistic work sprung from a selfless inspiration directed to the whole human community, which it enriches with new knowledge and with more powerful means of action.

Anyone who has been privileged to know a person with the genuine entrepreneurial gift can appreciate what Pius XII was talking about here. Such persons function precisely with the same drive, often forgetful of self, as dedicated scientists or artists engrossed totally in their undertaking. That is the kind of reality which the economic science must work into its understanding of the economic order: "Thus, in order to appreciate economic facts exactly, theory must simultaneously take into consideration aspects which are both material and human, personal and social and free, but which are completely logical and constructive because governed by a true understanding of human existence." Since the real man, unlike the surrealistic, mythical economic man, is indeed also a personal, and social, free being, the economic science operates in an unreal world when it disregards those aspects of human nature.

Again, "many men, without a doubt, are obedient in their daily conduct to the natural tendencies and instincts of their nature; but We would believe that few are actually incapable, at least at critical times, of making altruistic, selfless feelings predominate over preoccupations of a material kind." Indeed, "—even among the humble and lowly—self-sacrifice and fellowship are expressed in acts of moving, heroic generosity." So much for the profit-maximizing, ever-calculating, self-seeking *homo oeconomicus* portrayed or inferred as reality in many of the classical works of economics!

The Pope concluded on a spiritual dimension, indicating that "even as the subject of economy, man can never introduce a complete separation between the temporal ends he pursues and the final purpose of his existence." He referred repeatedly to the latter dimension as "this realistic level," and he concluded with some frank counsel for economists. "If all have the courage to face difficulty with honesty and without concealing or falsifying any aspect of reality, We have no doubt but that you will soon be able to congratulate yourselves on the result of your efforts."

Moral Guidelines for the Economy

A Papal Letter by the Deputy Secretary of State A. dell'Acqua
to the 29th Social Week of Italian Catholics at Bergamo
23 September 1956 [32]

This letter was read by the Substitute Secretary of State, Cardinal A. dell'Acqua on behalf of Pius XII. It may be regarded as a papal message on the economic order, in this case dealing specifically with certain principles which ought to govern that order. The members of the *Italian Catholic Social Week* had chosen "Economic Life and the Moral Order" as their topic.

Speaking for the Pope, and following the line of thought which Pius XII had been developing on this important matter of the economic order, Cardinal dell'Acqua referred again to the attempt to isolate, in the name of science, the moral aspect from any analysis of the economy; and he indicated that this was in line with the de-Christianization of the modern world. The thrust is to divorce social life from its source, i.e., from God, so as to contrive a culture without a soul, and thereby in a sense to make of man a mere extension of the machines he invented. We are told that the economy has its own laws, and man has only to observe those laws in forging economic life. What these laws add up to is a purely utilitarian calculation. What results is that fictitious construct—the "*homo oeconomicus*"—something which can only exist in the abstract since it is out of touch with reality. The painful experiences of recent decades have made it clear what dangers that entails also for the economic order, when moral values are subordinated to utilitarian values. They demonstrate how futile it is to expect that the fulfillment of economic interests is enough to satisfy the far more exalted demands of the human spirit.

Quoting what Pius XI had said in *Quadragesimo Anno,* the Pope's spokesman then reaffirmed the legitimacy of the Church's getting involved in social teachings. It did so recognizing well that man's eternal salvation—its proper mission—must be accomplished on this earth with the material bounty which it affords. Even though it has neither the mission nor the competence to involve itself in the technical aspects of economics, it definitely has a right to address the moral aspects of economic life.

What followed passed judgment on liberal capitalism as had become common in papal pronouncements before and since. Quoting St. Thomas (*De regimine principum* I, 15), the Cardinal pointed to the requirement that "an adequate supply of material goods must be on hand as is necessary for leading a good moral life." Following that mandate, which is an economic as well as a moral requirement, because otherwise there can be no "healthy economy," will enable us to "overcome that capitalistic order which is built on liberalistic principles." In that order, "the goal of economic activity is based almost exclusively on the highest possible entrepreneurial profit." That leads to the denial of spiritual values, along with an inhuman exploitation of labor and man's enslavement to the machine—all of which happens to be a hallmark of our age. That hallmark was expressed in the words which Cardinal dell' Acqua repeated here from *Quadragesimo Anno*: "Material goods leave the workshop ennobled, and man leaves there spoiled and degraded."

The traditional Church teaching about private ownership of the means of production (from St. Thomas) was recalled at this point, namely: that while the ownership of property is to be predominantly private, its use must in all respects be social, i.e., taking into account the needs of our fellow human beings and society in general. "The temporal goods which God grants us are ours as to the ownership, but as to the use of them they belong not to us alone but also to such others as we are able to succor out of what we have over and above our needs" (*Summa,* II-II 32, 5 *ad.* 2). That expresses the "twofold aspect" of private property: its individual and social aspect. And the Church in its social teachings has always insisted on this double aspect, whereas liberal capitalism was based solely on the individual one, with the socialists insisting exclusively on the social aspect. At this point the Cardinal referred back to a statement by Pius XII (*Radio Message* on Pentecost 1941) where the latter declared as poor a nation in which there is a great abundance of economic riches but where that wealth is poorly distributed; whereas a nation with modest wealth, but with a just distribution can be declared economically healthy. Many small European countries, like Ireland and diminutive Luxemburg, serve as examples of the latter.

At this point the principle of subsidiarity came up for review in the Cardinal's discussion of how a fair distribution of national wealth is to be accomplished. It cannot be left exclusively to private initiative, and even less so to "the free play of economic forces." That approach is based on "a false conception of the state and of man, and it leads inevitably to class conflict." At this point it is the state's responsibility, as custodian of the common good, to call the individuals to order reminding them of their social responsibility, and to conduct their economic activities always within the bounds of right and morality.

However, the other extreme, traditionally opposed by the Church in its social teachings, would be to turn all planning of economic life over to the state with a view to establishing some mythical equality among all people. The state is to intervene only by inciting and coordinating economic activity, and to the extent that this is necessary to safeguard the common good. And its citizens and lower social bodies are to do whatever is within their competence. The Cardinal once again quoted what Pius XII had said about this in an address on 7 May 1949: "The economy, like every other area of human activity—is by its nature not an institution of the state, but instead the living outcome of the private activity of the individual person."

The message turned to the microeconomic aspect of economic life. If efforts to direct it to the service of man are to succeed, then an honest and salutary relationship must be cultivated among the various orders of society, and in particular in the world of labor. These orders did not originate in order to combat each other, but to complement and harmonize activity in their undertakings. Worker organizations have been earnestly supported by the Church, not to engender conflict with employers, but to bring about harmony between capital and labor so that together they may accomplish their legitimate goals. Therefore, it would be a great fallacy to view the occupational communities as "a weapon" designed "for offensive or defensive warfare, so as to bring about reactions and repressions "like a river that overflows its banks and separates." Instead, they are to be a "bridge which unites."

Cardinal dell'Acqua turned his attention to certain new initiatives that would assign great responsibility to workers in their enterprises going beyond merely their monetary relationship. That requires of the responsible parties a greater sensitivity for improving the traditional distribution patterns, and a need to bring the workers into closer relationship involving greater responsibility in the everyday life of the enterprise and eventually some sharing in the earnings of the enterprise. It would involve a recognition that employees too share in the risks that their employers must face. Those entrepreneurs who insist on an unrestricted notion of private ownership ought to pay attention to the words of the Holy Father (Address on 7 March 1948). During that address Pius XII warned the employers who clung to the old notion of private ownership that they did a better job than their opponents (the socialists) in destroying this important and legitimate right. At the same time the Pope admonished the workers that they too have an obligation to live up to the legitimate claims which their employers have on their conscientious services.

The message concluded with a reminder that the much-sought healthy renewal of economic life is inextricably tied to a renewal of morals. At this point Cardinal Dell'Acqua presented a fine exposition specifically of the complementary roles that justice and charity play in the reconstruction of economic order. Religion constitutes the basis for economic life precisely in the way justice and charity are brought to bear. Charity incites just conduct in the various areas of economic conduct and policy, as in the production and distribution of goods, in the circulation of money, and in the realm of social services, unemployment, and the insecurity faced by the workers. Charity is to some degree a natural disposition in man's relationship to his neighbor. Christian charity transfigures such natural charity, and it motivates man to even go beyond the bounds that strict justice would require. There was an apt reference to what Leo XIII had said many years previously (*Rerum Novarum*): that the salvation of society in the final analysis will be the fruit of a widespread diffusion of charity.

The address ended with a well-placed quotation from St. Augustine.

> Society is not to be called happy solely because there are numerous heirs, or because of its adorable ladies, its fertile herds and fat oxen.... Some say: "happy such a country.'" But they delude themselves. Happy the nation whose Lord is God. (*Ep.* 45, 7)

Economics, the State, and the Personal Worth of Man
An Address to a National Convention of the Christian Union of Executives and Businessmen
7 March 1957[33]

In this discourse, Pius XII drew the businessmen's attention to difficulties they would be facing despite and, in fact, partly because of "the promise of magnificent developments" that lay ahead. Specifically, the convening group was dealing at the time with "automation and with agricultural units."

The time was 1957, and a new word—"automation"—had entered our vocabulary. Its implications for business, and for Italian business specifically, were worrisome. Among other things would Italy, not one of the world's stronger economies at the time, be able to compete in world markets? That applied with special force to its agricultural sector; and it involved "consolidation of our whole population, from more than a merely economic point of view."

The Pope referred to the emerging computerized era as "this technical transformation." Automation was an early application of computer technology.

His concern, as a spiritual father, in particular of the more vulnerable members of the human race, was directed to the working class. This prompted the Pope to counsel that, "wherever efforts are being made to increase productivity—the primary object of automation—now as always the ultimate determining factor should be the question of the personal value of the worker, whether he is giving orders or carrying them out, whether on higher or intermediate levels." At this early stage of that new "technical transformation" there were already signs that the personal value of the worker "seems to have been particularly neglected."

The Pope saw a "threefold threat" there. The "natural development of automation [would] be slowed," and "the laboring classes can be faced with unexpected unemployment crises, and eventually serious harm can be done to the whole national economy." Avoiding the manifold danger meant that, first of all, "business managers and directors must attend, from this moment on and with much more vigor than in the past, to the technical education of those employed in production."

There followed an astute observation that when the "changeover from a production system that was built around artisans to a mechanical-industrial system took place in the early 18th century, it seemed at first as if it would necessarily reduce the personal contribution of the worker to that of being a mere overseer of machines." Instead, said the Pope, "it resulted in a growing need for technical ability and training." The message by now was clear: "This need will be even greater in the case of automatic processes, not just during the period of transformation, but after as well, if the new machinery is to be maintained and function properly." The implications? "It is also foreseen that the age of automation will constantly reassert the preeminence of intellectual values among the productive class: knowledge, ingenuity, organization, foresight." Perhaps that was foreseen by Pius XII, but it appears as if all of that has still not been fully appreciated even a half century later. Nor is that problem any less relevant now if we consider these words: "There is no doubt that the period of transition may result in an increase of unemployment among older workers, who are less adapted to new training; but younger laborers as well are faced with the same danger whenever a nation is forced to hasten its steps toward automation because of competition with other countries." If one substitutes the more comprehensive, updated expression, computerized technology, for the word "automation," it is clear that the problem discussed by the Pope in 1957 is no less urgent now.

The remedy was suggested then, and it applies equally now. "In every case, producers must accept the principle that technology is at the service of the economy, and not vice versa." In other words, the subject of all of economic activity and the sole, ultimate purpose for it is man and the satisfaction of his economic needs. One could perhaps detect promotion of "demand-side" rather than "supply-side" economics in that statement by Pius XII. "This principle can be safeguarded only by taking into consideration the concrete conditions existing in each individual country, especially the conditions of the workers who constitute also a large part of the consumer sector." Indeed, one might even see there a certain hint of "Keynesianism" with its emphasis on maintaining buying power on the consumption side of the economy. However, what the Pope was saying goes back far beyond Keynes and his effort to revamp economic analysis. It was Leo XIII who promoted the cause of the working poor precisely because they make up the major segment of the modern economy (*Rerum Novarum*, par. 34).

Although this papal address was delivered in 1957, regrettably Pius XII could still say: "Even now, after more than a century, we have still not completely solved the crisis affecting salaried laborers which resulted from the first industrial transformation, when it sacrificed the primacy of the economy, and in particular the primacy of the objective aim of the national economy, the welfare of the people, to the dynamics of technology."

In pointing out the error involved, the Pope demonstrated once again that uncanny acumen which he enjoyed in the widest range of specialized fields—in this case, economics: "The error consisted precisely in trusting completely in mechanization (which was then believed to be the sole determining factor in the market), while neglecting other provisions (sometimes through a gradual process of depreciation) which would have regulated productive forces for the good order and advantage of the whole social body." In other words, the mechanistic approach to resolving economic problems ran roughshod over the humanistic approach, which places man and his needs and problems at the center of the economy. Progress came as a gift of Providence, and it was left to run rampant over the very people for whom God in His providence intended it. That was done in the name of the "market" or simply in the name of progress for its own sake.

Since this address was delivered in the early days of the European economic union, nations lagging somewhat behind in their economic development were threatened by the intended removal of all trade barriers among the members of the Union. Aware of that prospect, the Pope cautioned about the implications for Italy, which was then handicapped inasmuch as others were for the time being better supplied with capital and raw materials. An interesting bit of advice came with this: "At the moment, it seems that the Italian economy in the immediate future must be characterized by a deep interest in the superior quality of its products and in serving the genuine rather than the artificial needs of the people." In retrospect, there is no better example than Japan, a nation also faced with a chronic, endemic lack of raw materials and originally also of capital, which nevertheless struggled until it became a leading actor in world trade. Italy too has since made great strides in overcoming its still serious internal problems, to become a major trading nation.

The remainder of this important message is addressed to the demarcation between what people as individuals and in their various organizations ought to do to resolve their economic problems, and what the state could be required to do. In other words, the Pope concluded with an exposition, once again, of the principle of subsidiarity. Indeed, he warned about "an ever increasing tendency to call for intervention by the State, to such an extent that sometimes you get the impression that this is the only expedient imaginable." While allowing that "the social doctrine of the Church clearly holds that the State has a role of its own in bringing right order into social affairs," the Pontiff cautioned that "those who continually invoke it and who throw all responsibility onto it are leading it in the direction of ruin and serving the cause of powerful groups with interests of their own."

The address concluded with a strong defense of *personalism*, which had become a matter of special interest to this Pope in his economic messages. He told the businessmen and executives why he was confiding in them in this manner. It was because he felt sure, "that your particular position in life brings home to you daily the fact that what is most important is man personally; no factory system, no profession or legislative institutions, no vast organization with officials and meetings can create this personal value of men nor substitute anything for it." This includes "the notion of a State that must do everything and of institutions that take care of everybody," a notion which "has become widespread."

Poverty, the State, and Private Initiative
An Address to the "'Stations de Plein Air' Movement"
3 May 1957[34]

The "*Stations de Plein Air*" movement was the "Open Air Camps" movement founded by a Belgian priest in 1931. Its purpose was to offer recreational facilities and vacation opportunities for poor children. Beneficiaries of the group were brought to Rome and presented before Pius XII, where he delivered this address on the occasion. The Pope used the opportunity to express his disappointment that even in "the most developed countries of this continent, the income of a sizeable part of the population remains below the living minimum." That, despite what the Pontiff called the remarkable "progress made in recent times in family allotments, pensions, social security, housing policies." Indeed "some hundreds of thousands of people live constantly as prey to the direst necessities, deprived of decent shelter, tortured by hunger, struggling desperately to keep a little dignity and not to fall ultimately into black misery and despair." He was referring to the very large number of people who, according to the current figure of speech, "have fallen through the cracks" in modern society.

> Is it necessary to bring up the sad example of the exploitation of slum areas? Dilapidated, ramshackle houses without the most necessary hygienic installations sometimes yield a sizable income to their owners without costing them a penny. Inevitably, they neglect to make necessary repairs in them for years on end.

Although this message was delivered in 1957, it still has poignant relevance, as does the following. After mentioning the obvious dangers to the physical health of people reduced to such circumstances, the Pope turned to the moral damage. "But the moral injuries are still more serious: immorality, juvenile delinquency, the loss of taste for living and for working, interior rebellion against a society that tolerates such abuses, ignores human beings, and allows them to stagnate in this way, transformed gradually into wrecks."

The cost to society is obvious. "Because it did not wish to prevent the evil and to provide a remedy in time, it will spend enormous sums to keep up an appearance of curbing delinquency and to pay expenses for prolonged confinement in sanatoriums and clinics."

What follows appears especially, if not exclusively, relevant to those who today, because of the persisting racial and ethnic prejudice in American society, are excluded from full participation in the economic promise which our country purports to offer to all.

> One of the most disastrous results of unhealthy and inadequate housing is serious deficiency in the education of children. How many among them are morally abandoned by their parents, deprived of care and affection, forced to live on the street or in an environment stamped with vice! Inevitably, psychological and emotional instability is added to physical damage. Once disorder takes hold, evil tendencies lose no time in stifling the good and in making the person unfit for all normal social life. Thus, the evil, perhaps accidental at first, quickly takes root and grossly aggravates the task of re-education.

The insight of Pius XII was remarkably prophetic, in particular when he addressed the attitude of so many "persons of good faith who have only an inadequate knowledge of the matter." As he indicated, they "readily believe that the majority of those who live in the slums or who must be satisfied with an income below the essential minimum are there through their own fault or negligence, and that welfare organizations are capable of helping anyone in need of it."

While allowing an "important role" for "private initiative" in alleviating this massive social injustice, like the movement whose representatives he was addressing, the Pope summoned the help also of "public authorities."

> We should like, then, to draw the attention of public authorities to this persistent wound in modern society: there still remains a whole section of society—reaching from 10 to even 20 percent of the total population of the best provided countries of Europe—who cannot live a decent and really human life, who remain without protection against disease and moral corruption, and often become the victims of the unscrupulous. There follows for the states considerable financial outlay in order to stay the evils caused by the persistence of the slums.

It is worth noting that when the address was delivered in 1957, the drug traffic had not yet reached its present dimensions. The "victims of the unscrupulous" mentioned here by the Pope now include, specifically also in the United States, those who are lured into various aspects of the drug traffic because they have lost all hope of trying to gain acceptance in normal economic pursuits. A papal message, delivered in 1957, is still relevant in our time, if not more so at present in the affluent United States.

Christian Solidarity
Address to Members of the Catholic Union of French Railwaymen
17 September 1957[35]

This is the first of two messages late in the pontificate of Pius XII that address the virtue of solidarity. It was brief, and it is included here mainly because of the theme: *Christian solidarity*, one that has been emphasized with increasing frequency by Roman Catholic pontiffs beginning with Pius XII. Here he laid the foundation for what Pope John Paul II would designate many years later as the "Christian virtue of solidarity" (*Sollicitudo Rei Socialis*, par. 40). That virtue is in fact identical with *social charity* presented by Pius XI along with *social justice,* as ultimate regulating principles for economic life in a reconstructed social order. (*Quadragesimo Anno*, par. 88).

The Jesuit economist, Heinrich Pesch, whose thinking was of major influence in the modern social teachings of the Catholic Church, indicated that the doctrine of the Mystical Body of Christ underlies the solidarity which he placed at the heart of his outline for an economic system.[36] Pius XII here provides a singularly excellent and eloquent expression of this same underlying basis for Christian solidarity, and of its ramifications into everyday life—in the economic order and in society generally.

> There exists among Christians of the whole world a solidarity superior to all earthly bonds, for it is built upon the community of the supernatural life. Each

Christian supports and nourishes the others as members of the same body. He carries his share of the burdens; he has solicitude for the common good; he sacrifices himself for the needs of others. His faith never remains idle, but constantly diffuses itself in charity. Act thus in the exercise of your professional life.

There is not, in fact, any division among the activities of the Christian: it is the same faith and the same love of God that make him fulfill his social duties as a worker and his religious duties as a believer.

The Spirit of Christian Solidarity in the World of Work
Address to Italian Railroad Workers
22 February 1958[37]

It is noteworthy that this message on the theme of Christian solidarity is likewise addressed to a gathering of railroad workers. Perhaps the appreciation of the intensive cooperation among the great number of persons with various skills and responsibilities that is called for to operate a nationwide rail network was the reason why Pius XII chose that industry to illustrate the tremendous force of solidarity in economic life. Indeed, he characterized the railroad as "an enormous and multifaceted organism in which the wonderful harmony of the most modern accomplishments of science, the wise and determined application, and the effective cooperation of an enormous number of persons...are all combined." He indicated too that all of this vast network was put together in less than one century.

In fact, the Pope pointed out that the rise of the railroads was one of the hallmarks of the new era for humanity, being the first means on earth to convey large numbers of travelers to destinations at speeds until then undreamt of. He expressed his fascination with the great network of stations and control towers, along with communications required to make the system operate without delay and danger for the thousands of travelers involved. Clearly there is not much room for free-wheeling individualism there. The railroad is a practical exercise in solidarity among all of its personnel.

The Pontiff went on to use the railroad industry as a model also for the spiritual life, pointing out that anyone who embarks on a rail journey must first of all know precisely where he wishes to go. All other objectives involved must be subordinated to arrival at that destination. These include the speed, the comfort, the attractiveness of the countryside that is traversed, all of which become secondary to arrival at the chosen destination. "What would you think of a person who, because he cannot find comfortable seating decides to take another train which is headed in the opposite direction?" The analogy is clear. We all have a definite destiny: "to attain the beatific vision, the love and the possession of God!" To achieve that goal we have to sacrifice all else, no matter what the cost. This involves rejecting all other diversions no matter how attractive, because giving in to them could divert us irretrievably from our Destiny.

Once we understand where we are headed, we are obliged to demonstrate our concern also for all others who are seeking the same goal. Some of our fellow travelers may have lost sight of that goal, and it is our obligation to clarify it for them. Others spend too much time at wayside stations, and we have to urge them to come back on board. Still others are in a great hurry, but they are heading in the wrong direction. We ought to try to bring them back on course. This means enlightening those who are stumbling around in the darkness of error, and providing guidance for the ones who wander about in the fog of doubt and uncertainty. It also involves helping to their feet those who have been run down and have fallen by the wayside.

That brought the Pope to a rejection of individualism which had become standard in papal social teachings.

> Dear sons, do not say, what others do is none of my business. Are we not talking about friends? Do not say, like Cain, that you are not your brother's keeper. Do not pass by when you see your brother in need. That would not be human conduct, let alone Christian behavior.

The introduction of the concept, "solidarity," followed directly. Pius XII admonished his audience that they should not regard people as of no importance to them, but as members of a single great family; in fact, even as members of the one Mystical Body of Christ. Thus, "the members do indeed enjoy conscious, free, responsible individuality; but to achieve their destinies they live in common with others in such a way that they share in the joys, sorrows, and cares of each individual."

A striking definition of what it means to be a Christian follows:

> A Christian is one who regards no one in the whole world as a stranger. A Christian is one who is prepared to help all, as a member of the body comes to the assistance of every other member of the body. A Christian is one who patterns himself after the powerful expression of the Apostle Paul, to become all things for all people.

The expression, "solidarity," appears now for the first time in this message: "This solidarity which already finds expression when we are dealing with cares and concerns of our temporal life, is required even more when the interests and the destiny of souls are involved."

Having delivered that powerful endorsement of the virtue of solidarity, the Pope returned to the railroad analogy. He rejected the often-heard retort that whether or not a person is saved or damned depends on how he himself conducts himself in this life. We know better. Many a person has been rescued from disaster by the timely intervention and assistance of some "apostle." Conversely, how many suffer everlasting torments because they never had that opportunity? That is not unlike our journey here on earth which depends on a good conductor, an alert telegraph clerk, a conscientious section inspector who detects defects in rails in time to avert disaster.

Toward the end of this address there is this preview of a very remarkable prediction by Pius XII of a new "springtime in world history," which he presented before 100,000 young people of Italian Catholic Action in St. Peter's Square less than a month later, a few months before his death.[38] He anticipated that message here in concluding this address to Italian railroad workers. Encouraging them to work not only to save themselves, but also the countless numbers of their brothers, the Pope told them:

> In this way you will cooperate in bolstering the hope of a possibility that in the world of labor winter will end, and a new spring will begin.... Then those times will slip into the distant past, when a hopeless and depressing drama unfolded. For, that was a flight from Jesus, a distancing oneself from Him, a fear of approaching Him, as if drawing close to Him marked a kind of betrayal of one's own interests.

The Pope, nearing the end of his life, promised that a new age was coming when even "the slightest conflict between the world of labor and the redeeming teaching of Christ must end. "

Christianity and Social Progress
An Address before a Rally of Catholic Workers on the Feast of St. Joseph
1 May 1958[39]

In this message presented on the occasion of his last May Day address, Pius XII was largely laudatory and exhortatory. He praised the *Association of Christian Workers* for their cooperation with the Church and its social teachings. The Pope recalled the progress that had been made in many nations since Leo XIII addressed the "social question" in modern industrial society. And he noted how the First of May had been purloined early on by forces hostile to the Church, which would have made that day one of bitterness and conflict between workers and their employers. In the meantime, social peace "has been achieved without the shedding of your brothers' blood (as has unfortunately happened elsewhere—and without attaining this objective)...." One tends to think of the turmoil in relations between workers and capital where Marxian principles triggered violence between them. It is worth recalling, however, that there were many instances of violence and bloodshed in the early history of American labor relations, usually in the form of picket-line clashes during the course of bitter, prolonged strikes.

The Pontiff did get into a significant doctrinal issue while discussing the role of charity as "the most beautiful and characteristic flower of Christianity." In reference to workers' associations who felt that "Justice is enough for us," the Pontiff made an important theological point:

> Precisely the contrary is true. There is, in fact, no genuine justice which is not preceded and prepared for by the warmth of charity.

> Have you ever seen hard-hearted men do justice willingly, sincerely and completely? Certainly not, for selfishness is like ice which prevents any good seed from germinating and flowering.

That important lesson speaks directly to the question, why justice is no substitute for charity, any more than charity can substitute for justice. In its social teachings, the Church has always presented the two virtues of justice and charity, specifically social justice and social charity, as twin social virtues. That was especially clear since the immediate predecessor of Pius XII had introduced these virtues in *Quadragesimo Anno* as the ultimate regulating principles of the economic order.

The organization being addressed here is precisely the kind which Leo XIII and Pius XI have urged the workers to form in order to infuse the Christian spirit and principles into the discussion between workers and employers. The alternative is a situation "where places of work are subject to prejudices which regard religion and progress as incompatible, and Christianity as an 'ideology' replaced by Marxism, or to an even worse prejudice which would see in the Church an adversary of the workingman."

Notes

1. The complete text of this address may be found in Volume I of Vincent Yzermans, *The Major Addresses of Pius XII* (St. Paul: North Central Publishing Co., 1961), 30-36. Numerical references following statements are to page numbers of this address in that book. The text is also to be found in the periodical, *The Catholic Mind,* June 8, 1941.

2. Michael Chinigo, ed., *The Pope Speaks* (New York: Pantheon Books, 1957), 287-292. See also: A. F. Utz and J. F. Groner, O.P., *Soziale Summe Pius XII* (Freiburg, Switzerland: Paulusverlag, 1954-1961), 1: 341-355. (Translation from the German for all Utz & Groner quotations is by Rupert J. Ederer).

3. The renowned Austrian-born Harvard economist Joseph A. Schumpeter offered an early indication in 1949 when he remarked, not without sarcasm: "I believe that there is a mountain in Switzerland on which congresses of economists have been held which express disapproval of all or most of these things." [Cf. *Capitalism, Socialism & Democracy* (New York: Harper & Row Publishers, 1950) , 418.] He was referring to Mt. Pelerin where a society of free market-oriented economists, launched in 1947 by Friedrich Hayek, met at regular intervals. It included notable persons like Ludwig von Mises and Milton Friedman (d. 2006) of the University of Chicago. It was a reaction against Keynesianism and centrally planned socialist economies. The so-called Austrian School spun off from that under the guidance of von Mises and Hayek. Milton Friedman became a leading free-market economist who influenced both Ronald Reagan and Margaret Thatcher.

4. Utz and Groner, 1: 158-162.

5. Utz and Groner, 2: 1662-1666.

6. Utz and Groner, 1: 1251-1253.

7. *The Catholic Mind,* November 1949, 701-704.

8. Heinrich Pesch. S. J., *Lehrbuch der Nationalökonomie/ Teaching Guide to Economics,* trans. Rupert J. Ederer, vol. I, bk. 2 (Lewiston-Queenston-Lampeter: The Edwin Mellen Press, 2002), 305.

9. Utz and Groner, 2: 1760-1761.

10. *The Catholic Mind* 68 (August 1950): 506-510.

11. The macroeconomic approach focuses attention on such so-called aggregates as national income, fiscal policy, money supply, price levels, interest rates, and their management where necessary. Microeconomics deals with individual buyers, sellers, workers and entrepreneurs in business firms, and how particular prices and wages and profits are arrived at among them. The former lends itself more to management from the top, while the latter would involve action between individuals or smaller groups at the firm or enterprise level without significant intervention by government.

12. Utz and Groner, 2: 1762-1765.

13. Ibid., 1: 331-335.

14. *The Catholic Mind,* January 1953: 44-48.

15. That kind of papal statement, along with earlier statements by Pius XI about workers sharing in profits, management and ownership apparently led certain devotees of the Church's social teachings to arrive at unwarranted conclusions. They jumped from what were suggestions, to the claim that, e.g., co-ownership, was the workers' right. Pius XII was forced to deal with that gratuitous assumption. In an address to the Austrian *Katholikentag* in Vienna, on September 14, 1952, he stated: "We Ourselves have declined to deduce directly or indirectly, from the labor contract the right of the employee to participate in the ownership of the operating capital, and its corollary, the right of the worker to participate in decisions concerning operations of the plant (*Mitbestimmung*). In other words, while employers and workers may freely enter into such arrangements, there is no strict right to them arising from the labor contract. (Cf. *The Catholic Mind,* January 1953, 51).

16. In addressing the wage problem, Pesch stated that "an unbiased approach to this problem will show that what ethics determines to be the just wage is, at the same time, the economically correct wage." Pesch/ Ederer, *Lehrbuch/Textbook*, vol. V, bk. 2, 78).

17. *The Catholic Mind,* January 1953: 48-51.

18. *The Catholic Mind,* June 1954: 369-374.

19. Utz and Groner, 1: 1240-1247.

20. *The Catholic Mind,* September 1955, 564-568.

21. *The Pope Speaks,* Spring-Summer 1956, 45-49.

22. Cf. Alfred Marshall, *Principles of Economics* (New York: Macmillan, 1920), Ch. 12.

23. See Joseph Schumpeter, *The Theory of Economic Development* (Cambridge, Mass.: Harvard University Press, 1934).

24. Full text in Utz and Groner, 3: 3673-3677; excerpts in *The Pope Speaks,* Autumn 1956, 180-183.

25. *The Pope Speaks,* 3, 3 (Winter 1956-1957), 241-245.

26. These equations indicate what happens to the value of money as reflected in prices (P) based on changes in the various determinants of that value, its quantity (M), the velocity at which it circulates (V), or the cash balances which people choose to hold (K), for the transactions (T) which are to be made with money.

27. Barbara Ward, *The Rich Nations and The Poor Nations* (New York: W. W. Norton Co., 1962), passim.

28. Cf. especially John XXIII, *Mater et Magistra* (1961), and Paul VI, *Populorum Progressio* (1967).

29. Pesch/Ederer, *Lehrbuch der Nationalökonomie/Teaching Guide*, vol. I, bk.1, 1.

30. *Sollicitudo Rei Socialis* (1987), see ch. 5.

31. Cf. Heinrich Pesch, *Ethics and the National Economy* , transl. Rupert J. Ederer (Norfolk, Va.: IHS Press, 2004). See also: Pesch/Ederer, *Lehrbuch /Teaching Guide,* vol. II, bk. 2, 266-278.

32. Utz and Groner, 3: 3651-3659.

33. *The Pope Speaks,* 4, 1 (Summer 1957), 85-89.

34. *The Pope Speaks,* 4, 2 (Autumn 1957), 205-209.

35. *The Pope Speaks,* 4, 4 (Spring 1958), 431- 433.

36. Pesch/Ederer, *Lehrbuch der Nationalökonomie/Teaching Guide*, vol. I, bk. 2, 197.

37. Utz and Groner, 3: 2609-2614.

38. *The Pope Speaks,* 4, 4 (Spring 1958), 427-430.

39. *The Pope Speaks,* 5, 2 (Spring 1959), 209-213.

Chapter 5
Pius XII on the World of Work

One of the most frequently addressed topics among the discourses by Pius XII on the economic order were those dealing with relations between workers and their employers. This was a topic of great concern for the Pope, inasmuch as it deals directly with the Church's social teachings. Four years into his pontificate he delivered a message in Italian to a large group of workers from throughout Italy who came to honor the Pope on the occasion of his 25th episcopal jubilee.

The Church and Labor
Address to Workers in Rome
13 June 1943[1]

Even while World War II was still raging throughout the world and also in Italy, Pius XII drew attention to the need for "adjustment and improvement" throughout the "whole complex structure of society...thoroughly shaken as it is in its foundations." And the "labor question" he saw as being at "the nerve center" of the social body because "of the complexity and variety of the problems which it entails and the vast number of people it involves." That put the matter in proper focus, and along with the Pope's reference to "the doctrine of justice, equity, charity, mutual understanding and adjustment" it provided a proper keynote for the many occasions when he would address this important topic.

From that general introduction, it did not take long for Pius XII to get involved in what has since Leo XIII been a central issue in the Church's social teachings—the just wage doctrine:

> Our predecessors and We Ourselves have not lost any opportunity of making all men understand by Our repeated instructions your personal and family needs, proclaiming as fundamental prerequisites of social concord those claims which you have so much at heart: a salary which will cover the living expense of a family and such as to make it possible for the parents to fulfill their natural duty to rear healthily nourished and clothed children; a dwelling worthy of hu-

man persons; the possibility of securing for the children sufficient instruction and a becoming education; of foreseeing and forestalling times of stress, sickness and old age.

That is, if anything, an even more detailed presentation of what the just wage involves than the one provided by his predecessor, Pius XI in *Quadragesimo Anno*! It is followed by a forthright announcement that what Pius XI and Leo XIII before him had made a matter of the highest urgency over a century ago is still far from accomplished: "Now, however laudable may be various provisions and concessions made by public authorities and the humane and generous sense that inspires employers, who could affirm and maintain with truth that such ideals have been everywhere realized?" Indeed even now, another half century later, many nations of the world are still far from the goal, and even an allegedly wealthy nation like the United States finds itself receding toward a paltry wage level which forces both spouses to work outside the home with consequent devastating effects on child-raising. Thus, what the Pope pointed out then is as applicable now: no one should be led to believe "that all these questions are to be considered solved."

What follows is a veiled warning about the "false prophets of social prosperity who call evil good and good evil, and who, boasting that they are friends of the people, do not agree with those mutual agreements between capital and labor, employers and employed, which maintain and promote social concord for their common progress and advantage." At the time, Italy was governed by the formerly socialist Benito Mussolini. And it was involved in a wartime alliance with Germany which was ruled by what was officially known as—and many tend to forget this—the National *Socialist* German Worker Party (NSDAP)! Mentioning these by name would have been virtually suicidal for the Pope under the circumstances, since the Vatican City was at the time a tiny island on the vast Fascist sea. But the inferences are clear enough. "Such false prophets would have us believe that salvation must come from a revolution which shall overturn social order and assume a national character." At the time, communism was still masquerading as an international program for the working class, while Fascism and Nazism were explicitly *national* in their character and pretensions.

Lest there could still be some doubt as to whether Pius XII was directing his words only against Marxian socialism, he went on to say: "You see that the working class remains bound, yoked and tied to the force of State capitalism, which restrains and subjects all, not only the family, but even the conscience, and transforms the workers into a gigantic labor machine." Furthermore, "Like the other social systems and orders which it claims to fight, it classifies, regulates and presses all into a fearful war instrument which demands not only blood and health but also the goods and prosperity of the people." That appears to be a clear indictment of the totalitarian state, of whatever stripe, Nazi, Fascist, or Communist.

A warning follows: "No, your salvation, beloved sons and daughters, does not lie in revolution." Again:

Salvation and justice are not to be found in revolution but in an evolution

> through concord. Violence has ever achieved only destruction, not construction; the kindling of passions, not their pacification; the accumulation of hate and destruction, not the reconciliation of the contending parties. And it has reduced men and parties to the difficult task of building slowly after such experience on the ruins of discord.

Finally, the Pope felt the need to address one other unjust charge against the Church and himself personally: "Hence it is that propaganda of antireligious inspiration is circulating among the working classes that the Pope wished the war, that the Pope does nothing for peace." This, he termed "calumny" both "monstrous" and "absurd":

> Who does not know, who does not see, who is there that cannot ascertain for himself that no one consistently opposed the outbreak, the advance and the spread of the war more insistently than We have in every manner allowed Us; that no one has pleaded and exhorted more continuously than We have: peace, peace, peace; that none has sought to lessen its horror more than We have?

Now, many years later, it is, or should be, well known that the "sums of money which the charity of the faithful puts at our disposal are not set apart for, nor do they go to sustain the war, but to dry the tears of the widows and orphans, to console families anxious and sorrowing for their dear ones far away or missing, to succor the suffering, the poor and the needy." The Pope alluded to "the publication of documents," in the future when "circumstances of the times and human passions will permit," "concerning the constant activity pursued during this terrible war in favor of peace by the Holy See, which feared neither rebuffs nor opposition…."

Meanwhile, Pius XII called on

> …every Christian worker to renew his resolution to labor in obedience to the Divine command of work, whatsoever it may be, intellectual or manual, to gain by his toil and sacrifices the bread for his dear ones, to keep in mind the moral purpose of life here below and the happiness of eternal life, conforming his intentions to those of the Savior and making his work a hymn of praise to God.

The Future of Trade Unions
Address to Delegates to the Convention of the Italian Catholic Workers' Association
11 March 1945[2]

It was in the last weeks of World War II in Europe that Pius XII addressed this message to workers indicating why worker organizations with the prefix "Catholic" had a definite purpose. The reason he gave was because "Christ's enemies strive to make use of the difficulties and problems of the life of the worker in modern times, so as to confuse the Catholic worker's soul and conscience and to deprive him in the end of his Savior." From that point, such an association, if it fulfills its mission, "will produce true apostles, workers who will become apostles among their comrades, and will animate and impregnate with the Christian spirit all that surrounds the worker—his work, his home, even his leisure."

The Pope then addressed the question of what Catholic Worker Associations have to do in relationship to other worker associations. Indeed, a single, comprehensive Trade Union had just been established in Italy. He expressed the hope that it and all labor unions "shall confine themselves to the limits of their essential mission, which is that of representing the workers and defending their interests in labor disputes."

Experience in the United States had shown that when labor unions ventured into the political arena—at times even forming political parties—they succeeded mainly in dividing their members from the rest of society, oftentimes failing in their partisan ventures, and eventually discrediting their activities as labor unions. It is worth noting here that the patriarch of American organized labor, Samuel Gompers, steadfastly insisted on what came to be termed, "business unionism," meaning that the purpose of labor unions was to see to the bread and butter needs of their members, while leaving party politics to politicians. In Europe, of course, labor unions had the tendency to become even more ideologically charged than the various ventures into political unionism in the United States. As a rule they veered toward socialism, whether of the radical Marxian type, or the more moderate Fabian kind, such as in Great Britain.

Pius XII saw fit to warn labor organizations, therefore, that if they went beyond an inevitable measure of "influence on politics and on public opinion they would cause "great injury to themselves." Indeed, if "the Trade Unions, as such, and as a result of political and economic developments, take over the right to control workers entirely, as happens elsewhere, the very conception of the Trade Union, which is an association aimed at mutual assistance, would be altered and destroyed." Meanwhile, Catholic worker groups should concentrate on inspiring "that sense of responsibility and solidarity without which no organization of mutual assistance...can flourish." (The term "solidarity" was to come up again later in this address).

The central mission of unions and of this particular Association was certainly "to improve the living conditions of the workers." However, it has also, through its members made a "high spiritual contribution" and provided "Christian inspiration and spiritual activity...within the Confederation, to the good of all." The Pope suggested that this is entirely proper since the "spirit of the Gospel" represents "a fight that the principles of justice shall prevail in accordance with the order established in the world by God over the purely material force of circumstances; and that love and charity shall prevail over class hatred."

That brought the Pontiff to a specifically contextual portion of his address. The volatile conditions of the time, the closing months of World War II in Europe, brought to the surface again some old ideological "chestnuts" which the Church had dealt with previously under various aspects in its social teachings. Pius XII proposed now that "a mere agreement or compromise between the two parties, employers and workers," could not be made into "an inflexible principle of social order," no matter how just it was at the outset. In a shifting context it could become "an instrument for the oppression and exploitation of the workers," or be turned toward "what is today called 'the socialization of enterprise' or 'the democratization of the economy.'" Thus it would become "a weapon for the struggle against the private employer as such."

Socialization of the entire economy, widely proposed in some circles at the time, was not an acceptable option for an organization which used the identifying adjective, "Catholic." Thus, said the Pope, "The Catholic Associations support socialization only in cases where it appears really necessary for the common welfare; in other words, when it is the only means to remedy an injustice and to ensure the coordinated use of the same forces to the benefit of the economic life of the nation, so that the normal and peaceful development of that economic life may open the gates to material prosperity for all, a prosperity which may become a sound foundation for the development of cultural and religious life."

As for the "democratization of the economy," that is endangered on two fronts. One is represented by "monopolies—that is, by the economic tyranny of an anonymous conglomeration of private capital." The other involves "the preponderant power of organized masses, ready to use their power to the detriment of justice and the rights of others."

The remainder of this significant message comes close to proposing at least the broad outlines and principles for an economic system—even while his successor, Pope John Paul II, would later state that "the Church does not propose economic and political systems or programs, nor show preference for one or the other (*Sollicitudo Rei Socialis*, par. 41). How then are we to interpret the following?:

> The time has come to repudiate empty phrases, and to attempt to organize the forces of the people on a new basis; to raise them above the distinction between employers and would-be-workers, and to realize that higher unity which is a bond between all those who cooperate in production, formed by their *solidarity* in the duty of working together for the common good and filling together the needs of the community. If this *solidarity* is extended to all branches of production, if it becomes the foundation for *a better economic system*, it will lead the working classes to obtain honestly their share of responsibility in the direction of the national economy [italics added].

The term "solidarity" occurs twice in that paragraph, and it was used by Pius XII twice more in the brief remaining portion of this message to Catholic workers. As indicated previously, the Pope's leading advisor in matters dealing with the economic order was Gustav Gundlach, S.J.—a colleague and understudy of Heinrich Pesch, S.J. Pesch, who devised an economic system, was within his competence to do so, being a trained economist and mature scholar. In that task he functioned as an economist, not as a spokesman for the Catholic Church. Nevertheless, having been trained previously as a philosopher and theologian, he knew how, and made it a point, to develop his economic thought in keeping with that philosophy and theology which happened to be in complete harmony with what the Catholic Church teaches about man and society, and their relationship to God.

In the important paragraph presented above, and in the sentences remaining in this address to the Catholic workers of Italy, other notions that are central to Pesch's solidaristic economic system occur: the solidarity between the workers and their employers in the same enterprise; and that same "solidarity...extended to all branches of production," in fact as "the foundation for a better economic system."

Then the notion that is critical to Catholic social teachings dating back to Leo XIII recurs. "Thus, thanks to such harmonious coordination and cooperation, thanks to this closer unity of labor with the other elements of economic life, the worker will receive, as a result of his activity, a secure remuneration, sufficient to meet his needs and those of his family...." That is the same just wage doctrine which is central also to the Peschian system,[3] and which Pope John Paul II established as "the concrete means of verifying the justice of the whole socioeconomic system" (*Laborem Exercens*, par. 89).

Finally, in the concluding paragraph of this important address, there is yet another appeal to solidarity. "May the Italian Catholic Workers' Associations, in these times of misery, promote unity and solidarity among men in economic life." Finally, there is a significant reference to "building this temple of solidarity," which is to be "a sure guarantee of social justice and peace." The "best material for building this temple" is "the spirit of the Gospel, which flows towards you from the Heart of the Savior of the world."

The Church's Social Teachings and the Working Class
An Address to Catholic Action Delegates of Central and Southern Italy
29 April 1945[4]

In this brief message delivered a few days before Germany surrendered, thus ending World War II in Europe, Pius XII indicated that there are many ways in which religious and moral issues are germane to the social order. Therefore the Church has the right and the obligation to present its own teachings on that order. And although they are couched in general terms that are applicable to all times and places, they are nevertheless to be applied precisely in concrete historical circumstances wherever they are relevant. Thus, no Catholic may follow social theories and systems that the Church, in its teachings, has warned against. The Pope challenged the group's members to be vigilant and courageous, especially in the present hour, in defending and bringing to bear their own convictions.

He issued a second warning: Catholics should never tire of making it known everywhere that the Church has always spoken in defense of the working class and its interests. Pius XII expressed his awareness that the Church is accused, even among Catholics, of having triggered by its social teachings revolutionary systems, or of at least clearing the way for them. If such persons are unwilling to submit their thinking to the Church's authority, they have only to look honestly at what the Church has said about the worker problem. They will see that she has always rejected impractical socially and morally unacceptable programs which, while they make good propaganda, have little to do with the true and lasting interests of the workers.

Unity Between Employers and Employees as the Basis for Social Order
Discourse before Workers and Employers of the Italian Electrical Industry
24 January 1946[5]

Significantly, Pius XII addressed this gathering as a "useful meeting between two productive forces, the employers and the workers." He indicated that a flawed doctrine proposes that the workers and the owners of capital are by some natural law destined for an inevitable and bitter struggle against one another, and that in this way industrial "liberation" is to be eventually achieved. The Pope commented: "It takes only a moment of sober reflection to realize that any kind of sensible and human social harmony is not to be expected from a simplistic effort to eliminate one of the contenders by such combat: "That would be destructive of the kind of harmonious work which invigorates public and private economic endeavor."

He indicated that the proposed collective organization of society would by no means abolish strife among parties. Rather, there would then exist a different set of contenders. Although the conflict between workers and the private owners of capital is eliminated, it is replaced by a conflict between "labor and state capitalism." What takes the place of the previous conflicts are contentions over how profit is distributed, whether that is equal or on the basis of hours worked, or according to the needs of the individuals. What is more, working conditions remain a bone of contention also, because managers are never perfect. Then the working class is in mortal danger of becoming enslaved by the public authorities who control the system.

To bring about harmony between labor and capital, there should be a resort instead to the occupational organization and the labor union. However, these are not to be seen as "weapons for defensive or offensive combat, or as a kind of river that overflows its banks and separates people, but as a bridge which unites." The Pope recalled how he had on other occasions pointed out that, beyond the distinction between employers and workers, there is a higher unity which unites both groups in the productive process.

At this point he came back to a favorite element of papal social teachings, especially since Pius XI in 1931 included it in his program for reconstructing the social order. The labor union and the professional organizations of employers are "preliminary, auxiliary, transitional forms" for organizations which give expression to "that higher unity which binds together all who are involved in the productive process." The goal of such organizations is "the unification and solidarity of employers and workers for the common advancement of the general welfare and for satisfying the wants of the community as a whole."

What Pius XII was referring to here were the corporate bodies of persons working in the same industry that were identified explicitly by Pius XI in 1931. Indeed, the words used by the latter in *Quadragesimo Anno* are remarkably similar: "Such a bond of union is provided, on the one hand, by the common effort of employers and employees of one and the same group joining forces to produce goods or give service" (*Quadragesimo Anno*, par. 84). The important concept has been translated variously from the original Latin "*ordines*" as "vocational groups," "functional groups," "vocational orders," "corporate bodies" or "industry councils." What they are called is not so important as the essence of what Pius XI had in mind when he urged that "social policy" therefore must aim for their "reestablishment" (*Quadragesimo Anno*, par. 82).

The immediate successor of Pius XI was now telling the workers and employers at this gathering, in effect, that even the restoration of certain structures would not accomplish the immense task of social reconstruction unless there is a revival of spiritual and moral life in postwar society. He expressed the hope that the misery and destruction of World War II would instill in the loyal sons of Italy the dedicated urge to create peaceful relations among the various "groups and classes that make up the nation." He expected that the kinds of persons—workers and their employers—who appeared before him could certainly act as the "leaven" for establishing harmony in the work place.

The Socio-Religious Task of the "Christian Worker Youth (JOC)
Letter Addressed to the International Meeting of JOC
(Jeunesse Ouvrière Chrétienne) in Montreal, Canada
24 May 1947[6]

In this letter Pius XII acknowledged the importance of youth and the role this organization of Christian Youth would play in their apostolate among workers. He recounted how even before the recent "most destructive of all wars," large groups of young Christian workers had come to the Eternal City "for a paternal reception" by the Pope.

Now he urged these zealous young workers to begin their apostolate anew by their studies and "by frequent reception of the Holy Sacraments," along with "a firm bonding with the Church—this '*columna veritatis*'—'*pillar of truth.*'" That led to what was the crux of this message: "Did not Our Predecessor Pius XI, of blessed memory say in his famed Encyclical *Quadragesimo Anno* that "the workers will be the apostles to the workers"?

The message concluded with reference again to the notion of solidarity which was to become ever more prominent in this Pope's teachings: "We know that the problems in the future will no longer be tied to localities, but, as we suggested, are now a part of the world order" He continued: "The boundaries between the countries and even between the various portions of the earth are falling ever more, thanks be to God, so that the unity of the human race becomes ever more apparent. "Contributing also to this consolidation is "technical progress which promotes more and more interpenetration among nations."

The Prerequisites to Improving the Conditions of Workers
Address before a Group of American Officials Who Attended a Meeting of the International Labor Organization in Geneva
16 July 1947[7]

The *International Labor Organization* based in Geneva, Switzerland was established in 1919 by the signatories of the Versailles Treaty following World War I. It was intended, among other things, to work toward achieving certain common minimum standards for workers worldwide. Now after the Second World War had ended, a group of American delegates to a meeting of the *Organization* came to pay their respects to the Pope in Rome. Some of the objectives which the agency set for itself from its origins reflected the agenda which Leo XIII had proposed in *Rerum Novarum.*

That Pope's successor now encouraged the members of the ILO to continue with their task that they "undoubtedly recognized as a staggering and unending one." He reminded them that whereas "the Church does not have a commission to regulate directly economic life," nevertheless "the social and economic order cannot be divorced from the moral one." Hence the Church "has the prior right and the obligation to insist on and proclaim the unchangeable principles of morality." At that point Pius XII suggested the metaphor of a "Lighthouse in a storm-tossed sea of social disagreements" where the Church would always "shed its light to assist in healing social evils."

The Pope proposed that the "honorable worker does not seek to improve his own position at the expense of the legitimate freedoms of others which ought to be as sacred to him as his own." However, each and every worker does "nurture the legitimate desire for independent and secure ownership of all that is necessary to make possible for him and his family a level of living which accords with his own dignity and conscience." Therefore the Church will always "defend him against any system which denies him the inalienable rights which did not come to him from civil society but from his own nature." Here the Pontiff was also clearly directing his remarks to the socialist threat, which would lure workers into a "status of total dependence on the bureaucratic clique which gains possession of political power."

At that point Pius XII proceeded to pack a remarkable amount of social teaching into the remainder of this brief message. He told the ILO delegates from America that "any organization for improving the living conditions of workers would be a mechanism without a soul" so long as its approach does not include certain points. These were:

1. Respect for the human person in all regardless of their social status.
2. Recognition of the common obligations toward all of those who, created by the loving power of God, make up the human family.

3. The overriding requirement that in society the general welfare, the service of each to all, takes priority over personal profit.

The Pontiff concluded with the reminder that if "the human spirit is renewed and confirmed according to these truths, the living conditions of workers will also be improved." Again, "no power by the state will renew the spirit of man." That is the "sacred task of religion," and "any state which is founded on the principles of morality and religion will be the best protector and defender of the workers."

The Nobility of Work
Address to Ceramic Workers
27 March 1949[8]

In this address to a group of skilled workers, Pius XII spoke with some severity about persons, "who, without contributing any efficacious help, seem to have no other aim but to increase misery, to reduce to impotence those who wish to work and those who seek to provide work with just wages, to excite discontent and to build up an atmosphere of exasperation, harming the very interests of workers." He cited the Church's efforts, "not only to bring relief to those in need, but also to impress their responsibilities and duties on those who would quietly shirk them, frequently renewing Our severe admonitions." The Pope referred to the malefactors as "exploiters of misery." And notwithstanding the inherently noble quality of labor which is "in itself beautiful and ennobling," there are those who employ "anti-human and anti-social tactics...to make work seem hateful." He offered a preview of the *theology of work* that Pope John Paul II would present many years later in *Laborem Exercens* (1981). "Because it is productive, it continues the work begun by the Creator and represents the full collaboration of each one for the benefit of all." The lesson to be drawn is: "Such a thought should be sufficient to make all work agreeable, even the most monotonous and difficult."

After praising the special artistic quality of what ceramics workers do, in almost poetical terms the Pontiff expressed his admiration for their work. "Your art, regional and traditional for many centuries, has the noble character of every profession that works the earth." Then, tracing the sources of the material that they use, he stated:

> The farmer smears the earth with his sweat and sows seeds that germinate in its breast and furnish men with nutritive bread and delicious fruits. The miner toils to wrest from the earth its most deeply hidden treasures for the benefit of humanity. You work with this earth to make it from a dark and shapeless mass into something useful, beautiful and brilliant.

Comparing the creative work which these skilled craftsmen accomplish with the material of the earth to the work of the Creator Himself, Pius XII said: "He kneads it into the daily vicissitudes of life, and submits it to the fire of trials to make His greatest masterpiece out of the lowliest soul, the one most pitiable in the eyes of man." The Pontiff ended with the question, "If in your factory the earth could speak, do you think that it would lament the vigor of the hands that fashion it, or that it would complain under the burning caress of fire, which gives it hardness, beauty and splendor?"

Problems of Italian Workers
Address to 30,000 Members of ACLI
Workers' Section of Italian Catholic Action
29 June 1948[9]

This discourse was an exhortatory address by Pius XII to a group which had been formed and appeared before him just three years previously. The Pope invited them now to constitute an "apostolate among the workers, first of all among their own members and then among the others; an 'apostolate of the workingman by the workingman.'" (cf. *Quadragesimo Anno*). He inquired of them: "How fares at your hands that fervent apostolate of good example among so many—including the young—who drag themselves to work every day as though they were convicts, with no joy in their hearts, no noble aspirations of any kind?" And the Pontiff urged them, beyond looking for "the help of the State or the Church, through the channels of their relief organizations" to also "rely on their own efforts." By this time Pius XII had begun pointing out with increasing frequency the significance of solidarity; and he told the workers now that "they must count on their own mutual assistance, in the operation of which the basic point is the sentiment of intimate solidarity between those who give and those who receive."

There followed a stern and somewhat unique precautionary message about the need to curb "increasing wants," even while the Church has always stood by the workers in their demand for just wages. Pius XII Indicated that, while wages should certainly supply "food, clothes and housing; the children's education; wholesome recreation for soul and body," there are also "those other 'wants' which go to show how the modern, anti-Christian, immoderate quest for pleasure and heedless unconcern are tending to penetrate even to the workingman's world."

That *monitum* was present in papal teachings on the just wage from the beginning, but we find it presented here with particular, if not extraordinary, emphasis. Leo XIII in *Rerum Novarum* spoke of the just wage as one which would "support the wage-earner in *reasonable* and *frugal* comfort" [emphasis added]. He added that with such a wage the worker "will find it easy, if he be a sensible man, to practice thrift, and he will not fail, by cutting down expenses, to put by some little savings and thus secure a modest source of income." When he followed up on that presentation of the just wage doctrine contained in *Quadragesimo Anno* forty years earlier, Pius XII too qualified the just wage doctrine with a call for "skill and thrift," and for "living sparingly." In addition, what he stated in this message to the Italian workers about "the level of the wage or salary which the father of the family, and eventually also the grown-up children bring home," echoed what his predecessor had said. Pius XI mentioned the acceptability of having other members of the family contribute to the economic effort. "It is indeed proper that the rest of the family contribute according to their power toward the common maintenance, as in the rural home or in the families of many artisans and small shopkeepers." However, he added an important qualification:

> But it is wrong to abuse the tender years of children or the weakness of woman. Mothers should especially devote their energies to the home and the things connected with it. Most unfortunate, and to be remedied energetically, is the abuse whereby mothers of families, because of the insufficiency of the father's salary, are forced to engage in gainful occupations outside the domestic walls to the neglect of their own proper cares and duties, particularly the education of their children (*Quadragesimo Anno*, par. 71).

Pius XII reaffirmed that message about working mothers in this address by the statement: "But it is of greatest moment of all that the lady of the house should manage well the affairs of the home."

The remainder of the discourse dealt with the suggested relationship between the ACLI and other branches of the labor movement, "some of which attend to the defense of their legitimate interests bound up with the labor contracts—the proper function of labor unions—while others take charge of projects for mutual assistance in economic matters—such as the consumers' cooperatives." The Pope made it clear that the mission which this branch of the Christian labor movement had taken on was extremely important; in fact, "It matters more than any passing form of labor-union organization whatsoever," if the rank-and-file labor unions happen to go astray, e.g., seek "exclusive control in the State and society," or try to "have the workman completely in their power." The Pontiff even hinted at what were by then not uncommon abuses of labor union power.

> What must one think of refusing a laborer a job because he is not personally liked by the union? Of the compulsory strike for the attainment of political ends? Of getting lost along several other wrong roads which lead the working class far from its true advantage and from the unity to which it has been summoned?

Getting down to specifics, the Pontiff referred to the relationship between the ACLI and "the single Labor Federation." Reference was to the Italian Federation of Labor, and to indications that it showed tendencies to go down wrong roads: "There is indeed question today of important decisions and reforms in the national economy, in the face of which a class struggle based on enmity and hate would expose the labor union idea to mortal peril, if it did not bring it straight down to destruction." (It is necessary to recall that the Communist Party in post-World War II Italy was the largest one outside the Soviet Union.) Therein Pius XII saw the challenge for the group which he was addressing: "That is why you must see to it that Christian principles prevail decisively within the Federation."

He concluded that his words to the ACLI representatives were not "festive words," but "practical words" from a Pope who was "deeply concerned with the gravity of the present hour."

Labor's Dignity and Freedom
Address to 900 Representatives of Labor, Management and Catholic Action of Turin, Italy
31 October 1948[10]

On this occasion, Pius XII returned to the stereotypical challenge thrown before the workers by the obstreperous Communist element present in Italy. "It has been asserted, and continues to be asserted, that religion makes the workman slack and listless in daily life, in the defense of his private and public interests; that it puts him to sleep like opium, keeping him perfectly quiet with the hope of a life in the beyond." To that charge, he responded simply: "What an obvious error!"

Then the Pope offered this straightforward statement of the Church's position:

> If the Church insists always, in her social doctrine, on the respect due to the inherent dignity of man, if she asks a just salary for the workman in his labor-contract, if she demands that his material and spiritual needs be met by effective assistance, what prompts this teaching if not the fact that the laborer is a human person, that his productive capacity may not be regarded and treated as so much merchandise, that his labor represents always a personal service?

As if moving onto the offensive, the Pontiff offered a barbed comment:

> It is precisely those world reformers claiming for themselves the protection of the workers' interests as though it were their monopoly, and asserting that theirs is the only really "social" system, who fail to safeguard the personal dignity of the workingman and make of his productive capacity a mere object to be disposed of by "society" entirely as it wishes, completely at its discretion.

What followed was an affirmation of the Church's position on those great shibboleths of the modern world dating from the French to the Russian Revolution: liberty and equality. On liberty: "The Church.... tells you that human liberty has its limits in the law of God and in the several duties life brings with it; but at the same time she will spend herself to the utmost so that each one of you, in a happy home and in tranquil and decent surroundings may live your lives at peace with God and men."

Regarding equality: "The Church does not promise that absolute equality which others are proclaiming because she knows that life in human society always and of necessity produces a whole range of degrees and differences in physical and mental traits, in inward dispositions and inclinations, in occupations and in responsibilities." Instead, "she assures you full equality in human dignity, as also in the Heart of Him who calls unto Himself all those who labor and are heavily burdened and invites them to take upon themselves His yoke and find peace and rest for their souls."

That exposition of these two important, basically Christian principles, which were purloined and exploited by the architects of the French Revolution and later adapted to the goals of the Communist revolutionaries, followed in the tradition of the great teachings of Leo XIII in his important encyclicals of the late nineteenth century. And they provided the occasion for this Pope to make a scathing denunciation of the latter-day apostles of those revolutions:

> It is rather those reformers We have just mentioned who, while they flash before the eyes of the people the mirage of a future of fantastic prosperity and unattainable riches, sacrifice the dignity of the human person and the happiness of home life to the idols of a mistaken world progress, based on the superstition of technology and of organization.

That progress, the Pope pointed out, is "genuine and not artificial only when it is also a step towards God and His likeness." On the other hand,

> All purely earthly criterions of progress are an illusion—We were about to say a mockery of man—in the midst of a world which is subject to the law of original sin and its consequences, and which therefore, seeing that even with divine light and grace it remains imperfect, without this light and this grace would fall into an abyss of misery, of injustice, and of selfishness.

And if "God is the beginning and end, where the order that reigns in His creation is not a guide and measure of the freedom and activity of everyone unity among men cannot be achieved."

Obviously the Communist plan for society has another basis, and the capitalist system does so too, if only a bit less obviously. What they propose, Pius XII dealt with in the conclusion of this message: "The material conditions of life and labor taken in themselves, and resting upon an alleged uniformity of interests can never form the basis of the unity of the working class." The sad history of the world over the half-century which passed since this address was delivered to the working community of Turin substantiates what the Pope said here.

> Would not the attempt to build on such a foundation amount clearly to an act of violence against nature, and would it not serve merely to create new oppressions and divisions within the human family, at a moment when every honest laboring man yearns for just and peaceful organization in the private and public economy and over the whole range of social life?

The Pope concluded by offering the direction by which that yearning may finally be accomplished:

> To Him (Jesus Christ) let the tribute of your adoration and your gratitude go out. Put yourselves at His service, clearing for His "kingdom of truth and life, of holiness and grace, of justice, charity, and peace" a path among the ranks of

your fellow working men and women at the factory, so that in the radiant light which flows from Him—sun of justice and burning furnace of love—every sinful movement, all envy, hatred and discord may vanish; so that the peace of God may reign in hearts and homes and workshops, in town and country, between labor and management, among your own people and those of every nation.

Address to Catholic Employers
The Ninth International Congress of the International Union of Catholic Employers
7 May 1949[11]

In this brief, but urgent message, Pius XII offered, among other things, his oft quoted statement that employers and workers "eat, so to speak, at the same table, seeing that they must live, in the last analysis, from the gross or net profits of the national economy." He offers a refutation of the ongoing fallacy, nurtured in particular by Marxian ideologues, that management and labor are locked in "an irreducible clash of rival interests." Such opposition, said the Pope, "is only apparent." Actually, the parties "are linked in a community of action and interests." Above all, "Employers and workers are not implacable adversaries." Nor does such community "in any way imply that one is at the service of the other."

The Pontiff made the significant observation that whereas "in the accounting of private industry salary-totals may be listed under costs to the employer, in the national economy there is only one type of costs, which consists in the national resources utilized with a view to national production, and which must in consequence, be constantly replenished." That represents an early warning in the area of ecological concern, long before such consideration was in vogue as it became soon afterwards.

Clearly, some natural resources are non-replenishable. However, fortunately for the human race, a beneficent Providence also made available to us a great abundance of the kinds of resources which are indeed restorable, like forests, animals, and certain qualities in the soil; those therefore call for wise management. Human ingenuity, also providentially, is able to come up, time and again, with substitutes for the resources which may eventually be depleted, like some minerals in the earth. The Pope proceeded from the observation that "both parties are interested in seeing to it that the costs of national production are in proportion to its output," to the proposal: "[W]hy should it not be allowable to assign to the workers a just share of responsibility in the establishment and development of the national economy?"

That provided access to restating one of the key principles set forth by Pius XI eighteen years earlier. Pius XII now indicated that his predecessor "had suggested the practical and timely prescription for this community of interest in the nation's economic enterprise when he recommended in his Encyclical *Quadragesimo Anno* 'occupational organization' for the various branches of production." Indeed, the author of that encyclical felt, according to Pius XII, that "Nothing, indeed, appeared to him more suited to bring economic liberalism under control than the enactment for the social economy of a public-law statute based precisely on the common responsibility which is shared by all those who take part in production."

Unfortunately, that part of the plan for reconstructing the social order appears to have been too far ahead of its time. Objections abounded: some suggested that it meant "a return to the Middle Ages." Others felt that it went in the opposite direction, proposing that it was "a concession to modern political trends." There were indeed movements in this direction which were not always well thought out or even in basic harmony with the Church's teachings generally. There was talk of a "corporate state" in Fascist Italy, in Spain under Franco, in Portugal under Salazar, and in Austria under Dolfuss before that tiny country was occupied by the Nazis.[12] (The state intended by the martyred Austrian chancellor was even referred to by some as the "*Quadragesimo Anno* state.") Indeed, even in the United States, the early New Deal era saw the establishment of industrial codes under the Franklin D. Roosevelt administration. These were probably influenced to some extent by Msgr. John Ryan, and by Senator Robert Wagner, who was a convert to Catholicism and well acquainted with Catholic social teachings. Some of these initiatives lacked the balance required by the principle of subsidiarity so that they tended to become too statist in their coloration. In other words, they were imposed from the top, instead of being nurtured so as to grow more naturally from the grass roots where labor's relations with management took place. Others simply did not have sufficient time to mature. In any case, Pius XII indicated here that "at present that part of the Encyclical would seem, unhappily, to provide us with an example of those favorable opportunities which are allowed to escape for want of being seized in time."

Indeed, the same principle is invoked in the next paragraph, where the Pontiff rejects the ongoing "feverish attempts...to work out other juridical types of organization for the social economy." The "preference at the moment," he indicated, was for "state enterprise and the nationalization of industry." And while "there can be no question that the Church also admits—within certain just limits—state ownership and management,...to make of this state enterprise the normal rule for public economic organization would mean reversing the order of things." That is because "it is the mission of public law to serve private rights, not to absorb them." And in a virtual paraphrase of the subsidiarity principle, we find: "The economy is not of its nature—no more, for that matter, than any other human activity—a state institution." Instead, "It is...the living product of the free initiative of individuals and of their freely established associations." Clearly the "occupational organizations" suggested by Pius XI in *Quadragesimo Anno* and mentioned in this discourse by Pius XII were intended to be examples of "freely established associations." Fascist Italy, as well as Franco's Spain, tried to establish them by state mandate. What was allowable was the kind of "public law statute, which would encourage and legitimize the existence and operation of "occupational organizations." In the United States, for example, the anti-trust laws would have had to be amended to legitimize them, in the same manner as they were adjusted to allow labor unions, which are of their very nature monopolies. Instead, the Supreme Court ruled that industrial codes whereby industries regulated themselves were unconstitutional, since they were eventually imposed in some instances by the federal government.[13]

The Church was forced to deal also with overly zealous enthusiasts who viewed each business property as "a society with its personnel relationships determined by the norms of distributive justice to the point where all without distinction—owners or not of the means of production—would be entitled to their share in the property, or at the very least in the profits, of the enterprise." Pius XII refuted that notion on the grounds that it is "a conception stemming from the assumption that every business belongs naturally within the sphere of public law." He stated flatly: "The assumption is inexact." And that applies whether "the business is organized in the form of a corporation or an association of all the workmen as part-owners, or whether it is the private property of an individual who signs a wage-contract with all his employees." In any case, "it falls within the competence of the private-law discipline of economic life."

Finally, there was an appeal to the owner of the "means of production" whether he happened to be "an individual owner, a workers' association, or a corporation." Whereas he "must always—within the limits of public economic law—retain control of his economic decisions"; also, "…it goes without saying that his income is higher than that of his collaborators." There is intriguing economic insight in what follows. "The material prosperity of the entire population, which is the objective of the social economy, lays upon him, more than upon the others, the obligation of contributing by savings to the increase of the nation's fund of capital." Yet, "it is supremely advantageous to a healthy social economy when this accumulation of capital derives from the greatest possible number of sources," so that, "it is very desirable...that the workmen also should be enabled, by the fruit of their savings, to share in the creation of the capital resources of their country." That bit of wisdom corroborates the particular ingredient of the just wage doctrine calling for the worker to be able also "by skill and thrift" to "acquire a certain moderate ownership...." (*Quadragesimo Anno*, par. 63).

Pius XII, thus, seized the opportunity to reaffirm several of the salient features of Catholic social doctrine. In closing, he offered to his Catholic employer audience a sobering reminder that the "realization" of that doctrine called for "a strong dose of good sense and good will."

On Workers' Organizations

Address to Members of the Christian Workers' Movement of Belgium

11 September 1949[14]

This discourse makes several significant points with reference to labor organizations and their role in furthering the social teachings of the Catholic Church. First of all, Pius XII reaffirmed the legitimate role of "a strong trade union organization" in its role of "safeguarding...the rights of workers and...maintaining them at the level of modern requirements." He alluded to the historical note that they "arose as a spontaneous and necessary consequence of capitalism, established as an economic system." However there was also the significant qualification that unions received the approbation of the Church "always on condition, however, that, based on the laws of Christ, as on an unshakeable foundation, they would work for the promotion of a Christian order among the workers." The American reader may choose to question whether labor unions in the United States would meet that criterion, or whether unions here were instead predominantly secular and pragmatic!

Turning to what he called "a magnificent fruit from the tree of the Church's social doctrine..."the Pope termed an outcome of the Belgian Union "your National Federation of Christian Cooperatives." The cooperatives, according to the Pontiff, were "a work of authentic solidarity," and they offered "a great contribution...to the improvement and the security of the economic conditions of the worker and his family." The Christian Workers' Movement, therefore, went beyond typical union activities, in that it had a "special organization for helping those who are victims of illness." It also offered "institutions and unions for the training and education of the workers." In other words, it made efforts also "to develop the spiritual culture of the workers."

Pius XII, always a champion of the lay apostolate, scored as "ridiculous" and "hateful" the efforts of critics who "accuse the clergy of keeping the laity in humiliating inactivity." He seized on the alert and varying activities of the Christian Workers' Movement of Belgium as a refutation of that charge. And he urged the laity to "turn its attention to the family, social and scholastic questions," and to "become active in science or art, literature or the radio and cinema," as well as to "engage in political campaigns for the election of the legislative bodies or for the definition of their powers and their constitutional attributes."

The Pontiff concluded with some precautionary words about the "temptation to abuse" union power that "everywhere threatens the workers' movement." And he equated this with "abusing the strength of private capital," something with which workers were painfully familiar. The consequences could be dire, and rather than to bring about "stable conditions for the State and for society," they could be "doubly fatal for the well-being and the freedom of the worker, who would himself be hurled into slavery."

Finally, that admonition led the Pope to champion, once again, the "organization of industries and professions" by "the immediate drafting of a public law covering economic life and all society." These are the same "occupational organizations" which he referred to earlier in the same year (May 7, 1949) in his address to Catholic employers. He also recommended "an increase in the number of owners of private property, of medium and of small industries." He ended by appealing to the group to work "for the common good and with justice and charity," two virtues which, in their application to society, have its common good as their object.

The Social Worth of Labor
Papal Letter by G. B. Montini to the
President of the 26th Social Week of Canada
7 October 1949[15]

This letter was presented by the Papal Undersecretary who would later become Pope Paul VI. In it Pius XII expressed his praise that the Canadian group was addressing the "one theme" which "underlay the entire social question," *labor* or *work*. As Montini stated it, "The resolution of the problems which face the modern world in the area of industry, agriculture, commerce, and even in the liberal occupations depends for the most part on how one understands human labor or work." The *Canadian Social Week* earned papal praise, therefore, in dealing with this "essential element of all sociology, in its proper place within Christian thought."

That led to a proclamation of the traditional position of work as the human race's "not incontestable claim to nobility." It was of course a revolutionary departure from the way "pagan society, with its heavy reliance on slavery, thought of labor." Once again we find expressed the "theology of work" which Pope John Paul II would make the subject of a major social encyclical in 1981. The latter affirms that even in the terrestrial paradise before the Fall, work held a place of honor, notwithstanding the difficulties which came to be attached to it afterwards. Testimony to that dignified status of work is to be found in the words of St. Paul (Acts 20:34): "You yourselves know that these hands of mine have provided for my needs and those of my companions." Thus the nobility of labor was upheld by the "continuous defense and support for the sacred character of work and the condemnation of all forms, old and new, of slavery."

From those premises are derived "a great number of practical conclusions...about the personal and necessary character of work, its universality, and with regard to decent conditions, including the just wage, its legal protection, its relationship to capital...." Montini cited the Pope's *Christmas Message for 1942* where he insisted that, "The star of peace will rise and remain in place over the world" only if "human labor is accorded the dignity which God from the start assigned to it."

The discussion then switched to another aspect of human toil which "goes under the name, 'leisure,' and which also represents a requirement of human nature." "Rest and recreation should, if they are properly understood, strive toward an educational and moral goal." That is why Leo XIII already affirmed that "the right to daily rest and complete leisure on the Lord's day must be an express or tacit condition of every contract between employers and workers."

A new problem! Montini acknowledged that in our time Sunday rest and daily rest breaks have already, "Thanks be to God," become something of a civil right. Now the main problem appears in another form: what use is made of leisure time. He concluded by urging the Canadians also to devote serious study to this problem.

The Worker Apostolate
Radio Message to Young Christian Workers of Belgium (*JOC*)
3 September 1950[16]

This message was addressed to a meeting of the movement of young Christian workers who came to be known as the *Jocists.* Pius XII had addressed this group on previous occasions. He encouraged them in their apostolate directed toward re-Christianizing the working classes, while praising their success in getting members into positions of influence in labor organizations and even in government. The Pope noted that the movement had an influence beyond its own ranks, so that now even "materialists...who formerly preached class conflict" had progressed to where they were willing to instill "cultural value" in the workers. That presented a challenge to the young Christian workers, because those cultural values were often alien to what religion and the Church stand for. The Pontiff pointed out that the only way to instill true cultural worth in the workers was by way of religion, because it is their religious beliefs that provide the "divine spark" linking them with "the world of the spirit." Only by enkindling that spark can they be raised above "ordinary materialism and utilitarianism."

A warning followed. The Pontiff indicated that even among Catholics there is the temptation to "classify souls into categories.... No, there are not two kinds of people: workers and non-workers." "That," said the Pope, "led to a belief that the Church could win over the workers only if it agreed with all of their demands, no matter how impossible those may be." The Church cannot diverge from the "straight line of justice and charity, from the natural and supernatural order." It cannot ignore the fact that some of the selfsame distractions, which alienated many from "the other classes of modern humanity" also afflict workers. At this point Pius XII resorted to disturbing figures of speech, referring to "emaciated spirits," "sacrificial victims of an epidemic," and "mere shadows of human beings." They are ones who "never tire of visiting movies, sporting events, and which gorge themselves day and night with frivolous novelties, imagery and music."

Clearly this was a message addressed specifically to the youth of the emerging postwar generation. It was also prophetic in that the situation confronting youth, workers included, was to become much worse in the years ahead. There was a hint at the cold indifference which was to afflict a large part of mankind during the latter half of the century, which was just then at its half-way mark. The Pope suggested that many of such persons "may not even be hostile to religion, but—and this is almost worse—incapable of understanding it."

This, then, was the challenge facing these young Christian workers. They were dedicated to influencing a mass of non-Christian types, who, as Pius XII stated, "move along like a herd, with their eyes riveted to the ground."

The Worker Question and the New Social Order
Radio Message to the Workers of Spain
11 March 1951[17]

This message was broadcast to Spanish Catholic workers and employers who met together in various cities in Spain to commemorate the 12th anniversary of the coronation of Pius XII as pope. At the time, workers in Spain as elsewhere were being serenaded by the Marxian siren song. Referring to it as "the banner of liberation, the Pope urged them to remain loyal to the "banner of Christ." That the Church was ever at their side in their struggle, he reassured them by presenting three points.

He reminded them that no one can accuse the Catholic Church of having ignored them and their best interests. "Few questions have occupied the Church's attention more than these matters ever since Our great predecessor Leo XIII presented the workers in his encyclical *Rerum Novarum,* with the *Magna Carta* of their rights." The Pope pointed out that "the social question cannot be resolved without the Church, but neither can the Church do it alone." Needed also are the "intellectual, economic, and technical capabilities of those in public authority." The Church had "provided the religious-moral basis and carefully considered directions." Indeed "the social legislation in various countries is to a large degree nothing other than applications of principles established by the Church." That rather bold assertion was followed directly by the statement: "Do not forget that everything that is good and just which you now find elsewhere is already contained in Catholic social teachings." Indeed, "whenever the labor movement sets goals for itself which oppose the Church, then we are always dealing with defective objectives which sacrifice human dignity, social justice, or the real welfare of all citizens." That was perhaps a boast which the Pope would not have made before a less thoroughly Catholic audience than this assembly of Spaniards!

He then recalled how "in its 2000 year history, the Church has had to deal with the "greatest variety of social structures ranging from the ancient economic system with its slavery, until thé modern one which is identified by the words 'capitalism' and 'proletarian.'" And it has never preached "social revolution." "Yet, ever since the *Letter of St. Paul to Philemon* up until the social teachings of the popes of the 19th and 20th centuries, it has always insisted that people are more important than economic and technical accomplishments, and that all must do what is in their power to lead a Christian life worthy of human beings."

It was for that reason that the Church "held the right of private property as a basic, inalienable right." Yet, "she also insisted on the need for a just distribution of property, and condemned as unnatural a social situation where a small group of privileged and exceedingly rich persons stand opposite an enormous, impoverished mass of people." While there will always be inequalities, those who are in a position to influence how society develops "must always strive to bring about conditions where all will get enough to not only live, but also to save." That suggests again the just wage doctrine which was a central feature of his predecessors' social encyclicals. A specific affirmation of that doctrine followed:

> There are many factors which should contribute to a wider distribution of property. However, the most important one will always be the just wage. You know, beloved sons, that the just wage and a better distribution of the goods of nature constitute the two most urgent requirements in the social program of the Church.

Here the *pontifex* is at work once again. Pius XII was building the bridge between his predecessors who installed the just wage doctrine at the heart of their social encyclicals, and his later successor, Pope John Paul II, who made it "the concrete means of verifying the justice of the whole socioeconomic system and, in any case, of checking that it is functioning justly" (*Laborem Exercens*, par. 19). He pointed out that the Church also supported all initiatives which would make it possible for relations between employers and workers" to be structured in a more human and Christian way" and "marked by reciprocal trust." There is no room for class struggle here. While the specific term *solidarity* is not employed, it is implicit in the statement that "discussions between employers and workers must have as their main objectives concord and cooperation."

As the final point of his presentation, Pius XII committed what would now perhaps be regarded as a violation of some dimensions of the "ecumenical" spirit. "This work can only be accomplished by people who live the Faith and fulfill their obligations in the spirit of Christ." He added that "the solution of the social question was never easy." And now, after the "unspeakable catastrophes of this century, they have been made more difficult." What is called for is, among other things, "the reconciliation of the classes, the readiness to sacrifice and mutual respect."

The Pope concluded with words of praise for a training program for young workers in various areas of expertise. Such initiatives would, among other things, counter accusations that the Christian Faith does little besides console mortals with thoughts of the hereafter. He invited this Spanish audience to look at the "great past of their beloved Spain.... Who has done more than the Church to see that life in the family and in society would be established on a sound and stable basis?" And as for the present and the future: "No one has established a program for resolving the present social question that surpasses the Church's teachings in security, durability, and realism."

The address ended on a warm and interesting note. As the Spanish workers had hailed the Pope with a greeting: "Spain for the Pope," he responded with: "And the Pope for Spain."

To Italian Employers
Address to the Italian Catholic Association of Employers
31 January 1952[18]

Pius XII, in his address before this now five-year-old Association, took the opportunity to thank the employers for their patient steps toward instilling Christian principles into the area of labor-management relations. A key word appeared early in the discourse. The Pope praised the various employers in different industries for "not shutting yourselves off in individualistic segregation." And he commended them for proceeding, "moved by a most ardent spirit of *solidarity*...." That *solidarity* extended simply to the still small numbers of business executives who were "animated by the same desire": "the full, the lofty, the Christian management of our establishment penetrated with human sentiments in the widest and highest sense of the word." The Pontiff compared that with "the drop of oil in the gears," which must penetrate all the members and all the branches of industry: the executives, the assistants, the clerical employees and the workers of all ranks from the most highly skilled artisan to the lowest worker." Thus, he was content to speak at this point about solidarity within the individual enterprise. But he foresaw that as spreading gradually, perhaps like the leaven, to other business firms until they "become so many large families"; and then, "not content with their own separate existence as in a closed vase, they will unite among themselves all together," and "they will tend to form a strong and happy society."

That was, of course, a look into the future, perhaps the too distant future. As Pius XII indicated, "it would be certainly Utopian to imagine that this society could be formed by a single stroke." Yet, continuance on that course would eventually bring about "the greater consolidation and expansion of a vigorous, healthy Christian society."

Here too there is no "ecumenical" mincing of words: "The great misery of the social order is that it is not deeply Christian nor really human, but only technical and economic." That is an indictment which fits the then threatening socialist movement as well as the entrenched capitalistic system. Both lack the "really human," let alone the "Christian" perspective. The Pope challenged the employers before him to "introduce everywhere this human factor into business, in the various grades and offices which comprise it, and in economic and public life by legislation and popular education." Thereby they can "transform the masses...into a society whose members, while differing from one another, constitute, each according to his function, one united body." It is clear that the Pope was leading up to the Church's doctrine of the Mystical Body of Christ, which is, in any case, also the ultimate doctrinal underpinning of the virtue of solidarity. Indeed, he referred his audience to I Cor. 12:12 where St. Paul presents that exalted doctrine which is so significant for the Church's social teachings.

That brought the Pontiff to the apogee of this message to the employer audience. He urged them not to get too involved in the "talk nowadays about reforming the structure of industry" which directs its attention primarily to "legal modifications among its members." Because those endeavors "regarding eventual legal adjustments in the relations between the workers as members of the labor contract and the other contracting party" get bogged down in matters "of secondary importance...meanwhile, they pass over more or less in silence the chief part of the encyclical *Quadragesimo Anno,* which contains that social policy embodying the idea of an occupational, corporative order of the whole economy."

Pius XII had obviously not given up on the important concept of providing occupational organizations a major role in governing the operation of the economic order, while avoiding the predominance of the State in that governance. Also, he was aware that various initiatives toward employee co-ownership, while praiseworthy in themselves under certain circumstances, could, and in fact, did, divert attention from the eventual goal of the "corporative order of the whole economy." That was the reason for his questioning "[T]hose who set about treating questions relating to the reform of the structure of industry without taking into account that every single business is by its own purpose closely tied to the whole of the national economy." Meanwhile, the Pope encouraged the employers to proceed on their course of giving "a soul to personal relationships by a sense of Christian brotherhood." That would nurture "the personal dignity of the workers," and also "increase the efficiency of the business, not only materially, but also and primarily by gaining the values of a true community."

Preserving the Dignity of the Worker in the Workplace
Letter Read at the Opening Session of the Italian Social Week in Turin by Giovanni B. Montini, Substitute Secretary of State
19 September 1952[19]

This letter was, once again, read on behalf of Pius XII by the man who would later become Pope Paul VI. The theme for the occasion was "The Enterprise in the Modern Economic System." Msgr. Montini extended the Pope's thanks for the steadfastness of the Italian group in doing its part to find "a solution for those problems which are foremost in challenging minds and consciences at this historical moment in the political economic, social and moral life of the nation." He then proceeded to "recall here some of the teachings of the Sovereign Pontiffs on this specific theme of the Week."

The opening paragraph throws down the gauntlet to what must be regarded as still the predominant approach of contemporary economic thinking to what is cited here as "the fundamental problem of economic life, control of production and of the distribution of wealth." In the social teachings of the Catholic Church, that control is not to be left to either an all-powerful state, or to the forces of the free market as is still widely proposed. Instead, "This problem must be resolved in a way conformable to justice and the common good, and in a manner which safeguards the integrity and development of the human personality."

Then, in methodical fashion, are presented the "outstanding aspects of [business] enterprise" which are "evident to anyone who reads through the pontifical teachings on this matter." They are "the relation between the machine and the workers; the juridico-social position of the worker; and the relation between the enterprise and the state." From this there arises the necessity: 1) of studying special provisions for cases where the machine may increase unemployment; 2) of offering the workman adequate vocational training which will make him appreciate his own specific contribution to the goods produced (and on this point the action of public authorities toward the establishment and increase of professional retraining courses merits recognition); 3) of striving to better his moral consciousness and social sense through which he may become persuaded that his labor also fills a service to his neighbor; and 4) especially of strengthening religious sentiment through which the workman may regard his labor as a collaboration in the creative and redemptive action of God and, therefore as a means to his own spiritual perfection.

That was a remarkably detailed and specific program, but then the *Italian Social Week* was a purposeful operation dedicated to serious study of specific issues.

With regard to the "juridical-social position of workers in the enterprise" the Montini letter delved into a problem which was preoccupying the attention of Pius XII at just that time, and which he had a few days previously dealt with in an address to Austrian Catholics.[20] In the discussion of co-determination (*Mitbestimmung*) which was occupying the attention of workers and legislators in various countries at the time, certain errors had crept into the thinking even of those who professed knowledge of and loyalty to Catholic social teachings. Briefly, certain parties had proposed that worker co-determination and co-ownership were natural rights flowing from the labor contract. And they cited certain provisions in *Quadragesimo Anno* which seemed to them to support their position. Montini referred to how Pius XII "has many times referred to the juridico-social position of workers in the enterprise, distinguishing what belongs within the sphere of natural right and what forms part of the aspirations of the working classes and which, therefore, can be pursued by legitimate means as an ideal." He had in mind an address by Pius XII on 3 June 1950 to delegates to the Catholic International Congresses for Social Study and Social Action. There, referring back to Pius XI, Pius XII made it clear that workers do not 'have the right to economic co-management, especially when the exercise of this right rests in reality directly or indirectly with organizations managed from outside the enterprise." And here again, Montini reaffirmed that "in the main...there is actually no true right of a worker to co-management; but this does not prevent employers from granting participation in some form and measure to the workman, just as it does not impede the state from conferring upon labor the means to make its voice heard in the management of certain industries and in certain cases, where the overwhelming power of anonymous capital, left to itself, manifestly harms the community."

It requires only a moment's reflection to realize that laws which safeguard the existence and operation of labor unions in effect extend to workers the power to have a decisive say with regard to the conditions of their employment, i.e., in the management of the enterprise. That is what collective bargaining is all about. And employers are always free to extend to workers participation in management and, *if they wish*, even in the ownership and profits. But that is not the same as saying that: a) the wage contract is essentially unjust; or b) the workers have a natural right to share in ownership, management, or the profits of an enterprise.

Reference is made to an address by Pius XII to Italian Catholic Association of Employers on 31 January 1952.[21] The Pope encouraged "the profound spiritual modifications to be realized through humanizing and vivifying the relations between workmen and employers within the enterprise." That discourse appeared also to return to the persistent Pius XII theme of occupational organization. Thus: "if business firms, effectively penetrated with a truly human spirit, multiply and join with you, one after the other, if they become like so many great families, and if, not content with their own separate existence, as if in a closed vessel, they unite among themselves, they will, all together tend to form a strong and happy society."

The Montini letter continued with the promise: "Once the internal atmosphere of the business undertaking is transformed, those innovations which the professional abilities and the sense of responsibility of the workers, the keen and active sensibility of the employers and the needs of the common good might permit or require at a given moment, will be made possible and even facilitated."

Turning finally to the third aspect of the enterprise—the relationship between it and the state, we find affirmation of the centrist position of the Church and its social teachings. "If the so-called liberal conception is based on various erroneous principles, no less erroneous and dangerous is the notion which attributes to the state (the power of) a complete leveling of the economic world, for the added reason that it would lead to the crushing and death of fundamental human rights." Referring again to a statement by Pius XII, we find: "Whether this slavery arises from the exploitation of private capital or from the power of the state, the result is the same." The rights of private enterprise are then reaffirmed: "The economic world is primarily the creation of the free will of men; it pertains to the state, therefore, to create the conditions which enable private initiative to expand within the limits of the moral order and the common good."

The legitimate freedom of private initiative is more easily maintained in smaller-sized enterprises. Again quoting Pius XII we find "that the Church has benevolently regarded and encouraged those forms of business enterprise in which the personal initiative of all those engaged in it finds possibility for assertion and expansion, such as the craftsman's shop, the family-sized farm and the cooperative establishment." That does not automatically rule out the large-scale enterprise: "the Church also holds that it can be in conformity with right order that the large-sized enterprise remains in the realm of private initiative—when evident considerations of the common good are not against it." Therefore, the ultimate criterion for humane labor relations is not the size of the enterprise, even though the precondition would seem to be more appropriate in the smaller ones. In the final analysis, success in this area

>...depends on how well those responsible for the enterprises mentioned know their rights and duties both toward the civil community and their own personnel; and on how far the laboring classes, made aware of the negative aspects of state super-capitalism are allowed to assume an adequate responsibility in the cycle of the national economy, in professional life, and in the organs of production.

The letter ends with a significant quotation from an address by Pius XII to Italian Catholic workers on March 11, 1945:

>The time has now come to abandon empty phrases and to think with *Quadragesimo Anno* about a new organization of the productive powers of the people. Over and above the distinction between employers and workers, let men know how to see and recognize that higher unity which mutually binds all who collaborate in production which means to say, the unity and solidarity inherent in their joint duty of providing together for the common good and the needs of the entire community.
>
>Would that this solidarity be extended to every branch of production, that it become the foundation of a better economic order, of a healthy and just autonomy, and that it open the way for the working classes toward gaining honestly their share of responsibility in the conduct of the national economy! In such a way, thanks to this harmonious coordination and cooperation, and to this more intimate union of his labor with the other factors of economic life, the worker will come to find in his work a reasonable return which is sufficient to sustain himself and his family, a true satisfaction of the spirit and a powerful stimulus toward his own perfection.[22]

Those paragraphs synopsize an important portion of Catholic social teachings as found especially in *Quadragesimo Anno*. There is the appeal for a "new organization of the productive powers of the people." There is the call for "that higher unity which mutually binds all who collaborate in production;" and there is the reminder that a sound social order calls for harmony among the various "factors of economic life." There is a call for "solidarity" extended to "every branch of production, so that it would become "the foundation of a better economic order." All of that certainly reiterated the call by Pius XI for the organization of economic life along occupational (vocational) lines instead of into "an arena where the two armies are engaged in combat" (cf. *Quadragesimo Anno*, par. 83). There is the plea for *solidarity* which Pius XII invoked with increasing frequency and which was to become the leitmotif of the social teachings of Pope John Paul II. And with those elements in place, the goal of the just wage for all workers could finally be attainable which that same Pope called the "the concrete means of verifying the justice of the whole socioeconomic system and, in any case, of checking that it is functioning justly" (*Laborem Exercens*, par. 19).

The continuities linking three great men who each contributed much to their Church's social teachings is worth noting here. There was Pius XII represented and often quoted by Giovanni Battista Montini, who would one day succeed him as Pope Paul VI; and finally there was Pope John Paul II who added his own great trilogy of social encyclicals addressed to the economic order. We have here once again a splendid example of the development of the Catholic Church's moral teaching in this crucial area.

Unemployment
Address to Italian Worker Groups
1 May 1953[23]

The occasion for this talk was the congregation in St. Peter's Square of many thousands of workers on May 1, the feast of St. Joseph the Worker. Those in attendance included members of various groups from different parts of Italy, along with other workers who came singly on their own. Represented were workers from Frosinone and the economically hard-pressed areas of Southern Italy. Thus, Pius XII addressed the problem of unemployment of which many of those present had tasted the bitter fruit.

The Pope drew attention, even while labor is celebrated on this first day of May, to the plight of so many workers who suffer unemployment and underemployment, which he refers to here as "half-employment." In addition, even among those who are employed, many live in the constant fear of losing their jobs. Although parts of Italy were afflicted by this problem, he pointed out that at the time all nations of Europe were experiencing the same difficulty. Nor is it entirely the consequence of "malice or the abuse of power on the part of those who would be in a position to do something about it." In fact, circumstances "that had operated favorably for more than a century for economic development have now changed drastically." Accordingly, Pope Pius praised the initiatives underway to develop the hard-pressed areas in the South of Italy, including the construction of reservoirs in the mountains, waterlines and highways.

The Pontiff reaffirmed the Church's support for the workers whenever they suffer under an unfair labor contract, or when collective bargaining agreements are violated, and where their legal, economic and social circumstances can be improved without violating the rights of other parties. He indicated that in the light of ongoing efforts to establish the European Common Market, "the labor problem has become a more generalized one in which all of Europe is involved solidaristically.... No one could seriously propose that the interests of the worker can be served with the old methods of class struggle...."

Very pertinent to the nascent attempts to restore the old free market economic system is the Pope's next comment. "Doubtless the advantage to be gained by an integrated European economy cannot stem simply from unification of a larger area in which the so-called market mechanism would regulate production and consumption." What is more important "is that the competition will operate within the framework of a stable, genuine social life, with a healthful development of the family from generation to generation, and that according to this objective the natural criteria for organizing production in time and place, and a rational consumption will be brought about."

In speaking of that kind of goal for the then incipient European Economic

Community, apparently even this prescient pope did not foresee another grievous malady which would soon afflict Europe, including Italy along with the other developed nations of the world. He suggested that only with the aforementioned kind of rational economic approach to economic development could nations with large numbers of families that were "rich in offspring," bring to bear the important contribution of their wealth of labor resources and power as consumers. Since Pius XII's pontificate, after many years of anti-life propaganda and activity, most European nations, including nominally Catholic ones like Italy, have declined toward fertility rates well below even the replacement level.

Nevertheless the prophetic insights of Pius XII had not deserted him. At the close of this message to workers, he bolstered the spirits of the workers before him with a quotation from John the Evangelist: "Let not your heart be troubled" (John 14:1). He told them: "Even though it appears as though the will of a few powerful and arrogant persons seem to dominate and determine the course of events, ultimately and in truth everything is in the hands of God, and nothing can escape his strong and paternal providence!" That remains true even though "the times are such in our world that those who, lacking a vital faith while placing all of their trust in human beings and human calculations, can approach the future with confidence." "Not so for the faithful," said the Pope. Even while doing all in their power to defend their rights to a livelihood and to work, they must not lose heart while "trusting your heavenly Father to help you in all of your daily trials and needs."

Address to Italian Personnel Directors
6 May 1953[24]

In this brief message, predominantly spiritual in its tone, Pius XII offered special praise and encouragement to those entrusted with "negotiating labor agreements, the conciliation of collective controversies, the organization of workers, the distribution of unemployment subsidies and assistance to immigrants." He urged that they not run the risk of allowing their daily tasks to become "cold and without soul," and to not be "contented by narrow justice," or to allow "the end of your work be only one's own personal gain."

Probably aware of a temptation facing managers, especially in large-scale enterprises, to begin to look down on workers, in particular the most ordinary among them, the Pope cautioned that, "every one of you—managers, employees, experts of every sort—feel that upon your everyday work, if done with an understanding of love, the material tranquility and also the moral peace of so many families will be able to rely." He pleaded that, "We would prefer that persons and practices would never be considered by you as "least important things" which it would become acceptable "to not care about." Indeed, "this ought to be applied particularly on behalf of the most humble persons, because these are ordinarily more exposed to injustices, and have less opportunity and capability to defend themselves."

Thus, "A living and operative Christian love will always assure that this care for the 'least' things and for the 'little' persons is accompanied by the diligence and attention toward the 'prompt clearing up' of various actions." That is because "every sheet of paper that passes through your hands must place before your vision the weighty and urgent problem of daily bread that creates anxiety in so many men, and necessitates solutions by every possible licit means."

The Pope closed his address to those whose work is handling labor relations with the Pauline prayer, "May the love of Christ impel you!"

The Responsible Entrepreneur
Address to Participants in the International Congress of the Metal Industry
29 September 1954[25]

This address, though brief, afforded to Pope Pius XII an opportunity to remind managers of the vast industrial complexes comprising the metal industry about their obligations to the many workers under their supervision. He referred to the especially difficult working conditions in the metal processing industries, e.g., the steel mills of that time. While much has been done to improve working conditions, "the promptings of conscience make it obligatory to honor the inalienable rights of the human persons who, along with their families, derive their livelihood from the industry." The Pope reminded his audience that "the demands of competition which is a normal consequence of human freedom and ingenuity, can nevertheless not be the ultimate norms of economic life.... There are unimpeachable values which if violated or ignored may eventually lead to dangerous social and political upheavals."

In closing, the Pontiff quoted St. Paul who told the Romans: "Be not overcome by evil, but overcome evil with good" (Romans 12:21). He encouraged his audience to not allow their own interests to lead them to lose sight of the "real, material, and moral needs of those who depend on them." And he urged them to appreciate their problems and their legitimate demands, always allowing justice to operate to the extent that social institutions make this possible.

The Concern of the Church for the Worker Problem
Address to Workers from Barcelona
25 October 1954[26]

In this brief address to Spanish workers visiting Rome, Pius XII told them that they were especially dear to him because of their vital faith and their special loyalty to the pope. He reassured them that the Church is and always has been solidly behind them in their aspirations for a decent livelihood for themselves and their families. With those words came the reminder that "the Church has always concerned itself with the worker question and the social question, and that this involved above all the great principles which must serve as the only basis for a true resolution." It even got involved "to the limits of its capability in suggesting practical applications to the extent that these lay within its competence."

The Church wishes for those who work "to be able to achieve a decent livelihood, so as to lead a dignified Christian life while avoiding any excessive preoccupation with temporal concerns." This involves a "just distribution of the goods of this earth for which it has always campaigned on the basis of the principle of the just wage." Such a wage will "assure for you and your families your present life inasmuch as it makes possible savings as a guarantee for the future." That is of course, a reaffirmation of the just wage as a saving wage, as presented by both Leo XIII and Pius XI in their own social encyclicals.

Pius XII concluded by expressing the hope that he expected good results from the institutions and legislation that were then being developed in Spain.

The International Labor Organization
Address to the ILO Governing Body
20 November 1954[27]

In this address to members of the prestigious organization, then thirty years old, Pius XII commended them for the contributions the ILO had made to bringing about social legislation in various countries. He indicated that "while they do not possess legal force in the member countries," what they propose "may after ratification become real international treaties." And the Pope referred to the awareness of his predecessor, Leo XIII "of thc importance of international collaboration in labor questions," and of a general "realization that social safeguards and restrictions...would impose economic burdens and tip the scales against those countries that were willing to adopt them." That is a situation which was once again to became a burning reality a half century later when a renascent free-wheeling capitalism sought to avoid higher labor standards by exporting its manufacturing operations to countries with low or no labor standards.

Once the ILO came into existence following appeals by Leo XIII to, among others, Kaiser Wilhelm II of Germany on March 14, 1890, and after a private venture in 1900 that was later interrupted by World War I, it supported trade unions and their activities, among other things. "At the present time, the human factor, whose importance was neglected for too long—though not, however, by Catholic social doctrine—is attracting the attention of sociologists, and We know that you intend to make it one of your foremost concerns." That could be interpreted as an "instruction" by Pius XII to the ILO; or he could have been privy to something that was on its agenda. In any case, he pointed to the concordance between the objectives of the "Christian trade-union movement" and what the ILO stands for. "These objectives include, first and foremost, living conditions which safeguard the inalienable rights of man, as contained in natural law or as formulated in statutory law." However, the Pontiff pointed out that

> ...legislation by itself is a soulless standard, a mere barrier against wrong-doing.... The essential factor is the spirit that moves its defenders, the urge to improve upon the present, which, although it may be better than the past, is still overshadowed in many ways and burdened with the uncertainty of human weakness.

The specifically papal message was contained in the remainder of the address:

> If men are to strive with all their might to build a temporal society where private initiative can flourish without fear, where the rights of the individual are fully respected, so that the aptitude and abilities of each can find their full expression, and where everyone can adhere with heart and soul to the highest principles of morality and religion, they must put their faith in spiritual values, confident that these will triumph over the forces of dissolution and discord.

Finally: "What is at stake are not only the interests of the working class and its admission to the full exercise of its responsibilities, but the future of human society as a whole."

So far as the labor movement is concerned, the Pope warned that it cannot "rest satisfied with material success" and simply a "fuller system of safeguards and security and a greater measure of influence on the economic system." Nor should it "visualize the future merely in terms of opposition to other social classes or to the excessive subordination of the individual to the State." Instead, "It must seek its objective" where the ILO "has placed it, that is to say, on the plane of universality—as the Encyclical *Quadragesimo Anno* proposed—in a social order where material prosperity is the outcome of the sincere collaboration of all for the common good and serves as a foundation for the higher cultural values and above all for the indissoluble union of hearts and minds." That reference is, of course, what brought the specific impact of the Church's social teachings to bear on the entire discussion.

Accident Prevention in Industry
Address Before the First World Congress for Preventing Industrial Accidents
3 April 1955[28]

Pius XII pointed out to this group how the ILO which he had addressed just a few months previously included the matter of industrial safety in their agenda for the member nations, as had the social encyclicals of "Our predecessors, Leo XIII and Pius XI." He therefore congratulated those in attendance for confronting this serious problem. While appreciative of "the efforts of scientists, experts and all persons having a position of responsibility in regard to safe and hygienic working conditions," the Pope expressed his recognition that a "dispersal of strength must be avoided, that the results of experience and research in different fields must be pooled, that undertakings must be coordinated with the widest possible international extension." That was the praiseworthy purpose of this particular World Congress.

The Pope, however, would not have been the pope if he had not invited the participants to also reflect on "the more delicate aspect, namely, the intervention of human motives," in this important area. Recognizing that every "human work entails a certain risk, whether physical, economic or moral" and that up to a point that "may, or even must, be accepted when it does not pass the limits set by prudence," he suggested what those limits were when he indicated that "no one may, without serious reasons, compromise his own health or that of his fellows, risk his own life or that of others." Clearly, that is the serious problem involved here. "And yet, how much imprudence, how much culpable negligence, how may risks deliberately increased, occur as a result of the sole desire of avoiding the economic charges and material sacrifices presupposed by every application of safety measures...." Ah yes, the cost of installing and implementing devices for industrial safety! "The line of least resistance in this case is the same for all: in order to avoid waste of time and to increase production and profit, or even simply to save oneself an unpleasant psychological effort, all vigilance is relaxed, and sometimes even the most elementary precautions are neglected."

Pius XII then invited his audience to consider one of the subtler aspects of the matter under discussion. If "production and profit" were the crucial factors, then: "No one nowadays denies the part played in the worker's productivity by his subjective dispositions." That meant: "Non-recognition of the physical, affective and moral requirements of the human being ends by embittering him and turning him against those who despise his personal dignity." Consequently, "How can the interest each man has in his work, and the professional conscience which impels him to do it perfectly, how can these subsist when there is constantly imminent the threat of an accident which would deprive the individual and his family of that salary on which their material sustenance depends?" Thus, the Pope brought the matter back to the level of economic considerations. "Even on economic grounds alone, such reasons suffice in themselves to arouse in employers the will to assure their workers of satisfactory safety and hygienic conditions."

Beyond purely technical considerations for improving industrial safety, there are also more basic ones of "professional selection and training," the lack of which often leads to the kinds of problems addressed here. These were highlighted as a phenomenon peculiar to the post-war ambience. The Pope made mention here of a situation that had become widespread in post-war Europe: the importation of workers from other countries or localities, who were sometimes ill-suited for the industrial work whether by training or by lack of it. Thus, many immigrant workers "are sent to industrial tasks for which they have not been prepared by long apprenticeship, nor even by family or regional traditions." Nor were the workers themselves completely exonerated:

> These difficulties are often attributable to the very parties concerned, who do not understand the purpose of what is asked of them or the tragic consequences of actions forbidden to them, or else, while not denying the necessity of the rules laid down, gradually tire of observing them so that their good will needs

to be unceasingly stimulated.

The Pontiff concluded his exhortatory message by reminding those gathered before him: "Your intention, in its temporal domain, is related to that of the Church and of its Divine Founder, Whose life and death were consecrated to suffering mankind to apply a remedy to its ills."

Three Addresses to Railway Workers
17 May, 13 June, 26 June 1955[29]

Since the railroad industry offers an especially appropriate example of the urgency and outcome of solidarity among the persons involved in it, and of the overriding importance of the common good, Pius XII seized the opportunity to stress that point in his brief discourse before Spanish Railway Engineers. He told them "that the answer to the problems which beset the world is not to be found in division but in union; not in mutual ignorance, but in mutual comprehension; and not in hatred but in love."

The Pope suggested that the "railroad network is not unlike a blood stream which provides all of its related members, tissues, and cells with food, heat, and life." And "when it reaches into the outlying regions of a country and, in an efficacious manner, establishes contact with the neighboring networks, it is as if the same life were being infused into a much larger and a much more extensive body, as if it were, so to speak, being made available to all of humanity." That is indeed a significant analogy, and it provides an appropriate example of the solidarity which Pope John Paul II thirty-two years later would designate as a "Christian virtue" (*Sollicitudo Rei Socialis*, par. 40).

The address on June 12, 1955 to an Athletic Association of French Railwaymen continued on the same theme. After a few words in praise of physical exercise and the discipline required for athletes, the Pope pointed out that "If the railroads stop running for any reason, great trouble ensues: basic commodities are quickly in short supply; certain industries are promptly paralyzed; large numbers of workers become unemployed or cannot get to work; supply lines of cities are jeopardized; and long distance travel is rendered very difficult." In other words, here is an industry that is especially crucial for the overall well-being of the nation. In addition, the working person never loses importance despite the advances of technology. "The automatic control devices never fully take the place of the glance by a specialist or the competence of a chief who calculates and foresees."

The solidarity theme surfaces again in the following accolade for the railway worker. "He is aware of the fact that he is a member of a large entity, that he benefits by its resources, that he participates in its collective life; he and all his colleagues are interdependent, he is proud of their successes and saddened by their sorrows."

The address to the Railroad Workers of Rome on June 26, 1955 was the third to workers of this important industry within a two month period. This convocation of some 10,000 railway men at St. Peter's followed the consecration of a new chapel in Rome's new railroad station the day previously.

Here, Pius XII allowed himself one of the prophetic insights which became more common during the last years of his pontificate. He spoke of "the hope that better times are in store for the working classes." But at the same time he cautioned lest such a perception would lead to "a slowing down of effort and still less a ceasing to strive." Yet, he allowed himself to speak of "times which are coming and that the day should not be long delayed when, with "error overcome, and the clearly defined Christian solution of the social problem revealed in its fullness...it will be possible to inaugurate a true return of the ranks of labor to Christ Jesus the only Master and Savior."

That expression of hope followed the warning about the world of workers becoming victimized by "a cunning and divisive activity on the part of men eager to deceive the workers with false promises and pledged to draw them away from the practice of their faith and even to destroy that faith." This warning must be understood in the context of postwar Italy, which at the time had the largest Communist party outside the Soviet Union itself. Indeed, after alluding to the remarkable *solidarity*, i.e., interdependence, among all of the various personnel who make up the railroad industry, the Pontiff returned to what was an obvious threat to that solidarity among the railroad workers themselves.

There were those among them who were content to dedicate their attention "to the problems of material life," even while remaining "always faithful to Christian political principles." There are even those who propose that "men ought not to think of the soul so long as they have not suitably provided for the material needs of the body." The Pope reversed that order of thought. "The truth is that you ought before all else to be in your deepest convictions true Christians. Attachment to Christian political principles is then a natural consequence which comes almost automatically."

Indeed, the Pope had previously told the workers that "the harmonious action of all groups in the state is a Christian duty; no individual citizen ought to become a victim of the arbitrary act or tyranny of others." He told the workers that they "are therefore acting in full conformity with the Church's social teaching when," by all means morally permissible, you vindicate your just rights." Moral permissibility, however, means avoiding "acts of violence which damage the liberty and the goods of others...." It includes the workers using "the power of their organizations to win recognition for their rights." Such exercise of power always presupposes that "in the first place they use the means suitable for the negotiation of a peaceful settlement."

Following what seems remarkably similar to the conditions for just war, Pius XII added: "there must be taken into consideration whether the results being aimed at are in reasonable proportion to the damage which would result from force." Needless to say, the right to strike has been upheld explicitly in Catholic social teachings since the time of Leo XIII. For railway workers whose activity especially involves the broader general welfare, there is a "special weight" of responsibility because "your work—as We have said—has a vital part to play in the economy of the whole nation."

The Catholic Employer: Mission as Citizen and Christian
Address Before Seventh National Congress of Christian Employers of Italy
7 June 1955[30]

The employers group being addressed here by Pius XII had as its theme: The Employer and the Future of the South. The relative economic underdevelopment and consequent poverty of southern Italy was an ongoing long-term special problem for that country. It was also a problem to which various popes in their social teachings directed attention. All available resources were needed to come to grips with it, including the "government, as the interpreter of the common will of the nation," and also "citizens who possess considerable economic resources." That, for the Pope, meant "in the first place, management." In this context he seized the opportunity to restate the principle of subsidiarity:

> One of the essential points of Christian social doctrine has always been the affirmation of the primary importance of private enterprise as compared to the subsidiary function of state enterprise. This is not to deny the usefulness and the necessity, in some cases, of government intervention, but rather to bring out this truth: that the human person represents not only the purpose of the economy, but is its most important element.

That statement also expresses the intense devotion to personalism in economic life, which characterized the teaching of Pius XII in particular. The human person emerges here as both the *purpose* of economic life, and also as *its most important element,* meaning the dominant productive element in the economic order. Such personalism is an important element in the solidarist economics of Heinrich Pesch, S. J.

That emphasis reemerges again shortly. After referring to the importance of such factors as: "means of communication, housing, irrigation and soil conservation, development of agricultural equipment, improvement of existing industries and establishment of new enterprises" etc., the Pope returned to the personalist theme. Admonishing the Catholic employer to go "beyond the immediate rudiments," he reminded him: "Only on this condition will he be faithful to the principle which We have just recalled, that is to the maxims of Christian sociology concerning the transcendent value of the human person." That corroborates his earlier statement: "Here, indeed, it is not merely a question of investing capital, of perhaps running great financial risks, but especially of putting into action a social idea, a concept of economy, of its laws, of its aims and of its limits."

There was a warning lest there be substituted "for an old form of guardianship a new kind of subjection which, while freeing man from economic slavery, would impose upon him in exchange an even less bearable social dependence." And this would happen, "if employers, while working for the transformation of the South, were to subordinate its development to their own interests." If the employer intends "a truly Catholic meaning " to his action, then "you have the opportunity of practicing equity and charity in an excellent manner, because you have given them a social dimension through which they become a proof of the Christian spirit in the highest degree, a proof written in facts." "Equity and charity" as proposed here are, of course, the same social virtues—justice and charity—set forth as such by Pius XI in *Quadragesimo Anno* as the proper principles for reestablishing social order.

The discourse concluded with candid advice to the "head of a Christian firm," if

> ...he really wants to do his duty—to live intensely the doctrine to which he pays lip service.... The teaching of the Church which gives a clear formula of Catholic principles, runs the risk of being neither well understood nor applied unless it finds in the responsible head of a firm not a resigned and passive reception, but the fullness of an intense interior life, nourished by the sacramental sources of grace.

This means that "Christian social thought should be profoundly organic." And, "Far from being built up solely by starting from abstract pronouncements, it ought to correspond with constant fidelity to the intentions of Divine Providence as they are manifested in the life of every Christian and in the life of the community to which he belongs."

Returning finally to the theme of this meeting of Catholic Employers, Pius XII reminded them that there is at stake here a "twofold duty" as "Citizens and as Christians." As citizens there is the need for awareness "of having to collaborate for the unity and prosperity of the nations;" and as Christians there is the consciousness "of your co-responsibility in promoting the Christian religion and culture among those who are your brothers and sisters in Christ." Concern about the "problem of the South," gives expression of that twofold duty in "concrete form."

The discourse ended with one more bit of straight-forward papal advice to the people in his audience: "Perhaps employers were for too long a time accustomed to remain in the narrow circle of their own cares and their own economic purposes and not to take an active interest in the common life of society and of the state." That may have given "rise to and widely spread the rumor that the economy, or rather its managers, are the obscure power that from behind the wings directs everything upon which the fate of the people depends."

The Petroleum Industry and Human Relations
Address to the World Petroleum Congress in Rome
10 June 1955[31]

This address is one among many delivered by Pius XII demonstrating his remarkable grasp of, and insights into, technological matters. It sometimes seemed as if, disguised in papal robes, there lurked a could-be scientific genius. Along with the knowledge of what was going on in this specialized technical field, like the development of polyethylene with its important role "in the development of radar during the second World War," and the "Improvement in the performance of automobile motors resulting from a more rational construction of the explosion chamber and the introduction of additives to the motor fuel in order to prevent the formation of deposits," we find the use of terms like "catalytic agent" and "spectro-metrical methods," all of which suggested an expert rather than a layman in this field.

However, the Pope apparently demonstrated that knowledge of the specialists' field in the same way as Christ bemused the professional fisherman, Peter, by telling him on which side of the boat to cast his net. The Pontiff was about to lecture the petroleum industry specialists on human relations in their industry! He wanted "to call to mind the activity of many men whose fortunes are directly or indirectly linked to that of the industry, either because they are employees or because they are affected by the repercussions of the economic changes caused by the industry." That led to "reflection" on "the particular responsibility of those who fill the role of management in this industry." And the message was forthright: "At the present hour when one notes more and more the precedence that social problems must take over merely economic ones, when efforts are made to promote 'human relations' within business enterprises, no one has the right to limit himself to technical specialization or administrative work."

Once again that introduces a papal message of overriding importance for the concerns and treatment of the human beings who make industry work. Indeed, one section of this Congress "...is dealing with the training of personnel, and it has been fortunately emphasized that the concern of management is more and more with the men themselves who serve as its collaborators." There are responsibilities on all sides. "It is important that these men put forth all their initiative on behalf of the employers." However, "they will be led to do this only if industry first takes care to fulfill their basic human needs, which are not completely satisfied either by a just salary or even by the appreciation that is due their professional competency."

Finally, the Pope ventured into certain worldwide dimensions involved in the petroleum industry's special importance in the modern world. "The natural riches of a region, a country, or a continent are destined not just for the economic profit of the few, but for the improvement of living conditions—first of all material, but also and paramountly moral and spiritual—of the groups of human beings who must live by exploitation of the earth's resources." That foreshadows the theme which would be of great concern for future popes: the application of the social virtues also on the international level, especially in an industry whose importance has such critical worldwide implications. "The more and more apparent world character of economics and of the duties that fall upon privileged nations toward less favored ones will have their effect on the division of the goods produced." While Pius XII often suggested the international dimensions of justice and charity, John XXIII and Paul VI would subsequently devote much specific attention to that aspect in their social encyclicals.

The Managerial Employee in the Service of Social Peace
Address to a Conference of Italian Management Personnel
27 November 1955[32]

Pius XII was addressing a group here which, depending on circumstances, might properly be regarded as "middle management." In any case they are professionals who work at management without necessarily being owners or even part-owners of the enterprise. This particular organization, then just ten years old, already had some 800,000 members. The Pope appealed to them to continue their zeal for contributing toward a solution of "the social question which still causes great problems for a large part of humanity."

By virtue of their position in business operations, these people were clearly strategically placed to "help moderate the harshness of class antagonisms." They were in a position, the Pontiff suggested, that would "help all to find a way leading to an honest and flexible cooperation among all of the vital forces of the nation for the well-being of all...." Hopefully then "the social teaching of the Church would be recognized and applied as the means that is really in a position to put aside those deep-seated causes which promote hatred and nourish the class struggle."

Pius XII reminded his audience that "notwithstanding external appearances," their association was in fact comprised of actual workers, and it resembled in many ways a "labor union." Thus, they were not likely to "cover up or defend actions which would do harm to the ordinary workers." Yet, they also rank at the head of personnel in enterprises and "perform functions which were formerly done by the entrepreneur himself." Thus, the Pope suggested to these people that they were "in an ideal situation to cooperate in an effective manner for bringing about that cooperation among social classes which all right-thinking persons very much wish for."

The message concluded with a papal plea that these "beloved sons would spare no effort in this peacemaking role...in the name of justice and charity."

Ideals for the Businessman
Three Addresses
20 January, 4 February, 17 February 1956[33]

On January 20, 1956, Pius XII addressed the First National Congress of Small Industry in Rome, a group representing some 60,000 small businesses. This offered the Pope an opportunity to reaffirm the "indispensable functions of the private entrepreneur" as upheld in the social teachings of the Catholic Church. Indeed, he referred here also to the "spirit of free enterprise to which we owe the remarkable progress that has been made especially during the past fifty years, and notably in the field of industry." Whereas the legitimacy of *private* enterprise has never in doubt in Catholic teachings, the notion of *free* enterprise sometimes brought with it dubious implications. What the Pope had to say about the term "private enterprise" sheds light also on what the Church has always understood by the notion of *freedom* in owning and operating a business.

"The words, 'private enterprise' might be erroneously understood, as though this, in particular in the small business concern, were handed over, both as to organization and activity, to the sole discretion of the owner, who, it might be thought, is interested merely in the ventures of his private interest." Not so! "You, however, have explicitly affirmed your intentions, by emphasizing the fact that the safety of private enterprise and small businesses must be thought of in terms of the nation as a whole, with regard to which you have both rights and duties." To stress the importance of various small businesses to the "nation as a whole," the Pontiff mentioned a few of the industries where small businesses still predominated, like "the building trades, the clothing industry, produce markets, machine shops, or electrical works..."

The role of the individual business leader is especially critical in small businesses. Whereas in larger concerns, the management task is divided among "numerous subordinates and selected representatives of the owner," in small concerns "these functions tend to be exercised more immediately by the owner himself." And "technical, economic, and social problems nearly always end up by devolving upon one and the same person, who must answer for everything and must concern himself with particulars, with purely practical questions, as well as with the human problems of his employees."

Elucidating on this matter of "human problems," Pius XII warned that while "[M]any people show no lack of goodwill,...it must be observed at times that an overwhelming attachment to economic advantages attends more or less to blind men to a perception of the want of equity and justice in certain living conditions." At the level of practical suggestions for the heads of small businesses, the Pope told the group: "An indispensable prerequisite for the success of any small business enterprise is that the employer should be able to depend upon the faithful collaboration of his employees."

While that kind of collaboration suggests obligations on the part of the workers, it nevertheless reflects in an important way the kind of treatment they should get from the employer. "Let us say at once that the employer himself is the deciding factor in this; he is the principal source of the spirit which animates his employees." The reason? "If he is noticeably careful to place the interests of all concerned above his own private interests, he will have little difficulty in maintaining the same spirit among his subordinates." That is because "The latter will readily understand that their superior, under whose orders they do their work, has no intention of profiting unjustly at their expense, or of exploiting their labor excessively." Instead, "they will see that, by providing them and their families with the means of livelihood, he is likewise affording them an opportunity to perfect their own individual capacities, to engage in work that is useful and profitable, and to contribute according to their abilities to the service of the community as well as to their own economic and moral improvement."

All of that suggests a formula for success in business operations that may seem almost simplistic. However, any worker who has encountered the all too frequent situation where there are "depressing suspicions that they are being cheated," and who has felt the "consequent desire for revenge," will know that attaining such a level of human relations is not easy, and sometimes, in fact, elusive. Where it exists, on the other hand, "there will be restored among the workmen an atmosphere of alacrity, of spontaneity, of willing cooperation in the improvement of their common labors." Continuing on that important theme of labor-management harmony, the Pope stated that those "common labors" will "become interesting, intelligible, and constructive." Thus, "labor will regain all of its significance and nobility; it will become more truly human and will bring men nearer to God." Thus he regaled the attending businessmen with what may appear to be a deceptively simple formula for successful business operation.

Shortly afterward, on February 4th, the specific theme of human relations came up again when the Pius XII addressed the International Conference on Human Relations in Industry. This group included representatives both of companies and unions, so the Pope told them their initiative "represents an advance towards the union of the two great forces which collaborate in production, namely employers and employees."

After expressing due deference to "the human sciences of Sociology, Psychology or Psychotechnique," the Pontiff indicated that these nevertheless "encounter enormous resistance." They are aggravated over time by "the way institutions operate, by the accumulation of errors and various prejudices." Thus, the persons involved have a hard time making objective judgments. Also the freedom of the parties is handicapped inasmuch as powerful forces, like social pressures and competition in technology, exert tremendous pressures on decisions of the parties involved. Indeed, technology itself "vividly brought out the importance, so long ignored, of human relations in labor. At this point Pius XII repeated a statement by his immediate predecessor in *Quadragesimo Anno,* which he liked to quote in the context of industrial relations: "Contrary to the plans of Providence, labor, which was intended even after original sin, for man's material and moral perfecting, under these conditions tends to become a means of perversion: for dead matter emerges from the factory ennobled, while men are there corrupted and degraded" (*Quadragesimo Anno*, par. 135). A poignant papal lament followed: "We wish We could say that his no longer takes place anywhere in the world.... Alas! Everyone knows that progress is slow, much too slow on this essential point, in many countries and on whole continents."

That provided the entry for what is the Church's position on this matter. "For the Church all men are equal in dignity before God; therefore they should also be equal in the free or necessary relations which unite them." The business community is nowadays based on contracts between employers and employees. In the large industrial enterprises that imposes on the former a serious obligation in their dealings with the latter, since they make demands on them for a major portion of their time and their energies. Here follows what is certainly an expression of the central idea in Catholic social teachings with regard to labor-management relations. "It is not simply a matter of a worker hired and paid for his labor; it is a matter of a man, a member of human society, who comes to cooperate for the welfare of that same society in the given industry." Suggesting that a business enterprise, even of the modern stripe, is not "totalitarian," the Pope warned: "A business does not monopolize initiatives which are outside its particular scope of activity and belong personally to the workers." Nor does it "disintegrate into a game of technical functions coordinated in an anonymous manner." That line of thought led to the admonition that employers and their workers "must loyally render to each other a mutual service; and if the concern of employers is to treat the workers as men, they would not be satisfied with utilitarian considerations: productiveness is not an end in itself."

That lesson in labor-management relations by the head of the Catholic Church was a powerful one; and but a moment's reflection will make clear that it is no less relevant and cogent now than it was in 1956. Since the Church regards itself as an "expert on human nature," its head did not hesitate to lay before his audience the basis for its position. For it, "every man represents a transcendent and absolute value," which is based on the fact that "the Author of human nature has given him an immortal soul." What is more, "He became Man and identified Himself morally with everyone who looks to others for the needs of life that he lacks: 'As long as you did it to one of these, my least brethren, you did it to me.'" There, according to Pius XII, "is the origin of the high dignity of every human being and the responsibility of whoever takes a man into his service."

It is difficult to see how anyone could fault the Church for its position in the important area of labor-management relations as expressed in this significant discourse delivered on February 4, 1956. That is, unless one follows a narrow legalistic approach, or is captivated by a mechanistic free market ideology.

The last of these three lectures on various aspects of human relations in business management was delivered on February 17, 1956 before the General Italian Federation of Commerce. Here the Pontiff was addressing merchants who, unlike manufacturers, occupy an intermediary position in the economic process between the production of goods and services, and its costumers. He seized this opportunity to voice his concern about various kinds of criticism against businessmen, as well as about excessive regimentation by governments. It is good to recall that the mercantile businessman has had to fight a long battle for respectability ever since antiquity and through the Middle Ages so as to attain the kind of status he enjoys, by and large, today.

As Pius XII pointed out: "People sometimes question his usefulness to the community; they attempt to do without his services; they suspect that he is trying to derive enormous profits from his economic function." That was accompanied by what was perhaps a papal hint that "it would be worthwhile for businessmen to investigate whether these charges are well-founded or not." As for the principle of the matter, it is clear that "since the merchant exercises a specific function in society," it would "be a mistake to see in him only a middleman between the producer and the consumer." He is that, among other things, including his role as a "stimulating force in the economy," where he is "able to assure an opportune distribution of goods and services"; but "he likewise gives effective encouragement to the manufacturer to provide merchandise of higher quality and lower cost." So far as the buyer is concerned, the businessman also has it in his power to afford for him "a free access to the market."

The paragraph which follows merits attention in the matter of what may be regarded as a textbook statement of the pivotal position of the entrepreneur at the heart of the economy:

> Every exchange of products, in fact, quite apart from satisfying definite needs and desires, makes it possible to put new means into operation, arouses latent and sometimes unexpected energies, and stimulates the spirit of enterprise and invention. This instinct, which is innate in mankind, of creating, improving, and making progress explains commercial activities as much and more than the mere desire for gain. The businessman needs a thorough and well-balanced professional training; he must have a mind always quick to understand and follow up economic trends as they develop, in order to handle his business with success and to foresee the reactions of the masses of the people as well as their mental attitudes. These last considerations are frequently of great importance in the interplay of exchange.

There followed a brief lecture on certain "moral qualities" which are "no less indispensable to the businessman." They include "courage in a period of crisis"; tenacity "in overcoming public apathy and misunderstanding"; "a spirit of optimism in revising his formulas and methods of action.... These are the qualities which will enable you to be of service to the nation; with them you are entitled to the esteem and good opinion of the whole community."

As for the exterior context in which the businessman must operate, the Pope pointed out certain conditions which must also be in place. They include "an open field...where his way is not barred by too many obstacles set up by a regimentation that is too complicated or too strict." Also, the businessman "expects to face fair competition, operating under the same conditions in which he himself is placed...a competition that does not enjoy exclusive and unjustifiable privileges." The Pontiff mentioned also that favorite bone of contention among businessmen: "He dares to hope that an excessive part of his well-earned profits will not be taken from him by taxes that are too numerous and too heavy."

Turning to the legitimate demands of those who work in the establishments of businessmen, there is "a growing desire to assure to all classes of society guarantees that will preserve them from the mishaps and chances inherent in the fluctuations of the economy; guarantees that will protect employment and its rewards; guarantees that will provide for sickness and incapacitating accidents that may reduce a man to idleness and deprive him of the means of livelihood." These represent the kinds of social welfare measures that are widely sought and achieved in most of the advanced economies of our time. This desire, the Pope regarded as "quite justified." Indeed it is one that is not yet entirely fulfilled, since "the present system of social security has not yet succeeded in putting an end to difficult situations or in healing wounds that are always open."

At the same time, there is a papal *monitum* for those in the position to seek such benefits from their employers or from governments. Thus, "the anxious desire for security should not prevail over the businessman's readiness to risk his resources, to such an extent as to dry up every creative impulse; nor impose on enterprise operating conditions that are too burdensome; nor discourage those who devote their time and energy to commercial transactions." The Pope referred to that as "an all-too human tendency to seek out the way of minimum effort, to avoid obligations, and to exempt oneself from the duty of self-reliance in order to fall back upon the support of society and to live at the expense of one's fellows." They are "the easy solutions in which the responsibility of the individual is reduced to a minimum under the shadow of the nameless multitude."

What follows is a restatement in familiar terms of the principle of subsidiarity. First we have a prefatory common-sense acknowledgement that, "If the businessman has his own interests to defend and promote, if he bears the responsibility for his own activities, he will deal with and solve his own economic problems with greater enthusiasm, ability and wisdom." However, lest anyone be carried away by this stress on the reliance by individuals on their own resources, we are reminded that government maintains its vigilant and subsidiary role. "No one will deny the need for assurances and vigilance exercised by public authority in the interest of the businessmen themselves as well as in that of the public." Then we have a restatement by Pius XII of the actual principle which was first set down explicitly in *Quadragesimo Anno*:

> We may hope then, that the State will be able to remain within the limits of its function of meeting the needs of private enterprise, by keeping a watchful eye upon its progress, and by lending a helping hand, should the need arise. But the State ought not to try to take the place of private enterprise, so long as the latter functions usefully and successfully.

The concluding clause represents a crucial qualifying statement which is often overlooked in appeals to the principle itself, in particular by exponents of the free market. In that context, the subsidiarity principle is violated perhaps as much by omission as by the heavy-handed active intrusion by an overactive State. Indeed, it is the abuses resulting from a lack of the active practice of the social virtues by the individuals and businesses on the market, which eventually trigger a reaction—perhaps sometimes an over-reaction—by the public authorities responding to appeals by persons who are often in no position to help themselves. That is why Pius XII added: "An equilibrium must be maintained between these two component parts of the economic movement, namely the forces of progress and the element of organization; otherwise economic life will fall into either anarchy or stagnation." Unfortunately, in a historical context where the social virtues as practiced by individuals have been relegated to a past era, we have witnessed a tendency toward an almost rhythmic vacillation between economic anarchy and the kind of economic regimentation which characterized and eventually led to the decomposition of socialist society in the Soviet Empire.

That, ultimately, may be why the Pope then appealed to the businessmen to make use of "freedom of action not only to serve your own private interests or those of a definite class of society, but to promote the advantage of the whole country." He reminded them that, "Temptations, of course, are not wanting, if we consider the weakness of human nature; temptations to employ procedures that are not quite honest, to realize unlawful profits, to sacrifice moral dignity to the allurements of material goods." Those words are not time-bound in their implications, given that we are dealing with "the weakness of human nature." Present history bears this out. Now as then, the resolution of the economic problem presupposes that we cultivate "spiritual development" and "an earnest will to promote, among individuals and among social groups, true disinterestedness and a compelling desire to alleviate the sufferings and miseries of one's neighbor."

The urgent lesson—an ever contemporaneous one—is left to the end of the papal discourse. "Every man must be convinced that his destiny is not limited to procuring the most comfortable situation in his temporal life." If that is indeed our goal, we are told that we "will be unable to find sufficient energy to resist the ignoble impulses arising from [our] lower nature." In addition we will be forced to expend much energy in the need to defend ourselves from similar conduct on the part of others. The ultimate fate of a society in which individuals are unable to muster up "sufficient energy" will be an "ever-growing tendency towards a type of society whose economic and political organization constitutes the very negation of any sort of freedom."

The warning may seem to some as lacking in relevance to the present, now that the Soviet Empire has disintegrated. However modern history should serve as a reminder that society abhors chaos with the same predictability as nature abhors the vacuum. For good reason Pius XII concluded his address to businessmen, therefore with a fervent appeal. "Still we exhort you, merely in the defense and protection of your own interests, to exhibit a spirit of proper moderation, which takes account of the conditions of the national economy and of the numerous and delicate factors that enter into the regulation of the social structure." He urged them, in almost apocalyptic terms, "to not forget the really essential point, that is to say, the enduring values of the spiritual order, which are superior to all individualistic aims, and which remain the only means capable of assuring the survival of modern civilization."

The Christian Labor Movement
Address to a Catholic Labor Rally in Milan
1 May 1956[34]

This was one of what became, during the papacy of Pius XII, a series of May Day addresses. It marked the second year in which the feast of St. Joseph the Worker was celebrated throughout the Catholic Church.

The Pope noted with special enthusiasm the presence of representatives of Associations of Catholic Workers (*ACLI*) from Italy and elsewhere, a group whose spread he encouraged. Their intention was not to promote what he called "an imaginary international unity of the working class, but rather "the close harmony of Catholic workers who...are desirous of bringing the whole world of labor back to Christ." They are intended "to seek each other out, not in fear of other movements, nor in competition with them, nor even in that feeling of solidarity which draws together the members of a given class, but rather to act as Christ's apostles among your brothers who do not know, or who reject His saving message."

The Pope noted that there was at large "a certain embarrassment in their attempt to justify and, as it were, excuse the existence of Christian associations of workers." He asked bluntly: "To excuse it before whom and of what accusation?" And he volunteered what to him seemed like the weak-kneed answer: "To excuse it for the reason that they call it simply a labor movement; to excuse it for the supposed breach which the *ACLI* might bring to the movement itself!"

In those words lies a challenge to various Catholic organizations, which, especially in the post-Vatican II ambience, sought to conceal or even to disown any Catholic identity, perhaps on the grounds of a misunderstood ecumenism. That was unacceptable to Pius XII for at least two reasons. The first was that "...every social movement, hence the labor movement also, supposes as its beginning and end, man with his supernatural destiny, with all his rights and natural obligations, from which one may not prescind even when the proposed movement aims directly at economic and temporal goals." The second reason, specifically with regard to the *ACLI* , was that it opened "its doors to everyone."

In any case, the Pontiff indicated that "the unity of the labor movement as such in the world does not seem to have been favored by the course of history." And he mentioned specifically "industrial Europe and America during the last hundred and more years."

Anyone familiar with the labor movement in the United States will recognize that the Pope knew what he was talking about. One of the great weaknesses of American organized labor throughout its troubled history was its inability to gather all of even its dedicated unionists into one house, so to speak. Closest to the point in history when Pius XII delivered this address was the great schism that split American unions between the older, more conservative American Federation of Labor (A.F. of L.) and the more recent, militantly aggressive Congress of Industrial Organizations (C.I.O.) during the explosive 1930s. Notwithstanding that split, in the year just prior to this address, the historic merger of the two groups into the *AFL-CIO* took place. Nevertheless, much of the previous identity of the two federations persisted, as is evident from their hyphenated title. Moreover, at the same time some large national bodies remained outside the so-called "house of labor," while others, because of various disagreements, later separated from it.

As for industrial Europe, labor unions there tended to be more closely linked to political factions and parties. Being by-and-large more ideologically oriented and less pragmatic than American unions, some of them were more socialistically inclined than others. And for all of the talk about "workers of the world" and the common fate of "the proletariat," the fact of the matter was, as the Pope indicated: "the idea of international unity of labor classes has always failed because of national differences arising out of complications of war."

What followed was a prophetic suggestion which, however, even the more optimistic may be inclined to question. Speaking of "the longed for social peace," the Pope indicated that "the Christian workers...are perhaps not far from the day when they will be able to exercise the function of guide in the midst of the world of labor." Pius XII may have been speaking not about the immediate future but about the day after tomorrow! His reliance was on the eventual triumph of the truth. "The sound doctrine which they (Christian workers) profess, the upright feelings by which they are animated, are so many lawful claims to their becoming leaders of the labor movement of today." Who could foresee the storms of discord that would break out in the period following the Second Vatican Council within the very Church itself? Thus, society roundabout was deprived, at least for the historical moment, of the self-assurance provided by a secure Bark of Peter sailing on serene seas. The precondition established here by Peter's successor was soon to suffer a rude shock. He indicated that, "In you the unbiased person can readily meet honesty of principle, moderation in means adopted, a true notion of justice, and, above all your independence of outside influence and interests." Subsequently the ranks of the "unbiased" were severely thinned, and even those who claimed the title of "Catholic" became distracted by a level of internal dissension seldom surpassed in the Church's history.

However, what Pius XII proclaimed here remains a persistent mark of the Church in its long journey through history. "She wishes for and defends peace—internal peace between sons of the same country, external peace between members of the great human family." However, as the intervening years have demonstrated poignantly: "But She needs strong and determined cooperators in this tremendous undertaking." The alarming level of disharmony within her own house has, it would appear, delayed the desperately needed progress in that direction.

Christ's Kingdom and the World of Labor
An Address to a Pilgrimage of Workers from Prato
28 October 1956[35]

Here Pope Pius XII was addressing workers who came to him as pilgrims on the feast of Christ the King from the industrial city of Prato in Tuscany. Accordingly, he reached into the liturgy for the Mass of the occasion and reflected on "the coming of the kingdom of Christ" which "men—often without realizing it—are waiting for...." In the prophetic terms which became more characteristic of this great Pope's messages late in his pontificate, he dared to say that "in the midst of the miserable shattered fragments of countless scepters and the deserted halls of many palaces, Jesus alone is spreading His dominion ever farther and receiving new professions of loyalty from His subjects." This address seemed like a homily preached by a pastor to his flock on this special Sunday, the Feast of Christ the King. He asked that, in turn, that the Kingdom of truth, the Kingdom of grace and life, the Kingdom of justice, and the Kingdom of love and peace come into their lives.

The social message, as such, was contained in the appeal for the kingdom of justice and of love and peace. “May justice rule in your factories.” Here the Pope became specific, indicating that “We have in mind a special kind of justice—social justice,” and pointing out that “a hunger and thirst for it are stirring within men of the modern world as never before.” At the same time he indicated, “We must make clear once again that there will be no real justice in the field of labor without the reign of Jesus.” And employers were reminded that “while it is true that the Church condemns any unjust violation of the rights of property, she also warns that this right is not unlimited and absolute; for it carries with it some definite social obligations.” The key to this problem is deceptively simple: “it will not be particularly hard to live up to these obligations if you make it a point to adopt the same attitude toward your workers as you do toward your brothers.” Ultimately “They are persons with the same kind of nature as you, even if they are called upon to carry out different tasks in life.”

Turning to the workers, the Pope told them: “the Church is with you when you are defending yourselves against unjust contracts, or demanding that others meet their just obligations.” And it will “be with you in the future whenever you are using legitimate means to bring about an improvement in your conditions.” “But it can never take a stand with you when you are asking something that is wrong or when you decide to use unjust means to obtain it.” There followed the warning that took into account the attempts to influence workers in Italy at that time by the ever-present Communist Party: “those who pretend to be your friends while they go about sowing hatred and practicing violence.”

Finally, there was one more highly significant element of social teaching. Pius XII alluded to the difference between justice and charity, the twin virtues for social order. “Justice gives what is due, but love does more; someone who is in love gives all he has and all he is, he gives himself.” The model for that, of course, is “the Divine Savior” who “preached and practiced” this “science of complete and lasting love.”

Automation: Its Problems and its Prospects
To the National Convention of the Christian Association of Italian Workers
7 June 1957[36]

The then novel issue, automation, and its implications for workers and industry, was the topic of two addresses by Pius XII during 1957. This first was before the *ACLI* (Christian Association of Italian Workers) which made that the theme for the 1957 convention. The message contained in this important presentation is applicable to all aspects of the ongoing cybernetic revolution. It merits serious study and reflection specifically with reference to the computer age, which has since taken on episodic dimensions. Automation was to a degree an early application of computerization techniques to industry, along with all of its effects on the workers, their job security, and relations with their employers. And the fascination which it had for many in the 1950s is now being replicated on a far grander scale with regard to computers and their impact and implications for the future.

Basically, at its early stage, automation involved the transmission of previously programmed instructions to machines by punch cards or tapes. Once again, this involved, even if on a far more sophisticated level, the same basic problems that came with the earlier phases of the Industrial Revolution. Machinery, in brief, seemed to reduce the human workers to a lower level of importance, and it foreboded, among other things, the loss of jobs. The Pope, therefore warned that "you should approach this uncharted terrain not merely as scientists and technicians, but also as sociologists and Christians, since a mistaken approach to the question at issue might well have dangerous repercussions both in the material sphere and in that of moral and spiritual values." Once again, he revealed a remarkable familiarity with an area that was not directly germane to his role as a religious leader.

As always, man's experience and fascination with novelty led to various extremes of response. The Pontiff indicated that "the very word 'automation' divides thinking people into optimists and pessimists with regard to mankind and the world of tomorrow." In fact, "some people have gone so far as to assert that with automation there is coming into being a world completely 'made by man,' and that today for the first time, man, enlightened by the exact sciences, is taking the place of the Creator, as autonomous lord of the universe." He alluded to "the more extensive influence of the mathematical methods recently elaborated in research upon genuinely quantitative relations."

Typically, despite all pretense of being highly methodical, the scientists involved in this latest step in the Industrial Revolution seemed to allow themselves to be carried away by its novelty. Pius XII told his audience, "We read again and again that scholars have not yet reached a satisfactory definition of automation." Nevertheless, some "even arrive finally at the point of imagining or dreaming of a factory without any human beings." For the true Christian, it ought to inspire "a grateful admiration for the greatness of God the Creator and of His works." However, for materialists, especially those who are "in agreement with Marxist principles," all of this simply seems to reinforce their view that man and his social relations are ultimately determined by the "technical side of human life." This led to a "wake-up call" from the preeminent religious leader in the world: "However, man's development is always determined by the totality of his nature in the midst of society, and consequently by the manifold factors embraced in man's unity." In other words, "the technical factor cannot prevail over the general direction of the economy, nor against that of social life in general." As for automation, however great its influence may become, "it will remain limited by its very nature; it is one of the factors of the future, but not in itself a determining one nor a restrictive one."

There followed a sober and highly significant reflection on mathematics and its contemporary regency as the preferred tool also for the social sciences, "But for social reality and its stable ordering, statistical and mathematical programs will not suffice, however much the social sciences are inclined nowadays to such a unilateral conception of their purpose." According to the Pope, more is needed in the present post-Christian culture the Babylonian tower-builders are trying to establish. "Social life requires further and principally other forms of knowledge—theology, philosophy, and the sciences of man's spiritual life and of his history." And for all of automation's promise and fascination, "Man, as he reaches out toward domination of the earth, remains always to his own advantage circumscribed by limits." These "have been imposed by nature, or to speak more accurately, by the same divine Wisdom which set 'a law to the waters that they should not pass their limits'" (Proverbs 8:20). In the final analysis, automation "does not cease to be a ticklish problem, demanding reflection and prudence."

A major problem is offered for reflection by Pius XII. "Automation involves, above all, the danger of confusing technical productivity with economic productivity." By the latter, "we mean a lasting and sure attainment of conditions which will make possible the material and human well-being of every member of the population, and in which all those who contribute immediately—with their labor, their property, their capital—to the national economy will receive a return corresponding to their investment." In other words, this great surfeit of goods which production by automated technology should make possible, in the Pope's view, "ought to be capable of giving an easy solution to social tensions." That will involve a lot of factors, not the least of which is "an assured consumer's market."

What followed was a lament that came in the context of full-scale Cold War expenditures for armaments especially by the major powers. What automation had proven incontestable thus far was "its technical capacity to produce" armaments. For most countries, it can only prove itself when "disarmament frees capital and when the development of technology, accelerated mainly by the armament race, will no longer make obsolete tomorrow what was considered an advance yesterday." The temptation will be there for many nations, "when expenditures and investments are dominated by fascination with technical progress," to live beyond their means.

Another problem, close to the hearts of both Pius XII and his audience on this occasion was the specter of "technological unemployment which might well arise, according to circumstances with the introduction of automation." The term was assigned by economists to the loss of jobs due to the introduction of machinery, and it has been happening in all ages, but on an especially significant scale since the Industrial Revolution. In fact, because the economic science as such began in about the same time frame, economists were captivated by a simplistic notion that the economy would quickly adjust by counter-balancing natural laws to all disturbances in the ongoing equilibrium. The Pope was well aware of the standard cant. With regard to technological unemployment, he said, "Some believe that this would be experienced for a short time only, because in the long run other possibilities of employment would open up with the growth of new industries, with the adaptation of the working force to other positions, with the lessening of the hours of labor without any corresponding loss of wages."

There was always the disconcerting problem, however, regarding what happens to the worker—the human person—who is faced with short-run unemployment and displacement, and how short the "short run" will end up being. The fact is that vast numbers of workers have been impacted time and again by such unemployment with their lives devastated. All in all, "It should be asked whether these arrangements might not make automation burdensome for the economic productivity of the nation." Indeed, "[I]n this area it is not at all legitimate to adopt the false principle which in the past impelled certain statesmen to sacrifice an entire generation in view of the great advantages that would occur to succeeding ones."

Pius XII, it is clear, showed remarkable insights regarding the implications of automation, which would put some economists to shame. For example, he suggested also that "a national economy, when completely equipped in accordance with these new techniques, seems likely to be more vulnerable in its totality and much less versatile in a time of crisis or other disturbance." That suggested what the Pope saw as the central problem, "to harmonize the interests of employers and employees in order to make them conscious of their common share in a social economy that is developing the productive forces ever more harmoniously throughout the entire breadth and length of the nation." The governing principle here for the "organized parties to the labor contract," he proposed, was that "it is better to bargain than to fight one another."

Turning to the "question of wages," the Pontiff provided an intriguing insight:

> Up to the present the workman was at the heart of the productive process which was the contribution, measurable by results obtained, of the muscles and ability of the hired hand. But now the individual is at the head of the process of production and must cooperate incessantly, with close attention and technical 'know-how,' in order that this process might constantly go on and, should there be some disturbance, be resumed as soon as possible.

All of that, the Pope concluded, called for "new criteria" in estimating "the value of the paid worker," and "new types of workers will have to be considered." This could "present domestic problems for the labor unions and may even affect their present form, especially if it is borne in mind that, in certain sectors of the national economy, the working class will not in the future be notably affected by automation."

Since there were already those who felt that the great impact of automated production could only be resolved by the "formula of socialism," Pius XII concluded that "extensive planning will undoubtedly be necessary both in the national and the European economies." However, such planning "cannot and need not be identical with a directed planning that is more or less absolute." Such planning would destroy "the independence of the family and the freedom of the citizen," because those are "naturally bound up with a sound functioning of private property as a stabilizing social institution." Also, so long as "the bond of the common good makes itself felt" throughout the economy "in business firms, in the various fields of production, in the government, and in parliament, that is to say, wherever decisions are made that affect man and the economy," there is no need to resort to total central planning.

After such discussion of the economy overall, Pius XII returned to what was for him always the real core of the problem, and at the same time, the solution: "the human person, insofar as he is the subject and the object of every social change." He directed attention to certain promises held out to workers with the widespread introduction of automated production. "It is said that automatic machinery will free the workman definitively from the monotony of labor, from the endless repetition of uniform motions; that the advance of mechanism will no longer impose upon him and his fellows the inexorable rhythm of toil." Ever aware of the scriptural sentence, "In the sweat of thy face shalt thou eat bread" (Gen. 3:19), the Roman Catholic Pontiff felt the need to remind man that even automation will not abolish the curse of Adam: "However the hardships connected with labor will undoubtedly overtake him in another form." In a remarkably prescient manner he reminded the worker that, "There will be situations in which he will have to maintain his vigilance hour after hour, alone and with tensed nerves, over the wondrous functioning of automatic production." And as for the wider ramifications of that kind of production, we have more of the same remarkable insight:

> The laborer will no longer be able to specialize in only one field of work. He will have to be intellectually and professionally adaptable in order to comprehend the functioning and coordination of the most varied kinds of apparatus. In this way, judging from previous experience, the number of unskilled laborers will gradually decrease while the number of educated and fully trained workmen will continue to grow in the same proportion.

Inevitably, such preoccupation with the person of the worker had to turn the Pope's attention to the need to train him for the new age of automated production. "This means, of course, that there will always be a need of more intellectual versatility, vocational training, and confident readiness to assume responsibility." The kinds of people needed now "must be allowed to grow in their vocational education, as in every other form of education." That would involve "the long period of apprenticeship, followed by work in the shops themselves as well as in special schools." In other words, all could not be left to the "magical" workings of the market and its supposed capability to resolve the problem of technological unemployment in what economists like to refer to as "the long run." Clearly, all parties involved have to do whatever is possible to ease the transition of workers into the age of automation.

Finally, the Pope addressed what was another expected consequence of automated production: more leisure time. "A man who has thoroughly grasped the religious, moral, and professional meaning of labor, will likewise understand the meaning of free time and will be able to use it to advantage." He also warned of the false notion that "a man works in order to enjoy leisure.... In reality, a man has leisure—apart from the natural and honorable rest from toil, which is needed to enable him to perfect his faculties and to fulfill better his religious, social, and domestic duties—in order to make him physically and mentally more competent in his work."

Pius XII proposed that vocational training "has an important place in the education of the people and in developing a sound popular culture." Then he indicated that whereas a "high degree of income is relevant and important," its rational use is "more important." He applied the same reasoning to the possession of rights. Simply gaining more "extensive rights" is not so important as their "correct use"—all of which reflects back on "the internal stability of the man himself."

This major address could be regarded as the definitive papal statement on the mid-century development—automation—and its subsequent extension: computerization. Perhaps the cybernetic phenomenon taken altogether is simply the latest phase of the ongoing industrial revolution. The message that follows is already a sequel based on it.

Aspects of Automation
To the European Committee of Cooperation Among Machine Tool Industries
23 October 1957[37]

This gathering involving representatives of nine countries was one of the early instances of post-war initiatives to unite Europe, first economically, and eventually into "a European federation." Pius XII traced the development of the ongoing revolution in technology, indicating that now "the rate of invention and discovery has been accelerated to such a degree that there is a real race in the turnover of machinery, especially that used for the mass production of articles of industrial construction." While ascribing all due credit to man's genius, a paternal warning followed forthwith, that "it would be fatal for him to permit himself to become dazzled by material success which does not free him from servitude and from the tyranny of his passions."

In fact, the Pope introduced a significant perspective on one of the possible outcomes of the widespread introduction of automation. He said, "...one can hope that an ever-increasing number of workers will be freed who have until now been subjected to the performance of purely material and monotonous tasks." The earlier stages of the Industrial Revolution rendered many skilled trades obsolete, at the same time that it vastly increased the demand for unskilled labor and for the category which then came to be designated as semi-skilled labor. Automated production hopefully could now be expected "to be substituted for men in cases where the job has been reduced to a definite number of mechanical motions or to carrying out a purely material type of control."

All of that is as it should be, i.e., providential. "What technical capacities make possible today, economic circumstances often make necessary...because the growing needs of modern society demand an incessant increase in productivity." The Age of Discovery opened up new lands with bounteous natural resources for European peoples who had often mined to exhaustion their own scant resources. The Industrial Revolution provided the technology needed to maximize available resources, and employment possibilities for Europe's then large families which could no longer be absorbed on the small farms that prevailed on the Continent. Now, as the whole world was opening up to the economic potential which the ongoing technological revolution has presented, automated production appeared to be a logical sequel. Pius XII alluded to the switch, long underway from human or animal energy, to "energy of mechanical origin," and he proposed that this further necessitated "devices which can use available energy in ways that are economically advantageous." Next followed a predictable papal warning about how the expected bounty is to be used. If "man learns how to dominate his instincts and make good use of the ample means for developing his intellectual and spiritual life, there is nothing to fear from material progress."

This address was delivered in 1957, just 12 years after Europe began the task of digging itself out from under the devastation caused by World War II. However, the Pope already sensed, perhaps with his characteristic foresight, the first signs of what would come to be called "consumerism." Hence he warned that if "man learns how to dominate his instincts and make good use of the ample means for developing his intellectual and spiritual life, there is nothing to fear from material progress." Otherwise "he will gain nothing from it except another kind of slavery and a certain moral decadence." The lesson to be learned would be to use the "greater amount of leisure time available" to satisfy "the most profound needs of the soul."

In closing, Pius XII made those in attendance at this audience aware of their mission, along with a reminder of the Church's ancient teaching on private property: "You are destined to contribute to the necessities of the present world and to smooth the way for an order which can put into the service of the greatest number, the riches common to all mankind."

Concern about the Working Human Person in the Industrial Operation
An Address to an International Group from the Chemical Industry
10 January 1958[38]

During the last year of his life, there were no less than five papal addresses before various groups of industrialists and workers about their relations to each other and to society. This first address of the year was before an international gathering of representatives of the chemical industry from Western Europe and also North America. As was his practice on such occasions, Pius XII spoke to his visitors in French. Those before him were concerned about protecting their workers against the health hazards and injuries in their industrial operations, but they were also interested in the broader aspects of labor-management relations.

Among other things, the chemical industry felt a need to counter a widespread prejudice about what were ostensibly some especially grave health hazards in chemical production. In fact, actual available statistics disproved that supposition. Yet, the Pope urged those who were gathered before him to continue to exercise all due care so as to maintain and improve where possible the conditions in their industry, especially with regard to health and safety hazards that may face chemical workers in particular.

The Pontiff then turned his attention to the broader aspects of industrial relations, i.e., to the "humanization" of industry overall. He reminded his audience that whereas the relations between entrepreneurs and their workers is represented as an antagonistic one where opposing interests play themselves out, more recent research suggests that there is a deep underlying community of interests. On the surface it appears that business management is geared to getting as much production out of the workers as possible by the way it succeeds in regimenting their labor. At the same time, the workers are presented as interested solely in earning as high a wage as possible for their efforts. Actually, scientific studies of the worker-manager relationship are finding that purely economic considerations are ranked lower than impulses stemming from the deeper spiritual side of man's nature and from his emotional and intellectual needs. Experts are finding that when a person performs work which denigrates his abilities and his personality, his resultant attitude goes far toward negating the gains that have been made over the past quarter century by all of the impressive advances in mechanization. In fact, psychologists, in attempting to classify the factors which motivate the worker, have found that what ranks highest is the active interest in his work as incited by his feeling that his full human personality is appreciated and engaged. In other words, "the worker feels that he is not merely applying his muscular capacity, but also his entire self, and that his efforts are reckoned in terms of the pride which he can take in what he has contributed to the finished product." In other words, "his job is not to be viewed solely as a means to make a living, but as giving meaning to his life and value to his personal and social being."

If this viewpoint makes sense even merely from the standpoint of the improvement in worker productivity, it should appeal even more so to the person who operates on the level of human conscience and the responsibility stemming from that. At this point, Pius XII injected the specifically Christian perspective into the discussion:

> A man with a heart, and above all Christian, respects the human person and his inalienable rights; and he recognizes the deep bond which associates him with even his humblest fellow human being. Therefore, he will not simply admit that economic factors and social circumstances are to be judged in a deterministic manner according to blind laws, or as the inevitable result of historical evolution. In fact, he suffers greatly when he sees how the worker of today all too often regards himself as tied to his work like a slave in irons, instead of as a human person whose work contributes to his development, no matter in how humble a manner.

The Pope closed with a fervent exhortation that the distinguished members of his audience would not rest until they had done their best to bring about a condition where it would be possible for each of their workers to develop their personality fully according to his or her potential. That should take place, not by occasional condescension, but with continuous concern about the well-being of the other person and his personal and social fulfillment in the order ordained by God.

Praise and Encouragement
A Greeting to the Rupert Mayer League of German Industrialists
2 May 1958[39]

This is a brief message of welcome to a group of German industrial leaders who named their organization in honor of the famous German Jesuit victim of the Nazi persecution of the Catholic Church in Germany. Rupert Mayer, now venerated widely as the "Apostle of Munich," was beatified by Pope John Paul II on May 3, 1987. He had been arrested and imprisoned on several occasions after refusing to remain silent in the face of Nazi slander against his Church. While he did not achieve a "red martyrdom," he suffered the "white martyrdom" of being removed from his active apostolate and put in the Sachsenhausen Concentration Camp. There the frail health of this decorated chaplain of World War I, in which he had lost a leg, began to fail. The Nazis, fearful of his great popularity among Bavarian Catholics, released him from the camp and sent him into protective custody at the Benedictine Monastery in Ettal for the remainder of World War II. After being liberated by American troops, the *victim* became the *victor* in a sense. He commented wryly that, "A one-legged Jesuit has outlived the thousand year *Reich!*"

Pius XII related to his audience that he had known Fr. Rupert Mayer personally, while he, as Eugenio Pacelli, was the Papal Nuncio stationed in Munich during the Weimar era. He complimented those present for their efforts to impress upon the membership the need for professional competence along with Catholic witness in their working lives. Referring to them as "the Catholics of a highly industrialized country," he told them that they were responsible for "imparting the Christian aspect and form to this new world of industry, to your workshops and offices, to your installations and operations."

There were no specific recommendations, as were typical in many of the other addresses to industrialists. This was mainly a pastoral "pep talk." Pius XII seized the opportunity to make known his esteem for the courageous Jesuit whose good influence obviously persisted also in the organization whose members stood in his presence.[40]

Industrial Workers as Objects of Materialistic Propaganda
Address to Italian Iron Workers from Naples
4 May 1958[41]

Pius XII greeted a gathering of workers from the vast and important ILVA iron works of Bagnoli near Naples. Along with an expression of support for their efforts to improve the lot of the workers, the Pope also presented them with a warning. While praising the great technical progress, as well as the many steps to improve the security of its employees, and relations between them and management, he admonished the members of this vast enterprise to remain steadfast in improving the safety standards in their always somewhat hazardous operations. Beyond that, the Pope warned against the ongoing and persistent hatemongering and agitation. The powerful Italian Communist Party was, of course, active at the time in its endeavors to overthrow the existing social order.

Like the address to German industrialists two days previously, this too was principally a message of pastoral admonishment and encouragement. The great Pope was now approaching eternity. Coincidentally or not, his addresses appeared to reflect more and more a predominantly spiritual tone.

Women and the World of Work

Frequently during his pontificate, Pius XII addressed the problematical aspects of women in the world of work outside the home. Throughout the social teachings of the Church, since *Rerum Novarum,* there was a presumption in favor of having most women fulfill the role of wives and mothers who would work at doing the many tasks involved in that calling. Anyone who has observed the care required by just one infant, let alone by the larger number of children as would be normal in a non-contraceptive society, will appreciate that motherhood requires full-time devotion and presence. Consequently, an integral part of the just wage doctrine which, with reference to its application in modern industrial society first appeared in *Rerum Novarum*, called for an income that was sufficient to support the mother and children in the home.

In earlier times when rural society still predominated, the mother was generally at home. There, in addition to the work involved in raising children, she also helped with the many tasks that were a normal part of farm life. In the neighboring cities and villages, small retail and craft shops run by individual proprietors were also the rule. There too, typically the wife and mother was on the premises taking care of the children along with also apprentices who among master craftsmen were often quasi-members of their extended family.

One of the perhaps less salubrious by-products of the Industrial Revolution was a system of production which coaxed workers in ever-increasing numbers out of their small shops and off their farms, into centralized work places called factories. These were separate from and often distant from their homes. Historically, the liberal economic philosophy unfortunately entered the stage of history at the same time. Its leading emphasis was on the pursuit of one's self-interest, and it relied for control solely on no-holds-barred, free competition. In that socially warped milieu, female and child labor soon became an attractive option for the capitalist owners of mills, mines, and factories. With an increase in the supply of labor, the price of labor—the wage—became ever lower, so that mothers and even children were frequently forced to abandon the home, and entire families had to work in order scratch together even a subsistence wage.

Most unfortunately, the revival of that same liberal economic philosophy in recent times—Pope John Paul II referred to it as "neoliberalism"—brought with it a revival also of female and child labor with the same horrendous aftermath. Once again, several family members have to work outside the home in order to earn enough to survive. Propagandists for the new *status quo* defend and encourage this disorder now as a hallowed aspect of the "emancipation of women." Ironically then, while the Soviet system with its state-provided day-care for children has broken down, capitalist society now increasingly adopts the same day-care culture, often without significant state-support, but with the same attendant devastating effect on family life.

It is a forgone conclusion that there were and always will be women who do not marry, are widowed, or for other valid reasons work outside the home. The popes in their social teachings did not regard that in itself as a problem area in the social order. They have always defended the rights of women as workers, including their right to a just wage and the right to equal pay for equal work. However, there were persistent allusions to the problems presented when mothers, especially those with young dependent children, work outside the home by choice or because of economic necessity. Pius XII was especially vigilant about this development, as the selections presented below indicate.

Work and the Family
Allocution to Working Women
15 August 1945[42]

This address sets forth precisely the position of Pius XII and the Catholic Church regarding the role for which most women are destined by their own nature, as well as for serious sociological and demographic reasons. "The woman is the heart of the family: the care of the home, in which she is queen, is the center and stage of her principal activity." That states the basic principle which underlies sound social order where the family is the cell unit of society with the mother at its "heart."

Then comes the acknowledgment of present-day reality, bearing in mind that this address was delivered at the close of World War II in 1945. "But in the present state of affairs, industry with its tremendous progress has brought about a transformation without precedent in the history of civilization." One aspect of this was, "it has taken over a noteworthy part of the domestic duties which belong by nature to the woman." And "it has obliged great numbers of women to leave the home to work in the factories, in various enterprises." That, the Pope said, "is an accomplished fact from which at present it is impossible to prescind," notwithstanding that "not a few people deplore this change." He then addressed what may be regarded as some of the "deplorable aspects of what had happened": "We know well how arduous it is, while remaining faithful to the law of God, to fulfill the duties of a working woman in some public enterprise and at the same time those of mother of a family." Recognizing how difficult the situation is for women who are caught in that economic trap, the Pontiff recalled: "[T]he efforts of the Church on behalf of a wage sufficient for the sustenance of both the worker and his family had and have precisely the object (often very difficult of realization) of bringing back as well the wife and mother to her proper calling in the home."

Later in the same address we find stated the principle of "equal pay for equal work" which was, it seems, rediscovered far more recently by secular society:

> First of all, We need not remind you, with your wide experience of social affairs, how the Church has always supported the principle that to the working woman is owed for the same amount of work and production, a salary equal to that of the working man; that it would be an injustice and contrary to common good, to profit without consideration from the work of the woman, only because it is available at a lower price.

Few statements by this Pope resonate more amazingly in recent times. "This would harm not only the working woman, but also the man, who would thus be exposed to the danger of unemployment."

There followed a stirring reminder of how the Catholic Church has been in the forefront of the battle for social justice for a long time. It is worth presenting verbatim.

> "If I must boast," We would say with St. Paul (2 Cor. 11:30): Who can point out a social program as solidly founded as rich in content, as vast and at the same time so well proportioned and just, as that of the Catholic Church? Who has battled like the Church, from the moment when the proletariat first appeared in industry, in a loyal struggle for the defense of the human rights of the workers? In a loyal struggle, because it is an action in which the Church feels herself obliged before God, by the law of Christ. In a loyal struggle: not to excite class hatred, but to guarantee to the worker a secure and stable position, like that which other classes of people already enjoyed; and so that the working class might take its place in the social community with rights equal to those of its other members.

New Duties
An Allocution to Italian Women
21 October 1945[43]

Just two months after the address to all working women, Pius XII delivered another to Italian women which ranged more widely than the world of work. For example, it dealt with marriage and the family, and woman's role as "man's partner" in married life, as well as the vocation of the celibate woman whether in religious life or not. And it alluded to the end for which "the Creator has fashioned the whole of woman's nature: not only her organism, but also and still more her spirit, and most of all here exquisite sensibility." The Pope pointed out that "social and political conditions today are, unfortunately, fraught with danger to the sanctity of the home and therefore the dignity of woman."

In a highly significant portion of this address, Pius XII explained how "various political movements" seek women's support in contending for dominance in the world. First there is a clear reference to the system in the Soviet Union which, as one of the victor nations in World War II, was just then embarking on the expansion of its empire throughout Europe:

> A certain totalitarian regime tempts here with marvelous promises: equality of rights with men; assistance during the period of gestation and labor; communal kitchens and other public services relieving her of domestic burdens; public *crèches* and other institutions, maintained and administered by the State and local authority and exempting her from her maternal obligations towards her children; education without fees; public assistance in the case of illness.

Lest there be rush to judgment of that vile system which has since succumbed to its own inherent flaws, "the regime in which capitalism is dominant" was to receive papal attention shortly. But first, Pius XII indicated: "We have no wish to deny the advantages to be derived from certain of these social measures, provided they are administered in a proper manner." Clearly he was not advocating a universal day-care culture. Instead he recalled that "we have...Ourselves insisted that, for the same work and the same service rendered, women have a right to equal pay with men."

Then turning his attention to the alternative regnant system, "capitalism," the Pope asked, "Does it offer a prospect of real welfare for woman?" The answer seemed to him a forgone conclusion, because he suggested that "we have no need here to describe the economic and social consequences of this system." Nevertheless, the Pontiff did recall a few: "the excessive crowding of the population into the cities; the ever-growing and all-invading power of big business; the difficult and precarious conditions of other industries, especially the crafts and even more especially agriculture; the disquieting spread of unemployment."

These words, it seems, are strikingly appropriate to describe capitalism also a half century later as it revived under the "new liberalism" which Paul VI and Pope John Paul II, each in turn, would later warn about. Indeed, the so-called "emancipation" of women (actually from the home and from child-bearing) that has become a hallmark also of present-day capitalistic society was an urgent part of the Communist program as outlined by Lenin long before it was imported into Western society.[44] It appears therefore that once again the two great secularized societies often end up with the same results while approaching from what are in some ways opposite directions. In any case, Pius XII offered a radically different agenda: "Restore woman as soon as possible to her place of honor in the home as housewife and mother!"

Notes

1. Vincent A. Yzermans, *The Major Addresses of Pope Pius XII* (St. Paul: North Central Publishing Co., 1961), vol. I, *Selected Addresses,* 50-58.

2. Pius XII, "On the Future of Trade Unions," *The Catholic Mind* 45 (December 1947), 707-711.

3. Heinrich Pesch, *Lehrbuch der Nationalökonomie/ Teaching Guide to Economics,* trans. Rupert J. Ederer. vol. 5, bk. 2. (Lewiston, NY: The Edwin Mellen Press, 2002), 77-114.

4. Arthur-Fridolin Utz, O.P., and Joseph-Fulko Groner, O.P., *Soziale Summe Pius XII* (Freiburg, Switzerland: Paulusverlag, 1954-1961), 1: 44-46.

5. Ibid., 2: 1705-1708.

6. Ibid., 2: 1480-1483.

7. Ibid., 1: 329-330.

8. *The Catholic Mind* 47 (September 1949), 564-565.

9. *The Catholic Mind* 46 (October 1948), 609-616.

10. *The Catholic Mind* 47 (May 1949), 303-305.

11. *The Catholic Mind* 47 (July 1949), 445-448.

12. Fr. Johannes Messner, *Dolfuss : An Austrian Patriot* (Norfolk, Va.: Gates of Vienna Books, 2004).

13. Schechter vs. United States, 1935. This decision involved a New York business which processed live poultry according to kosher standards for orthodox Jews. The Schechter brothers had been found guilty in a lower court of filing false sales and price reports and of selling diseased poultry. This put them in violation of their industry code established under the National Industrial Recovery Act. The U.S. Supreme Court ruled the Law unconstitutional, thus putting an end to the codes drawn up by various industries to regulate competition.

14. *The Catholic Mind* 48 (January 1950), 58-61.

15. Utz and Groner, 1: 148-151.

16. Utz and Groner, 2: 1488-1492.

17. Utz and Groner, 1: 331-335.

18. *The Catholic Mind* 50 (September 1952), 569-572.

19. *The Catholic Mind* 51 (January 1953), 53-56.

20. See Chap. 3, note 10: Pius XII, *Address to Austrian Catholics*, 14 September 1952.

21. See note 17 above.

22. See note 2 above.

23. Utz and Groner, 1: 336-340.

24. *Discorsi e Radiomessaggi di Sua Santità Pio XII,* 1953, 129-131.

25. Utz and Groner, 3: 3685-3686.

26. Utz and Groner, 3: 3528-3530.

27. Utz and Groner, 3: 3613-3618.

28. *The Pope Speaks*, 2, 2 (Summer 1955), 169-172.

29. Ibid., 141-142, 142-143, 163-167.

30. Ibid., 154-158.

31. Ibid., 159-162.

32. Utz and Groner, 3: 3697-3698.

33. Ibid., 45-53.

34. *The Catholic Mind,* 54, 1123 (July 1956), 403-408.

35. *The Pope Speaks,* 3, 4, (Spring 1957), 411-416.

36. *The Pope Speaks*, 4, 2 (Autumn 1957), 147-155.

37. Ibid., 4, 4 (Spring 1958), 409-411.

38. Utz and Groner, 3: 3703-3706.

39. *Discorsi e Radiomessaggi di Sua Santità Pio XII*, 1958 (2 March to 9 October), 149-150.

40. The author of this work, born in Munich in 1923 while the Jesuit was immersed in his apostolate there, was named by his parents in honor of Father Rupert Mayer. That apostolate involved also encounters with Nazis and Marxists who were both engaged in a contest to take over Germany, starting with Catholic Bavaria.

41. Utz and Groner, 3: 2687-2692.

42. *The Woman in the Modern World* (Boston: Daughters of St. Paul, 1959), 124-142.

43. Ibid., 127-142.

44. Cf. a little-noted book edited by Lenin's wife, entitled *Lenin: On the Emancipation of Women*, published in 1934. It is a part of the English-language publication of Lenin's *Collected Works,* first printed in 1965 by Progress Publishers in Moscow. It already contained all of the standard jargon employed by the militant feminists in the Western world in our own time.

Chapter 6
On Agriculture and Farmers

Frequently throughout his pontificate Pius XII addressed farmers, demonstrating his concern for the problems which faced them as an especially important group within the national economy overall. As indicated elsewhere, in this respect he anticipated John XXIII, who was the first pope to devote specific attention to the agricultural sector in a social encyclical.[1] Commentators have noted how that popular Pope's own roots in a poor agricultural region of northern Italy may have influenced his special insight as reflected in his influential encyclical, *Mater et Magistra.* In any case, here, as so often, Pius XII, who issued no specifically social encyclicals of his own, was the forerunner of many important teachings by his successors.

The Basis and Importance of a Healthy Agricultural Class
Address to the National Farmers' League of Italy
15 November 1946[2]

After brief quotations from the Roman poet Virgil (*Eclogues* and *Georgics*) and Plinius (*Natural History*) about the virtues of rural life, Pius XII affirmed the critical importance that a class of farmers, integrated in an orderly manner in society and firm in its religious convictions, has for the moral health of nation. Farmers comprise not only consumer communities, but also, and especially, producer communities who make available the bounty that a benevolent Creator has stored for us in the earth. From their ranks come upright citizens who take their places in all walks of life, providing also religious vocations.

From a healthy peasantry come those virtues which maintain the strength of a nation: a capacity for hard work, a simple and honest lifestyle, respect for authority, especially of parents, love of the homeland and faithfulness to traditions which have been so beneficial over the centuries: mutual assistance not only within the family, but among families, from homestead to homestead, and finally, true religious spirit without which all of that would not endure, but yield instead to unrestrained profit-seeking. He expressed the hope that an upright fear of God and confidence in Him along with a vital faith as expressed in family prayer would govern the everyday lives of farm families, and that the Church would remain the heart of the village.

Alluding to the still prevalent family farm enterprise, the Pope stressed its right to a return that would support its members in decent style. What he was speaking of was, in effect, the right to a just family wage as applied also to the hard-working farm family. It would not do, therefore, to strive simply for the highest possible and quickest return for the benefit of the national economy, or for the cheapest possible provision of farm products, while sacrificing the farm producer's own welfare and sustenance to those ends. He indicated that farms, in particular as family enterprises, are entitled to all of the advantages which other businesses enjoy, even while avoiding the handicaps that face them. Thus farm operators should be adaptable, alert and diligent cultivators of their domestic lands, using these but never exploiting them. He should be progressive also in applying capital, whether his own, or that provided by others, to the extent that this is of advantage and does not endanger the future of the family. They should be honest as sellers, not greedy calculators who harm their own nation.

After setting forth an almost idyllic picture of what farming and farm life should be, Pius XII established the grim, present-day reality that its people often face in our time. There is the ever-present temptation to look for easy gain that speculates at the expense of neighbor, instead of being content to earn one's bread by the sweat of one's brow. Sometimes it is even the fault of parents who fail to provide proper spiritual training and education for their children. Also the schools and professional training may be at fault. Unfortunately, there are those who feel that the farmer does not need a basic and appropriate training for work that is so varied and subject to the changes of season.

Whereas original sin made working the land tedious, it did not introduce such work into the world. Before the Fall, God had entrusted the earth to man for him to cultivate and manage. It was intended to be a most noble and honorable occupation. But the sin of our first parents persists in its effects, and also our own sins have gone on to make life ever more burdensome. The land was harmed over the course of the ages by floods, earthquakes, pestilence and wars, so that the soil often was turned to infertile desert waste where work became uncommonly difficult. For example, in our own time the land often conceals deadly land mines left from warfare, which remain buried under the soil awaiting their victims. And so it no longer lavishes its fruits without great effort on man's part: "The earth is gravely wounded; it is gravely ill." Thus, "the farmer expends his care not like the slave bent over the clods of ground, but like the doctor bent over his patient with loving care." However, even that "loving care" is not enough by itself. What is necessary in addition is careful examination of the parcel of land "to ascertain what harmful seeds lie buried, what rodents are at work, what worms eat its fruits, what weeds are harmful to the harvest of crops, what minerals are lacking, so that a proper rotation of crops can be applied."

So much for nature and what are, to some extent, the ravages of original sin and the sinfulness of mankind afterwards. There is also the question of reforms in the way property ownership has emerged. However, the Pope warned that before such measures are undertaken, there is a whole other area that requires attention. Especially today, great caution is called for, lest actions are inspired by "pure demagoguery," which then prove harmful instead of beneficial. Too often in history, the peasantry has been seduced by the "cries of agitators" so that they ended up as "hapless objects of exploitation." In our time the dichotomy between urban and rural life presents a special difficulty in this area, especially to the extent that the life of the farmer is rooted in the family and is close to nature.

Thus, we are faced now with the steady growth of large cities with dense habitation. And that, said the Pope, is the outcome of the "predominance of the interests of big capital over economic life; and not only over economic life, but throughout all of human culture."

That, incidentally, suggests a proper and accurate definition of capitalism, which is superior to those found or intimated in many economic textbooks, even though this happens to be close to the Marxian conception.[3] However, Pius XII was referring here to his predecessor, Pius XI, who cited the predominant role of capitalism and profit-seeking in the encyclical *Quadragesimo Anno.* In the capitalist milieu "the quest for profit rather than the human needs based on the objective and natural meaning of economic life come to decide which wants are to be satisfied and to what degree." Thus, "human work which is directed to the common good does not take capital and press it into its service, but the reverse happens: capital takes on labor and people themselves and puts them into play like a ball." Powerful words, those! And since, unlike Marxist doctrine, Catholic social teaching does not denigrate human labor to the status of a commodity, it is vastly more vibrant and valid as a doctrine. But there is more:

> Even while the city dweller suffers from this unnatural condition, his status contrasts even more to the intrinsic condition of farm life. For, despite all of the difficulties facing the latter, the farmer still reflects the natural order intended by God: the human person and his work still predominate over material things, instead of things predominating over human beings.

Now we move to the crux of the precarious relationship between the city and the countryside surrounding it. Pius XII stated that city life "actually forms different kinds of people" than country life.

> And that contrast becomes the greater, the more capital falls short of its noble purpose—promoting the welfare of society in all of its families. It injects delusion into the life of farmers parading before their eyes gold and glitter and a life of ease. Thus they are tempted to abandon the land and move into the cities which by and large offer them only disappointments, cause them to use up their hard-earned savings, and all too often cost them their health and vitality, joy and honor, in fact even their very souls.

And what about capital? It exploits the abandoned land and turns it from the object of love, which it was for the farmers, to an object of cold exploitation. What follows is a bleak picture. "The same land that used to provide nourishment for the cities as well as for the country people now produces merely for speculation, and while the people suffer from hunger and the farmer is burdened with debt, moving toward ruin, the economy of the nation is drained by having to import food supplies from other countries at a high price."

The Pope warned that socialism scarcely provides a remedy for this juxtaposition of farm and city people. In other words, abandoning private ownership of land in favor of state ownership only makes matters worse, since the love and interest which farm owners had for their land is now lost. Besides, where the state appropriates the capital and means of production completely, once again the interests of industry and foreign trade that were of primary concern to cities predominate. "What gets lost in the process is the basic teaching found in the Church's social doctrine, that the economy of a nation constitutes an organic whole where the productive forces of the nation must be developed in a healthy reciprocal relationship to each other." Had this concept been recognized and acted on, the opposition between the city and the country would never have reached its present proportions.

Those thoughts lead into a proposal by Pius XII in addressing the representatives of farming interests. Given their importance in the economic order, what is needed is a sensible economic policy and appropriate legislative structure to assist them. Then a precaution! First and foremost they must help themselves by means of their cooperatives and their systems for providing credit. Then the rural economic sector may even be instrumental in restoring the health of the entire economy.

The parting admonition recalls what is basic in Catholic teaching with regard to the social order. Pius XII affirmed the importance of the economy as a working community. Farmers with their families assisting them constitute such a community. But they are a part of the wider agricultural community. And ultimately they should strive to integrate themselves into a working community made up of all other occupational groups in the nation, since that is the order corresponding to what God and nature require. That, said the Pope, is "the true Catholic concept of work." Work is destined to unite people for common service in meeting the needs of all the people of a nation, "because such common effort is intended for one's fulfillment and for the honor of the Creator and Redeemer."

In that context, the basic just wage principle is affirmed again as having its proper place also in the context of farm life. "Your work is to be regarded as the contribution of yourself and your family to the national economy." Therefore, "you have the right to an adequate income to provide for the needs of yourself and your family in accordance with your human dignity at the given cultural level." This presupposes "the recognition of the requisite bond with all other occupational groups which also work to provide for the various needs." That, according to the Pope, constitutes the farmers' "contribution to social peace."

This was a most powerful message! In addition to a clear reference of the just wage doctrine as implicit also in agricultural life, and the other traditional teaching about harmony among occupational groups in the economy, there were timely warnings against the socialist siren song about socialization of land ownership. At the same time, there was a scorching indictment of what capitalism has wrought also in the agricultural sector of economic life. Beyond that there were substantial reflections of "the theology of work" that would be presented in definitive form many years later in the encyclical *Laborem Exercens* by Pope John Paul II. We find human work as the predominant active factor of production, with capital as merely an "instrumental cause." We have here an altogether pace-setting message specifically for the people involved in providing their fellow citizens with food and other basic sustenance. Additional messages would follow. Few would excel it in its sweep and incisiveness.

The Farmer's Status as a Pressing Problem of Social Order
Letter to the Leaders of the Social Week of Canada
31 August 1947[4]

The occasion of the 24th meeting of Social Week of Canada afforded Pius XII his second opportunity to address the pressing problems facing agriculture, its important place in the national economy, and the trials facing hard-working farm people. He opened with a lament that sociologists and politicians appeared in our time to prefer devoting attention to problems related to the aggregation of huge industrial complexes.

While making due allowance for the importance of that sector of economic life, the Pope insisted that one of the main causes of distortion in the world economy and "at the same time in civilization and culture overall," is to be found in the decline and even defamation of agricultural life in all of its various aspects. Once again, as in the previous message, he alluded to ancient Rome as a starting point for the discussion. Here he suggested that there is a connection between the denigration of rural life and the decline of Rome and its civilization. However, alarms were already sounded precisely in areas where industry was making great strides, suggesting that a "healthy, vigorous farm population with deep-seated Christian convictions" was essential for society.

As for the religious and moral aspect of this issue, it is clear that farm work of its nature promotes the "physical and moral health" of society. That is because nothing bolsters "the resiliency of body and soul like this beneficial direct contact with nature.... The earth does not deceive; it is not subject to the caprices, the temptations and artificial, feverish fascinations that characterize city life." Instead it is marked by "constancy, rhythmic regularity, a deliberate pace, the majesty of the change of seasons, all of which are reflections of the Divine Nature."

Beyond those qualities of rural life, there are also the economic and technical aspects to be considered, in particular as they involve "social justice and the general welfare." Serious consideration of the elevation of the rural workers' status was all the more important at this point in history—just two years after World War II ended. The world was still hard pressed by hunger that urgently called for increasing the yield of agriculture, while at the same time improving the lot of those who undertake to grow food for a hard-pressed world. Only prompt attention in this area, according to the Pope, would at the same time stem the great exodus from the farm by assuring rural people of the significance of their role and instilling the requisite pride in their important and noble calling.

The Question of Agricultural Reform
Papal Letter Transmitted by J. B. Montini to the 22nd Social Week at Naples
September 15, 1947[5]

The future Pope Paul VI once again acted on behalf of Pius XII to deliver this message to the conferees in Naples. The very nature of the gathering demonstrated, he said, that the issues involved are "religious, ethical-moral, as well as economic and social problems." He indicated that nowadays even rural life, "where in the past the purity of the air normally reflected the purity of the morals, was tainted by that moral neo-paganism which is the greatest danger of our time."

Following the tremendous disruptions in the equilibrium of economic life and life on the farm caused by World War II, the issue of agricultural reform also became an issue in Italy where various proposals were forthcoming. Italian Catholics who are aware of and cherish the Christian social teachings proposed in papal encyclicals seek to avoid "both of the false and harmful extremes, namely those of agnostic-liberal 'individualism,' and Marxian 'collectivism.'" There is a stern warning against the "extravagant promises and deceptive hopes arising from the agitation of demagogues on the one hand, and the blind rejection of any changes at all." The latter course is associated with "the egotism of those who have abundance, so that they identify the status quo with what is just and right, thereby opposing the kinds of reforms which are actually called for by the common good."

Here the message recalls the twofold character of private ownership: the individual function and the social function. "The former operates to fulfill the legitimate needs of those who own property;" and the other must serve also to see to "the essential needs of all members of the human family."

That general principle applies to every kind of private ownership, but it has special importance in the area of land ownership, which is "the first source of life and of the general welfare."

Here the message referred back to the encyclical *Rerum Novarum,* where Leo XIII indicated that the land, even though it is divided up among private owners, remains dedicated "to the well-being and service of all, since there is no one on earth who does not derive nourishment from it." And Pius XI in *Quad-*

ragesimo Anno reaffirmed that double aspect of private property, adding that it is within the legitimate power of the state to intervene so that the use of land will in fact serve all. Finally, there is reference to the 1942 *Christmas Message* by Pius XII which made "access to the goods of the earth normal and natural on the basis of personal human dignity." Thus, while the right of private ownership is basic for all, the manner and form which that right assumes is subject to change and may be more or less restricted.

The message ended with a stern reminder that the Lord has entrusted to "all Catholics, clerical and lay, the social teachings of the Church as a talent which no one may bury without incurring the severe punishment meted out to the 'wicked and slothful servant' mentioned in the Bible." (Matt. 25: 26)

Economic Policy and Agriculture
Address to the FAO
21 February 1948[6]

This was a brief message of approbation and encouragement to the Food and Agricultural Organization recently established in Rome as an organ of the then scarcely three year old United Nations Organization. Pius XII credited the FAO with aiding nations in overcoming the fear which dire poverty causes and the indignity of having to beg for subsistence. All are placed in a "position of reciprocal solidaristically related debtors and creditors."

The Pope pointed out that it is entirely proper to direct special attention to improvements in the conditions facing the rural population. In good times they are in the forefront among those who nurture us all, but they also tend to be the first victims of natural disasters as well as of wars, when some areas become unworkable because of their location. He recommended the Church's social teaching to the audience, indicating that it by no means clashes with natural ethics. Indeed, there is a resonance here with Christ's own assurance that he came not to abolish the law but to fulfill it. At the same time, the Church has always followed the example of its Founder who took pity on the multitude and multiplied the loaves and the fish, even while reminding them "that man does not live by bread alone."

Problems in the World of Agriculture
Address Before the First International Congress for the Problems of Agriculture
2 July 1951[7]

On this occasion, Pius XII spoke before a group that was devoted to Christian principles and Catholic social teachings, seeking to determine how they should be applied in the world of agriculture. That world included not only the actual farmers who raise crops and livestock to nourish their fellow human beings, but also others who lived in rural areas where they rendered various services to the primary producers. He pointed out that, as a matter of fact, the majority of the human race still lives in a rural ambience, whether on farms, or in rural villages and market centers. Furthermore, what affects such a large portion of the population directly has a great impact also on the rest of mankind. Accordingly, the state itself is affected and concerned, as is the Church, by the influence which rural life has on man's biological, intellectual, spiritual, and religious development.

Once again Pius XII referred to his predecessor Pius XI and his encyclical *Quadragesimo Anno.* The latter had spoken of the beneficial and harmful consequences of the "economic system of industrial capitalism." In considering the influence which that system had on the overall development of the economy—an influence which, the Pope indicated, still continues inasmuch as it had a tremendous impact also on "the spiritual, social and material conditions of the rural population." Indeed, he pointed out, the fate of all of mankind could be said to lie in the balance. So, "will it succeed or not in harnessing this influence properly, allowing the spiritual, social, and economic life of the agricultural world to retain its own physiognomy so that it will be able to play, if not a dominant, nevertheless an equal role in human society overall?"

The Pontiff pointed out that there is no legitimate occasion for conflict between the industrial and agricultural sectors. The division of labor and of functions in the economy do not, of themselves, give rise to such conflicts. Indeed, everyone must concede that the economic system of industrial capitalism has contributed immensely to increasing agricultural production, and that it has led in some parts of the world to greatly improving the bodily and spiritual lives of the rural population. Thus, there is no cause to overthrow that system, but only to beware of the danger that it would try to alter rural life by impressing its own character on it to such a degree as to make of it simply "an extension of the city."

What followed was a keen observation of how Marxism has sought to accomplish that blending of farm production with what the Pope called here "the superstition of technicalizing and exaggerated industrialization." He was referring, of course, to the "collectivization" of farm labor into "a kind of factory, degrading the rural area into a mere reserve of labor power for industrial production." So much for Marxism! Pius XII was quick to point out: "the basic principles of economic liberalism lead to the same result once the craving for profit on the part of finance capitalism takes hold of economic life, and when the principles of the national economy look one-sidedly on the market as a mere price mechanism." Then the rural population suffers the same consequences as the industrial workers: it becomes a "mere reserve of labor power or it drifts toward a miserable existence that is subjected to the most dangerous tensions."

Even if industrial capitalism is not "the sole cause of flight from the land that is now taking place almost everywhere, this dominant role of the interests of industrial capital in production and in the distribution of income does play a large role." And it would be foolish to shrug it off as merely an "abandonment" of the land, since it is actually more like "a flight." That often results in large tracts of land remaining uncultivated, or subject to exploitative cultivation which eventually damages the natural fertility of the soil, with consequent serious harm to the national economy. Now we are faced with decisions whether to continue pursuing short-term, one-sided gain, or whether we want to even this out to embrace the entire economy. For example, there are measures like the support for "backward areas," agrarian reform proposals that have already been undertaken here and there, agreements on emigration and immigration, and a better distribution of productive resources nationwide. Wherever such steps are taken, the Pope urged that they should take into account preserving the special character of the rural population, to enable them to retain "their own particular influence and value in the economy and in society."

Pius XII followed that warning about harm which may befall the rural population, with what remains a most impressive cataloging of the downside of industrialization. It is worth presenting verbatim:

> In considering the harm which may befall the rural population, we must take a hard look at the mistakes and frictions in human relations stemming from the working world of industrial capitalism. We lament the fact that work has "lost its soul," i.e., the personal and social sense of human life; we complain that it is oppressed on all sides by a giant network of organizations, and that human life in this context has been transformed into a huge automatism where people become mere small, unconscious cogs in the machinery; and we object that technology has "standardized" all motion to the detriment of the individuality and the personality of the worker.

While avoiding the most extreme ramifications of distributism, that warning is almost Chestertonian in its dimensions. What better antidote to the predominance of that kind of world than the family farm? Pius XII indicated that while there is no single panacea for resolving the problem, the work of the farmer certainly erects "a mighty wall" against it. And he was referring specifically to the "family farm enterprise." While not rejecting "the usefulness and sometimes the necessity of larger farm operations," or the undeniable benefits of "modern technology," he nevertheless extolled the special advantages of the family farm. It is there that we find a kind of people who are in constant direct contact with nature as God has created it and controls it. Thus they know from daily experience out in the field that "human life rests in the hand of the Creator." No other portion of the work force is "so suited to family life as a spiritual, economic, and legal unit, even with reference to production and consumption." The work may be hard, but "man is still the lord of his world by his activity in the midst of society."[8]

Pius XII concluded this discourse by disclaiming adherence to any "romanticism which is out of touch with reality." He warned that it would take great patience and resourcefulness to restore the agricultural world to a sound condition, and to overcome the attraction among rural people to a world in which they are strangers. In addition, modern social legislation must extend its benefits to them also, with due regard for their special character. That would include, among other things, the possibility of getting proper training in their chosen occupation. And for Catholics, the Pope added the proviso that they should be assured a "solid Catholic education."

Once again, this great teaching Pope set the pace for his successors, especially John XXIII. The value of the family farm and measures to assure its continuance would soon be the objects of special attention in *Mater et Magistra.*

The Social Importance of Farmer Associations
Address before the Members of the Italian Farmers' Association
29 February 1952[9]

The association in question here was the *Confederazione Nationale dei Coltivatori Diretti.* Its leaders had come before Pius XII previously in November of 1946 when Italy, like much of Europe, still lay in the desolate ruins left by World War II. The organization was founded to help lift Italian agriculture from the desperate condition in which it then found itself.

Here the Pope presented an interesting reflection on certain traits peculiar to the rural population. Country people tend to be more pensive and therefore less likely to be swayed by promises of quick solutions, while at the same time preoccupied with the interests of themselves and their families. That, he pointed out, has a positive as well as a shadowy aspect. The farmer tends to be somewhat slow in taking action. And he wants to deal with his own problems by himself. Thus his horizons tend to narrow, while failing to take into account that his destiny is tied to what is happening around him. He fails to recognize sometimes that if others are having a difficult time, he will eventually suffer also. That was a handicap which hampered the group previously, but it had grown in size and importance.

Pius XII then offered three "paternal guidelines" for the Association. The first, once again, involved a Roman classic—Virgil's *Aeneid*—"*Audentes fortuna juvat*:" "Fortune comes to the assistance of the venturesome." Another version might be: "God helps those who help themselves." Translated for the situation at hand, the Pope proposed that the organization should make a special effort to arouse the interest of young people in the rural areas. Specifically, they should be offered courses of study that would sharpen their skills in agricultural pursuits, while at the same time indicating what the obligations were in that area.

The second proposal stressed the importance of the family as the solid foundation of the economy. It is "the source of your bodily and spiritual strength, the secret of your influence and your importance in the state and in politics." Then came this rather dramatic proposal: "To save the family, direct your attention to the rural proletariat: it must disappear!"

The third point: "reflect on God and love Him." "No one can accomplish anything without Him." And "no one can forget him, least of all the farmer." That is because no one more than he senses his daily dependence on God's largesse for rain and sunshine. "Even the wonderful advances in technology are of no avail if God, in His goodness and mercy, does not support our efforts." And while it is true that God permits the sun to shine and the rain to fall for both the good and the wicked, it is a mistake to take His bounty for granted as though we had it coming to us. We have an obligation to pray and to show our gratitude.

The Value of Agricultural Science for the World Economy
Address to the Ninth International Congress of Agricultural Industries
29 May 1952[10]

As occurred with increasing frequency during the pontificate of Pius XII, this address too included an endorsement of the principle of solidarity. It opened with praise for the "reciprocal assistance" implicit in the goals of this organization, which "affirm the bonds between man and man and between nation and nation for the benefit of all mankind." Indeed it is the "ever closer and more clearly discerned reciprocal interdependence among all groups of people which evokes the exchange of information and material assistance." He warned that while "the largest part of humanity cannot get enough food, with many regions experiencing periodic hunger and starvation, an egotistical denial of the available advantages which would alleviate such problems is simply not acceptable." The needy people, in fact, "have a legitimate right to them."

The specific expression, "solidarity," the meaning and dimensions of which were clearly indicated in the opening portion of this address, was used by the Pontiff in the closing paragraph. Pointing out how the deeper understanding of nature by scientists and technicians has led to ever-improved means for assisting one's neighbor, Pius XII suggested that while following the law of work imposed on mankind by God, people gain an ever deeper understanding of the wise plan of Divine providence: "It enables them to perceive better that close solidarity which binds all people and makes them dependent on one another, recognizing that the material life of each is to some degree the work of all."

The Pope concluded with the supplication: "May the awareness of this solidarity spread and deepen; may cooperation in research, the increase of information, the occupational quality of the researchers, the noble selflessness of the individuals and of the various groups multiply the daily exchange and make the useful knowledge, experiences and assistance accessible to all!"

The Pope thus forecasted here remarkably the precise definition of solidarity offered by Pope John Paul II in his encyclical *Sollicitudo Rei Socialis,* many years later.

Agriculture as an Integrating Segment of the Economy Overall
Address to the Members of the International Association of Agricultural Producers
11 June 1953[11]

The broad scope of this particular organization, which incorporates national groups from some 30 nations, provides further evidence of that selfsame solidarity elaborated on in the previous message. Here, however, Pius XII alluded to the great difficulty involved in getting across even "the most useful ideas once they run afoul of vested interests." He indicated how experience has certainly demonstrated that often, unfortunately, "common sense is not enough to gain the acceptance of rational solutions." What is needed also is great determination and dedication. Thus, anyone who represents the interests of others and works toward their realization "must be absorbed by the will to serve." Also, "he must be firmly convinced of the rectitude of his action, and plod ahead without stopping to count the costs."

In praising the goals of this organization—helping those who provide the essential means of subsistence for the rest of mankind—the Pope returned to the theme of the terrible imbalance between sectors where production must be cut back because it is unprofitable, and entire nations in which people face malnutrition and starvation. The remedy lies in "a restoration and sensible stabilization of economic relations among nations, and that does not apply only to agriculture."

Anyone who is familiar with the Church's social teachings "is able to detect an essential flaw ever since the advent of modern industrialism." It lies in the fact that "the economy has become a mere appendage of industry and, above all of the market." The Pope therefore urged the members of this organization to work for a "better organization of the markets, for a strengthening of trade, and improvement in the living standard of the great family of agricultural producers."

Economic and Cultural Self-Help on the Part of the Rural Community
A Letter to the Organization of Irish Agricultural People
14 July 1954[12]

Here we have a letter addressed to the head of an Irish agricultural society—*Muintir na Tíre*—headed by John M. Hayes and founded 17 years previously. Pius XII commended the group for not allowing "the children of the light" to be outdone, as his predecessor Pius XI had mentioned in *Quadragesimo Anno,* " by "the children of darkness." He was referring to its earnest study and application of the Church's social teachings. And he praised specifically the members' attempts to "put into practice justice and charity…in a spirit of self-help, while contributing to the general welfare even at significant personal sacrifices." The theme, "reciprocal aid" as applied not only in one's own family, but "from family to family and from house to house," was repeated here, along with the reminder that "the most important and most basic element in genuine agricultural culture is a true religious spirit."

St. Pius X is not usually cited for social teachings, since he issued no "social encyclicals" in the strict sense of that term. Yet, Pius XII did refer here to that Pope whom he had canonized a short time before, citing a significant passage from his encyclical *Il Fermo Proposito—On Catholic Action in Italy* (1905). In it the Holy Pope indicated that he wanted the motto of his pontificate—*To Restore All Things in Christ*—applied in such a way as to "take to heart the interests of the people, especially those of the working and agricultural classes, not only by inculcating in the hearts of everybody a true religious spirit...but also by endeavoring to dry their tears, to alleviate their sufferings, and to improve their economic condition by wise measures."

Pius XII concluded with his blessing on the Irish organization for its ongoing efforts to improve the lot of the farmers of their land. He cited again the special advantages and virtues that went with agricultural life, as well as the threats posed to it by flight to the cities, especially among the young.

Farming: Model of Human Effort
Discourse to the Italian National Federation of Farmers
18 May 1955[13]

Pius XII noted that this was the third time he addressed the organization founded in 1944, which he characterized as representing "one of the most substantial social and moral supports of the nation." It was a group "in accord with the principles of Catholic social doctrine," that "respond[s] most completely to human life, both in its natural and its supernatural aspects." They are principles that "give rise to the search for a solution of the problems emanating from the rapid development of the economy and the general conditions of society." Accordingly, they would lead to "the building of a world less harsh, less saturated with materialism, less a slave to the constant seeking of mere personal advantage."

The message also contains the ever-present words of paternal counsel. The Pope saw the Federation as rendering a valuable service in that it makes its members "...fully aware of the part that concerns them in the economic life of the nation." One can discern the drift toward papal concern about solidarity. He cautions its members to "free themselves from a 'local loyalty,' sometimes rather tenacious and easily understandable in the worker on the land, who is strongly attached to his own earth and not easily led to lift his gaze to wider horizons." It is a widely accepted fact that farmers, by the nature of their work, which involves so much self-reliance, tend toward an individualistic outlook. Therefore, Pius XII urged them to concern themselves also with "the general good," and to apply their energies also to the "national interest." He then mentioned again the specific term, "solidarity": "Your organization, by giving strength to the sense of solidarity among farm-owners, brings to their activity an increased efficiency and a breadth which are justified by the lofty virtues of their familiar traditions and their attachment to their native soil."

There is praise for the "personal risk" which is a part and parcel of the farmer's vocation. It is seen as "exposed to risk precisely because it is the model—at present insufficiently recognized—of human effort, an effort which always gives to the life of nations the guarantee of continuance and fruitfulness."

The Pontiff expressed his approval of the Federation's efforts to get social benefits extended to farmers, such as insurance against illness, against disability and old age. In addition there had been action "for the stabilization and protection of produce in times of emergency." He was gratified that the group had apparently taken action also on certain of his recommendations to them in 1952 with regard to the farm family. There were initiatives directed toward young people, specifically in the area of training courses "which will equip them later on to fulfill their noble task with competence." Long before the contemporary strident feminist movement appeared on the scene, this progressive Pope urged the "farmers' union to strive to get rural women to take part in the life of the union." That was "in addition to their role of wife and mother, a part more or less important in the work itself."

Involving the family as the "foundation of your economy" helps to "overcome the great temptation of our time to which so many yield." Pius XII was talking about the excessive concern about simply

> a higher living standard and constantly increasing productivity as the fulfillment of man's desire for prosperity.... Mere abundance of goods at low prices, the mere lightening and lessening of the strain of work are doubtful benefits, as they do not remove anxiety for the future; rather they increase it to the extent that they arouse inordinate desires, and never satisfy man.

That followed a statement, pregnant with significance, the more so a generation later when people seem unsure of even a proper definition of "the family." Pius XII said that "...even in the economic field, the family stands for what is lasting, for what assures the continuance of future generations."

He concluded with encouragement for the Federation's assistance in "the formation and development of small estates." That was in response to land reform, which provided "many families of farm-workers" with "a bit of land." Among them there were praiseworthy efforts to develop cooperatives, "a powerful instrument for the preservation and progress of the new rural communities."

A Farmer's Three Duties
Address to the Confederations of Italian Tenant Farmers
11 April 1956[14]

This address is unique among those addressed to farmers, in that it was directed to those who do not own farms, but who work on land owned by others. Tenant farmers, like other workers, are vulnerable to what Pius XII called here the "suggestions and programs of all sorts...being continually offered." Thus, "they are often unable to distinguish between what is just and what is unjust, between their rights and avarice, between freedom and slavery." He proposed as the proper criterion: "whether these programs are in accord with or in opposition to the principles of Christian social teaching."

What followed was an excellent litany of the qualities of that teaching. It is

> the result of the fullest vision of reality; it is based on the eternal order established by God, and manifested in nature; it is designed to safeguard the dignity of the human person, which is the beginning and the end of relations between men; it is not restricted to the unilateral interests of a single class; it reflects the just hierarchy of values; it does not sacrifice one good for another, but tends to harmonize them all in justice and in charity.

The Pope then presented a most cogent reason why his audience, in fact anyone, should pay close attention to the principles of Catholic social teaching. "From it you can learn what your duties are, as well as your rights in a well ordered society."

There followed a disclaimer that has become a standard whenever the Catholic Church ventured into teaching about the economic order. "It is not Our business to define the particular provisions that society ought to adopt in order to fulfill its obligation of coming to the assistance of the rural population." However those proposed by this particular Confederation "are in accordance with the duties which society has towards you." And they actually amount to an exhaustive and quite detailed program for agricultural reform. Included are: "a wider diffusion of agricultural ownership and its productive development; the placing of farmers who are not property owners in the position of salaried employees working under contract with an income sufficient to insure their stability on the lands cultivated by them, and to facilitate their rise to full property rights, preserving, of course, the regard due to productivity, to the rights of the owners, and above all to their investments; encouraging them with concrete assistance to improve their method of cultivating the soil and their patrimony of livestock in such a way that it will increase their income as well as the prosperity of the nation; by promoting in their favor those forms of assistance and insurance which are common among other groups of laborers, but administered according to the special conditions of the farmer; promoting the technical training, especially of the young men, in keeping with modern rational methods which are in continual progress; and finally, taking pains to remove the acute difference between agricultural and industrial income, which is the cause of the abandonment of the countryside to the great disadvantage of an economy which in a country like yours, is based in large part upon agricultural production."

Exhaustive as that listing may be, Pius XII took the liberty to add to the agenda a few programs which he felt "derive from the particular conditions which prevail in your country districts." They include "adequate housing, with roads, with schools, with aqueducts, with electric power, with visiting doctors."

Any migrant farm worker in the wealthy and powerful United States would welcome the realization of even a small portion of those proposals! That all comes with a precautionary admonition by the Pontiff. Admitting "your right to ask the nation for these and other services," he warned the tenant farmers "not to ask for them without taking account of what the nation can actually do, or with the impatience of those who regard the State as the mere servant of individuals or of particular classes."

The Pope then proceeded to present what was the paternal core of this message. He outlined "three duties" for his sons and daughters who toil on the landed estates of others: "cultivating yourselves, as laborers, as members of society, and as sons of God."

As for the role as "laborers," this involves certain adjustments. While "it is commonly said that 'nature does everything' in the fields," one may not overlook the fact that "nature waits to be assisted and directed by the intelligence and hands of men in unfolding its almost unlimited energy to the advantage of mankind." Therefore, since the farmer's work "is a kind of cooperation with the creative work of God," it is necessary to be "aware that modern science has discovered and is constantly opening up new methods of reinforcing man's collaboration." Hence, farm workers must "know, study, and apply the methods suggested by science," and they must be willing to abandon "primitive systems of trial and error, which constitute not only a waste of human energy, but a serious loss of results" which are "the more deplorable where, as is the case among you, the land is inadequate for the number of its inhabitants." They must allow themselves "to be guided by those who recognize in agriculture a science and an art." And closely related to that acceptance, "the young must be encouraged to acquire modern professional training, by being provided with the time and the means for it."

The role of farm workers as members of society stems from the fact, as Pius XII told them here, "that they still continue to be the good sap of a mighty tree." In other words, agriculture, "especially in Italy, has been and is the very basis of the national life, whether one considers its important contribution in the economic sphere, or the wholesomeness, vigor, and sound morality by which it is distinguished." He went on to catalogue its contribution of "countless saints and famous scientists, artists, political leaders and patriots." An awareness of that was clearly intended to bolster the self-esteem of farmers who, since they are "somewhat isolated," may develop a feeling that they are "in a position that is inferior to that of other citizens."

Then the Pope turned to the young people "who are so frequently tempted to abandon the countryside by a deceptive dream of an easier life in the cities." He admonished them to not be taken in by "echoes," which "come to you from the large cities, by means of the press, the radio, the television, and the cinema," which have a "tendency to obscure your vision of reality." He also made them aware of a "law of compensation" at work here. For example, "the high wages in the city are decimated by the easy opportunities of spending;" and "the spectacular amusements are not worth the loss of serene hours spent in a peaceful family circle." "Nor do abundant conveniences compensate one for the loss of independence, of health, of security for the future, which are the prerogatives of life in the country." Another warning counseled the young that, if they feel that they must change their occupation, "take care not to base your choice on glittering and empty appearances."

Finally, a painful awareness of certain moral and spiritual dangers that all too often confront rural workers led Pius XII to the third duty facing them. While it is "commonly said that the farmer is nearer to God because he assists, as it were, hour by hour in the marvels of God's providence," the overall picture is not that idyllic. On the minus side there is, "the farmer's unending work, lack of facilities, and even distance from church," which may "prevent the religious seed planted in his heart from germinating and ripening into fruits of instruction, of religious practices, and of genuine sanctity."

While the Church in modern times has made it a point to send "zealous priests to establish themselves in the rural districts and to attend to their spiritual needs," there are "new conditions of rural life" that "have raised not a few problems, spiritual as well as material...." Apparently referring to a modish alienation between rural dwellers and their priests, the Pope urged them: "keep yourselves in close contact with your priests," and "break the ice of frigid hostility if it exists."

In a bucolic conclusion, Pius XII told his audience: "And whenever the melodious sound of a bell, in harmony with the whisper of the wind, the murmur of flowing water, and the chirping of the birds, is heard abroad, like a voice calling upon you to think of heaven, and promising God's blessing upon the furrows and the crops watered by your sweat, elevate your thoughts to God in a fervent prayer of thanksgiving and propitiation."

This ranks among the foremost of the Pope's messages to the agricultural community. Its structure is excellent; its message, cogent; its pretensions, realistic.

The Modernization of Farm Life in the Spirit of Christianity
A Letter to the Participants in the First General Meeting of International Movement of Farmers and Rural Youth
August 2, 1956[15]

The first international gathering of this youth group was held in the Netherlands. Pius XII related how its members would "undoubtedly be the ones who would experience the consequences—immediate or eventual—of new technology in the operation of farms." And he challenged them to accept their responsibility as Christians. "Is it not the business of the Church's children to be active amid the ranks of working humanity, so as to safeguard it from threatening aberrations, and to work toward the establishment of the kingdom of Jesus Christ in the spirit of faith and of charity?"

The Pontiff also encouraged them to study the impact of technology and of social patterns on youthful spirits, and how that would influence their religious life. At this point he challenged them to also rely "with supernatural trust on the riches which belong to you," referring to the "treasury of your Church's teachings." Those teachings were a part of the ever-young message of Christianity which could renew also the vibrant perspective of youth. "They must provide the soul of a rural culture which includes the progress envisioned by the application of technology, while at the same time preserving the ancient values of respect for family life, for authority, for hard work, for a simple life, and reciprocal help, among others." And although all of that involves the preservation of tradition, it does not mean being "egotistical or blind defenders of outmoded forms.... Christian teachings provide a depository from which it is possible continuously to draw new and old treasures for the well-being of the entire community."

The message ended with an appeal that youth would serve as the leaven for their agricultural communities, and be a "reservoir of spiritually and physically healthy people"—a "Christian generation providing a confident glimpse of the future."

The Problems of Rural Life
An Address to the Social Week of Italy
September 18, 1957[16]

Alluding once again to the agricultural sector of society as one of the most valuable sources of physical and spiritual strength for a nation, Pius XII referred to the characterization of agriculture by St. Augustine as "the most innocent of all of the arts" (*Omnium atrium innocentissima*). He therefore endorsed the desire of the Social Week to have the rural population share in the progress which efforts "to promote a fuller measure of what social justice has brought for the other working classes."

Actually, the problems confronting agriculture can no longer be viewed in isolation from the other sectors of economic life. The impact which scientific and technological developments have brought also to the rural economy, altering work patterns and increasing dramatically the productive yields, have revolutionized the life style there. Among other things, this has made the agricultural sector an ever more important part of economic life overall. Therefore, the pressing problems facing it have assumed greater importance than in the past when there was a tendency to relegate these to the background.

At the same time, the Pope pointed out once again, "the influence of the city with its illusions of an easy and greater income along with a higher living standard, the greater conveniences of urban living," is a well known fact in Italy. That leads to an uncontrolled migration from the country areas, bringing with it "weighty moral and religious problems."

Clearly then, what needs to be done goes beyond considerations of a merely technical and economic nature, and of how a more equitable distribution of land and an increase in productive capacity will resolve the problems facing farmers. Many of those who leave the land do so because they see no prospect of improving their social status. That involves matters like home ownership, schools, and decent medical facilities. It reflects also a feeling that, "in comparison with those who work in other occupations, farmers are entitled to live with the same dignity and measure of convenience, and that their contribution to the economic community merits the same recognition."

Pius XII then turned again to the two opposed false philosophies which have frustrated all endeavors over the past two centuries to bring about lasting solutions to the problems facing the economic order, including its agricultural sector. He excoriated experiments that were based on "the principles of liberal individualism and materialistic collectivism." These he termed "two extreme forms of egotistical exploitation of labor and of human dignity." The Church, on the other hand, has approached the matter differently, in that "it took into account the human person more so than the economic and technical aspects." And in considering the reconstruction of economic conditions, it put "the importance of the spirit in first place."

The Pope encouraged the Italian Catholics participating in the Social Week at Cagliari to announce how "Catholic social teaching holds high, more so than any other teaching, the torch of legitimate freedom and of human dignity." He extolled the riches of teachings, which the Church in her "ancient and maternal wisdom" has been propagating with regard to the essential and durable values of rural life, as the best means to avoid errors in trying to establish a new order in the agricultural world.

True to the principle of subsidiarity, Pius XII challenged the farmers themselves to remain in the forefront of all efforts to improve the status of agricultural life. And repeating a theme that occurred previously in his addresses to farm groups, the Pontiff warned about a kind of "particularism" which is a temptation especially peculiar to them, "because of the nature of their bonding to their own land." He urged them to "lift their sights toward the wider horizon" as their organization prompts them to do. In that way they will gain from the prospect of broader cooperative support, and contribute "to the welfare of the whole." That kind of "solidarity" will make it possible to take advantage of the "technical and occupational preparation of farm workers" which "is ever more urgent today, given the progress in agricultural science." Such preparation is required so that "a saving in human energy and an increase in working capacity and more intensive productivity may be possible in the Italian soil which is otherwise no longer capable of providing for the number of its habitants."

However, remaining true to the principle of subsidiarity, Pius XII did not hesitate to call on the state to lend a hand in this urgent matter. It was to do so "without setting aside the personal activity of the parties themselves in their various groupings." But its role would serve to "coordinate and awaken their various energies, at the same time that it would enhance the general prerequisites, including public education, the transportation system, and the various social security measures." The latter would "where possible serve to avert antagonism among the various classes so as to assure a positive and continuing economic and social development." At that point the Pope injected the Church's social teaching into what has always represented a controversial position for some. "If the particular distribution of private property stands in the way of how it is supposed to function—which it by no means does of its very nature and always—the state must regulate its use; and where it becomes necessary, it must even redistribute it, always providing fair compensation to the former owners."

The Pontiff encouraged Catholics to strive earnestly for the fulfillment of the objectives proposed in Catholic social teachings. That would include whatever measures were needed to bolster farming, and in particular the preservation and spread of the economically beneficial family farm operation, along with the various cooperative and occupational associations, which complement it. It was that type of farm that the Church has traditionally supported as "a bulwark of healthy freedom, a dam against the danger of organization, and an effective contribution to the continuation of the genuine traditions of a nation."

Enter, once again, the priest and the parish organization in defense of the farm and, in particular, the family farm. Pius XII urged the rural population to retain its close bonds to their parish churches and priests. The parish priest in rural areas had a close familiarity with both the daily and also the longer-range problems that farm families faced. At the same time, he enjoyed their confidence, as perhaps no one else. Meanwhile, with improvements in transportation, he also experienced first hand the influence—not always salubrious—which contact with neighboring cities and city life had on his parishioners, especially the young. Beyond that, the Pontiff pointed out that there was also "the propaganda which was hostile to religion" that had weakened the faith of many in the rural areas.

Therefore, it was up to the priests to be alert and aware of what was going on. By improving the contact between the rural people and their parishes they could bring about a "renaissance of the country areas." That would involve overcoming a certain "passivity not only in the social, but also and even more so in the religious area." And the farmer will come to understand better "that the interests of the Church are also his own." Thus "he will come to cooperate with others and to abandon any kind of egoism, while dedicating himself to the service of his neighbors, thereby cultivating the social virtues." He will learn from the Church "that Christianity becomes the translator for his deepest aspirations, helping him to fulfill himself as a human being and as a working person."

The Pope concluded with a hope that the Church with its parishes, its priests, and its teachings, would once again become, as it had been in past centuries, a "pathfinder for progress, not only in religious matters, but also in the civil and social area." That suggested more than nostalgia for a more innocent time, but rather a well-founded hope for the future of, among others, its beloved country people.

The Farm Problem
To the Food and Agricultural Organization
9 November 1957[17]

The brevity of this address may suggest that the problems facing agriculture and the farm populations of the world had been dealt with frequently and at length by Pius XII throughout his long pontificate. However, the sad fact remained that a world preoccupied with other matters, in particular, with the industrial sectors of national economies, still had not satisfactorily resolved the long-standing ones confronting the farms and their people.

This gathering of the FAO was addressing the problem of "impoverishment of agriculture in the world economy," with special reference to the diverging trends in the price of manufactured goods which "continues to rise," even while the "price of agricultural products since 1952 has progressively continued to decline." Thus the farmer who is caught in this divergence finds that "his purchasing power shrinks little by little." This aggravates other long-standing problems like "the depopulation of the rural areas, especially in Europe." Also, it "creates a new series of social and religious problems." Deeply affected is "a large, courageous, and deserving class of people whose qualities of stability and fidelity to the best of traditions are more necessary now than ever before to stabilize a rapidly evolving society."

Time and again, this Pope and his successors indicated their reliance on the farm populations, and admiration for their sound qualities and traditions. John XXIII would be the first to address farmers and the agricultural sector of the economy with their problems specifically in a social encyclical: *Mater et Magistra* (1961). Both he and Paul VI after him (*Populorum Progressio,* 1967) would include mention of the problem caused for farmers by so-called "free markets" which operated one way for industry, and another way for farmers.

The Vocational Tasks and the Cultural Mission of the Farmer
Address to the Italian Farmers' Association
April 16, 1958[18]

This was the last address by Pius XII before general farm groups, i.e., other than specialized groups such as dairy farmers or beekeepers. Here the Pope was addressing the 12th National Congress of the Italian Farmers' League in Rome—a group whose efforts he had followed with interest and encouraged since its inception in 1946. It, in fact, approached what was for farmers the kind of occupational organization which Pius XI had encouraged for the various trades and industries in *Quadragesimo Anno.* Pius XII praised its steadfast affirmation that "the Italian farm family is traditionally and by conviction Christian, and that the material and moral elevation of farm families is only possible in the light of Christianity." It was, therefore, fully committed to the principles contained in "the Christian social school of thought."

Such specific commitment has by no means hampered the efforts of the organization to improve the lot of their members. For example, it was instrumental in getting insurance for the disabled and the aged extended to independent farmers as well as to tenant farmers. The Pope praised the group for successfully establishing some 2233 branches where members could avail themselves of educational facilities for improving their occupational competence.

Here the Pope outlined the way in which the status and calling of the farmer took its place within the overall community. Properly carried out, and "using all legitimate means to improve his own lot" the vocation of the farmer is no less than a "full-fledged fulfillment of a holy obligation." "It is, in fact, a genuine act of worship, an expression of love for God, and for one's neighbor." At this point, the Pontiff alluded to the doctrine of the Mystical Body of Christ, of which all Christians are parts, and of which Christ is the head. The proper fulfillment of this role has less to do with what particular station one occupies as a member of the Body, than with how well he fulfills the function which is his own to perform.

Then the Pope turned to some specific aspects of the role which farmers have in the economic order overall. They must "make every effort to improve the living standard of those who devote themselves to agriculture." That would involve improving the soil, and also "a proper and healthy land reform." And the spread of independent farm ownership is listed as a step in that direction. Also, the farmer must apply himself to increase and improve production, so that rigidities in the way production is accomplished and consequent restrictions in supply do not react on prices "in such a way that demand for farm products is harmed and your actual income decreases."

Here Pius XII made an appeal for "one special group, which, among all others, is the most economically deprived and the least socially advantaged and protected." He was talking about "the group of day-laborers whose living conditions seem to deteriorate ever more because of the burden of unemployment and underemployment, especially in the areas where small, divided estates prevail."

Turning then to the more specifically spiritual dimension of life among agricultural people, the Pope warned of the spread of religious indifference, which at one time became common especially in certain intellectual circles. Unfortunately, even after there was a "return movement" among intellectuals, that affliction had now spread also among the working classes, including even the rural population. While not wishing to exaggerate this, he also warned against underestimating it. Pius XII therefore encouraged farm people to hold fast to their "healthy religious traditions." And he expressed confidence that among them "atheistic materialism would run into a stone wall and crumble." He attributed that assurance, among other things, to the family-oriented character of their operations.

The Pontiff concluded by praising the organization he was addressing for providing a tangible example of how intense activity for achieving material goals at the same time foiled the blandishments of those who found that incompatible with Christian beliefs. "It represents proof positive of the untruth of claims that Christianity, in its truths and in its practical norms, blocks or retards true progress."

Notes

1. The encyclical *Mater et Magistra*, which appeared in 1961, is usually entitled in English as *On Christianity and Social Progress.* Its paragraphs 123 to 156 deal more or less specifically with the agricultural sector of the economy and its problems.

2. Arthur-Fridolin Utz, O.P., and Joseph-Fulko Groner, O.P., *Soziale Summe Pius XII* (Freiburg, Switzerland: Paulusverlag, 1954 -1961), 1: 1197-1205.

3. Frequently, capitalism is simply lumped together with private ownership of the means of production even though that being a more or less natural phenomenon has prevailed throughout most of human history. Marx, who gave the initial impulse to the meaning of capitalism, had in mind the actual total dominion over society, including its economy, its politics, and even its broader culture including, for example, religion. That did, in fact, describe the state of affairs which came to prevail to an increasing degree after the landed nobility and other landowners began gradually losing their dominance in society to capitalists after the 16th century. Heinrich Pesch also accepted the latter notion of capitalism as valid.

4. Utz and Groner, 1: 1206-1208.

5. Utz and Groner, 1: 1215-1219.

6. Utz and Groner, 1: 1739-1740.

7. Utz and Groner, 1: 1209-1214.

8. This easily could be, even though it is not, a direct quote from Pesch's chapter heading, "*Man as Lord of the World within the Framework of Society.*" Cf. *Pesch/Ederer, Lehrbuch/Textbook*, vol. 1, bk. 1, p. 31.

9. Utz and Groner, 1: 1220-1223.

10. Utz and Groner, 1: 1228-1230.

11. Utz and Groner, 2: 1701-1704.

12. Utz and Groner, 3:, 3352-3353.

13. *The Pope Speaks*, 2, 2 (Summer 1955) 173-176.

14. *The Pope Speaks*, 3, 2 (Autumn 1956) 169-174.

15. Utz and Groner, 3: 3347-3349.

16. Utz and Groner, 3: 3336-3346.

17. *The Pope Speaks*, 4, 4 (Spring 1958), 442.

18. Utz and Groner, 3: 3365-3370.

Chapter 7
Pius XII on Food and Population

At various times throughout his pontificate, Pius XII addressed the problems of hunger and population. Somewhat ironically, during the period immediately following World War II, in the course of which some 40 million people had lost their lives, a massive propaganda campaign was launched about the imminent dangers of overpopulation relative to the capacity of the earth to feed its people. The white peoples of the world had, in the main, already headed into a declining mode of procreation. For a time the Catholic populations of the world were an exception, which is why some suspect that there may have been religious as well as racialist overtones in this campaign.

The realities included, first of all, the undeniable fact that the world's population was indeed growing, in some areas at an unprecedented rate. Also, there was hunger, often to a catastrophic degree in various parts of the world, especially in the economically underdeveloped nations. It was easy for the undiscriminating to link the two phenomena as cause and effect. In fact though, birth rates overall were not rising; and in many instances they were lower than in the previous generation. Death rates, on the other hand, were declining due to the spread of the advances in medicine, sanitation, and other benefits of the technological revolution that was ongoing since the 18th century. So the rise in population levels was due to declining death rates and not to rising birth rates. It should have been obvious that the decline in death rates which was largely responsible for what appeared to be a phenomenal population increase could not continue indefinitely, since everyone who is born must eventually die. Therefore, unless there were to occur an atypical rise in birth rates, i.e., in family size, population levels would eventually stabilize even though at a higher level. The decisive issue then was whether food supplies could increase to match that higher level. All of the evidence suggested that with the spread of modern technology also to agriculture, which in many parts of the world had continued to operate at a virtually stone-age level, the world would be able to feed easily many times its present population.[1]

Pius XII was the first among modern popes to address this matter. As was frequently the case, he broke ground for his successors, including John XXIII and Paul VI, who were to devote specific attention to the matter in social encyclicals. What he had to say was contained specifically in six addresses during his pontificate.

The Specter of Famine
A Radio Message to the World
4 April 1946[2]

This Radio Message addressed to the entire world was an anguished plea for aid to the millions of people who suffered severely from the lack of food in the immediate aftermath of World War II. Pius XII cited the disruption in the normal flow of production and distribution both in the nations directly affected by the hostilities, as well as in parts of the world where food imports would normally occur from countries left prostrate by the devastation of nearly six years of warfare. The problem was aggravated enormously by the flood of migrants and displaced persons throughout Europe, as well as by sparse rice harvests in East and Southeast Asia along with drought in South Africa.

The Pope cited individual nations which had demonstrated great generosity, and from which even more could be expected. Providentially great agricultural surpluses in the United States and Canada were applied with great generosity for relieving this worldwide shortage. The Pontiff also mentioned Latin America, in particular Brazil and Argentina, which he referred to as "granaries of the world," and which had experienced recent significant increases in agricultural productivity. He saw them in the role of Joseph of the Old Testament in charge of the Egyptian granaries at a time of great need.

Finally, the Pope appealed for fraternal solidarity among peoples as the solution to this immediate serious problem of world hunger. There was no time to attempt to assess blame for the problem, or to bicker over who might be entitled to more or to less assistance. Above all, this was not a time for wastefulness among those who were in a more fortunate situation than the millions of God's children who lacked the basics. Even worse was the guilt of those who may have exploited shortages here and there for their own speculative gain—in other words, those who would conduct "business as usual" despite the desperate situation of their fellow human beings.

Pius XII concluded with warning against the grim prospect of adding millions of additional casualties caused by hunger, to those already left in the wake of the disastrous war. He cited appropriate scripture passages from both Old and New Testaments. "The little ones have asked for bread, and there was none to break it unto them" (Lam. 4:4). Then there followed the grim warning: "Depart from me, accursed ones...for I was hungry and you did not give me to eat" (Matt. 25:41-42).

The Economy of Worldwide Food Production
Address Before the FAO
23 November 1950[3]

This address was one of many by Pius XII to annual gatherings of the Food and Agriculture Organization (FAO) of the United Nations, which was headquartered permanently in Rome. While the immediate extreme emergency of the post-war period as addressed in the previous message had passed, there was now the ongoing pressing imbalance in the world which would engage the attention of this Pope and his successors in the years ahead. Until now, the blame had not been shifted to alleged overpopulation. Instead attention was still focused on the failure to transfer the available technology from one narrow sector of the industrialized world where food surpluses were common, to the vast regions of the underdeveloped nations that were still trying to cope with the sustenance problem while using primitive technologies.

Although the full-scale assault against alleged overpopulation had not yet started, the Catholic Pope began to move in the direction that his Church would take on that matter. He suggested to the FAO experts that the great need itself should serve as a "powerful incentive" to put all forces in motion for a resolution of the admittedly grave problem. Pius XII hinted that much had to be done not only in the matter of increasing the production of food, but also in improving the methods of storage, of distribution and of transporting, as well as in making available the vastly improved fertilizers. All of these avenues were to facilitate making use of the "immeasurable riches of the earth and of the sea, of the forests and streams, of the farms, fisheries, and animal husbandry." That indicated the direction the Catholic Church would take in the forthcoming propaganda war waged by those who saw population control exclusively as the preferred solution to the problem of world hunger.

A subsequent suggestion by Pius XII indicated yet other sources of the difficulty as well as possible avenues for solution. He referred to the plight of certain nations that are remarkably endowed by nature itself, while remaining unproductive because better methods and tools are lacking to them. At the same time there are others "which are in desperate need of one or the other absolutely necessary foodstuff, whereas they are in possession of other products which they cannot trade because they have no means of transportation."

Such "anomalies and problems" can only be resolved by effective international agreements and cooperation on all sides. That was the substance of the Pope's plea to the members of the organization established to deal with the critical, persistent problem of the post-war world: basically a distorted distribution of its existing economic potential.

The Problem of Overpopulation
A Papal Letter Presented by G. B. Montini
On the Occasion of the Social Week at Palermo
27 September 1953[4]

By this time, the well-funded and concerted campaign was underway to prove that overpopulation was a critical problem facing the post-war world.[5] Thus, the Catholic Church was now confronted by a proffered solution to an acknowledged problem—world hunger—but a solution which was in direct conflict with its own perennial teachings on birth control. Pius XII lost no time in expressing his Church's opposition in a message delivered on his behalf by Giovanni Battista Montini, then the papal undersecretary of state, later to become the archbishop of Milan, and then pope. As Pope Paul VI, Montini would confront this issue head-on with two encyclicals. *Populorum Progressio* (1967) would call with the utmost sense of urgency for help from the rich nations of the world to the poor nations for their economic development. The second, *Humanae Vitae* (1968), would provide the occasion for great turmoil within the Church by, among other things, reaffirming its opposition to contraceptive birth control, thus foreclosing on that route for solving the alleged overpopulation problem. As so often, it becomes clear once again that here the groundwork for the position which the Church would take on those matters had already been prepared by the great teacher whom Pope John XXIII would refer to in his own first *Christmas Message* as the *Doctor Optimus*: Pope Pius XII.

The task, as the Pope proposed it to the group before him for their study, was to look at "the burning population problems in the light of the Church's teachings, and to study the relationship between population growth and economic development, while discerning the causes of the distortion between the two phenomena and ascertaining how the situation is to be remedied."

> While it is a fact that society is already devoting much attention to these thorny issues, the Church also has a vital interest in a correct solution. That is precisely because the propagation of human life is involved here, and therefore the family, the cell unit of society from which the Church expects the basic education of its members.

The Pope pointed out that there was not merely an economic problem here, "but a question of a moral and religious character for Catholics." Indeed, there is even a relationship between establishing a proper balance between population density and the means of subsistence, and the entire matter of world peace. Here he cited the Augustinian definition of peace as "the tranquility of order."

From that point on, the Church's position on the issue of "overpopulation" emerges clearly in the form that it would maintain during successive pontificates, specifically those of Pope John XXIII and Pope Paul VI. "World peace is something that must be sought by a better balance between the number of people and their means of subsistence." As this message indicates, Pius XII already proposed that in his Pentecost Message of 1941 while World War II was still raging. At the time he had envisioned a "better distribution of population on the earth's surface...a surface which God provided and destined for all men."

And now the war against natality began to manifest its one-sided solution to the imbalance between a growing population and the way in which the earth's potential to provide for it was engaged. In this message, the Church showed that it was abreast of the situation. The future Pope Paul VI made clear reference now to how the concern about the rising "population curve of humanity" led in many circles to suggesting "birth control as the only solution." His actual words referred to: "...the enhanced propaganda for the neo-Malthusianist method which is directed against the sources of life itself, a propaganda which uses pseudo-scientific notions to advance ideas and practices which pose a grave danger for public morality, and which introduce into society an ever more burdensome and unhealthy weakening of moral-religious foundations." The prophetic quality of those words should be painfully evident to anyone who would be witness a half century later to the deterioration of family life and the moral wreckage round-about, brought on in large measure by the contraceptive mentality.

The message urged the participants at the Palermo conference to stand fast on their principles in searching for solutions to the "population problem." They were warned that no remedies which did not acknowledge "the sacred and inviolable value of human life" were acceptable. The reader will note that these words came two decades before abortion became widely legalized as a standard solution to the alleged overpopulation problem. Yet, the warning was already present that "any attack against human life in its progression from the parents to the cradle is a crime which no political or eugenic considerations could possibly justify." That admonition applied not only to the "direct killing of the innocent," but also to any attempt to "sidestep the purposes of nature which reflect the will of the Creator."

There followed a quotation from an address by Pius XII to the Swiss nation on September 20, 1946: "If the deep-seated sense of the common good is the soul of a healthy and strong state, then the dignity and sanctity of marriage and family life are its backbone." And "if that suffers serious damage, then the vitality of the state is severely impaired and the nation will sooner or later head towards its doom." Prophetically in that same address, the Pope scored as "contrary to God's plan, to sacred scripture, and also to sound reason and natural sense" the modern disdain for the ideal of a large family.

But given the unquestionable pressure of growing populations against given food supplies, how were we to address the problem? The answer lay in recourse to another requirement. It was in our seeing that the goods provided by the Creator and destined for the use of all mankind be managed in accordance with the principles of justice and charity. The message referred now to the encyclical *Sertum Laetitiae* that was addressed to the United States in the very first year of Pius XII's pontificate. It left no room for "calculated, limited self-interest whereby the goods of this earth that were intended for the use of all mankind would deny access to them by less well-endowed nations."

The program dictated by justice was therefore clear. It called for careful study of the disposition of the means of subsistence in relationship to population density, and a solution of the problem which takes into account the solidarity of all peoples. This means, in effect, that after eliminating the artificial obstacles that separate peoples, an improved exchange of peoples, capital, and material goods will be possible: "By that kind of subordination of the individual national economies to the overall good of the community of nations, national boundaries will cease to be walls, but instead bridges which unite, so that material goods will begin to fulfill their natural destiny, serving the needs of all."

At this point, the expression "solidarity" occurs for the second time with reference now to the 1952 *Christmas Message* of Pius XII. Herein is a very important passage which prefigured precisely the social teachings of his two immediate successors: Pope John XXIII, and Pope Paul VI.

> But also to nations as such, We extend our invitation to render operative this sense and obligation of *solidarity*; that every nation develop its own potentialities in regard to living standards and employment, and contribute to the corresponding progress of nations less favored. Although even the most perfect realization of international *solidarity* would hardly bring about perfect equality among nations, yet there is an urgent need that this *solidarity* be put into practice at least sufficiently to change perceptibly the present situation, which is far indeed from attaining a just harmony. [Italics added]

The message made it clear that the "natural wealth of the world offers immeasurable potential for utilization; human intelligence and work open up prospects in terms of which the dire predictions of the neo-Malthusian prophets find no justification at all." And even if one or the other region appears for the moment to be suffering from overpopulation, "that is not due to some natural law, but to a shortfall in the solidarity among peoples and nations."

The warning recurred that "all efforts to remedy a distorted balance between the means of subsistence and the growth of population must in no way interfere with the laws of life and lead to limiting the natural growth of the human family." That was because "[S]uch measures kill the noblest aspirations of the human spirit"; and "furthermore the declining birth rates that come with such systems signify for the destiny of nations that resort to them sooner or later a decline and judgment."

Finally, the prospect of emigration/immigration is considered. Involved here are "as yet underutilized regions," and emigration to them could among other things "relieve the heavy burden of unemployment." Thus, both the recipient nation and the nation that loses population can under the right conditions benefit from the movement of immigrants to new locations. "Families acquire land and property, so that the recipient nations in truth become a 'fatherland' to them. And the densely populated countries experience relief at the same time that they acquire new friends in the foreign countries." Also, "the countries which gain immigration benefit by acquiring diligent, working citizens."

This important message is significant in various ways. First, it confronted directly the neo-Malthusian campaign that resurfaced in the 1950s. Also, as indicated earlier, it contained important ideas which would later appear in the two social encyclicals by Pope John XXIII: *Mater et Magistra* and *Pacem in Terris*. In addition, the then Undersecretary of State at the Vatican who presented the message to the Social Week in Palermo, would later, as Pope Paul VI, make these teachings central features of two of his most significant encyclicals. Finally, the concept, solidarity, which Pope John Paul II would some years later designate as a "Christian virtue" in *Sollicitudo Rei Socialis* features prominently in the resolution of the imbalance between population and the earth's copious resources—which came to be designated simplistically as "overpopulation." From this point on, the Catholic Church was on record as opposed to accepting the problem of world hunger as, in fact, due to overpopulation. And it was clearly opposed to the solutions that came to be widely proffered, up to and including the eventual abortion holocaust that then still lay some 20 years ahead.

Food for the World's Peoples
An Address to the United Nations Food and Agricultural Organization
6 December 1953[6]

This address was, in essence, an earnest, direction-giving "pep talk" for the FAO during the course of its 7th session. Pius XII alluded to the enormity of the task the organization faced. However, he stressed the real nature of the problem as "characterized by a marked imbalance between developed areas and countries which are still insufficiently developed." Thus, there are countries, on the one hand, where "production is increasing rapidly, the level of consumption is rising again and exports are mounting." On the other side are countries, "particularly in the Far East," where production "remains inadequate, food insufficient and imports limited." While there is no mention of overpopulation, the Pope conceded that "it is necessary to take account of the continuous growth of the population." What that calls for, he noted however, "at the risk of making the evil worse," is "a parallel increase in the goods to be consumed."

Therein lies the task of the FAO, not in "proving that there is not enough food in the world," as was suggested by a critic.[7] Unfortunately, the focus of the organization's work tended to gravitate towards a view that the only remedy to the "imbalance," referred to here by Pius XII and later by John XXIII, was population control. Lost sight of was the counsel by the Pope that "The essential part of your work consists in acting effectively in the field of agriculture and also of exploiting the fishing and forestry industries." This meant, "directing toward underfed peoples, who make up seventy per cent of the world's population, the surplus production of the more favored nations, thereby assuring the latter of stable markets." Even more important was providing "for increased production in the very places where scarcity makes itself felt."

Pius XII became quite specific about details, suggesting that "In order to do this you desire first to reduce the often considerable losses due to the inexperience of farmers, and to epidemics." Also, "then you want to increase production through improvement of cultivation methods, the use of fertilizer and the selection of plant species." And beyond that, "you look forward to putting into use lands that are still uncultivated, especially by means of irrigation." Regrettably, much of the energy of the FAO came to be directed toward population control by means unacceptable to the Catholic Church.

Coincidentally, the opposing viewpoints were reflected dramatically in the differing responses to world hunger and poverty by two visitors to India. Paul Ehrlich, an American academic person, went to Calcutta, saw the deplorable conditions, and returned with an anti-natalist view that turned him into a zealous propagandist for population control.[8] Blessed Mother Teresa, on the other hand, went to Calcutta and became a world-renowned missionary working in the streets to alleviate in whatever way possible the misery caused by gross mismanagement of the country's enormous economic potential. India has since became a food exporter, proving that the continuing problem there lay not in an inability to produce enough food, but in a failure to address not only the technical and economic problem, but also the serious social dimension underlying India's misery.

Indeed, what Pius XII suggested next was attention precisely to the social aspect of the technical problem of improving the food and agricultural conditions in poor nations. Simply showing people in poor countries how to increase production is not enough. Indeed, it can be frustrated by such people's failure to see an improvement in their lot as they become technically more proficient. "To stimulate interest and personal initiative, to show that the good of the community will not be achieved at the expense of the welfare of the individuals, but to their profit, and to see to it that this is really the case, are certainly elements of primary importance for your success." That, the Pope said, added to the Organization's economic tasks, is "a no less decisive social one."

The now ever-recurring theme of solidarity applied among all nations, rich and poor, was expressed in a concluding remark. Action to improve the lot of all "obliges nations to consider themselves both the beneficiaries and the benefactors of one another." And the positive approach to the problem is emphasized again in the closing paragraph: "The civilized world always looks with great sadness at the pitiful picture of hunger victims at a time when the earth is capable of feeding all men." In that position, the Catholic Church has been unrelenting, whereas much of the world has all too often leaned toward the easier, but misleading solution of population control.

Population in True Perspective
Message to the World Conference on Population
9 September 1954[9]

In this very brief message, Pius XII designated as "young," "the science of population." He was referring to demography, which, like the other social sciences, is indeed young in terms of the 2000 year lifetime of the Church and as compared, for example, with theology and philosophy. Nevertheless, in the Pope's words, "it is basic since it touches immediately on human life and it can clarify some of the most serious individual and social problems."

That appears to be a reference to the problem of alleged overpopulation, and to the matter of begetting new life that confronts each individual married person. Pius XII reassured his audience that "the Church is not ignorant of these problems," nor is it "indifferent to their anguishing aspects." That is evidenced "by the many documents which have been issued recently by the Holy See on family life, national economy, and the relations between peoples." Specifically, he mentioned "the relations between peoples, some of whom find themselves abundantly furnished with riches, while others remain in tragic conditions."

The crucial point which he restated here is that "the Church has always wanted to place the problems of population in their true perspective: that of a moral, personal destiny, which through courageous and even daring action in time, is to find its accomplishment in the eternal possession of God." Specifically, he was proposing that Catholics must study and act in this area "with fidelity to Christian doctrine, in communion with the many men and women who, enlightened by their reason and sustained by a proper confidence in Providence, fully conscious of difficulties which they are facing and of duties toward the community respect the creative vow which is to be found at the very heart of love and of life." It is that "creative vow" which increasingly became the stumbling block for many who studied and proposed solutions to what they perceived to be the demographic problem of our time.

Food, Agriculture and Human Solidarity
Address to Delegates Attending the Eighth Conference of The United Nations Food and Agricultural Organization
10 November 1955[10]

There is scarcely a hint in this message about the growing obsessive concern at large with overpopulation and a virtual abject surrender to the belief that the problem of world hunger cannot be resolved except by Draconian population control measures. Pius XII continued to affirm instead that the aims of the FAO. "...were, and still are...to raise the levels of nutrition and standards of living of peoples, to improve efficiency of production and distribution of all food and agricultural products and to contribute towards an expanding world economy." He indicated that the Holy See, which had been made a "permanent observer" of the Organization in 1950, recognized full well that "over half the population of the world was underfed." Since this meant that "to meet the needs of mankind food production had to be doubled." the FAO set about at its outset, working "in nine war-ravaged countries in order to restore their agriculture."

Eventually, this reconstruction effort involved "increasing the productivity and raising the standard of living of rural populations." But, the Pope indicated, that was "bound up with the social conditions under which the farmers work," which led the FAO into also "reforming the agrarian structure and the related question of agricultural credit." Much good came from these efforts over the years after the War, but much remained to be done to reform and enhance the performance of the agricultural sector of national economies. Ultimately the factor, human solidarity, needs to be recognized so that effective action on the part of all the various segments of national economies and among all of the nations of the world will come to bear on the enormous problem still facing the human race. Otherwise, "peoples favored by nature or the progress of civilization are in danger of being rudely awakened one day, if they do not take the trouble henceforth to secure for the less fortunate the means to live in accordance with human dignity and to develop on their own account."

The papal appeal to "collective responsibility" led into the specifically Christian aspect of what is involved here. It foreshadowed the special emphasis which John XXIII was to place on farming for the first time in a social encyclical, and in particular his call in *Mater et Magistra* for intersectoral balance within national, and also worldwide, economies. It also clearly anticipated what was to be the specific theme of the Paul VI encyclical *On the Development of Peoples* in 1967. Finally, the appeal for "worldwide activity, intended to effect not a privileged class, but the often powerless and defenseless multitude," as being "an authentic aspect of the charity which Christ illustrated by His life and death..." indicated clearly that charity had not simply an individual, but also a social dimension. That is the *social charity* which Pius XI proclaimed as a regulating principle for social order in 1931; and it is the selfsame *solidarity* which Pope John Paul II would then refer to in 1987 as a "*Christian virtue*."

Notes

1. Cf. Colin Clark, *Population Growth and Land Use* (New York: St. Martin's Press, 1968). The distinguished British economist demonstrated in this carefully researched work that the world could indeed support many times its present population level once the careful, advanced methods of agriculture in use in countries like the Netherlands, Japan, etc. came to be applied around the world, especially in the then technologically backward nations. India proved this subsequently when it became a food exporter! Cf. also: Rupert J. Ederer, "Overpopulation: a Study in Relativity," *World Justice,* September 1967.

2. Arthur-Fridolin Utz, O.P., and Joseph-Fulko Groner, O.P., *Soziale Summe Pius XII* (Freiburg, Switzerland: Paulusverlag, 1954 -1961), 1: 1741-1747.

3. Utz and Groner, 1: 1748-1750.

4. Utz and Groner, 2: 1649-1700.

5. While still a youthful economics professor, I recall receiving in my college mail a booklet with a sinister-looking black cover, entitled *The Population Bomb.* The organization which promoted and sent this propaganda piece to all who were in a position to influence the thinking of the young in particular was the Hugh Moore Fund in New York.

6. *Catholic Mind,* March 1954, 187-189.

7. A commentator in the British publication, *Economist* (23 August 1952), sarcastically described the FAO as "a permanent institution devoted to proving that there is not enough food in the world."

8. Ehrlich's book, *The Population Bomb,* first published in 1968 and continuing through many editions, persuaded an entire generation that population growth must be

halted even by radical means. Such means, with all of their ominous implications, were later applied in Communist China where couples are allowed to have only one child, and they are punished severely for violating the norm.

9. *The Pope Speaks,* Third Quarter 1954.

10. *The Pope Speaks,* Winter 1955-56.

Chapter 8
The Middle Class

For a long time the so-called "middle class" has been the subject of concern among social scientists generally, and in a special way for sociologists and economists. At the same time it became for Marxists an object of considerable disdain—the *bourgeoisie*—it being the class which put a maximum premium on the ownership of private property. One problem that arises in discussing the "middle class" is its precise meaning. Where is the line between "the poor" and the middle class? Where does the middle class fade into "the rich"? And what is to be made of such designations as "upper middle class" and "lower middle class"? In earlier eras when one's function in society was a widely accepted criterion for class status, that was somewhat easier to determine. In more recent times when such matters came to be judged increasingly in monetary terms, i.e. income and wealth, the matter has become more complicated. In the United States where we do not have an aristocracy based on bloodlines, at least explicitly, or a landed gentry in the older established sense of those terms, class distinctions came to be identified increasingly with income brackets. Using the standard bell-shaped curve employed by statisticians, the majority of our citizens do tend to cluster into an area which one could with some legitimacy call the middle class. Even the sometimes juxtaposed classes, like the "working class" and the wealthy classes lack any real scientific precision, since most persons judged to be "middle class" work for their livelihood, as do even many of the very wealthy. The latter group, however, often earns a much larger portion of its income from the ownership of earning assets rather than from its work. But by and large most middle class persons work for the major share of their income. Nevertheless, the notion, middle class, persists, alongside the concept, working class, which is also not precise since, as indicated, middle class people generally work for their living. Even though a precise, generally accepted definition for "middle class" seems to be lacking at present, the concept does persist, as do judgments about its value in society and certain dangers alleged to be threatening it.

The Worth and Dignity of the Skilled Crafts
Address to Participants in the Congress of the Association of Christian Craftsmen of Italy
20 October 1947[1]

Skilled craftsmen typically enjoy a somewhat higher level of pay and also a greater degree of economic independence than rank-and-file workers. Therefore they are being included here as a part of the "middle class." Pius XII noted that difference when he recalled that, "over the past half century the Church in its social concern about workers has mainly but not exclusively addressed the problems facing the industrial workers." Yet, it never "surrendered its concern and love with regard to craft work…."

The Pope alluded to the "corporate groups" which over the centuries occupied a position of benevolent activity. Indeed, they "were actually at the same time religious fraternities which attended to obligations now performed by various Catholic associations." He had in mind the craft guilds, which in addition to regulating the economic aspects of their trades, also undertook significant charitable works in the medieval cities.

Pius XII noted that there is also "a deeper and more basic underlying basis for the relationship between the Church and the crafts, as also with farmers." He saw in these classes the possibility of providing a "barrier" against the "predominance of the machine and the constant growth of large-scale industry," because of what these developments are doing to modern man. There is praise for the work of persons who make things from raw material into the finished product, imparting to it their "technical ability and artistic capacity along with fine taste and the skill of their hands." That is contrasted with the impersonal and monotonous mass products as turned out in the typical large factory. It is a difference which makes the class of craftsmen "virtually an elect group for preserving the dignity and the personal character of the worker."

Proceeding from that discussion of the nature of their work, the Pope turned attention to another beneficial aspect of it. "Whereas there is often an unnatural and bitter combat between employers and workers, the crafts have in general been spared such antagonism." Indeed, the small workshop "often retains the imprint of the family." "Workers and apprentices labor under the management of the owner or the master craftsman...." There followed a remarkable kind of "ordination" of this class of workers. "The crafts therefore constitute a kind of chosen militia for protecting social peace and for the restoration and well-being of the national economy."

There followed a rather remarkable appeal that "the crucifix should never disappear from your families and your businesses, where it should serve as a witness of an always lively faith and a reverential fear of God." Indeed, the Pope encouraged the craftsmen that they should "not forget to pray in your workshops, where you should always thank the Father in the name of our Lord Jesus Christ."

Pius XII concluded with two "wishes" for craftsmen. "For over a century, the crafts have had to fight for their survival against the power and the strides made by large-scale industry." Thus far, they have "not only survived, but even carved out an important niche within and amid large factories even in great industrial regions." So their future appeared secure. He urged them to continue in their efforts, and he also admonished them to "fight to preserve the Christian character of your association." Otherwise the "strong religious and moral forces which are present among the Christian crafts would be excluded from having an effect in public life and they would be stifled."

The address closed characteristically with a blessing for those present and for their families. But there was also a reminder that Christ Himself worked for many years as a skilled craftsman, as did Joseph, His foster father.

Concern About the Middle Class
Address to the Spanish Social Week
13 April 1951[2]

This address may actually help to sharpen the concept, "middle class," which is used widely and often imprecisely. Once again, it was delivered on the Pope's behalf by the future Pope Paul VI, then his Undersecretary of State. G. B. Montini addressed this problem the *Spanish Social Week* in Barcelona assigned for study in 1951 by describing his audience as a social group of the "widest extent," embracing people in industry, agriculture, handicrafts and commerce. Some of them are employees and others are in the liberal occupations. "It is a significant portion of the population with characteristic qualities, and its social influence merits special attention."

He then went on to identify the "peculiar attribute of this class." It is "their economic independence which puts it in a position to assure social stability and the production of goods." Thus, it represents a fortunate harmony between personal work and private property. The middle class person is in a position where "he establishes his autonomy and his dignity by his personal efforts and by his own work." He does not have to "beg for his sustenance." According to Montini, this middle class establishes a "healthy and just division of property" which therefore helps to keep at bay "the various forms of a nameless collectivism." It does this by maintaining the true function of a pillar of social order," i.e.,private property.

In recent times there have emerged a series of circumstances which pose a threat to the middle class. These include great accumulations of wealth, and also inflation, which discourages savings; and there are also excessive fiscal burdens. Pius XII directed Montini to encourage and bless the persons involved in the *Spanish Social Week* who are directing their attention to these problems, since the Church has always encouraged the maintenance of a vigorous middle class.

The Small Retailer as an Economic and Ethical Factor in Society
Address to Members of the Association of Italian Tobacco Dealers
23 September 1955[3]

The essential element involved here is the small retailer, regardless of what specific merchandise he deals in. The group that appeared before Pius XII happened to be what were referred to in Italy as *Tabaccai* or tobacco dealers. These shops handled all products which were reserved as state monopolies, and the Pope mentioned specifically also "cooking salt, postage stamps and stamped paper." They were spread across Italy in some 49,000 concessions involving the welfare of a quarter of a million people. Such small business families whose status allowed them a decent income may legitimately be included among what we are calling here the "middle class."

The especially significant aspect of the Pontiff's address to this group is his reference to the "occupational organization which safeguards your legitimate interest and represents your occupation, in its dealings with other merchants or with public authority and public service groups." Thus the notion which his immediate predecessor had made an essential part of his plan for social reconstruction (*Quadragesimo Anno*, 1931) came up repeatedly in the social messages by Pius XII throughout his pontificate. Especially significant is the way the Pope introduced this discussion by using the expression, "It is altogether natural...." And he concluded by indicating the kind of items such an occupational group could legitimately have on its agenda. They could include "many questions of a technical, economic, and social nature." Specifically, this group was then concerned about "reducing administrative costs, simplification of business procedures, and the matter of vacations, a weekly 'free afternoon,' and greater effort on the part of the state in the area of health insurance as well as old age and disability insurance."

There was a concluding exhortation, whereby Pius XII admonished the group that it should always provide good example with the many people with whom their business brings them into daily contact. He urged them to show that they are "not merely middlemen in the service of the state," but persons of principle "true to your religious convictions and concerned about whatever threatens your national institutions." In other words, once again the Pope was telling this group to live up to all the traditional virtues attributed to the "middle class."

Small Business in Today's Economy
Address to Catholic Associations of Small and Medium-sized Businesses
8 October 1956[4]

This especially significant address involved a congress of several groups in Belgium, Holland, Italy, and Germany, all of which had in common their status as associations of Catholic small businessmen and who regarded themselves as of the "middle class." They comprised a significant organization representing some 110,000 members.

Pius XII praised them for their "spirit of initiative, ingenuity, and courage."

And he pointed out how "small and medium-sized businesses directed by Christians can more easily than others perceive and put into practice concrete solutions to this serious problem." The "problem" which the Congress had chosen to address on this occasion was "how small and medium-sized business interests help to inject man into society and the economy." More specifically, the persons in attendance were concerned about how "each member of the social body [could] be granted the opportunity to live fully as a man, to have at his disposal the means of assuring himself—through an equitable subsistence—access to culture, to play a role in proportion to his ability and devotion in the functioning and organization of society, and to participate, finally in the decisions upon which his political, economic, and social fate are dependent."

The Pope then moved on to what are widely regarded as some singular merits and advantages of middle class business types for society. "You like to point out that the large number of medium-sized businesses in which the head is at the same time the owner and occasionally the founder, assures a very broad distribution of private property, which is the essential condition of stability for society; while guaranteeing the independence and dignity of individuals and families, it does not confer upon them exorbitant economic power which would carry them beyond the scope of their true responsibilities."

One of the pitfalls of modern capitalism is precisely the accretion of the kind of "exorbitant economic power" referred to here, and a narrowing of the distribution of private property instead of its "very broad distribution." One can sense what is perhaps papal disapproval of that aspect of capitalism in the endorsement of smaller-sized business enterprises. Indeed, the Pope recognized advantages for the "greater good of the community" in the way the "private businessman, merchant, and farmer see to it that the value of their property is increased through their work," and in how "they see their labor directly sanctioned, as also the negligent acts or errors which they commit."

What followed such exaltation of the smaller sized businessman's status was straightforward admonition on behalf of his workers. "But if the owner of a business finds therein the means to maintain and to consolidate his social position, is it not proper that he should strive to enable all those depending upon him and giving him the support of their work to benefit from the same advantages?" Almost sternly, the Pope asked: "Do they not also have the right to occupy a stable position in society, to possess material necessities for themselves and their families, to enhance the value of their property through their initiative, and to derive there-from a legitimate profit?" Referring to the stake which workers sense that they have in the success of their enterprise, the Pontiff indicated: "It is certain that the worker and the employee who know that they are directly involved in the successful operation of the business, because a part of their wealth is invested and fructifying therein, will feel themselves more intimately obliged to contribute to it through their efforts and even their sacrifices." The implicit partnership between workers and their employers plays an important part in the success of the business since "they will feel themselves more fully men, trustees of a greater share of responsibility; they will realize that others are beholden to them, and thus they will apply themselves with greater courage to their daily task, in spite of its often harsh and tedious character."

That, incidentally, was a clear endorsement of what his predecessor had proposed in *Quadragesimo Anno* 25 years earlier. In reaffirming and developing further the just wage doctrine first proposed in its modern form by Leo XIII, Pius XI wrote: "We deem it advisable that a wage contract should, when possible, be modified somewhat by a contract of partnership, as is already being tried in various ways with significant advantages to both wage earners and employers" (*Quadragesimo Anno*, par. 65).

Then, as if to moderate the notions of certain enthusiasts who would seize on that papal suggestion to infringe on the business owner's right to manage his enterprise, Pius XII stated: "The head of a business values above all his power to make autonomous decisions; he foresees orders, and directs, assuming responsibility for the decisions which he makes." For, that is where "[H]is natural gifts, his previous theoretical training, his technical competence, and his experience find employment in the function of leadership, and serve as a basis for the development of his personality and for creative joy." Yet, by the same token, "will the head of the business deny his subordinates what he esteems so highly himself?" And "will he limit the role of his daily cooperators to that of simple executants, who cannot turn their own experience to account as they would like, and who remain wholly passive with regard to the decisions which govern their own activity?"

Here we find another instance where Pius XII acted as a true bridge-figure—*pontifex*—between his predecessors and his immediate successor. In one of his major social encyclicals, John XXIII devoted a significant portion to "an innate need of human nature requiring that men engaged in productive activity have an opportunity to assume responsibility and to perfect themselves by their efforts." Indeed, in that part of *Mater et Magistra* (pars. 82-104) dealing with "Participation of workers in medium-size and large enterprises," Blessed John XXIII quoted directly from this Pius XII address his statement that, "The economic and social function which everyone aspires to fulfill, requires that efforts of individuals be not subjected to the will of others." (*Mater et Magistra*, pars. 92).

The address continued with what could be considered a textbook lesson on good labor-management relations—a lesson especially adaptable for smaller scale enterprises. Pius XII indicated that while a "human conception of business should no doubt safeguard for the common good the employer's authority...it cannot tolerate such a grievous attack upon the profound value of the agents of execution." Suggesting an all too common lack of appreciation of the importance of worker input also in the successful implementation of "technical improvements or concerted efforts to increase productivity," the Pope pointed out that "it will be necessary to call upon the indispensable cooperation of personnel."

In such matters the position of the "small and medium-sized business" is especially relevant, because "contact between the employer and his employees is more direct and more immediate." There, in particular, the executant should be informed and listened to," and "consideration should be given to his desires and his suggestions, ...the reason for a denial should be explained to him, ...the technical and economic problems upon which the return of the business depends should be made known to him," and "...he should have an opportunity to contribute to their solution."

In concluding this portion of the message, Pius XII offered what may well be included in a good manual of personnel administration: "In such a way the erection of a wall of prejudice, incomprehension, and unjustified criticism between management and employees will be avoided." And so: "...many conflicts based upon misunderstandings or ignorance of the real situation will be forestalled."

The Pontiff turned to a problem related to their competitive situation about which smaller businesses often complain, not without justification. "The evolution of the modern economy to the accompanying rhythm of discoveries and innumerable applications which stem there-from accentuates the uneasiness of small and medium-sized businesses with respect to their bigger competitors." Showing once again his keen understanding of areas which transcend his position as head of a large religious body, Pius XII cited what typically causes this competitive difficulty: "[T]he modernization of mechanical equipment and more rational methods of mass production and distribution work quite frequently work to the advantage of enterprises which have large amounts of capital on hand."

For coping with that difficulty, seen here as a real one, smaller enterprises may seek remedy "from inside and outside" their own group. As for the "outside," the Pope apparently saw no violation of the subsidiarity principle in having small employers seek support from the state. The reason given was that the state "possesses in you an important factor of stability." The kind of help to be sought would include "the domain of credit and the tax structure." True to that principle of subsidiarity, however, "inside" help remains, "your principal support," "[t]hat is to say, from your associations themselves."

That opened the way for Pius XII to propose again what had at this point become one of his favored themes: solidarity. He pointed out that the "middle classes are often reproached for their exaggerated individualism, their desire for total independence, and their scorn for whatever runs counter to established customs." We have here virtually a recitation of what some critics of the middle class have come to regard as stereotypical "bourgeois" flaws. The lecture continued in its stern tone. "If social life presupposes in individuals all the independence compatible with the good of the whole, it demands to an ever greater extent cooperation, mutual agreement based upon confidence, the renunciation of certain privileges and of certain somewhat narrow and selfish points of view." Almost predictably, that set the stage for the papal remedy.

"May the principle of solidarity assert itself more positively!" Specifically, in its application that would imply its application "not only within each of your businesses, but also between similar enterprises, so as to avoid a waste of energy, useless expenses." It could serve "to bring together in a compact unit the scattered elements of a considerable economic potential which, by its present division is deprived of an effective energy in proportion to its true value."

No one could accuse this Pope of vague generalities while avoiding specifics. These proposals were directly relevant to the groups he was addressing. In his parting comment he reminded them that, "It is to the advantage of all that small and medium-sized businesses be well organized in all domains, and cause their distinctive qualities to be shown to better advantage."

No matter how remarkably specific this man became in addressing problems facing the great variety of groups who came before him for his support and blessings, he always concluded with profound spiritual advice. That was because: "Nothing has been accomplished if, while assuring the improvement of economic conditions one has neglected to deepen cultural, moral, and religious values." The spiritual advice was: "Each of you, each of those who are dependent upon you, is called as a son of the Church and a member of the Body of Christ to the fullness of human and divine life." Furthermore, "It is your responsibility to see to it that the treasures of this life are henceforth increased, not only in you, but equally well, in each of your brothers over whom Providence has granted you partial authority."

The Middle Class

An Address to the International Institute on the Middle Classes

25 October 1956[5]

The group appearing before Pius XII here was founded in Germany in 1903 to study economic questions relating to the middle classes. That country, which this Pope had served as Apostolic Nuncio, had made substantial contributions to the developing body of the Church's social teachings, especially in the persons of Bishop Wilhelm Emmanuel von Ketteler (1811-1877)[6] and Heinrich Pesch, S.J. (1854-1926). Popes since Pius IX have gratefully acknowledged the work of such men and the various study groups like this Institute. Pius XII told its members, "You represent great national and international organizations of the middle classes, which is to say, 'a large and very important part of mankind.'" And he reminded them of the "special position" which his predecessor, Pius XI had "brought out in his account of the profound changes that the economic regime has undergone since Leo XIII."

Referring to the middle classes, the Pontiff recalled that "the development of large-scale capitalism, on the one hand, and of the wage-earning classes on the other, have evoked a body of regulations and institutions which too often disregard an essential segment of the citizenry of each country." He proceeded to identify them as "those who generally contribute to production through their work and personal capital: craftsmen, independent trades-people, owners of small and medium-sized businesses, the majority of farmers, professional men, certain categories of civil servants and military men, and most persons who live on independent means." That, in fact, happens to offer a very comprehensive listing of persons who comprise the "middle classes."

The Pope acknowledged the legitimacy of what preoccupied the group before him on this occasion: "the consequences of fiscal measures applied indiscriminately to small and medium-sized businesses and to the craftsmen, the military, and the professional men of the various countries you have studied." He also apparently sanctioned the ambition of this Institute to "play the same role" for the middle classes that "the *International Labor Office* plays for the laboring class: to be a center for research and study for the middle classes, since your problems are as specialized as is your function in society."

That "function" stems from the "intermediary position you occupy, the large numerical place you hold in the population, the virtues proper to your place in life," that "make you an element of moderation and equilibrium which is in danger of being stifled if the obligations which encumber it exceed its real resource." Pius XII recognized the legitimacy of the group's concerns, as he did the important role which the middle classes play in society, notwithstanding the increasing polarization toward "large-scale capitalism on the one hand," and hard-pressed "wage-earning classes on the other." The role comes to the fore in the "share of personal responsibility which you normally exercise in your activities, the family scale generally assumed your enterprises," which maintain and develop within you a sense of work well done, thrift, and foresight." In other words, we have here the oft-related and praised middle class virtues, sometimes made light of, especially by Marxian critics and by those who, wittingly or not, are influenced by Marxian criticism of "bourgeois society."

The Pope noted that countries where "the middle classes have been too restricted and too weak are often exposed to serious and violent political excesses." The middle classes, however, "favor stability and arbitration based on distributive justice." That is a social role which characterizes them and "you must fulfill it with a lofty sense of the general good."

Overall, this may be considered a laudatory exhortation for the middle classes and organizations like this one, which represent them and their interests. The Pope left his listeners with the message that they "ought also to be agents for moral well-being," because they possess along with a "love of a just liberty, a high ideal of the personal dignity and respect due others, without which social life turns into a struggle of selfish and blind passions." That presupposes that they will be guided in their "thoughts and actions according to the maxims of wisdom taught by the Gospel." Pius XII told his audience that "Society's proper balance has its surest basis in moral order which is inspired, not by cold calculating logic concerned exclusively with equitable distribution of material goods, but rather by justice and generous charity, by the example of Christ, which is to say by that generous love which entails forgetfulness of self, renunciation and sacrifice."

The Skilled Trade Operation, An Ideal Form of Business for Promoting Human and Moral Fulfillment

Address Before Italian Craftsmen

15 February 1958[7]

Unlike the previous messages to various groups with regard to middle class problems and prospects, this one is addressed to one specific category of middle class workers: skilled craftsmen as represented by the Congress of Italian Craftsmen. Indeed, this group of workers seemed to many to be an especially embattled one whose future often seemed to be in jeopardy.

Pius XII opened with the jubilant observation that despite all of the predictions of experts, including economists, at the close of the last century, skilled trades were in 1958 still very much a vibrant part of economic life. It was the growth of factory-type production that prompted also leaders of the socialist movement to announce that small craft operations were doomed. Actual events proved them wrong, even while it is true that the proportion of such enterprises has decreased. And even in the large enterprises such as construction firms, a large percentage of the workers are skilled. Once again, demonstrating his keen awareness of what was happening in the world beyond the walls of the Vatican, the Pope referred to the fact that this was going on even in highly industrialized nations like Germany. There such recent innovations as automation created a demand for even more highly trained workers.

The Pontiff then turned to certain advantages the skilled crafts brought with them in the world of work and in society generally. He acknowledged that the Church in its social teachings had indeed devoted more attention to the industrial workers in large enterprises, and to their relations with employers. That was because the nub of the problem appeared to be there, which called for prompt attention and solution. Yet, there was always a good rapport between the Church and "the world of skilled trades," one which could be called "a good, natural, and close understanding."

The Pope said that he wished to draw attention to two particular points that illustrated the Church's concern about skilled crafts and their survival and well-being. The first is the apparent growing dichotomy between a person's private life and his occupational one. Living and what one does to earn a living are sharply compartmentalized, as though there were no integral relationship between them. One works to earn a livelihood, without any significant joy in one's work, while at the same time counting the hours and days until there is free time. Regrettably this attitude is found not merely among office workers and workers in large-scale operations, but even among skilled workers in their various crafts.

Again displaying his keen insights into what was going on in the world of work, Pius XII offered some possible explanations for this phenomenon. The tasks of the individual workers have been divided to where what each does is merely a small part of the entire operation. Thus, what each does no longer appears to be of much importance. The sense of performing a vital function and contributing toward a significant end result gets lost.

Therein one can see one great advantage of the skilled craftsman. He usually has undergone some serious training and schooling, so that he is able to do a job from start to finish. That applies also even where the worker is not independent, but employed in a larger operation, e.g., construction. The Pope indicated that the Church rejoices in that aspect of skilled labor, since it avoids the sharp separation between one's private life and one's work. That involves the kind of satisfaction which the craftsman shares with the farmer who works his own land with his family nearby, and the teacher, the physician, the nurse, etc. Meanwhile, in those occupations where there is a loss of unity between what one is expected to do for a living along with pride in one's occupation or profession, there is increasing loss of interest and eventually a shortage of workers develops.

The Pontiff indicated that he is not surprised when workers in such occupations seek their fulfillment and enjoyment elsewhere, often even with bad moral consequences. That may involve dire implications for one's sense of responsibility toward neighbors and for society. He told the skilled craftsmen that he was pleased with how their kind of work protects them from such dangers, and that they continue to derive satisfaction from their work.

The second point about the skilled craft occupations that Pius XII found to be very positive is the fact that in their kinds of business operations it is possible to retain a closeness and a familiarity among those who are involved. He made it clear at the outset of the discussion that he was not yearning for a restoration of patriarchal structures. Instead, he regarded it as acceptable "that the relationships between entrepreneurs, workers and apprentices were established on a contractual basis in full harmony with applicable social legislation." Indeed, the Pope deemed it good if the entrepreneur would "take an active part in the operation of the business, remaining among his workers to guide them, encourage them and to instruct them." In that way a "familial atmosphere is introduced into the business operation." Thus, "not many words are required, but mainly good example and vigilance regarding the true welfare of the personnel." That would lead to a "feeling among all workers and apprentices that there is a good spirit at work in the operation which fosters reciprocal respect and a willingness to be helpful."

A rather unusual and very admirable bit of advice followed. The great Pope asked whether it might not be possible to instill a Christian spirit in the enterprise by perhaps installing a crucifix in the shop." In fact, would it even be possible and advisable to start the day with a common prayer to invoke the blessing of God on your daily toil?" And continuing in this vein, the Pontiff reminded the older workers that they should strive to avoid the kind of language, all too common in workshops now, which would give bad example to the younger workers and apprentices. In fact, one should not be surprised to find the leader of the world's largest Christian body making those kinds of suggestions.

Nor should it be surprising then, if in closing, the Pontiff cited in his blessing on the workers the example of Joseph the head of the Holy Family. He reminded them that St. Joseph and Jesus were craftsmen in the contemporary sense of the word "who owned a small operation as so many of you."

The Problems of the Middle Class in the Economic Order of Today
Papal Letter to Leaders of the International Middle Class Congress of Madrid
3 May 1958[8]

This letter was delivered by the Substitute Secretary of State A. dell'Acqua on the behalf of Pius XII as the Pope neared the end of his life on earth. It was addressed to the International Institute for Social Science and Policy then meeting in Madrid in association with the International Middle Class Congress.

This Pope had a special interest in the topic of the middle class, as he had addressed it on previous occasions. He expressed concern in particular about the need for "representatives of this social group—in commerce, the crafts, and in small and mid-sized industrial concerns—to take their proper place in the economic life of the present time." Threats facing the middle class had appeared, given "the growth of large-scale industrial capitalism." Yet its "irreplaceable function in the economic and social order as a balancing element in society" was also well established. Given that we live now amid altered circumstances, even while the important role of the middle class persists, "we had better not waste effort on futile lamentations about the advantages of handicraft production, or about the question of social ranking." Better to see to it that there is established a structure where we find "the spirit of initiative and the free cooperation at all levels of occupations, and which affords to these vital economic resources an area of opportunity where they can play their role in the service of the general welfare fully and completely." The letter quoted from a previous address by Pius XII (8 October 1956), where he stated that "the various elements which represent important economic potential must be firmly joined together, because fragmented they cannot achieve the effectiveness of which they are in fact capable."

The letter continued indicating that the concerns which at present rightly concern the middle class with regard to its service to the general welfare and its place in the nation warrant the support which it expects from public authorities. Citing the same earlier address to the middle class, it recalls that "the state which has in you a powerful force for balance, may not deny you the help which you count on, above all in the area of credit and in the tax system." That came with the warning that such help should, however, not endanger "the values which come along with the various occupational groups that include themselves under the designation, 'middle class.'" As a matter a fact "the general welfare which they propose to serve" requires that in their organizational combinations "they safeguard the ideals of freedom and moderation, and also the capacity for human relationships which come as part of their traditional advantages." Is it possible, in other words, that "too much concern for success and power could lead to the kind of excesses which have brought with them so much disorder and discord among the other sectors of the economy?"

The letter continued then, quoting from an address by Pius XII to representatives of the middle class on 25 October 1956:

> The personal responsibility which is a normal part of your activity, and the character of enterprises that are usually conducted as family operations, entertain and develop in you the sense for solid work and for thrift and providence,

beneficial by-products of a relative amount of independence, all of which you rightly regard as essential features of your social status.... You stand or fall with this social role; and you must fulfill it with a vigilant regard for the general welfare.

Notes

1. Arthur-Fridolin Utz, O.P., and Joseph-Fulko Groner, O.P., *Soziale Summe Pius XII* (Freiburg, Switzerland: Paulusverlag, 1954 -1961), 1: 1254-1256.

2. Utz and Groner. 2: 1599-1601.

3. Utz and Groner, 3: 3711-3713.

4. *The Pope Speaks*, 3,4 (Spring 1957), 405-409.

5. Ibid. 401- 403.

6. According to biographer Ludwig Lenhart, Leo XIII referred to Bishop von Ketteler as his "great predecessor," remarking, "It is from him that I have learned." Cf. Ludwig Lenhart, *Bischof Ketteler* (Mainz: Hase & Kohler, 1966), 1: 47. For an English language translation of Bishop von Ketteler's basic teachings, see Rupert J. Ederer, *The Social Teachings of Wilhelm Emmanuel von Ketteler* (Washington, D.C.: University Press of America, 1981).

7. Utz and Groner, 3: 3415-3421.

8. Utz and Groner, 3: 3723-3725.

Chapter 9
The World of Money and Finance

Money is the lubricant without which a modern economy could not remain modern, which is to say, function at a high level of productive effectiveness. The economic system would be forced to operate at a primitive pace with barter as the principal arrangement for accomplishing the all-important exchange process. In logical sequence, exchange is the second step in the economic process leading to the process of satisfying man's temporal wants—the purpose which an economy is intended to accomplish. Moving beyond the most primitive level of production that is intended directly for the producer's consumption, exchange is required in order for producers to make use of goods and services which they turn out in surplus as specialized producers. That means trading them for the goods and services other specialized producers provide in quantities that exceed their own needs. Exchange can take place directly, without the use of a medium of exchange and standard of value, but that kind of exchange, i.e., barter, is severely limited in its potential and scope. It presupposes a coincidence of wants. Producers would be required to always find other producers who have the goods and services which they want, but who at the same time need the surplus goods and services they themselves have to trade. Such exchange is conceivable in a very close-knit, limited economy. It is cumbersome at best, and it would restrict economic life severely within a narrow range of goods and people's wants for them. Once a medium of exchange—money—was devised to facilitate exchange and enable it to move beyond such a very narrow range, economic life became richer, more varied, and at the same time more complex, and sometimes also more precarious.

Allowing that we may place the dawn of the capitalist era somewhere near the start of the modern era in Western history during the fifteenth century, that soon led to the beginnings of modern banking. By modern banking we have in mind the kind of institution which began in various ways to create money, i.e., add to the available supply of it. The earliest banks were simply safe places to deposit surplus money. Eventually they added the function of transferring such funds among their depositors on their books without the need for withdrawal and redeposit. Thus, the latter were provided with a convenient service enabling them to make payment to third parties with whom they engaged in business transactions. As one might expect, the added practice of lending out idle funds soon put in its appearance. When the two functions of lending and transferring deposited money on the banks' accounts were combined, the potential for increasing the available money supply was present. It could not have been long before that occurred, given the increasing pace of trade and business that accompanied the commercial revolution and rise of capitalism.

The movement by banks into money creation resulted partly from the astuteness of bankers in recognizing the chance for great gain by careful exploitation of the opportunity which presented itself. Meanwhile they did in fact fill a void caused by the absence of a sophisticated criterion available to statesmen of the time for providing the needed money supply. The traditional reliance on gold and silver acquired by mining or by other sometimes less savory means was no longer capable of filling the need for an adequate medium of exchange for the rapidly expanding commerce during that era.[1]

Clearly, there was always a moral dimension in banking even in its most primitive function of providing a safe depository for idle money. As banks progressed from being a useful ancillary institution to the sophisticated status of a major determining force in economic life, various moral implications came into sharper focus. The Catholic Church entered into the discussion with encyclicals by Pope Benedict XIV (*Vix Pervenit,* 1745), Pope Leo XII (*Caritate Christi,* 1824), and Pope Leo XIII (*Rerum Novarum,* 1891). In all of those the question of usury was eventually addressed. Pope Pius XII offered frequent insightful messages with regard to these institutions, which had developed such important and powerful status in modern economic life.

The Social Function of Banks
Address to Officials and Employees of the Bank of Naples
20 June 1948[2]

Early in the post-World War II era, Pius XII took the opportunity to admonish a gathering of Bank of Naples personnel who visited him in Rome. He reminded them of the tension which exists between what transpires in the world of banking and Christian sensibilities expressed at various points in the Scriptures. For example, there was the juxtaposition between God and Mammon, the reminder that where your treasure is, there your heart lies, and the Pauline warning that: "those who seek to become rich fall into temptation and a snare and into many useless and harmful desires which plunge men into destruction and damnation." (1 Tim. 6:9).

Nevertheless, the Pope stated that whereas the possession of and quest for money has its pitfalls, as those who labor in banking are well aware, money also has its beneficent side. The banks which administer wealth are in a good position to see that it is directed toward the well-being of the people and the nation.

He alluded to the especially difficult circumstances that the country found itself in during the period of reconstruction in the post-war period. And he acknowledged that the "influence and the responsibility of the banks is enormous," since they serve as "the mediators of credit and the providers of capital to agriculture and industry." Also, "one cannot understand the economic order without the factor, money." Since the banks direct the flow of money, they are required to avoid "unhealthy economic undertakings which violate justice," and to "harmonize their actions with sound public economy and genuine culture."

Throughout, there was evidence of clear papal recognition of the importance of money and of the banks as its administrators. While money and the banks are neutral agents in economic life, its use and their performance are nevertheless subject to special spiritual hazards.

The Work Ethic of Bank Officials
Allocution to Directors and Employees of the Bank of Italy
25 April 1950[3]

On this occasion, Pope Pius XII gave a "pep talk" to the banking personnel of the Bank of Italy, who had just concluded a retreat in Rome. He admonished them that they should consider their "...work, not in a purely materialistic sense but according to its true dignity and profound worth." For others, professional work of any kind can become "a burden which a man seeks to avoid so far as possible, or else an end in itself," "an idol of which a man makes himself the slave." But that must not be so for the Christian, for whom it is "a manner of serving God." The Pontiff pointed out that at the root of "so much discontent, so much indifference and irresponsibility" among workers today is the fact that "a clear and true concept of the Christian value of work no longer exists."

There is a perhaps oblique reference to the just wage principle in the statement: "A man's work ought to give to him and his family a sufficiency of daily bread." And as previous popes (Leo XIII and Pius XI) had indicated, that wage is a *family* wage. Also, bankers' work in particular "ought to contribute to the common good: it should testify to the sense of responsibility of each for the well-being of all." In other words, there is not only commutative justice involved here on the part of those who pay wages, but also social justice due from both the payers and receivers of those wages.

Perhaps one may detect in this address reference—likewise oblique—to another essential of papal social teachings on the economic order: the organization of all workers in a particular occupation, industry, or trade, i.e., the occupational or vocational order. "How is it that an organization such as yours is a real community, and not a mere existence in common, unless it is that all of you, from the first to the last, are conscious of working with a Christian loyalty for the good of all?" The Pope indicated that, "We insist on the social aspect of your profession, since this consideration ought to lead you to esteem and love it, and to practice it assiduously and conscientiously."

He concluded by pointing again to the "social function of the bank" which makes it possible "for the individual to render his money fruitful, even if only in a small degree, instead of dissipating it, or leaving it sleep without any profit, either to himself or to others." The inclusion of "to himself," is significant in terms of the Church's traditional teaching on interest and usury. In the context of modern society where opportunities to put money to work are virtually ongoing and ubiquitous, what Pius XII says here would seem to uphold the title to interest which analysts since the late Middle Ages already approved under the title: *lucrum cessans*. That is: interest may be charged for funds which, if loaned to another, lead to forgoing definitely possible gain for the lender who could have put it to other uses.

The other functions of banking which are invaluable for society are listed as: "to facilitate and encourage savings; to preserve savings for the future, at the same time rendering them productive in the present; to enable savings to share in useful enterprises which could not be launched without them; to make as simple and easy as possible the regulation of accounts, exchanges, commerce between the State and private organisms and, in a word, the entire economic life of the people; and to establish in some sort a mechanism which helps to surmount difficult times without running into catastrophe." That last function applies specifically to what is known as a *central bank*, in this case the Bank of Italy. A central bank is one to which other banks may have resort if they are in difficulty; i.e., it is among other things a bankers' bank.

Banks deal also in a special way, even if not exclusively, in administering the resources of wealthy people. Therefore, Pius XII reassured such persons that "In the Holy Gospels, the Divine Master does not condemn justly acquired riches." Instead, "[H]e praises or reproves the conduct, good or bad of man in their regard." However, there are reminders from Sacred Scripture, that "it is not possible to serve two masters;" and about the "bad rich man who lived only for pleasure without a glance of pity at poor Lazarus who, covered with sores languished at the gate." But there is also reference to "the reward for the good and faithful servant who made fruitful the money he received; while on the contrary, blame and punishment for the lazy servant who hid his master's money in the earth, instead of confiding it to bankers and receiving a return on it."

The Christian World View and Banking
Address to the Personnel of the Bank of Rome
18 June 1950[4]

The pilgrimage in this instance involved personnel of the prestigious Bank of Rome, which was marking a jubilee by a visit to the Holy Father. He reminded the gathering of various institutions to which banking personnel of both high and low estate are subject, as though dealing with money on a grand scale might tend to corrupt them. The Pope, for one, does not accept their "guilt" as an established fact. Instead, he urges all connected with the Bank and banking, whether of high or low estate, to acknowledge only the one Master, and to serve him conscientiously in their everyday dealings.

Pius XII reminded the bankers of the dignified function of the banking system and of its great importance for the national economy. And he recalled that it is a function that goes back in history to the times of the Assyrians and Egyptians. Indeed, time has done nothing but reinforce the significance of the role which banks play. The Pope introduced an interesting analogy. If money is regarded, "not unfairly, as the lifeblood of the economic organism, then the banks may be compared to the heart which regulates the flow of that lifeblood through the system...for the great welfare of individuals, of families, and of social groups, all of which together make up the body that is the national economy."

He concluded with the warning that such power and responsibility brings with it "the danger of abuse as there are copious instances in real life." But that simply presents all the greater challenge for the Church, the faithful, as well as for the banking system and the personnel who function in it. The Pope reverted to his analogy urging that those who undertake "the function of the 'heart' assure that they should therefore provide pure and healthy 'blood-flow' throughout the entire social economy."

The Role of Family Saving
Allocution to Employees of the Savings Bank of Rome
3 December 1950[5]

Here is a historic institution which was established under the auspices of Pope Gregory XVI. Savings banks represent a special kind of bank, which, generally speaking, did not formerly go beyond the safe-deposit and lending functions. Thus, the traditional savings bank did not combine the transfer-on-account by the use of checks, with lending so as to end up, in effect, creating additional money in the economy. Also, it had as its clientele predominantly people of modest means in the lower income groups. As the Pontiff pointed out here, its goal "is to enable people of very modest incomes slowly to increase their small savings and make them productive."

There followed paeans of papal praise for the kinds of families that patronize the traditional savings banks. Such banks encourage the type of thrift which implies a "virtuously courageous life." Courageous, because that is "without doubt necessary—in every age but never more than in our own—in order to resist perseveringly the thousand temptations to pleasure and joy and comfort and self-love which, even though falling short of a debilitating luxury, leave one with a disposition to do only what is strictly necessary." Though many people are able to save only small amounts, "those are not rare exceptions who, within the narrow margin between what is absolutely necessary and what is barely superfluous, manage to save, penny by penny, and confide to you what they have been able to put aside—very modest sums, it is true, but by no means negligible."

The Pontiff indicated that "such a manner of life notably contributes to maintain in a family a spirit of unity and a spirit of joy, amid a serene simplicity and moral dignity."

He reiterated what appears like approval of interest payment based on the title *lucrum cessans* as mentioned in a previous address to personnel of the Bank of Italy (see above). Savings banks too, "by informed and prudent administration...find a productive use for the modest capital of your depositors, not only to their private advantage, but also to the profit of undertakings which promote the public well being in which your clients become useful."

The Task of the Bank in the Service of the People
Address to the Personnel of the National Worker Bank of Italy
18 March 1951[6]

In this address, the Pope was dealing with a specialized kind of lending institution which provided credit for small and mid-sized enterprises, and originally also for farm cooperatives. He took the opportunity to stress the importance of agriculture for the well-being of the national economy; and the beneficent effect which the farm had for promoting family life as well as private ownership and cooperative work in and among families. It was a theme which Blessed John XXIII was to devote special attention to ten years later in the encyclical *Mater et Magistra.* Indeed, Pius XII suggested here that the role which this bank was fulfilling was specifically in keeping with the Church's social teachings.

He indicated that this particular banking institution, while still true to its original purpose, had expanded its field of activities to include "mid-sized and smaller industries." The credit they were able to get from these banks also constituted a "fortunate and practical application of the social teaching of the Church." That included now also lending which made possible home ownership, a prospect which was especially dire in the period following World War II. That urgent issue was addressed in the *Christmas Message* of 1942 where Pius XII had spoken of the need of families for "space, light, and fresh air."

While the somewhat technical work which banking personnel perform brings with it decent remuneration, the Pope alluded to the prospect of additional compensation in the realization that these banks are rendering an especially important social function in the life of the nation.

The Social and Moral Significance of the Credit System
Address Before Participants in the International Congress of the Credit System
14 October 1951[7]

The Pope drew the attention of the people attending this Congress to the fact that they are not simply functionaries in the field of credit, but that they are advisors. That makes them instrumental in avoiding the waste which comes along with the craving for luxury and sterile consumption, or which leads to mere accumulation without bringing in any profit. Pius XII made an interesting remark here in referring to the "egotists and lavish consumers" on the one hand, and "short-sighted *Geizhälze und Angsthasen*" on the other. Translated literally, these are "tightwads" and "scared rabbits" respectively. Both categories are devastating for the economy; and astute bankers are in a position to minimize their presence by making them aware of fruitful uses for their surplus funds. Indeed that can make the difference between whether "money flows or sleeps." The Pope encouraged them to make the rank-and-file depositors into active factors in the economy whether "as bondholders or stockholders in enterprises whose prosperity can be of great advantage for the community overall, whether we are talking about industrial activity or agricultural production, public works, or the construction of homes for people, educational or cultural activities, welfare or social institutions."

Whereas bankers have been accused, sometimes rightly, of being interested only in their own "dividends," a wise and healthy placement of capital constitutes a "social work of the first order." There followed the interesting observation that if bankers allow themselves to turn into impersonal clerks or "counter tenders," they may end up making themselves obsolete, given the development of sophisticated accounting machines. Pius XII referred to "these mechanical or electrical brains where the customer only has to push buttons to accomplish the purpose for which he came to the bank." Always the humanist with great concern for the personalist aspect in economic life, he contrasted such mechanical banking to the banker who carefully analyzes the customer before him, his needs and those of his business, in arriving at a decision about what is best for all concerned.

The Pope went into considerable detail describing the valuable function that the conscientious lender is in a position to render for individuals who come seeking credit. On the one hand there is the great responsibility to safeguard funds left in their care by investors. They expect such safety along with the prospect of some honest profit. On the one hand there are legitimate credit seekers: "a young inventor, a person with entrepreneurial spirit, a person who is a benefactor for humanity." On the other hand, their clients deserve to be protected from the "unrealistic dreamer" and the "scoundrel." There are also persons who experience "a bad year, a poor harvest; or damage…sickness" or some misfortune not of their own making, who can be rescued by a temporary loan. In such astute judgment about people we see the critical, important role which credit providers play. "They can be of great material assistance, along with providing moral support, for such people."

Finally, the credit provider—mediator—can even have an impact that goes beyond service to one or the other person. By a wise disposition of capital the periodic crises in economic life can be tempered and kept under some control, even if not averted completely.

All of that, the Pope offered to provide some solace to the people before him who often encounter suspicion, if not outright hostility in their occupation.

The Savings Bank in the Service of the People
Address Before the Administrative Council of the International Institute for Savings
16 May 1955[8]

In this address before a group of French bankers, Pius XII once again outlined the important role which savings banks as credit mediators render to the economy. Here he depicted them as assuming "in some way the function of a relay station between the small investors, on the one hand, who by their daily, astute and persevering labor have gained a modest holding, and, on the other hand, the state, the financial societies, the enterprises which need considerable capital in order to fulfill their economic functions. The savings bank brings these two factions together thus rendering a valuable service for the "general good." "It is important for a country to be able to use the resources accumulated by individuals but too widely dispersed to be of immediate use for purposes of the general good."

Pius XII took the opportunity to stress what is of the essence of good banking, as he put it, "the delicate problem…of the use of capital." In essence, this means avoiding "errors which would alienate the confidence of the depositors" so as to "defeat the ultimate purpose of the institution."

It is in the process of providing credit to the state, to industry, or to other lending institutions that the general welfare is served. Inasmuch as savings banks were established originally to help the "laboring classes," they may wish to continue helping especially to provide credit for agricultural operations, for craftsmen, and also for cooperatives and those who provide loans for home-building. Also, there are individual small enterprises which need credit periodically for raw materials and tools for their operations. Thus, there is encouraged cooperation between capital and labor of a kind that is especially helpful for workers.

The Good Administrator
An Address to the Directors and Staff of the Bank of Naples
29 May 1955[9]

In this message Pius XII extolled specifically how the Bank of Naples was aiding the "southern regions," always economically more hard-pressed than the more prosperous northern sectors of Italy. He presented the problem here as involving not merely making "abundant capital available," but just as importantly knowing "how to employ it wisely, according to the suggestions of a sound, clear-sighted financial policy" which would not "favor individuals to the disadvantage of the common good."

This suggested to the Pope the very important role of a "Bank such as yours" as "the soul of an economy returning to life...." Not at all reluctant to give prudential advice to bankers, he told them: "It is necessary to prevent the precipitous path of development in one direction from resulting in damaging stagnation in other fields, or certain industries from being favored for reasons not justified by genuine necessity." And as for sound labor relations, there was the added counsel that: "Each worker in some way shares the responsibility for the total success."

As their spiritual father, Pius XII closed with a warning, along with a word of encouragement. Informing this audience that "those who handle money in the materialistic environment of contemporary society must be deeply conscious of their responsibility, deeply rooted in the spirit of honesty in order to be on guard against temptations from within themselves as well as from without." At the same time, bankers should find "help" in their difficulties stemming from "the comforting realization that your function is important to society and benefits the national community in numerous ways." He closed with a reminder of the "good administrator" in Matthew 25:21, who was entrusted with greater amounts because he had been "faithful over a small thing."

Small Credit Banks in the Service of the Economy and Culture
Address to French Participants in the Eight International Congress of Credit Populaire
9 June 1956[10]

The institutions involved here are specifically credit cooperatives, or what in the older American context would embrace mutual savings banks and credit unions. The Pope recalled the history of such institutions which, unlike the international association which represented them here, date back well over a century. They were established, above all in Germany, to serve small businesses, agriculture, trade, and crafts by providing these with operating capital, among other things to keep such businessmen out of the hands of usurious lenders who, as the Pope says here, are still at large. He mentioned as especially active in their establishment, *Schulze-Delitzsch* and *Raiffeisen*. The principle at work here was mutuality, cooperation among people of modest means and, in a manner of speaking, "in the same boat."

These institutions involved large numbers of such people putting their hard-earned, modest savings together. Such accumulations of loanable funds were then available to the members whenever they found themselves in need, all the while avoiding undue speculative undertakings that were deemed too risky. That this kind of institution was worthwhile was suggested by their rapid spread and growth. As Pius XII pointed out, in Italy alone there were then some 200 establishments with nearly 400,000 members. Indeed they had by then achieved the status of first-rate lending institutions for craftsmen and small industries. He admonished the directors and administrators of such establishments that the safety of the members' deposits was the prime consideration, because they were managing their property. Personal ambition or the desire for great financial gain was not to be a factor as might be the case in other private business ventures. For the members too, a "solidaristic bond" ties them into a "social community" where thrift is encouraged by the existence of such institutions, along with prudent reliance on their resources.

Finally, by their earnings such organizations traditionally supported works of charity and those serving the public interest, which in one way or another foster the economic or cultural progress of their communities. Thus, their members should not be disappointed if their banks "spend a substantial portion of their profit for educational objectives which yield no immediate gains, but which foster the enhancement of the intellectual and spiritual level of the population." That, ultimately, is why they were established.

Public Finance

During his nineteen-year pontificate, Pope Pius XII delivered two significant addresses related to the topic of public finance. It is a subject that is especially relevant to his position as the leading world spokesman on the application of ethical norms in the various areas of economic life where morality is of critical concern. The ethically sensitive areas involve justice in the way taxes are assigned to the various sectors of society, as well as in the manner that citizens fulfill their tax obligations. Involved here are *distributive justice* and *legal justice* respectively. The former is binding on public authorities in the way in which they allocate benefits and obligations, including tax burdens, among those subject to their authority. The latter binds those subject to authority with regard to their fulfillment of their obligation, including tax payments, to the community. These represent two different aspects of social justice, since they both have the common good as their object.

On Public Finance
An Address to 100 Delegates Attending the Congress of the International Institute of Public Finance
2 October 1948[11]

Pius XII, perhaps semi-humorously, suggested to his audience that public finance "has always been the object of special attention on the part of not only intellectuals and technicians but, so to speak, of everyone." Yes, everyone sees his prosperity nurtured or threatened by the way taxation and public spending are managed. Indeed, the Pope displayed a special sympathy for the persons who are entrusted with the serious actual responsibility of managing the fiscal apparatus of the state. He again indicated his keen appreciation of what faces those who are expert in this field by the following interesting comment:

"Through self-interest, partisan spirit, or considerations more of sentiment than of reason, many people, in fact too many people—makeshift economists and politicians—approach and treat financial and taxation questions with all the more ardor and earnestness, assuredness and airy manner, the greater is their incompetence." In other words, this is an area where everyone is a self-styled expert. "Sometimes they do not seem even to suspect the necessity, in order to solve these problems, of deep studies, investigations and numerous observations of comparable experiences."

There followed a hint at a generalized violation of the principle of subsidiarity. Speaking of the tremendous increase in the financial needs of "nations, large or small," the Pope suggested that, in addition to international complications and tensions, this "is due also, and perhaps much more to the huge increase in the State's activity." And he made it clear that such increase is often less than wholesome, since it is "dictated too often by false or unhealthy ideologies," so that it makes "financial policy" and particularly "taxation policy an instrument serving preoccupations of a quite different order." Thus, "the science and art of public finance will descend to the role of a technical and purely formal manipulation for lack of clear, simple, solid fundamentals." In the Pope's estimate, "that is what one sees today in several fields of public life—a clever and bold framework of systems and procedures, but without elasticity, life or soul."

That was a rather stern indictment of what appeared to Pius XII to be happening in this important area of public finance. Again, "[t]he individual is coming to have less and less understanding of the financial affairs of the State." The age of innocence, in other words, appears to be over, and cynicism becomes commonplace. "Even as regards the wisest policy, he always suspects a mysterious maneuver, a malicious ulterior motive which he should distrust and protect himself against." The consequences are more serious, perhaps, than meets the eye at first glance. "It is there, in short, that one must seek the real reason for the decay of the moral conscience of the people—people of all classes—in matters of the public good and in taxation matters principally."

Pius XII made it clear that he regarded what was happening here as "a crisis of conscience." Accordingly, he appealed to the experts appearing before him: "In the name of human conscience, do not destroy morals from the top." Specifically, he asked them to "[F]orego those measures which, despite their technical virtuosity, shock and wound the people's sense of the just and unjust, or which relegate to the background their vital urge, their legitimate ambition to harvest the fruits of their own labor, and their anxiety over family security, all considerations which merit first place in the mind of the legislator and not the last."

The specific ethical application followed. It tied the workings of the economic system to the higher ends and purposes which confront the human being. "The financial system of the State should aim at reorganizing the economic situation in a manner that would assure the people the material conditions for what is indispensable to follow the supreme end assigned by the Creator, the development of intellectual, spiritual and religious life."

Thus, it was the task and duty of the expert to "defend financial policy against the maneuvers of the ambitious and the demagogues." The Pope urged them to remain "devoted to the greatest impartiality, ardent to find not popular favor but the true good of the people." That would bring them, "at least the approbation of a select few who understand you...." In addition, there will be "the testimony of your conscience and God."

Taxation

An Address to Participants in the Congress of the International Association for Finance and Taxation

2 October 1956[12]

The theme which this group of experts chose for themselves included the question of double taxation in the area of the turnover tax, the matter of what reciprocal influence there is between how businesses are taxed and the particular juridical form they adopt, their nature and their expansion, and finally the legal safeguarding of those subject to taxes against the tax authority. The outcome of these considerations were then to be presented to the various countries for their practical consideration in tax policy. Such highly technical deliberations, one might expect, would intimidate even Pius XII who during his pontificate addressed a wide range of expert groups with amazing acuity about their various fields. Instead, he coolly recounted the history of this organization of tax specialists, and encouraged them in their complex deliberations, once again displaying his remarkable genius. Nor did he hesitate to make certain suggestions in keeping with his own authority as a moral teacher.

Tax laws in modern states, he informed his audience, did not always stem from "rational and precise criteria." Instead, there were "the necessities of the moment," and "the political or economic inclinations of those who happened to be in power." "In fact even the administration of tax laws follows a far from uniform pattern, often straying from the intent of the legislators." Hence, the results display a lack of simplicity and consistency. Worse still, there is often a "practical disregard of the principles of justice which ought to guide tax legislation."

Getting down to specifics, whereas citizens clearly have the obligation to share in meeting the cost of public outlays, the state has corresponding obligations, as it is entrusted with protecting and assuring the general welfare of its citizens. Hence, it is not to impose immoderate burdens, nor should it try to rectify deficits "caused by unreasonable measures," or "to favor one industry or branch of commerce at the expense of another that is equally useful."

The Pope then addressed the tendency of modern states during the postwar era to "extend their activities into economic life, and to take over a growing number of services..." That involves more direct control over the economy and "the social protection of various categories of workers." Of necessity the administrative apparatus becomes larger and costlier. "Private initiative can thereby be stifled by the increasing tax burdens, to the extent that "the development of industry and commerce are retarded." He expressed his gratification at proposals this group had made to eliminate harmful provisions in tax legislation, which go counter to the "true interests of the individuals and families, as well as to the normal progress of commerce and industry at the national and international levels." The Pope also approved the group's efforts to establish uniform legislation among nations so as to eliminate "double taxation and barriers in the international circulation of capital and goods." They were also at work providing legal protection for taxpayers in dealing with the tax authorities, which would avert their demoralization and tempt them to tax evasion.

Pius XII went further in his appeal for tax reform. He called for a thorough reexamination of existing tax legislation to rid it of what he referred to as "a very troubling empiricism." Also, it should express clearly the basic moral principles underlying the right to tax, so that both the taxing jurisdiction and the administrators of the laws may apply these. In that way taxes will not seem always to be excessive and arbitrary, but appeal instead to the taxpayers' understanding of its realistic dimensions. In that way people will grasp the reciprocal obligation they have one to another: "their civil solidarity and the relationship of all to all." In other words, "the wisdom of those who govern and the efficiency of a sacrificial and incorruptible administration would make it absolutely clear that the burdens imposed on the taxpayers represent an actual recognizable service which bears its fruit."

The Pope concluded with a reminder of the task this group had taken on itself, and what great benefit their successful management of it would render for society. "By benefit of the experiences of various countries you will be placed in a position where you can always improve on the theoretical basis of the tax system, and their various applications." And, "...inasmuch as you fortify the inner organization of contemporary society, you help to clear the way for much higher values which have been stymied or endangered by misunderstandings or hostility, and which at times drove a wedge between public authorities and the citizens, even bringing about hostility between nations." All such action contributed to what the Church sought for passionately: "the internal strengthening of nations and their effective cooperation at the international level." Without using the expression at this point, the Pope was clearly talking about solidarity within nations and among them.

Notes

1. For an examination of how money evolved from barter, and then from money issued by governments to bank-created money, see Rupert J. Ederer, *The Evolution of Money* (Washington: Public Affairs Press, 1964).

2. Arthur-Fridolin Utz, O.P., and Joseph-Fulko Groner, O.P., *Soziale Summe Pius XII* (Freiburg, Switzerland: Paulusverlag, 1954 -1961), 1: 1301-1304.

3. *The Catholic Mind*, May 1951, 331-333.

4. Utz and Groner, 1: 1298-1300.
5. *The Catholic Mind*, May 1951, 330-331.
6. Utz and Groner, 1: 1308-1310.
7. Utz and Groner, 1: 1293-1297.
8. *The Pope Speaks,* Summer 1955, 143-145.
9. *The Pope Speaks,* Summer 1955, 145.
10. Utz and Groner, 3: 3451-3455.
11. *The Catholic Mind,* vol. XLVII, no.1035 (March 1949), 189-190.
12. Utz and Groner, 3: 3883ff.

Chapter 10
Various Topics

Housing

Economic Policy and the Need for Housing
Address to Members of the International Labor Organization
25 March 1949[1]

Anyone familiar with the housing situation, following the virtual moratorium on home construction, in addition to the widespread destruction in many countries during World War II, will appreciate the lament expressed in this address by Pius XII. He took the occasion to deliver a pertinent stern lecture to the members of the ILO who came before him in this audience. The Pope indicated his awareness that in the immediate aftermath of the War most of the affected nations were concerned about getting their agriculture back into operation and in reestablishing their often depleted capital structure. Nevertheless the Pope made an appeal for "the great masses of the population" that desperately "need housing just as much as they need clothing and nourishment." That, he said "is a common need of all people without regard to income or status." Therefore, it is a need which calls for legitimate satisfaction from any normal economy that is directed toward its proper goal, with help especially from private initiative."

What follows is a seemingly barbed remark about "the highly regarded modern economy that is proud of producing ever more and always better, and always at lower cost." How is it, the Pope asked, that such economies "have thus far been unable to satisfy this genuine and by no means artificial pressing need of people, and above all of families...." It is as though "we are content with the primitive shelter of the primitive man or the nomad, or with the tidy little house that is equipped with all modern comforts, but where there is no room for the child." The Catholic Church, which was persistent in its denunciation of the artificially limited family, was also keenly aware of the connection between inadequate housing and the contraceptive mentality beginning to permeate society.

What followed was a polite papal suggestion that the housing industry should "pay more attention to satisfying this basic need of people, than to concern about the movement of prices on the market." Indeed, if it did that it would be doing a "social work, because it would be leading back the economy itself from the fallacies of an aimless competition to the level track of cooperation in a truly social order." While acknowledging that there was enormous work to be done in the postwar reconstruction period, Pius XII appeared relentless in his insistence that this particular problem is not to be lost sight of in the process.

The Pontiff concluded by recalling that the Church's interest in this matter stems from the fact that its social teachings are oriented in the first instance to "the interests of the family." And proper housing, in his view, presented an especially great "incentive for the progress of the economy and of technology." What is more, "an economy, a technology which is geared to the basic needs of people has no reason to be concerned about a number of the inhabitants being too large or too small." Thus, the proponents of the emerging overpopulation hysteria were already forewarned that the Catholic Church and its teaching popes would not be misled by the diversion which their campaign would put in the way of dealing with the true economic needs of mankind.

On Housing
Address to the Autonomous Institute of Public Housing of Rome
21 November 1953[2]

This address was originally published in *The Catholic Mind* under the heading: "On Public Housing." That was misleading. Pius XII was addressing here members of the *Istituto per le Case Populari,* which translates to "Institute for Popular Housing" or more loosely yet even more accurately, "Institute for housing for the people." It is clear that what Pius XII was presenting here was not primarily an appeal for publicly financed housing.

Inadequate housing is a special aspect of the overall social problem the Catholic Church had been addressing in her teachings, especially since the time of Pope Leo XIII. It represents a dark side of the period following the Industrial Revolution, and it is tied in with the some of the moral problems the Church has had to deal with since that time. As rural life diminished and urban life became a larger part of the social setting, housing for many of the people who left the rural setting with its characteristically large families was all too often inadequate from the start. Pius XII was addressing here an organization which had begun to help deal with this problem a half century earlier. It concerned itself with a situation which, Pius XII said here, "has been painful from the very beginning and has remained so even to this day." Needless to say, the "consequences of the War rendered it more difficult and made the need of help still more urgent." And it is a problem to which, he pointed out, his predecessor had already drawn attention in *Quadragesimo Anno,* where he said: "It is horrifying to consider the impediments that the altogether unbecoming state of housing offers to the union and intimacy of family life."

The Pontiff made clear the sinister connection between the housing problem and family life according to Catholic moral teaching. He stated that "the family must be a spiritual and moral, juridical and economic unity; and that strict and imprescriptible laws regulate the birth and the development of new life." Anyone who experienced the housing problem especially as it affected the working classes throughout Europe after World War II could understand the grave temptation it afforded to wink at the moral law with regard to procreation. Pius XII was keenly aware of this: "The Lord alone knows how often under such conditions, human weakness has hindered souls from leading a Christian life and injured them also in their faith!"

Incidentally, the expression "consumerism" describing the inordinate urge to "lead the good life," was not yet in vogue when this gathering was held in Rome in 1953. Yet, the straws were clearly in the wind less than 10 years after World War II ended with its scars still evident throughout Europe. Pius XII, in any case, saw what was happening. "Morally healthy people...do not let themselves be dragged into a consumption without restraint, the cancer of present-day social economy." Also, they do "not stand in the ranks of those who expect or demand everything from the state." This suggests at least the potential for violation of the principle of subsidiarity also in this matter of providing housing.

"Public authorities ought, in regard to housing, as in other matters, seek to favor, and in no case oppose, private enterprise." In fact, "they should favor the enterprise of cooperatives." Yet, amid "the difficulties of the postwar period...there must always be a strong public power that will methodically and energetically take action." At this point the Pontiff became quite specific, indicating once again his keen awareness of what was going on in the world outside the walls of the Vatican. He was suggesting that there is clearly a place for public authorities to intervene to prevent speculative activities from putting land prices out of the reach of ordinary people. "Therefore oppose, with every means that the common good justifies, usury in property and all economically unproductive financial speculation involving a good so fundamental as the soil."

On the negative side, the Pope blamed those "who bear responsibility for the common good and for the preventive measures that this good requires," for the aesthetically flawed—not to mention often physically and ethically unhealthy—monstrosities which pass for popular housing, especially in urban centers. Here Pius XII referred specifically to "bee hives," and "barracks," as well as to "grottoes," the "little caves," and the "roosts in cellars and other uninhabitable places." Some of these "monstrosities" are even the results of misguided ventures in "public housing," whereas others simply result from lack of proper public intervention in such matters as proper building codes and the enforcement of other laws with regard to healthy housing standards.

The Pope praised the Institute for its work on these issues at the regional, and ultimately at the national level "for the general good of the nation." Their activity on behalf of the Italian people was deemed "in harmony with the fundamental principles of the social doctrine of the Church."

Near the end of the discourse there was a significant reference to the destructive effect of "economic liberalism": "The country, the territory that is inhabited by a people united in a state and linked together by the common good, is not merely, even from an economic viewpoint, as economic liberalism would have it, the expanse of lands where the mechanism of momentarily lower costs and more favorable conditions of trade determine the destiny and the appointed lot of men." Although Pius XII did not use the expression "solidarity," that is clearly the issue here, since the common good is ultimately what links people together at the various levels of society up to the level of "the state" which is under discussion here.

Immigration

On the Immigration Question

Address to Political Personages from the USA
13 March 1946[3]

The Utz and Groner anthology of Pius XII's works does not identify what kind of "personages from the USA" he was addressing here. It seems clear that they were persons who had some responsibility in the area of immigration. It was then less than one year since World War II had ended, and Europe in particular was faced with a staggering refugee problem. As it had done so often in the past, the United States was again welcoming victims caught in the midst of heart-rending situations, and the Pope took the opportunity to praise the American nation for its generosity toward immigrants. At the same time, he pointed out the enormous contributions immigrants had made to the cultural and religious formation of that great land.

Pius XII indicated his awareness that "changed circumstances had brought about a certain restriction on immigration from abroad." That, he said, was understandable since, "in this matter, it is not only the interests of the immigrants, but also the well-being of the country itself that must be taken into consideration." Yet, in the next breath, the Pope seemed unrelenting. "We hope that along with such restriction, Christian charity and the feel of human solidarity [*Zusammengehörigkeit*] which involves all people, will not be lost sight of." His concern was that, "Immigration can contribute to the solution of one of the saddest human problems Europe has ever faced—a problem that was intensified in an inhuman manner by the forceful displacement of helpless and innocent peoples."

Immigration to North America, Then and Now
Address to Members of the U.S. Congress
31 October 1947[4]

In a second address on this matter of immigration during the years directly following World War II, Pius XII was addressing members of a Congressional Committee on Immigration. His message was poignant. He reminded his audience that their country "offered an unimpeachable proof that the peoples of various nations and races are able to live side-by-side and to cooperate in an orderly, peaceful, and fortunate society." Indeed, the Pope suggested, "It is the history of the rise and progress of your country." Furthermore, "No one can deny the vital role which the immigrants played in this history." He called it "an inspiring and encouraging history." The Pontiff was aware that the American Congress was considering amending their country's laws with some view to restricting immigration. He recognized that now there were "entirely new problems," just as he appreciated that the welfare of a country must be taken into account along with the interests of those who wish to immigrate." Yet, in these situations there are also pressures by local interests which can affect legislation. "Wise legislation will always remain aware of humanity and the poverty, the misery and the suffering which are its heritage."

That was plainly an appeal for generosity, and recalling the "spirit of sympathy for the unfortunate and the helpless suffering persons which is so characteristic of your nation," Pius XII reminded his visitors that their "brief journey to Europe has certainly revealed to you some of the pressing needs of humanity."

International Trade

International trade has been a perennial political and economic issue especially since the emergence of modern national states a half millennium ago. It has been a dominant issue among economists since their science began to take shape during the 18th century. Even before the Physiocrats and Adam Smith, the Mercantilists made trade across international borders a pivotal consideration in their approach to making their own national states wealthy and powerful in contention with rival states. Adam Smith's *Wealth of Nations*, first published in 1776, made free trade one aspect of his overall liberal economic philosophy which installed individual freedom in pursuit of self-interest as the ultimate source of national prosperity. And ever since Smith's work came to be accepted as the original classic for the infant economic science, there were and continue to be followers who insist, in nothing short of absolute terms, on unrestricted free trade both domestically and also across national borders. More recently this belief finds expression in the term "globalism."

The Catholic Church in its social teachings has taken a dim view of that view of unrestrained liberty—i.e. liberalism—as a correct guiding norm in the various aspects of economic life. Near the end of the 19th century, Leo XIII reacted in his pioneer social encyclical to the consequences of uninhibited self-interest and free competition. While *Rerum Novarum* and its later commemorative encyclical by Pius XI, *Quadragesimo Anno*, dealt mainly with the disintegration of social order in the domestic economy, successors, starting with Pius XII, had something to say about the implications of free trade both for one's own country and abroad, for example in former colonies. The two addresses below once again provided a bridge to the great works of his successors John XXIII, Paul VI and Pope John Paul II.

Christian Principles of International Trade
Address to the Congress of International Exchange
7 March 1948[5]

The opening statement to this group was an especially challenging one: "None is in a better position than you to appreciate the contrast between the disorder in the field of economic relations—which has reigned in many countries for some time past—and the law, order and harmony that God has imprinted on all creation."

Clearly his was not simply a routine welcome for visiting groups in Rome, anxious for a few words and a blessing from the Holy Father. What these visitors heard was something like a definitive statement on what economic activity is all about:

> The goods of the earth, whose exchange ought to stabilize and maintain economic equilibrium among nations, have become the object of political speculation. This applies not only to material goods, but alas! to man also. He has, in many instances been reduced to the level of a commodity to be exploited.

Had that statement been made by a Marxist, no one would have been surprised. But the world should by now have become aware that the teachings of the Catholic Church on social order were more genuinely radical by far than the dubious and often inconsistent rantings of Karl Marx. Marx observed the ravages of liberal capitalism and came up with a remedy worse than the disease. Roman Catholic popes saw the disease as well as the cure proposed by the socialists, and they opposed both with their social teachings. The observations by Pius XII were direct and to the point: "Unfortunately we are often witnesses to the interplay of policy which is nothing more than a race for power and supremacy." Thus, "what remains of economic relations between nations is, strictly speaking, no longer an exchange, the mutual action and reaction which could do good everywhere." Instead, "these relations are now limited to a unilateral flow of goods under the impulse of Christian charity, or a more or less disinterested benevolence towards nations in need." That, the Pope indicated, is a "far from abnormal state of things wherein exchanges of goods between nations is at one and the same time the necessary complement to the respective national economies and a tangible sign of their flourishing condition."

Pius XII suggested that present difficulties in this area "would not be so great, nor would their solution be so difficult, were it not that there has been added uncertainty and disagreement as to objectives." These include "a return to a world economy as was practiced during the last century." "Others support regional or inter-state unions for individual economies." That was probably a reference to the initiatives then underway to promote the European Coal-Steel Union which would later develop into the European Economic Community. The former situation was trade according to the rules of international gold standard under the hegemony of leading powers like Great Britain, which had enjoyed since the Industrial Revolution the clear advantage in international trade. Still others—and the Pope appeared to have had in mind the Communist states—"seek the centralization of all economic life—including even the activity of human labor."

Not wishing to get involved in the details of "the practical side of these problems," Pius XII drew attention to "the deeper roots and causes" of "this sharp division of opinion." These include "a deplorable want of reflection, that seems satisfied with an easy and superficial empiricism," and "a really fundamental difference of views as to what social economy is or should be, and how man should approach and treat it." That may have been polite language for: People don't seem to really understand what economic life is all about! What followed then was a significant lecture on basic economics in four "lessons."

1) "*Economic life means social life*." Its "essential scope—to which individuals are equally bound to help in the different spheres of their activity—is to assure in a stable manner for all members of society the material conditions required for the development of cultural and spiritual rights." Then came a telling indictment of the neoliberalism which was to infect economic thinking in the years ahead.

> But satisfactory results are not possible apart from an external order and social norms which aim at lasting achievement of this objective. *An appeal to an automatic and magic law is a mirage*, no less vain in the economic order than *in any other sphere of human activity*. [Italics added].

That may be as significant and clear a statement on the social order as is to be found throughout the Church's social teachings. It clearly foreshadows what Paul VI was to say about the "renewal of the liberal ideology" (*Octogesima Adveniens*, par. 35) in 1971, and what Pope John Paul II would say about "neoliberalism" in 1999 (*Ecclesia in America*, par. 56). The theme recurs in the second lesson.

2. "*Economic life means social life—the life of human beings*. Hence it cannot be conceived without liberty." That echoed the great stress Pius XII placed on the human person—the *personalism* which he stressed throughout his teaching pontificate. Nor was he thinking in the first instance about the blatant and obvious denial of liberty in the totalitarian socialist world. He stated: "This lib-

erty can never be the seductive but deceptive formula of 100 years ago—the purely negative liberty from the regulating will of the State." He continued, "Nor is it the pseudo-liberty of our day—the submission of oneself to the dictate of mighty organizations." What then is the liberty of which he spoke?

> Genuine and true liberty can only be that of men who feel themselves bound to the objective goal of social economy and enjoy the right to demand that economies be ordered socially so as to guarantee and protect liberty rather than restrict even in the least degree the choice of means to that end.

Foreshadowing the great emphasis by Pope John Paul II in 1981 on the subject-role of the worker (*Laborem Exercens*, par. 6), we find: "As regards the end of the social economy, every productive member is the subject and not the object of economic life."

3. "*National economy, being the economy of a people within the unity of the State, is itself a natural unity.*" So far as the international economy is concerned then, we find: "Accordingly, international economic relations have a function which, although positive and necessary, is only subsidiary." What is more, "upsetting of this relationship between national and international economy was one of the great errors of the past." Yet, given "the circumstances under which a large number of people are forced to live…it would perhaps be opportune to examine whether or not a regional union of different national economies would render possible a more efficacious development of the forces of production." Again, it was during this period that, partly because of the destructive consequences of the two World Wars, Germany and France were exploring with neighbor nations, first a combination of the coal and steel communities, and later the broader market which we today know as the European Economic Community (EEC), or European common market.

In that proposition, as in the previous one and in the one to follow, we find, once again an exact concordance with the thought of the Jesuit economist, Heinrich Pesch. Pesch stressed the primary role and responsibility for the *national* economy, explaining why unrestricted free trade is not an acceptable option, and adding precisely that while foreign trade must obviously play an important part in the relations of nations to one another, it must be kept within the limits of what is best for the national economy. And with regard to the role of the working human person, for Pesch he was not only the dominant factor of production, but he was, in fact, much more than a mere factor of production. That is: he is not only the *means*, but the *subject* and goal for which all economic activity takes place. It was, of course, Pesch who made *solidarity* the dynamic principle of economic life, as well as of social life generally. And it was he who demonstrated the critical importance of applying the *principle of solidarity* (a Christian virtue according to Pope John Paul II) at various levels of society. These included the solidarity of all of mankind, as well as of all citizens united in one political society. That provided the basis for the national economy, and for the international one which Pius XII positioned here as having a "subsidiary" role to the economic life of the nation.

Solidarity was then mentioned explicitly in the fourth of the Pope's lessons in economics.

4. "*Above all, there must be victory over the evil principle of utility as the basis and rule of what is right in economic life.* This means victory over those occasions of conflict which arise from glaring disparities, maintained at times by compulsion in the world economy." Also, "It means victory over the spirit of cold egoism, so as to bring about that sincere solidarity, both juridical and economic, which implies fraternal collaboration according to the precepts of the divine law among nations assured of their autonomy and freedom."

Pesch stated in his work that while solidarity makes good common sense, i.e., is in accordance with the natural law, a solidaristic system of economy would have its best chance of success in a Christian culture. At this point Pius XII appears to have confirmed that position when he stated: "Faith in Christ and observance of His commandments of love alone can bring about such a salutary victory."

There were four "fundamental concepts" about economic life. It would appear that only the conditions in a society which was fast becoming post-Christian could have led a teaching pope to become that specific about details for what is basically a secular science. The question needs to be asked whether the world was already at that stage in 1948. Pius XII seemed to think so.

He had two more observations to make which bear that out. But in true Ciceronian fashion, he would not mention them: "We preferred not to speak of the fatal inconsistency of those who, in proposing free world traffic for their own goods, deny to others this natural liberty." Great Britain, for one, climbed to the pinnacle of its vast economic power and wealth on such a hypocritical posture through much of the nineteenth century and before. The American colonists were early victims of that kind of policy—a difficulty that continued to confront them after they, in desperation, finally declared their independence.

There was then a second kind of conduct which Pius XII "preferred not to speak of": "We preferred to refrain from characterizing the conduct in practice of certain champions of the rights of private property." Then followed this momentous and challenging statement: "These persons so interpret the use and relationships of private property that they succeed—even better than their adversaries—in overturning this very institution, so natural and indispensable to human life, and especially to the family." Like his predecessors Leo XIII and Pius XI, and his successors, John XXIII, Paul VI, and Pope John Paul II, Pius XII pointed out how the exaggerated, self-serving, interpretation of private property as an absolute right by those who decry the Marxian solution serves to drive desperate men precisely into the arms of those socialists who propose a "cure" worse than the disease.

Finally, having assumed the role of the dutiful schoolmaster, the Pontiff urged others whose full-time responsibility it was to teach economics, to carry on: "It remains but to conclude Our address with the wish that in professional schools and universities these principles of economic life be properly taught."

By his closing words he appeared to be intimating that time was running out: "The urgent need of overcoming the materialistic spirit of our day, which also affects the field of economics makes this imperative."

Freedom in Commerce
Address to Participants of the 1st World Congress of the Chambers of Commerce
27 April 1950[6]

After praising his audience as "in fact the elite in the world of commerce," Pius XII followed with a suggestion that it is "entirely proper that you crown your technical and legal works by a serious moral consideration of your role and responsibilities." He then offered the intriguing parallel between Mercury to whom "mythology provided wings"—and the "desire for freedom of movement which the businessman needs both within and beyond the boundaries of his country." The Pope credited his businessman audience with an appreciation that this is by no means an "unlimited freedom that is irreconcilable with the purpose and the requirements of the national economy, and with the constant concern for the material welfare of all." He conceded generously that "it is precisely with a view to this welfare that you strive for a fuller freedom for commerce."

The Pontiff was by no means leading up to a plea for "free trade" or "free enterprise" in the *laissez faire* sense as proposed by both the paleo- as well as the neoliberal school of economic thought. He was simply reaffirming what is basically the Church's centrist avoidance of the two extremes of riotous economic libertarianism and the harsh collectivistic regimentation of economic life. The unacceptability of the latter was made clear in the following:

> There are even countries where a policy has been adopted more or less absolute, that places commerce in the hands of public authority. Let us affirm this clearly: this is a tendency in opposition to the Christian conception of social economy. Commerce is fundamentally an activity of the individual, and it is this private activity that gives a man his first impulse and lights the flame of his enthusiasm.

Pius XII set forth the basic economic gospel of the legitimate limits of freedom and the important role of incentive in triggering effective economic activity and progress. That is affirmed further in what follows, where the role of the individual is put in its proper perspective: "As a businessman, he must also consider himself a servant of the community." In other words, he must work for the general welfare of all, prompted in the first instance by his own good conscience rather than by state compulsion. Nevertheless, "you will not obtain the goal you wish, which is the general prosperity, without putting into full effect the individual exercise of commerce for the service of society's material well-being."

Rejected is the kind of egotistical free enterprise that was often inferred in so-called classical economics. "To have no other ambition except always to make more money and to enrich himself, is to betray his vocation, since one can well call by name (vocation) this mission that God has assigned to him, the particularly difficult calling of a merchant." With even greater severity, Pius XII continued: "He would thus play the game of the evil-minded who strive to make of commerce a living vampire at the expense of all economic life." Karl Marx once referred to *capital* as a "living vampire that is fruitful and multiplies." Unlike Marx, the Roman Catholic Pope was not condemning an entire class of people. He was censuring a purely chrematistic approach to business where money-making was the sole, over-riding goal.

What is expected of the good merchant is the endeavor "to circulate worldly goods, destined by God for the advantage of all," and to take "them where they must serve and in a manner to make them serve well." Then, he will be a "good and true servant of society, a guarantee against misery, a promoter of general prosperity."

In appropriate papal fashion, Pius XII concluded with a scriptural allusion. He referred to the passage in Matthew (13:45) comparing the kingdom of Heaven to that "single pearl of great price" which the shrewd merchant acquired by selling all of his goods.

The Activity of the International Chamber of Commerce as a Contribution to World Peace

Address to Participants in the 16th Congress of the International Chamber of Commerce

4 May 1957[7]

It is clear that Pius XII always did his "homework" whenever some specific organization came to him in Rome for a few words of greeting and paternal counsel. The International Chamber of Commerce held its second Congress in Rome in 1923, and it had since then, in the Pope's words, "grown in importance for its study and defense of the interests of the private economic sector." Indeed it had by now gained status in the Economic and Social Council of the United Nations because of "the prestige and authority of its technicians." Because of its access to an enormous amount of information, it has been able to play a part in the way agreements are arrived at between nations.

Characteristically Pius XII would cite the activity and the services rendered by organizations like the International Chamber of Commerce as support, in principle, of their potential. Typically, admonitions then follow.

> The realistic goals which you pursue will not permit you to lose sight of the human problems which arise in the area of international economic development: the exercise of individual freedom in the area of economic competition provides a productive incentive for all; but experience has demonstrated all too often that it leads to bitter battles in the process of acquiring new markets.

Enter here, the leading teacher of the largest Christian denomination in the world, the Pope of the Roman Catholic Church as he recalled the Scriptural warning: "For what does it profit a man if he gain the whole world but suffer the loss of his soul?" (Matt. 16:26).

Pius XII pointed out: "The personal damage, as irreparable as it may be, still provides only an incomplete picture of the evil brought about by the quest for gain, a quest which often leads to a true economic warfare, leaves behind irremediable damage, and brings with it the sad consequences of disruption in family life and in society generally." He suggested that "fortunately the time of unrestricted economic liberalism is past, while now the opposite excess seems to be the threat." Subsequent events would prove that this usually prescient Pontiff was being premature in this observation. His successors, starting with Paul VI, would have to warn precisely about "a renewal of the liberal ideology" (*Octogesima Adveniens*, par. 35). Nevertheless when this address was delivered, there was indeed a pronounced tendency, even in the so-called "free economies," toward centralized planning based to a degree on the momentary success of the so-called Keynesian revolution. The neoliberalism which Paul VI warned of then followed in pendulum-style reaction.

Pius XII returned to his positive appraisal of what the *International Chamber of Commerce* was attempting. "Everywhere you propose a solution that is reasonable and free of partisan political tendencies, with a view to the advancement of economic progress and the general welfare in terms of free international solidarity." That led into the theme which was moved into the forefront of discussion by this Pope in the last year of his pontificate, and which was soon to become a central preoccupation in the social teachings of his successors, John XXIII and Paul VI: "We are pleased with the notion that the underdeveloped nations are not lost sight of among your concerns, and that you are especially concerned about including them among your studies and practical objectives." That, the Pope concluded, would provide "the best assurance for a stable peace among the great economic powers, and we nurture a legitimate hope for a happy development of economic relations in the world for which you, with your know-how and unselfishness, will make your contribution."

Statistics

The architect of solidarist economics, Heinrich Pesch, considered statistics as one of the most important auxiliary sciences for economics. The application of statistical techniques to the data that is gathered and evaluated by economists is certainly of the first order of relevance in the progress of economic analysis. During his nineteen-year pontificate, Pius XII addressed experts in a vast range of disciplines, including also a gathering of statisticians during the early 1950s.

The Social Utility of Statistics
Address before Members of the Central Institute for Statistics
16 May 1951[8]

Pius XII encouraged the assembled statisticians whose occupation is often equated with "coldness," as one often hears the expression, "cold, hard statistics." He assured them that such an evaluation is likely to be made only by persons who have slight if any acquaintance with the craft. The expression, "a picture is worth a thousand words," may truly be applied also to the valid use of statistics. Indeed, the Pope recalled for the gathering that his predecessor, Pius XI, once spoke enthusiastically about the "poetry of numbers."

While its application to a particular set of circumstances can indeed give the "impression of dryness," the Pontiff proposed that since statisticians first organized themselves into a forerunner group in 1861, the science had developed in a most fascinating manner. As the physician relies on an accumulation of data in arriving at his decisions in treating sick people, the sociologist, the legal expert, as well as moralists and educators all refer to statistical data in reaching conclusions about problems germane to their disciplines.

Pius XII referred to the ongoing fascination with highly complex machines then referred to as "mechanical brains." While that remark preceded in time the arrival of the specific computer age when the so-called personal computer became as ubiquitous as the telephone, the straws were already in the wind indicating the remarkable transformation of the manner in which information would be processed and transmitted. "For all of that, we still required a human brain to put those mechanical brains into motion in order to render valid service to the human beings by obediently carrying out their intelligent directions." What he said then about those "mechanical brains" is entirely appropriate for the cybernetic revolution foreshadowed by what the Pope was talking about before the assemblage of statisticians.

On Statistics
Address Before the International Institute of Statistics
10 September 1953[9]

The Pontiff referred to the appearance before him of the Italian Central Institute of Statistics just two years previously, while expressing his pleasure in "receiving the participants in great scientific congresses who, after completing their work, come to visit Us." This address, unlike the previous, which was largely exhortatory, contained significant warnings with regard to the application of statistics, specifically the use to which certain social sciences were putting it increasingly. Rather than to risk misinterpreting or to raise the suspicion of misinterpreting the important counsel offered by the Pope in this address, significant portions of it are quoted directly.

Pius XII first took the opportunity to note the significant shift from "the domain of the natural sciences wherein reigns the determinism of matter (which) offers an appropriate field for such intellectual activity and lends itself quite easily to the elaboration of precise laws...." Then he moved into the present when, "without ceasing to study nature, we are turning more and more towards the sciences of man and particularly towards those whose object is human society." He warned that in those human sciences, "given the intervention of personal and free causes, a great number of facts escape appraisal by classical mathematical analysis, and seem to defy all attempts at rational and systematic explanations."

That *monitum* was undoubtedly directed to growing efforts by social scientists to analyze and depict society and its various phenomena in their relationships increasingly, and in some instances exclusively, in terms of mathematical formulae. However, in the natural sciences "wherein reigns the determinism of matter," so that mathematics provides a suitable language, in the human sciences the variables are too many, and the directions in which the human will moves are too various and unpredictable for the kind of precision suggested by the language of numbers. This does not apply to statistics, always a highly useful auxiliary science to the various social sciences, but it indicates definite directions and limitations in how it is applied, e.g. for prediction. At this point the Pope's allocution became quite intense and specific:

> Moreover, it is obvious that the application of statistics to an examination of economic and social questions involves something more than a certain mathematical skill; it also requires a knowledge of man, of his spiritual nature and psychological reflexes. In fact, if the intervention of the statistician is already justified when chance or imponderable elements make explanation of a phenomenon through its causes difficult, then it is particularly indicated when the uncertainty which must be removed depends on human factors, that is to say, on a complex of ideas, affections and different emotions in individuals, which may be constantly changing within the same subject.

With regard to "collecting data," "it is essential to know how to interpret them correctly, how to give true values to figures which, in themselves are inexpressive." Furthermore, "They must by an intellectual effort be placed in a living context, from which they emerge and about no single aspect of which do they give a false idea." That is a necessity "imposed on statistics because, as We have just said, in social matters the judgment of man and his feelings have a great importance." There followed a highly relevant example directed perhaps especially at economists: "Let us consider, for example, the price fluctuations of commodities under the influence of collective optimism or of an anguished shock produced by international events."

Another very specific *monitum* was directed to statisticians with regard to certain directions in which modern psychology has misled some social scientists in their use of statistics.

> When the statistician is forced to express in mathematical quantities the whole

> complex of phenomena in which freedom is involved in part, his great temptation will be to misunderstand that freedom and to attribute to social matters an integral determinism which they do not, in fact, possess, but which his calculations presuppose because of their methodological principle. There is real danger here to which We should like to draw your attention. The 'law of probability' in no way disproves the free will of individuals.

Thus, precisely the kind of determinism which the Pope alluded to in his previous reference to the "domain of the natural sciences" has come to be regarded by some as valid also for the human sciences!

To the credit of statistics, Pius XII pointed out then how the gathering and presentation of statistical data "make situations tangible which might otherwise escape even the keenest observer." That is so because "great human misery clearly appears in disheartening data when its dispersion over vast areas would not otherwise have permitted an appreciation of its real dimensions." And the availability of such data also makes it possible at times for whole populations, suddenly given access to culture, to insistently demand major improvements in their material and intellectual standard of living.

There followed one additional warning. "Since statistics proposes to give the most exact information possible, within the limits of its own methods, we expect from the person who practices it, besides the professional competence We mentioned above, a loyalty and sincerity which is above all suspicion." In other words, "It is useless to perfect methods if in the end they will serve to deceive the public more efficiently." Who would do such a thing? "Now the temptation is great when there is a strong desire to support a thesis, to twist results in a certain way, to dissimulate the truth or even, for financial gain or propaganda purposes, to falsify embarrassing or damaging results."

All in all, this presentation on statistics dealt in a most forthright manner with what Pius XII referred to as "the difficulties of its correct use and the dangers faced by those who do not use it in an orderly way."

Miscellaneous Topics

There were many allocutions by Pius XII which do not fit precisely under the above headings. They are nevertheless clearly related to the economic order. These are presented below.

The Threefold Task of the Catholic Young Man in the Cultural Contest With the Present-day World

Address to the Young Men of Catholic Action of Italy
12 September 1948[10]

In setting forth this challenge to Catholic young men of the Catholic Action movement of Italy, Pius XII began by recounting how "their sisters" of the same movement had knelt before him on the wet, hard pavement on the previous Sunday. Teasingly, the Pope quoted Ovid: "If the heavens are covered over with clouds, you will be left alone." But he felt confident that under similar circumstances these young men would give an equally valorous account of themselves. Then he proposed a threefold task to them.

First, the youth of today are called to achieve a victory over Godlessness. Pius XII reminded his audience that today the very "fundamentals of religion, of the Church, and of the Incarnate nature of Christ are attacked and denied. That may seem absurd and hard to understand, given the unprecedented manifestation of the presence of God through "the remarkable progress in the natural sciences."

The second victory which needs to be achieved is the victory over matter. The Pope referred to our time being designated as "the century of technology." Instead of technology becoming the great benefit for man which it was intended by its Author to be, it becomes "in the hands of violent people and parties which govern with brute force in all-powerful suppressive states a frightful tool for injustice, slavery, and horror, and it enhances modern war with the pain and torture of peoples to an unbearable degree." It is up to this generation of young people, therefore, to bring this power under control, so that "the order of values established by God the Creator, in which matter does not control, but serves, is scrupulously observed, and technology is subordinated according to the will of God to the dignity and liberty, the peace and the temporal, but above all the eternal happiness of man."

The third victory to be achieved is "victory over social misery, which is to be accomplished by the power of justice and charity." "The social question," said the Pope, "is undoubtedly also an economic one, but it goes beyond that to a problem which has to do with the regulated order of the way human beings live with each other." Therefore it is also one that is "at its roots a moral and therefore also a religious question." What it comes down to is this:

> Our people—from the individual, to the nation, to the community of nations—have the moral power to bring about the kind of public conditions where in social life no one and no single nation is a mere object, meaning without any right and subject to exploitation by others, but that instead all are also subjects, meaning that they regularly participate in the structuring of the social order, and that all, according to their own craft or occupation can live serenely and happily, with adequate means of support, effectively protected against the transgressions of an egotistical business, in the kind of freedom that is limited only by the common good, and with human dignity which each honors in another as in himself.

That great challenge, according to Pius XII, can ultimately be met only by reliance on "one source." The source is "the Catholic faith, providing all of its requirements are lived up to, and that it is nourished by the supernatural streams of grace which the Divine Redeemer Himself bestows on man."

Having proposed this great threefold mission to the young men of Italy, their Pope reminded them that these things can only be accomplished by prayer. "Only a host of prayers can achieve victory in the present battle between truth and falsehood, between good and bad, between faith in God, and the denial of God." And "only a host of prayers [those who pray] can bring social peace." The Pontiff urged his youthful audience to make a common front "against hatred, national as well as class hatred." "Hatred can only destroy." "Love builds up." He concluded with a reference to the horsemen of the Apocalypse. "The second, the third and the fourth are war, famine, and death." Who is the first rider on the white horse?" "It is Jesus Christ." That way lies victory!

The Meaning and Limits of State Intervention
Address to Scholars of the Science of Public Administration
5 August 1950[11]

This address is an explication of the principle of subsidiarity before a group dedicated to the study of the science of public administration. This address is included, because of the important position that principle occupies also in the teachings of the Catholic Church on the economic order. It therefore has a significant tangential relevance to Pius XII's economic thought. There is a message also for those who seem to recognize only positive aggression against that hallowed principle of social order.

Pius XII began his address with the reminder that next to the family, the state is the next most essential social institution being rooted as "one of the constitutive elements of the natural law." There has been much loose commentary since the revival of liberalism in social thought suggesting that the state is to be minimized as though it represented an evil, and that instead of offering a solution to our problems, it is itself actually "the problem." Meanwhile, the negative violation of subsidiarity tends to be neglected completely, i.e., the failure of individuals and of the lower social organs of society to live up to their social responsibilities, thereby forcing the state to get involved in matters which *could* be handled more effectively at a lower level.

The year 1950, when this discourse was taking place, still gave witness to much excessive incursion by an all-powerful state. As the Pope remarked, "and with what consequences!" Yet, he cautioned, "no one will contest the need for the state to extend its activity especially in the field of social activity, and even to increase its power there." He indicated that all of that could happen "without danger if there had been equivalent progress in the understanding and appreciation of the purpose and function of the state." In that case, "the state would have found a regulator and a control which could have prevented it from extending its power for reasons, other than economic and social needs, into areas of a cultural nature which would best be left to the free enterprising spirit of the citizens." Instead, all too often this grasp of what the state's purpose is "grew in inverse relationship to the increase in power, not only among those who see in the state only their source of profit, or among those who suffer under it, but even among those who have the responsibility to give the state its form and constitution."

The true concept of the state lies in being a "moral organism" which is based on the moral world order. "It does not have plenipotentiary power that suppresses all legitimate autonomy." Again: "Its function, its noble task is to promote the active cooperation of its members so as to forge, support and bolster a higher unity among them who will serve the welfare of the whole community so long as they respect their subordination to the state's purpose…." This means that "neither the individual nor the family is to be absorbed by the state…. Each is to retain its freedom of action to the extent that this does not pose the risk of harming the common good." The Pope offered specific examples of areas where this freedom of action is to apply: "the right to one's good name, the right and the freedom to honor the true God, the natural right of parents to raise and educate their children." He regarded it as a good omen and he likened to the sunrise the fact that some new constitutions have embodied these ideas.

Pius XII concluded with a warning about luxuriant blossoming of "plans" and "standardizations," all of which are acceptable within proper bounds. What he opposed is "the exaggerated intervention by the state," especially since its actions are all too often left to " pure technicians in the area of organization."

The Church and the World of Commerce
Address to the International Society of Schools of Commerce
10 September 1953[12]

In this address, Pope Pius XII began with the centuries-long connection between missionaries who traveled to the farthest points of the world and the commercial routes which they often made use of on their journeys. He mentioned specifically St. Paul, and also St. Francis Xavier who traveled as far as Japan in the company of an intrepid merchant. Even now, the Pope said, "the pioneer of world commerce and the pioneer of the Catholic faith always meet on the same streets." In their dealings, both are impressed by the similarities and unity among peoples.

Thus, the Church always insisted on 'the high moral worth of this occupation." Often it is the traditional ban on usury that comes to mind when there is talk of the relationship of the Church to the world of commerce, frequently with criticism. Nevertheless, a very significant point in this relationship is the Church's insistence on the important role of the merchant as "a provider of the material goods and services in the best way possible." Accordingly, rather than harboring "a long-standing opposition to commerce," as is often suggested, its moralists always affirmed the connection with the businessman's profit and the valuable service he rendered.

As the Pontiff pointed out, a widespread, nagging skepticism regarding the occupation of merchant still persists. The Church, for one, has long since corroborated that "he does indeed render a real service to his customers." The temptations he faces are considerable, given threats to which sound markets are prone, given the artificially induced wants, and also fluctuations in the value of money and on the foreign exchanges, along with the fascination with unsound speculation. All of that casts a shadow over the genuine service among honorable businessmen and customers, so that merchants are accused and lose people's respect.

The Pope concluded by pointing out that, now more than ever, businessmen need to focus on offering genuine service to their customers. Their training, more than ever before, requires great technical and economic know-how; as well as knowledge of languages and the many qualities which are normally expected of businessmen: "organizational ability, zeal, energy, and the willingness to take risks. But more important than ever, he now needs "an appreciation of the true nobility of his calling and of his function in the national economy." This involves, among other things, remaining open to all of human values, and developing "a mature character that is morally responsible."

The Material and Spiritual Blessings of the Cooperative System
Address to the Italian Association of Cooperatives
10 May 1956[13]

Cooperatives, while never proposed as a panacea or as substitutes for the basic reforms required in the social order, have always had the support of the Catholic Church in its social teachings. One may regard them as appropriate microeconomic measures for dealing with certain social ills. In this brief discourse, Pius XII reaffirmed that, and he congratulated the *Confederazione Cooperative Italiana* for the growth it achieved in extending its benefits to more than 2,150,000 members. He praised them for their awareness that "the production and distribution of material goods must never be an obstacle to the moral and spiritual progress of the human person, nor must it hinder their freedom or stand in the way of their eternal destiny. What they do accomplish is an increase in the members' share of what they produce; and they avert unnecessary expenses, while also safeguarding them against misfortune and unexpected difficulties." At the same time "they support an understanding of what the common good is and calls for, and sharpen the sense of social responsibility."

Human Claims on Economic Expansion
Letter to the President of French Social Week
10 July 1956[14]

This letter was delivered to the 43rd meeting of *Semaine Sociale* in Marseilles, France on the Pope's behalf by Msgr. dell'Acqua, the Substitute for the Vatican State Secretariat. It was addressed to the theme of the meeting: Human Claims on Economic Expansion.

The letter opens with a reference to what the Holy Father had said several months before (4 Feb. 1956), echoing words by his immediate Predecessor. It dealt with the fact that while work is intended for the material and moral fulfillment of man, all too often in modern industrial life it becomes "a tool for his corruption." At the same time "everyone knows that the gains to be derived from industrialization have been far too slow in reaching many countries, in fact entire continents." Here we have an indication of the direction in which the application of the Church's social teachings would be going, as these were subsequently developed by the successors of Pius XII, notably John XXIII and Paul VI.

After referring to "something like a second economic revolution," the Pope indicated that it would be "utopian" to try to reverse the force which modern technology has unleashed. This includes exploiting all of the potential for investment and the technical applications and new kinds of organization in the way the land is cultivated. Indeed, the message suggested clearly that all of the technological advances are a providential counterpart of the "population growth and the desire of peoples for a better life." Therefore, the whole range of developments in this economic expansion must be viewed with a "healthy optimism," since growth is, in fact, "the normal sign of the economic health of a nation, and it would not be reasonable or even Christian to try to stand in the way of future development."

"Actually, the Church encourages its faithful to see in remarkable scientific progress the realization of the plan of God who placed in man's hands the discovery and use of the riches of the universe." (Genesis 1:28) There is mention of the great strides in mechanization which have taken over not only physical functions formerly performed by workers, but even memory and control functions, with a reminder that for all such progress, thanks are owed to God.

The danger is, of course, that blind faith will be accorded to such developments and economic expansion. As the Pope recalled in the same previous message, "Productivity is not an end in itself, nor does it regulate itself." That clearly refutes the persistent economic liberalism which stubbornly clings to the myth of an economy as a self-regulating enterprise in which all will turn out well so long as the self-interest of enterprising individuals is in no way restrained. Characterized as vain are notions that "technology and organization will make it possible to forever reduce costs, to increase output, to forever raise living standards, and to continuously satisfy whatever increasing wants may occur to people the world over." The reason for this latter problem is because "the more exclusively and continuously the tendency to consumption is increased, the more the economy will cease having the real and normal human being as its object—the person who directs the wants of his earthly life to his final goal, and assesses it in terms of God's law." That repeated a warning note by Pius XII in an address commemorating *Rerum Novarum* on 14 May 1953.

There followed a reminder that all of the increases in productivity have by no means always been directed to increasing the standard of living overall, but rather "to increase the anticipated profits." But at the same time as care must be taken so that the workers will share in the gain in such increases in production, we must also be vigilant that they will use such gain for their cultural and spiritual advancement. It is a fact that in some countries enhanced mechanization and technology has shortened the hours of labor for workers. But even while it is true that increased leisure time is a healthy thing, it is also true that "idleness can ferment into a socially destructive force." In fact, therefore, "a kind of production that is disordered in its objectives would end up not serving man, but instead doing him a disservice."

The economic expansion which comes with the ongoing technological advances brings with it additional problems for the future. These involve not merely concern about the significant investments that are required, but also the human aspect of how the lives of the workers may be affected. Industrial renovation and constant modernization also in agriculture and commerce should not take place at the workers' expense. "A totalitarian economy may set about to assure the future at the expense of the present generation.... A Christian too can call for sacrifice, but he never has the right to sacrifice his brother." Here the papal message made the clear reference to "examples in recent times [which] have demonstrated that the danger of mass unemployment can be the result of a sudden modernization of factories." It then cited an earlier address (7 March 1948); "With regard to the high destiny of the social economy, each producing member is a subject and not an object of economic life."

Another problem which rapid economic reconstruction and technological advance had brought with it, especially in Europe by the time of this papal message, was the use of migrant foreign laborers. Large numbers of workers, sometimes accompanied by their families, migrated from economically poorer southern countries (Italy, Yugoslavia, Turkey, Spain, etc.) to countries like Germany. As may be expected, they received a welcome that was sometimes better, sometimes worse. Even in the best of circumstances the condition of a "guest worker" represented generally a difficult dislocation process; and it called for a good deal of Christian consideration on the part of the host peoples. The papal message expressed concern that all would "do everything possible to alleviate the problems facing the least of our brothers."

Marxist Threat to an Italian Community
Address to the Working People of Terni
18 November 1956[15]

These words were directed to a group of workers from the Italian city of Terni who were on pilgrimage to Rome. (In the Utz-Groner *Soziale Summe Pius XII* anthology, it was entitled somewhat less ominously: *Technical and Moral Resources for Overcoming Economic Hardships*). The Pope's own words will suggest which of the titles is more indicative of the heart of his message to these workers.

To put the matter in its proper context, the Umbrian city is, in the words of Pius XII, "one of the most privileged parts of Italy," and "an object of admiration to everyone who visits it, even from distant lands." Specifically, the region was "an industrial center of prime importance." The surrounding area by then included "68% of the industrial firms and 98% of the power stations, and nearly half the inhabitants in an area that constitutes less than 20% of the entire province."

Indicating further that Pius XII had "done his homework" in preparing for this address, he recalled that the area "became the principal target of the enemy offensives," the city of Terni having "suffered one hundred and eleven air raids which destroyed nearly two-thirds of the city." The Pope was also keenly aware that because of "vigorous competition between Italian and foreign goods," the "managers of the largest firms found no other way to cope but by modernizing their plants and reducing the number of manual workers." Anyone who is aware of what the prevailing political currents in Italy were at that time will now recognize why the chosen title above is probably the more relevant! Many will also recognize how what happened to this traditional industrial area foreshadowed what occurred later and quite recently in other parts of the world which had come to rely heavily on specific kinds of industry in earlier eras.

The Pope commiserated with the people of the Terni area when it was undermined with a high volume of unemployment, and he recognized well that their desperation provided attractive bait for Marxist agitators. He praised initiatives by certain industrialists and political leaders to, for example, diversify the economic base of the area. At the same time he warned that while basic economic principles must be observed in structuring and, in this case, restructuring economic life, that does not rule out "human understanding and Christian charity."

There followed a statement which should serve as a perennial guideline for economists, and specifically for those entrusted with shaping economic policy. "We must not lose sight of the fact that, by introducing the principles of ethics into our investigation of economic facts, we do no violence to the economy, but rather contribute effectively to the correct solution of the problems that it poses and confronts."

Next, there is an appeal to "the right to life [as] one of mankind's sacred and inviolable rights," in a historical context that preceded by many years the current ongoing struggle against the crime of abortion. This suggests, among other things, that the classical "right to life" transcends even the most elemental threat against it in the form of killing the defenseless unborn. It is a *right,* as indicated in teachings by subsequent popes, which touches also on the right of people to earn decent wages to assure a dignified observance of their right to life. Here Pius XII indicated specifically that it is a right which requires "that the efforts of all—the State, private enterprise, labor unions—should be united and should cooperate efficiently in order to overcome this embarrassing condition of hardship and unrest." That, not surprisingly, brings us to the Marxist threat. All of the aforementioned hardship creates a situation for "those at Terni and throughout the district generally who will profit from the misfortunes of the people in order to sow in their midst the cockle of discord and hatred."

The Pope then mentioned first, the One who always lurks behind "discord and hatred," and then specifically who his agents are in this particular situation. "We have often observed that the enemy of mankind is one and, at the same time, a multitude." But now he "presents himself with a well-defined countenance and with a name that is widely known." As for Terni, then, in 1958: "Whether because of the ability with which he conceals his tactics and hides his strategy, or through the fear that he is able to inspire, as well as by the hopes that he has aroused, the atheistic Marxist has penetrated your ranks and is at this hour solidly entrenched in his position."

That the Deceiver has done his work well, is clear from the remarks of Pius XII which follow:

> Our heart is troubled and tears come to Our eyes whenever We ask Ourself how it is possible that there should still be such acquiescence and such obstinacy in a sizable portion of the otherwise worthy working class. Is it possible that nothing will serve to open their eyes and move their hearts? They wish to remain with the enemies of God and reinforce their ranks, cooperating thus in aggravating the chaos of the modern world.

The Pope warned that "individuals and whole nations have allowed themselves to be led astray by Gods' enemies, because the latter have promised a better distribution of material goods and proclaimed that they desire to preserve liberty and protect the family." And in even more blunt language he stated "They assure their dupes that eventually the people will seize power, the workmen will own the factories, and the peasants will possess the land." Ah yes, the well-known hammer and sickle!

Grim reality, on the other hand surfaced inexorably. That message to the workers of Terni was delivered in 1956, when the Soviet Empire was perhaps at the peak of its power and prestige, and when its disciples were hard at work spreading their "gospel" throughout the world. Thus, Pius XII could illustrate what he was saying about the Marxian dream by alluding to the then ongoing agony in Hungary: "What is happening during these days to the sorely tried Hungarian people is bloody evidence of the extremes to which those who hate God are prepared to go."

Returning to bedrock reality, the Pontiff reminded workers that social progress *is* possible, and that men and the new machines they are able to devise can be instrumental in bringing such genuine progress. He explained how the kind of unemployment which occurs when new machines and process are introduced is indeed temporary, with all manner of new jobs eventually created by new technology. "The progress made in physics, for instance, has created, and will continue to create, a constant need for an army of workmen of every sort—from the engineer and the nuclear physicist to the qualified worker—to build reactors, nuclear piles and accelerators. And "[I]n the meanwhile, the application of these inventions to industry, to agriculture, and to defense continues to multiply." There were other specific examples, like "what has happened in the field of transportation, where the daily flight of tens of thousands of airplanes engages the services of countless specialists and workmen in various capacities." And on, with "electronics," and what it has done to "radio and television"; and "organic chemistry" with, for example, what "synthetic resins" have done to transform the textile industry. All of such changes called for flexibility and a willingness to reorganize where necessary. "It will be necessary for certain industries to insist less upon a fixed type of production." Also "people must not grow unduly anxious in the face of the inevitable dislocations caused by new enterprises, nor should they indulge in unwarranted pessimism."

That was followed by what was, in fact, a significant, optimistic note later in the message. "We are going forward to a better tomorrow, when, as can readily be foreseen, human labor will be ennobled by being freed from the necessity of exerting mere brute force." However, there was also a final sober note of warning.

> We are convinced that men will accomplish little or nothing if they continue to erect the edifice of this world while remaining aloof from God. Only He can build the house which humanity longs for; unless the Lord build the house, they labor in vain who build it.

That admonition may serve to explain the unusual final blessing: "May God bless you and protect you! God! God! God!

Economic Assistance to Developing Nations: A Moral Obligation
An Address to French Government Officials
13 April 1958[16]

Nearing the end of his life on earth, Pope Pius XII addressed a group of French government officials on a topic which was to be a major theme of his successors, John XXIII and Paul VI: an economic helping hand offered by the rich nations to the poor, developing nations. World War II and its aftermath ushered in the end of traditional colonial empires including the French empire. The Pope noted here "particularly the many representatives of the territories of Africa and Madagascar."

Mincing no words, the Pontiff pointed out: "A closeness more effective than protestations of friendship will result from the common development of the considerable riches the Creator has placed at the disposal of human industry in the soil and subsoil of the African continent." His favorite theme, solidarity, was clearly implicit in the statement, which directly followed: "Working together has always been a beneficial means of becoming acquainted and developing mutual esteem." All of that would be so, if there were a "rational concern for the general welfare" even though "differences of immediate interests may arouse temporary conflicts."

The proposal that the "contribution of capital and technical aid from Europe is an invaluable service which will hasten the economic development of the countries of Africa" seems commonplace now, a half century later. But in the immediate post-colonial years this was new ground on which both parties trod carefully. Indeed, nine years would pass before Pope Paul VI issued his encyclical *On the Development of Peoples* (*Populorum Progressio*). In the jargon of the times, what are now called more euphemistically, "developing nations," were still referred to commonly as "underdeveloped nations." Indeed, that term appeared in the statement by Pius XII that, in the modern world, economic development has become so urgent "that an underdeveloped country cannot enjoy complete freedom."

Characteristically for a great teaching pope, the discourse ended with a statement that "The unequal division of the gifts and treasures of nature gives men a moral obligation to aid one another, each according to the understanding and strength he has received." What is more, "This obligation constantly increases in proportion to the increase in power at the disposal of the social or national group."

It is heartening to note that the nations of Europe, recently preoccupied with working out from under the desolation and destruction left in its wake by World War II within their own boundaries, were nevertheless concerned about aiding the poor nations of the world. They are not to be faulted for recognizing that their own interests were also involved in such efforts. Their concern and actions indicate a growing awareness of their reciprocal solidarity, and that the virtues of social justice and social charity were potent motivating forces among them.

That papal message came near the end of nearly 20 years of Pius XII teaching all nations the gospel as it must be applied also in the very important area of economic life. This great teacher whom his immediate successor, John XXIII, referred to in his first Christmas address as the "Doctor Optimus," set the tone for the future social teachings of both Blessed John XXIII and Venerable Paul VI, as well as for the Second Vatican Council. Pope John XXIII made economic assistance among nations an important element of his own two social encyclicals, *Mater et Magistra* (1961) and *Pacem in Terris* (1963). And Paul VI made it the exclusive theme of his one encyclical addressed to the economic order, *Populorum Progressio* (1967).

The Socioeconomic Importance and Moral Obligations of the Broker and Commercial Representative

Address to Participants in the Second National Congress of the Association of Italian Brokers and Commercial Representatives

22 June 1958[17]

Pius XII candidly indicated his awareness that the occupation represented here was subject to suspicion because of the presence in their ranks of unscrupulous operators. Hence he expressed from the outset his assumption that the people involved here were Catholic and therefore operated according to Christian moral principles. That put him in the position where he could reject the neutral stance suggested by the oft-heard expression: "business is business." He proposed instead that as in any human action, divine and positive laws apply, suggesting the applicability of moral norms here as in other human actions. That includes the brokerage function, which is "a conscious and free human action."

The Pope began a rather scholarly explication of the origin of the brokerage function, indicating that there was no Latin expression for the term—broker—in the present-day sense of the word. Also, during the Middle Ages there were no instances of this kind of professional activity, aside from mediatory actions for resolving disputes among people. The function in its present form was clearly present in the city ordinances of the Italian City States. Pius XII described it in terms that would satisfy a moral theologian as to its legitimacy and economic value. The conclusion was: "The broker has not only a claim to being estimated as valuable, but also to the gratitude of all honorable people." In addition: "From the responsibility of the broker and the importance of his function, it is clear that he must have certain abilities and moral qualities without which business mediation would be morally evil and socially harmful."

Overall, the requirements for legitimate brokerage activity which Pius XII set forth in this address go well beyond the exhortatory genre of many such allocutions before various occupational groups. He offered here a carefully structured analysis of what the brokerage function involves and the various norms that are to be observed, drawing specifically on the Italian Civil Code. As indicated, what is contained in this address deserves to be included in the treatment of the matter by a moral theologian.

The discussion had an interesting and unexpected outcome. Pius XII did no less than to present Jesus Christ as the model for all brokers—He being the great and perfect mediator between His Father and mankind. He depicts Him as the "only real mediator between God and man—the man, Jesus Christ." That is because "any human individual as such, because of unworthiness and sin was incapable of standing in the middle between God and man."

The address ends with significant quotations from St. Augustine (*City of God*). Christ is the "good broker, because he reconciles enemies": "*bonus medius, qui reconciliat inimicos*.... The Devil, on the other hand, also stands between God and man, to prevent man from achieving blessed immortality." That makes him "a bad broker, who keeps friends apart—*medium malus, qui separat amicos*."

Brokers are exhorted to be like Jesus "the mediator.... Then the business world which is subject to so many and difficult temptations will also be a world which belongs to Christ and which will be a truly Christian world."

Notes

1. Arthur-Fridolin Utz, O.P., and Joseph-Fulko Groner, O.P., *Soziale Summe Pius XII* (Freiburg, Switzerland: Paulusverlag, 1954 -1961), 2: 1736-1738.
2. *The Catholic Mind,* May 1954, 309-310.

3. Utz and Groner, 2: 2066-2067.
4. Utz and Groner, 2: 2071-2072.
5. *The Catholic Mind,* 46, 1027 (July 1948): 421-424.
6. Utz and Groner, 1: 1248-1250.
7. Utz and Groner, 3: 3863-3865.
8. Utz and Groner, 1: 946-948.
9. *The Catholic Mind,* January 1954: 58-61.
10. *The Catholic Mind,* January 1949, 51-55.
11. Utz and Groner, 2: 1762-1765.
12. Utz and Groner, 1: 1251-1253.
13. Utz and Groner, 3: 3726-3727.
14. Utz and Groner, 3: 3667-3672.
15. *The Pope Speaks,* Spring 1957, Vol. 3, No. 4, 417-422.
16. Utz and Groner, 3: 3877-3878.
17. Utz and Groner, 3: 3403-3408.

Chapter 11
Conclusion: A Springtime of History

There has been increasing talk of late about a "new springtime" for our troubled world. The idea is not a new one. On March 19, 1958, a few months before he died on October 9, 1958, Pope Pius XII told some 100,000 young Italians of *Italian Catholic Action* gathered in St. Peter's Square:

> Look around you, O youth, spring of humanity, spring of life. Make our hope yours and tell everyone that you are in a springtime of history. May God grant that it will be one of the most beautiful springs man has experienced—after one of the longest and bitterest winters, a spring which precedes one of the most brilliant and rich summers.[1]

Consider that the man who first made that prediction was born Eugenio Pacelli in 1876, and that he lived through the two deadliest wars in human history. He served as papal nuncio to Bavaria and then to all of Germany during the years when Nazis and Marxists were battling in the streets while seeking to take over that country after its defeat in World War I. World War II began just six months after Cardinal Pacelli was elected pope on March 2, 1939. What is more, he was making that statement about a "new springtime" during what came to be known as the Cold War—when two superpowers had thousands of nuclear-tipped missiles targeted at one another's cities. Small wonder if some commentators indicated that his family name, Pacelli, was a diminutive form of the Italian word for *peace*, therefore meaning *little peace*.

Amid all of the misinformation about Pius XII spread by enemies of the Catholic Church in a campaign which started a few years after his death, certain aspects of his true stature have been obscured. Among them are his great magisterial role as well as certain prophetic aspects of his papacy. For example, as mentioned in the Preface, his teachings represent the most frequently cited single source in the sixteen documents of the Second Vatican Council. That indicated among other things how this Pope already anticipated in many ways the course the Catholic Church would take following the Council. John Paul II alluded to that in his encyclical *Tertio Millennio Adveniente* in 1994. Referring to the sense of newness in what Vatican II brought with it he noted: "This is true, but at the same time it is difficult to overlook the fact that the Council drew much from the experience and reflections of the immediate past, especially from the intellectual legacy left by Pius XII" (*Tertio Millennio Adveniente*, par. 18).

Beyond that aspect of his papacy, it is worth noting that popes since Pius XII have reaffirmed the aforementioned prediction about a glorious new springtime for the Church and for mankind. His immediate successor, Blessed John XXIII, spoke of a "new Pentecost. " In his opening address to the Second Vatican Council, after voicing his disagreement with "prophets of doom," he suggested that "the human family is on the threshold of a new era."[2] At the close of the first session of the Council, he expressed his hope that after the decisions and the laws established by it are implemented and obeyed, "[T]hen doubtless will dawn that new Pentecost which is the object of our yearning...."[3] Succeeding pontiffs have also used the Pentecostal metaphor to suggest what lies ahead. Meanwhile Pope Paul VI made an intriguing prophetic statement to the bishops of Eastern France during their *ad limina* visit on December 5, 1977, a few months before he died. He told them:

> Is not the Church when the Spirit breathes in her something like nature when spring returns? Our predecessor John XXIII was right in thinking so. The spring will return! For a while yet we must endure the winter. Please believe that We know what We are talking about, placed at this post which God has assigned to us![4]

During his long pontificate, Pope John Paul II often indicated his sense of a "new springtime." For example, in addressing the Pontifical Missionary Union in St. Peter's Basilica on 11 May 1991 he said, "I am certain that because of your contribution a new missionary age will arise, a new springtime for the Church."[5] He reaffirmed conditionally that expression of hope also in the encyclical *Tertio Millenio Adveniente.* In anticipation of the start of the new millennium, he indicated that what popes since the Council had accomplished "has certainly made a significant contribution to the preparation for *that new springtime of Christian life* which will be revealed by the Great Jubilee, if Christians are docile to the action of the Holy Spirit" (*Tertio Millennio Adveniente*, par. 18).

It is possible that such prophetic indications are not unrelated to the spectacular events at Fatima in Portugal during World War I. In one of a series of apparitions to three shepherd children in 1917, the Virgin Mary told them that after much turmoil, including a second war that would be worse than the first, there would eventually be a "time of peace."[6] Pius XII never visited Fatima as his successors Paul VI and John Paul II did subsequently. But it was reported in the October 25, 1950 issue of *La Domenica del Corriere* that while walking in the Vatican gardens during that month he witnessed privately a less spectacular version of what has become known as the "miracle of the sun."[7] That remarkable phenomenon which had occurred on October 13, 1917 was the culmination of six apparitions in Fatima. Since it had been pre-announced by the Mother of God herself, it was witnessed by some 70,000 people who came from far and wide.[8]

Since peace according to the prophet Isaiah (32:17) is the work of justice, and according to Pope John Paul II, also of solidarity—*Opus solidaritatis pax* (*Sollicitudo Rei Socialis*, par. 39)—it is clear that the peace which the world professes to crave entails among other things a basic reform of the social order. This would mean an overhaul of attitudes culminating in what the great Polish Pope has referred to as the "culture of death" and the "structures of sin" based on them. In the economic order, in a world grown small and more interdependent than ever before in history by virtue of the marvels of modern technology, this involves first of all an acknowledgment of that *interdependence* both within national economies and extending across national boundaries. Greed, celebrated in recent centuries as the "profit motive" or as "self-interest," must give way to justice in the way all honest labor everywhere is remunerated. That change will be based at last on a keen awareness of the common good that involves all human beings, no matter how humble their status, wherever they toil to provide a decent living for their families.

The social teachings of the Catholic Church have been in the forefront of the struggle to bring that about. They have been lost sight of for too long amid the chaos and the ensuing tumult. Free marketeers championed, and continue to do so, a continuance of the dominance of the capitalist class. They urged reliance on the convenient myth that if certain "laws" of the market are allowed to operate unencumbered by human institutions like the state and labor unions or guilds, just wages as well as just prices would automatically result. There was an underlying supposition that enough crumbs would fall from the bounteous table to sustain and placate the working class. The scheme failed, first within national economies as highlighted dramatically by the worldwide depression in the 1930s. Then after a second great World War, the maldistribution of the wealth made possible by the providential marvels of modern technology has led toward another great calamitous situation where entire nations classed as "poor," come to be aligned against others termed "rich." Amid the celebrated free competition within and among the nations, an ever-growing number of workers in the "rich" nations find themselves impoverished as they are either unemployed or forced to compete with workers in the "poor" nations earning wages at or below a bare subsistence level. All of that demonstrates cogently the *de facto* interdependence among all people, which is now more than ever worldwide.

Great teaching popes since Leo XIII, have addressed that "social question" for over a century. In the meantime Karl Marx and his cohorts came onto the sorry scene halfway through the nineteenth century. Disdaining all religious talk of justice and charity as the "opium of the people," they proposed instead class hatred. In opposition to the free market mythology, they established myths of their own, like the classless society. When they found themselves in a position to do so in 1917, they installed a hellish system which eventually cost tens of millions of lives of rich and poor alike—but in fact mostly of the latter!

Perhaps because Pius XII never wrote an encyclical designated specifically as *social*, his social teachings have been largely overlooked. Nevertheless he contributed greatly to that body of teachings, expanding on those of his predecessors, with certain ones bearing his own special imprint. One of these that I would like to indicate specifically here is the concept of *solidarity*. It is an expression which has appeared with significant frequency in the social teachings by all popes ever since the Pius XII pontificate. Although never mentioned specifically by Pius XI, the concept occupied a central role in that Pope's important encyclical *Quadragesimo Anno* (1931) which remains a quintessential blueprint for reconstructing the social order. That became clear in the light of what Pope John Paul II wrote sixty years later in *Centesimus Annus* (*Centesimus Annus*, par. 10). In his discussion of the "principle of solidarity," we find: "Pope Pius XI refers to it with the equally meaningful term 'social charity.'" Accordingly we may equate the "principle of solidarity" with the concept cited in *Quadragesimo Anno* as a principle for regulating the social order along with social justice (*Quadragesimo* Anno, par. 88). However, Pius XI did not supply a specific definition of social charity so that a sense of what it means had to be derived contextually.

For a definition of the concept of *solidarity* (and therefore of the virtue, *social charity*), John Paul II referred us back to his previous social encyclical *Sollicitudo Rei Socialis* where he also termed it "undoubtedly a *Christian virtue*" (*Sollicitudo Rei Socialis*, par. 40). There throughout the entire fifth chapter the Polish Pope provided an extended explanation along with specific applications. Essentially it is a "*firm and persevering determination* to commit oneself to the *common good*; that is to say, to the good of all and to each individual because we are *all* really responsible *for all*." And that is based on a recognition of the *interdependence* which is a fact of life in the contemporary world throughout its various "economic, cultural, political, and religious elements" (*Sollicitudo Rei Socialis*, par. 38) [All italics as in the original].

This outstanding Pontiff came to be hailed as the *Pope of Solidarity*, originally because of his support of the Polish labor union which faced down and finally prevailed over the Soviet Goliath. It is merited as well because of his exposition and clarification of the Christian virtue of *solidarity* in his great trilogy of social encyclicals, where he integrated it with teachings by previous popes.

It is especially gratifying for me personally to find the exposition of the concept *solidarity* as a culmination of more than a century of social teachings dating back to Pope Leo XIII. Along with my lifelong study of papal social teachings, I devoted more than a quarter of a century translating into English the works of the German Jesuit economist Heinrich Pesch (1854-1926).[9] He developed the *principle of solidarity* as the underlying basis for his social philosophy—solidarism—to serve as the foundation for his solidaristic economic system which he offered as an alternative to individualistic capitalism and collectivistic socialism. Shortly after his death, one of Pesch's Jesuit understudies, Oswald von Nell-Breuning played a leading advisory role in preparing the encyclical *Quadragesimo* Anno of Pius XI. A second, Gustav Gundlach S.J., was a lifelong advisor to Pius XII in matters relating to social teachings. And as a professor of social ethics at the Jagiellionian University in Poland, Father Karol Wojtyla, who went on to become Pope John Paul II, was already well acquainted with Pesch's work. That familiarity became evident later in his great trilogy of social encyclicals: *Laborem Exercens, Sollicitudo Rei Socialis*, and *Centesimus Annus*. It is nowhere more evident than in his use of the precise term and concept, *principle of solidarity*; and the term itself became common currency in the social teachings of the Catholic Church beginning with Pope Pius XII.

I prepared this book in the sincere hope that future generations will appreciate more than our own how much that is sound and orthodox we owe to the brilliant and saintly Pius XII. That applies in a special way to his social teachings. Even though he did not write an encyclical designated specifically as "social," the contributions of Pius XII in that area are profound and vast, as I have tried to indicate throughout the text. As I examined these teachings, I came to share wholeheartedly the expectation expressed by Blessed John XXIII shortly after his immediate predecessor died that, "Apart from any official declaration which would be premature, the triple title, '*Doctor optimus, Ecclesiae sanctae lumen, divini legis amator,*' would be most suitable to his memory." The enthusiastic John XXIII was well aware that to be declared a doctor of the Church one must also be a canonized saint. I pray that both honors will be bestowed without further delay!

Notes

1. Pius XII, "The Springtime of History," *The Pope Speaks*, Spring 1958, 430. It is noteworthy that the succeeding article in this issue of *The Pope Speaks* is an address by the same Pope to a Catholic Union of French Railwaymen entitled: "Christian Solidarity."

2. Staff of *The Pope Speaks* Magazine, eds., *The Encyclicals and Other Messages of John XXIII* (Washington, D.C.: TPS Press, 1964), 427.

3. Ibid. 444.

4. Paul VI, "The Present State of the Church in France," *The Pope Speaks* 23,1 (1978), 71.

5. Cf. *L'Osservatore Romano* (Weekly English Edition) 13 May 1991, 2.

6. William Thomas Walsh, *Our Lady of Fatima* (Garden City, N.Y.: Doubleday/Image Books, 1954), 82: Translated from Lucia's exact words: "In the end my Immaculate Heart will triumph. The Holy Father will consecrate Russia to me, and it

will be converted and a certain period of peace will be granted to the world." (The "period of peace" in the original Portuguese was "*tempo de paz.*")

7. For an artist's presentation of Pius XII witnessing of the "miracle of the sun" while walking in the Vatican Garden, see Sr. Margherita Marchione, *Shepherd of Souls*, (Mahwah, N.J.: Paulist Press, 2002), 177.

8. Walsh, "Foreword."

9. The original five-volume *Lehrbuch der Nationalökonomie* by Heinrich Pesch, S.J. was published by the *Herder Verlag* in Freiburg, Germany in several editions between 1905 and 1926. An English edition is available as *Lehrbuch der Nationalökonomie/ Teaching Guide to Economics*, trans. Rupert J. Ederer (Lewiston, N.Y.: Edwin Mellen Press, 2002-2003. Pesch's original (1898-1901) two-volume work entitled *Liberalismus, Socialismus, und christliche Gesellschaftsordnung* has been translated by Rupert J. Ederer in five books as *Liberalism, Socialism, and Christian Social Order* (Lewiston, N.Y.: Edwin Mellen Press, 2000-2006). Heinrich Pesch, S.J., *Ethik und Volkswirtschaft*, (1918), is also available in translation by Rupert J. Ederer as *Ethics and the National Economy* (Norfolk, Va.: IHS Press, 2004). It presents in 182 pages a brief but comprehensive synopsis of Pesch's thought.

Bibliography

Abbott, Walter M., ed. *The Documents of Vatican II.* New York: The Guild Press, 1966.

Carlen, Claudia IHM, ed. *The Papal Encyclicals 1939-1958* (vol. 4 of 5). N.p.: McGrath, 1981.

Carrier, Hervé. *The Social Doctrine of the Church Revisited.* Vatican City: The Pontifical Council for Justice and Peace, 1990.

Catechism of the Catholic Church. Washington D.C.: United States Catholic Conference, 1994.

Chinigo, Michael, ed. *The Pope Speaks.* New York: Pantheon Books Inc., 1957.

Compendium of the Social Doctrine of the Church. United States Conference of Catholic Bishops, Washington D.C., 2004.

Coulter, Michael, et al. *Encyclopedia of Catholic Social Thought, Social Science, and Social Policy.* 2 vols. Lanham, Maryland: Scarecrow Press, 2007.

Dalin, David. *The Myth of Hitler's Pope.* Washington D.C.: Regnery, 2005.

Dempsey, Bernard W., S.J. *The Functional Economy.* Englewood Cliffs, N.J.: Prentice-Hall, 1958.

Doctrina Pontificia III (*Documentos Sociales*). Madrid: Biblioteca de Autores Cristianos, 1964.

Ederer, Rupert J., *Economics as if God Matters.* South Bend: Fidelity Press, 1995.

——, *The Evolution of Money.* Washington, D.C.: Public Affairs Press, 1964.

——, trans. *Heinrich Pesch on Solidarist Economics.* Lanham, MD: University Press of America, 1998.

Haas, Francis J. *Man & Society.* New York: Appleton-Century-Crofts, 1952.

Halecki, Oscar. *Eugenio Pacelli: Pope of Rome.* New York: Farrar-Straus, 1951.

Lapide, Pinchas. *Three Popes and the Jews.* New York: Hawthorne Books, 1967.

Marchione, Sr. Margherita, *Papa Pio XII: An Anthology on the 70th Anniversary of His Coronation.* Vatican City: Libreria Editrice Vaticana, 2009.

——, *Pope Pius XII: History and Hagiography.* Vatican City: Libreria Editrice Vaticana, 2010.

——. *The Truth Will Set You Free.* New York and Mahwah, NJ: Paulist Press, 2008.

Masse, Benjamin, S. J., *Justice for All.* Milwaukee: Bruce, 1964.

Messner, Johannes. *Das Gemeinwohl.* Osnabrück: Verlag A. Fromm, 1962.

——. *Social Ethics*. St. Louis & London: B. Herder & Co., 1964.

——. *Die Soziale Summe.* Innsbruck: Tyrolia Verlag, 1964.

Murphy, Paul I. *La Popessa.* New York: Warner Books, 1983.

Pesch, Heinrich. *Ethics and the National Economy.* Trans. Rupert J. Ederer. Norfolk, VA: IHS Press, 2004.

——. *Lehrbuch der Nationalökonomie/Teaching Guide to Economics.* Trans. Rupert J. Ederer. 5 vols. Lewiston/Queenston: The Edwin Mellen Press, 2002-2003.

——. *Liberalism, Socialism, and Christian Social Order*. Trans. Rupert J. Ederer. 5 vols. Lewiston: The Edwin Mellen Press, 2002-2006.

Principles for Peace: *Selections from Papal Documents.* Washington, D. C.: NCWC, 1943.

Rychlak, Ronald. *Hitler, the War, and the Pope*. Huntington, IN: Our Sunday Visitor, 2000.

Seven Great Encyclicals. Glen Rock, NJ: Paulist Press, 1963.

Smit, Jan Olav. *Angelic Shepherd.* New York: Dodd, Mead & Co., 1950.

Utz, Arthur F. and Groner, Joseph F. *Die Soziale Summe Pius XII* (3 vols.). Freiburg (Switzerland): Paulusverlag, 1954, 1961.

Yzermans, Vincent, A., ed. *The Major Addresses of Pope Pius XII.* 2 vols. St. Paul: North Central Publishing Co., 1961.

Index

About the Author

Rupert J. Ederer is Professor of Economics *Emeritus* at the Buffalo State College branch of the State University of New York. He was born in Munich, Germany in 1923, and immigrated to the United States with the Ederer family in 1926. After serving in the U. S. Army during World War II, he earned his M.A. (1950) and Ph.D (1954) in economics at St. Louis University. He taught successively at St. Bonaventure University (N.Y.), Quincy College (Ill.), Canisius College (Buffalo, N.Y.), and Rosary Hill College (Amherst, N. Y.). Professor Ederer also served as Lecturer in the Extension Division of the Cornell University School of Industrial and Labor Relations, and for four years as Research Director for the Switchman's Union of North America. He has published widely in various journals, and there are also several books. These include: *The Evolution of Money* (1964); *The Social Teachings of Wilhelm Emmanuel von Ketteler* (1980); *Ethics and the National Economy* (1988, 2004); *Heinrich Pesch on Solidarist Economics* (1998). After retiring from teaching in 1985, Professor Ederer translated into English Heinrich Pesch's five volume *Lehrbuch der Nationalökonomie*, and his *Liberalismus, Sozialismus, und christliche Gesellschaftsordnung*. The former was published between 2002 and 2003 in ten volumes as the *Lehrbuch der Nationalökonomie/Teaching Guide to Economics*. The later appeared in five volumes as *Liberalism, Socialism and Christian Social Order* between 2000 and 2006. Both were published by the Edwin Mellen Press of Lewiston, N.Y.

www.ingramcontent.com/pod-product-compliance
Lightning Source LLC
LaVergne TN
LVHW101445200926
848483LV00001B/55
9780810877979